HANDBOOK OF ENERGY AUDITS

HANDBOOK OF

ENERGY AUDITS

ALBERT THUMANN, P.E.

THE FAIRMONT PRESS, INC.
P.O. Box 14227 • Atlanta, Georgia 30324

*This book is dedicated to one of the
first energy conservationists and his wife,
my parents.*

Contents

Acknowledgment

A wide variety of authorities in their field have contributed material to this Handbook. In addition several "classic" government publications have been incorporated into appropriate chapters. This assimilation of "state-of-the-art" energy audit material has made this a comprehensive reference which should help any individual who is performing an audit.

In addition to the chapter credits, special appreciation is given to the following individuals and organizations for their contributions to the energy audit field and this Handbook.

John Baumgartel
Energy Conservation and Management Division
New Mexico State Office of Energy

Robert J. Brown, Ph.D.
Pennsylvania State University

Mark Caplan
Xenergy

Chicago Federal Executive Board

Nick Choksi
Certified Test & Balance Company, Inc.

Richard Fessler
Marriott Corporation

Edward D. Howell
Carborundum Corporation

Robert D. Rinehart
Fuel and Energy Consultant

Rudolph R. Yanuck, P.E.
EER Associates

1

What Is An Energy Audit?

Energy audits mean different things to different individuals. Lacking a clear definition, the term "energy audit" has in itself caused confusion. This chapter reviews the background of energy audits and defines how they are presently being used.

WHERE IT STARTED

The term energy audits was used in the *Federal Register*, Vol. 42, No. 25, June 29, 1977, dealing with Energy Audit Procedures. For each State Energy Office to qualify for financial assistance, they had to submit a Supplemental State Energy Conservation Program (SSEP) containing procedures for:

(a) Carrying out a continuing public education effort on implementing energy conservation measures.
(b) Insuring effective inter-governmental conditions.
(c) Encouraging and carrying out energy audits for building and industrial plants.

With respect to energy audits, section 420.104 (c) (2) of the *Federal Register* specifies as a minimum eligibility require-ment for financial assistance that States offer mini-energy audits (described as Class A energy audits) in at least one city in at least one of the institutions, hospitals, hotels and motels, indus-trial plants, office buildings, restaurants, retail stores, and ware-houses and storage facilities. To the extent feasible, States are expected to offer "do-it-yourself" energy audits (described as

Class C energy audits) in the rest of the state in the category selected for Class A Audits. Class C energy audits are also expected to be offered throughout the state in the remaining categories to the extent considered feasible.

A third category of energy audit was also introduced in the *Federal Register*, namely a Class B information audit.

The three audits differ in the way the audit is to be accomplished. The Class A audit essentially requires an on-site visit by an auditor and the auditor's evaluation. The Class B audit is accomplished by a questionnaire which the building owner completes and which is evaluated by the state. On the other hand, the Class C energy audit is accomplished by the building owner with the help of a "do-it-yourself" workbook.

The following workbooks were prepared for use by State Energy Offices as a tool in assisting owners and managers of various types of buildings in performing Class C information energy audits to identify energy conservation measures:

DOE/CS-0041/1   Energy Audit Workbook for Apartment Buildings. Sept. 1978, 91 p., NTIS, PC $6.00; MF $3.00;

DOE/CS-0041/2   Energy Audit Workbook for Schools. Sept. 1978, 84 p., NTIS, PC $6.00; MF $3.00;

DOE/CS-0041/3   Energy Audit Workbook for Hospitals. Sept. 1978, 99 p., NTIS, PC $6.00; MF $3.00;

DOE/CS-0041/4   Energy Audit Workbook for Hotels and Motels. Sept. 1978, 100 p., NTIS, PC $6.00; MF $3.00;

DOE/CS-0041/5   Energy Audit Workbook for Die Casting Plants. Sept. 1978, 81 p., NTIS, PC $6.00; MF $3.00;

DOE/CS-0041/6   Energy Audit Workbook for Office Buildings. Sept. 1978, 95 p., NTIS, PC $6.00; MF $3.00;

DOE/CS-0041/7   Energy Audit Workbook for Restaurants. Sept. 1978, 79 p., NTIS, PC $6.00; MF $3.00;

DOE/CS-0041/8   Energy Audit Workbook for Bus Stations. Sept. 1978, 81 p., NTIS, PC $6.00; MF $3.00;

DOE/CS-0041/9   Energy Audit Workbook for Warehouses. Sept. 1978, 95 p., NTIS, PC $6.00; MF $3.00;

DOE/CS-0041/10   Energy Audit Workbook for Bakeries. Sept. 1978, 89 p., NTIS, PC $6.00; MF $3.00;

DOE/CS-0041/11   Energy Audit Workbook for Retail Stores. Sept. 1978, 77 p., NTIS, PC $6.00; MF $3.00.

The following two Instruction Manuals are companions to the workbooks and were prepared as general guidelines by which energy auditors can assist owners, managers, or operators of buildings and industrial plants in performing Class A information energy audits:

DOE/CS-0041/12   Instructions for Energy Auditors, Vol. I. Sept. 1978, 235 p., NTIS, PC $9.50; MF $3.00;

DOE/CS-0041/13   Instructions for Energy Auditors, Vol. II. Sept. 1978, 321 p., NTIS, PC $11.75; MF $3.00.

NTIS: National Technical Information Service, U.S. Department of Commerce, 5285 Port Royal Road, Springfield, Virginia 22161.

In addition to energy audits enabling the state to qualify for financial funding, energy audits were also to be used for "loan guarantee" or verification audits. Thus the audit terminology developed with financial assistance and funding in mind.

By abstracting several statements from the first generation of Class C workbooks, energy audits may be defined as follows:

"The energy audit serves to identify all of the energy streams into a facility and to quantify energy use according to discrete functions.

"An energy audit may be considered as similar to the monthly closing statement of an accounting system. One series of entries consists of amounts of energy which were consumed during the month in the form of electricity, gas, fuel, oil, steam, and the second series lists how the energy was used; how much for lighting, in air-conditioning, in heating, in process, etc. The energy audit process must be carried out accurately enough to identify and qualify the energy and cost savings that are likely to be realized through investment in an energy savings measure."

TYPES OF ENERGY AUDITS

The simplest definition for an energy audit is as follows: An energy audit serves the purpose of identifying where a building or plant facility uses energy and identifies energy conservation opportunities.

There is a direct relationship to the cost of the audit (amount of data collected and analyzed) and the number of energy conservation opportunities to be found. Thus, a first distinction is made between cost of the audit which determines the type of audit to be performed.

The second distinction is made between the type of facility. For example, a building audit may emphasize the building envelope, lighting, heating, and ventilation requirements. On the other hand, an audit of an industrial plant emphasizes the process requirements.

Most energy audits fall into three categories or types, namely, Walk-Through, Mini-Audit, or Maxi-Audit.

Walk-Through—This type of audit is the least costly and identifies preliminary energy savings. A visual inspection of the facility is made to determine maintenance and operation energy saving opportunities plus collection of information to determine the need for a more detailed analysis.

Mini-Audit—This type of audit requires tests and measurements to quantify energy uses and losses and determine the economics for changes.

Maxi-Audit—This type of audit goes one step further than the mini-audit. It contains an evaluation of how much energy is used for each function such as lighting, process, etc. It also requires a model analysis, such as a computer simulation, to determine energy use patterns and predictions on a year-round basis, taking into account such variables as weather data.

QUALIFICATIONS OF AUDITORS

The guidelines for Class A energy auditors were spelled out in section 450.22 of the *Federal Register* which states:

§   450.22 Auditors.

(a)   A person who conducts a building verification audit shall—

(1)   Be a licensed professional engineer or architect;

(2)   Have an engineering degree from a college or university accredited by the Engineers Council for Professional Development in addition to 4 years of subsequent experience in one or more of the following—

(i)   Heating, ventilating and air conditioning installation or design work;

(ii)   Building operations, including operation of the environmental systems;

(iii)   Design of the building systems which are to be modified; or

(3)   Be a Certified Public Accountant in the State in which the audit is performed and use building and building systems data provided by—

(i)   A Test and Balance Engineer as certified by the Associated Air Balance Council; or

(ii)   A Testing, Adjusting, and Balancing Supervisor who is qualified by, and employed by a firm that is certified by, the National Environmental Balancing Bureau.

(b)   A person who conducts a verification audit of a residential building having less than three dwelling units shall meet—

(1)   The requirements specified in paragraph (a) of this section; or

(2)   Subject to the approval of FEA, other requirements which shall be prescribed by a Federal agency whose program utilizes such audits.

(c)   A person who conducts an industrial process verification audit shall—

(1)   Be a licensed professional engineer, or

(2)   Have an engineering degree from a college or university accredited by the Engineers Council for Professional Development in addition to 4 years of subsequent experience with a relevant industrial process.

In determining qualifications of energy auditors some states are adopting the criteria set forth above for both the Class A energy audits and audits resulting from the enactment of the National Energy Plan.

IMPACT OF THE NATIONAL ENERGY PLAN (NEA)

In addition to the funding which each state receives from the Supplemental State Energy Conservation Program, NEA encourages energy audits and conservation through additional funding. Highlights of NEA are summarized in this section. Of particular interest is the $900 million grant program for energy audits of schools and hospitals. This program makes available funds for information-type audits as well as technically-assisted audits.

The National Energy Conservation Policy Act of 1978, as it relates to energy audits provides for:

Utility Conservation Program for Residences—A program requiring utilities to offer energy audits to their residential customers that would identify appropriate energy conservation and solar energy measures and estimate their likely costs and savings. Utilities also will be required to offer to arrange for the installation and financing of any such measures.

Weatherization Grants for Low Income Families—Extension through 1980 of the DOE weatherization grants program for insulating lower income homes at an authorized level of $200 million in FY 1979 and 1980.

Solar Energy Loan Program—A $100 million program administered by HUD which will provide support for loans of up to $8,000 to homeowners and builders for the purchase and installation of solar heating and cooling equipment in residential units.

Energy Conservation Loan Programs—A $5 billion program of federally-supported home improvement loans for energy conservation measures; $3 billion for support of reduced interest loans up to $2,500 for elderly or moderate income families, and $2 billion for general standby financing assistance.

Grant Program for Schools and Hospitals—Grants of $900 million over the next three years to improve the energy efficiency of schools and hospitals.

Energy Audits for Public Buildings—A two-year, $65 million program for energy audits in local public buildings and public care institutions.

Appliance Efficiency Standards—Energy efficiency standards for major home appliances, such as refrigerators and air-conditioning units.

Civil Penalties Relating to Automobile Fuel Efficiency—Authority for the Secretary of Transportation to increase the civil penalties on auto manufacturers from $5 to $10 per car for each 1/10 of a mile a manufacturer's average fleet mileage fails to meet the EPCA automobile fleet average fuel economy standards.

Other Provisions—Other provisions in the Act include the following:

- Grants and standards for energy conservation in Federally-assisted housing.
- Federally-insured loans for conservation improvements in multifamily housing.
- $100 million for a Solar Demonstration program in Federal buildings.
- Conservation requirements for Federal buildings.
- $98 million for solar photovoltaic systems in Federal facilities.
- Industrial recycling targets and reporting requirements.
- Energy efficiency labeling of industrial equipment.
- A study of the energy efficiency of off-road and recreational vehicles.
- An assessment of the conservation potential of bicycles.

Solar is considered a renewable resource and is covered by most of the programs as a measure for reducing energy consumption.

In the Residential Conservation Service (RCS) Program of NEA the following opportunities are encouraged:

CONSERVATION AND RENEWABLE RESOURCE MEASURES AND PRACTICES

The RCS Program applies to existing single- to four-family dwelling units with a heating and/or cooling system. The proposed rule divides the energy conservation measures into two categories: (1) energy conservation measures which conserve energy but do not use a renewable energy source, and (2) renewable resource measures which make use of solar and wind energy. The conservation measures covered by the RCS Program, according to NECPA, include:

- caulking and weatherstripping of doors and windows
- furnace efficiency modifications
- clock thermostats
- ceiling, attic, wall and floor insulation
- water heater insulation
- storm windows and doors
- heat-absorbing or heat-reflective glazed windows and door materials
- load management devices

This list of measures was expanded to include measures which are eligible for residential energy tax credit provided in the Energy Tax Act of 1978. The additional measures are:

- duct insulation
- pipe insulation
- thermal windows

Replacement gas burners are eligible for tax credits but are not included in the RCS Program because they are usually installed to replace oil burners. The RCS Program does not include measures which require changing from one fossil fuel to another, or in switching from fossil fuel to electricity.

The renewable resource measures covered by the RCS Program include:

- solar domestic hot water systems
- active solar space heating systems
- combined active solar space heating and solar domestic hot water system
- passive solar space heating and cooling systems
- wind energy devices
- replacement solar swimming pool heaters

The RCS is seen as a major program to increase consumer awareness and purchase of renewable resource measures.

THE IMPACT OF NEA ON ENERGY AUDITS

As a result of the NEA, several additional definitions of energy audits arise purely out of funding considerations. Since in most cases the state is responsible for implementing the program, these definitions and funding aspects sometimes get confused.

Figure 1-1 illustrates several programs involved in energy audits. The Supplemental State Energy Conservation Program previously discussed should be considered separate from the NEA programs described even though there is an overlap.

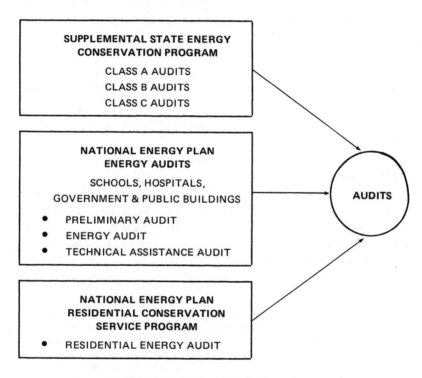

Figure 1-1. Energy Audit Programs

Residential Audits—The Residential Conservation Service (RCS) is primarily accomplished through services offered by utility companies. In some states public service commissions have mandated additional building audits by utility companies.

Schools and Hospitals Audits—The $900 million schools and hospitals program illustrated by the center block in Figure 1-1 indicates three types of audits.

- Preliminary or Information Audit
- Energy Audit
- Technical Assistance Audit.

In order to qualify for the bulk of the $900 million funds both the preliminary and energy audit steps must be completed.

Preliminary and Energy Audit—The definitions of a Preliminary and Energy Audit are given in the *Federal Register*, Vol. 44, No. 64, Monday, April 2, 1979 as follows: "The 'Preliminary Energy Audit' is in essence an information gathering phase." Specific content of the Preliminary Energy Audit is illustrated in Figure 1-2.

The second phase requires that all no-cost, low-cost energy conservation measures be implemented before Technical Assistance can be applied for.

Specific content of the "Energy Audit" is illustrated in Figure 1-3.

Notice that in either case auditor qualifications are kept fairly loose with the final decision resting with each state.

It should be noted that in the computation of BTU/square foot, the electric conversion factor is 11,600 BTU per Kilowatt hour. This is a "source" conversion and takes into account inefficiencies in transmission. Thus electricity will in essence be penalized over other fuels.

CONTENT OF A PRELIMINARY ENERGY AUDIT—The "Content of a preliminary energy audit" section defines the information requirements for this activity. This includes identification of the institution, basis for eligibility, description of the functional use of the building, owner of record, size, age, operating schedule, major energy using systems, building characteristics related to the potential use of solar energy or renewable resource measures, energy use and cost data by fuel type, energy use in Btu, an energy use index, and a brief description of energy conservation activities. Preliminary energy audits are to be conducted by States to establish the information base needed for development of State Plans which will be used in the subsequent phase of the grant programs to administer technical assistance and energy conservation measures, including solar energy or other renewable resource measures.

Figure 1-2. Detailed Contents of Preliminary Energy Audtis

AUTHOR QUALIFICATIONS—The person conducting an energy audit must be familiar with the systems and operations of the type of building to be audited. He or she must also have received State training, or have education and experience such that the State determines training is unnecessary. The energy audit is to be conducted using materials provided by the State. The auditor need not be a professional architect or engineer so long as he or she meets the qualification requirements established by the State.

§ 450.42 **Contents of a preliminary energy audit.**

(a) A preliminary energy audit shall provide a description of the building or complex audited and determine its energy-using characteristics, including—

(1) The name or other identification, and address of the building;

(2) A statement that the building meets the requirements of one of the following categories—

(i) A school facility;

(ii) A hospital facility; or

(iii) A building owned and primarily occupied either by offices or agencies of a unit of local government or by a public care institution, neither of which shall include any building intended for seasonal use or any building used primarily by a school or hospital;

(3) A description of the functional use made of the building identifying whether it is a—

(i) School—

(A) Elementary;

(B) Secondary;

(C) College or university;

(D) Vocational;

(E) Local education agency administrative building; or

(F) Other;

(ii) Hospital—

(A) General;

(B) Tuberculosis; or

(C) Other;

(iii) Local Government building—

(A) Office;

(B) Storage;

(C) Service;

(D) Library;

(E) Police station;

(F) Fire station; or

(G) Other; or

Figure 1-2. Detailed Contents of Preliminary Energy Audits (con't.)

(iv) Public care building—

(A) Nursing home;

(B) Long term care other than a nursing home;

(C) Rehabilitation facility;

(D) Public health center; or

(E) Residential child care center;

(4) The name and address of the owner of record, indicating whether owned by a public institution, private nonprofit institution or an Indian tribe;

(5) The size of the building, expressed in gross square feet;

(6) The age of the building;

(7) Approximate daily hours of operation, including periods of partial use if applicable;

(8) An indication of whether the building is partially used during vacation periods or other times when the building is not fully utilized, for periods of a week or more, by quarter;

(9) An identification of major energy-using systems, including—

(i) Type of heating system or cooling system or both;

(ii) Fuel used for heating system, cooling system;

(iii) Fuel used for domestic hot water, such as electric or natural gas;

(iv) Special energy using systems, such as food service or laundry; and

(v) Lighting, such as incandescent or fluorescent;

(10) Fuel use in physical units and cost data by type for a preceding 12 month period, by month if practicable, using actual data or an estimate if actual figures are unavailable;

(11) Total annual energy use expressed in Btu's per gross square foot. Energy use shall be calculated using the conversion factors set forth below—

(i) Electricity—11,600 Btu per kilowatt hour.

(ii) Natural gas—1,030 Btu per cubic foot.

(iii) Distillate fuel oil—138,690 Btu per gallon.

(iv) Residual fuel oil—149,690 Btu per gallon.

(v) Coal—24.5 million Btu per standard short ton.

(vi) Liquified petroleum gases including propane and butane—95,475 Btu per gallon.

(vii) Steam—1,390 Btu per pound.

Conversion factors may be taken from engineering reference manuals for fuels not listed.

(b) A preliminary energy audit shall provide a brief description of activities which have been undertaken to conserve energy in the building or complex being audited, including whether—

(1) A person has been designated to monitor and evaluate energy use;

Figure 1-2. Detailed Contents of Preliminary Energy Audits (con't.)

(2) Work partially or fully satisfying the requirements of an energy audit has been performed;

(3) Detailed studies have been conducted by architects, engineers or architect-engineer teams of energy use and energy conservation; and

(4) Any major energy conservation measures have been implemented, together with a listing of such measures, and estimates of their costs and energy savings if available.

(c) A preliminary energy audit shall provide information regarding site, building, and heating and hot water systems related to solar energy or other renewable resource potential including—

(1) An indication of whether open land, such as fields, yards and parking areas, is available within the immediate vicinity of the building which is not heavily shaded by tall buildings, trees or other obstructions;

(2) A statement of whether the building is located generally within an urban, suburban or rural area;

(3) An approximation of whether more than half the building's roof area or southern oriented wall surface is heavily shaded by shrubs, trees, buildings or other obstructions for more than about four hours per day;

(4) The number of stories;

(5) A general description of the building's shape, such as square, rectangular, E-shaped, H-shaped or L-shaped;

(6) An indication of whether the roof is flat or pitched, and if pitched whether it has a southern orientation;

(7) Whether there are existing roof-top obstructions, such as chimneys, space conditioning equipment, water towers, mechanical rooms, stairwells or other permanent structures;

(8) An indication of the exterior material of the southern facing wall, such as masonry, wood, aluminum;

(9) An approximation of the proportion of glass area of the southern facing wall, such as less than 25 percent, 25-75 percent, more than 75 percent;

(10) Location of primary space heating and water heating systems—

(i) Whether outside of or within the building;

(ii) If within the building, whether on the ground floor, in the basement, or on the roof; and

(iii) If within the building, whether centrally located, in multiple units, or a combination thereof.

Figure 1-2. Detailed Contents of Preliminary Energy Audits (concluded)

CONTENT OF AN ENERGY AUDIT—The energy audit is a brief on-site survey and analysis of a building, its energy use patterns, identification of opportunities for saving energy through implementation of operating and maintenance changes, and an assessment of its need for implementation of energy conservation measures, including solar energy or other renewable resource measures. The information regarding energy use patterns is the same as that required by a preliminary energy audit, except that it should provide further data needed for analysis of energy conservation potential. In addition, some data elements have been added as a result of concerns expressed by several comments that the proposed rule did not provide an adequate basis for making a judgment about solar or renewable energy resource potential. The identification of operating and maintenance procedure changes which could save energy is important because there are many such actions that can easily be identified and frequently save substantial amounts of energy. Finally, the energy audit is aimed at making an overall estimate of the potential for retrofit and solar or renewable resource applications. Some simple energy conservation measures may be analyzed to obtain an approximation of their costs and benefits. The results of the energy audit, in addition to providing recommendations to owners and managers concerning actions they can take to save energy at little or no cost, also provide basic information which will be used to select buildings to receive technical assistance grants under the later phases of the programs. In this respect, it is extremely important to audit as many buildings as possible because the information gathered serves as a basis for indicating priority of need for technical assistance which rigorously evaluates both solar energy and other conservation actions.

§ 450.43 **Contents of an energy audit.**

(a) An energy audit shall contain the information required for a preliminary energy audit, in accordance with § 450.22, and shall also include a description of—

(1) Major changes in functional use or mode of operation planned in the next fifteen years, such as demolition, disposal, rehabilitation, or conversion from office to warehouse;

(2) For a building in excess of 200,000 gross square feet, if available—

(i) Peak electric demand for both daily and annual cycles; and

(ii) Annual energy use by fuel type of the major mechanical or electrical systems if the information is available or can be reasonably estimated;

(3) Terminal heating or cooling, or both, such as radiators, unit ventilators, fancoil units, or double-duct reheat systems;

(4) Building site and structural characteristics related to solar energy or other renewable resource potential, including but not limited to—

(i) Climatic factors, specifically—

Figure 1-3. Detailed Contents of Energy Audits

(A)   Average annual heating degree days and cooling degree days;

(B)   Average solar insolation by month;

(C)   Average monthly wind speed; and

(ii)   Roof characteristics, including—

(A)   An identification of primary structural component such as steel, wood, concrete; and

(B)   Type of roofing material such as shingles, slate, or built-up materials; and

(5)   A description of general building conditions.

(b)   An energy audit shall—

(1)   Indicate that appropriate energy conservation maintenance and operating procedures have been implemented for the building, supported by a demonstration based on actual records, that energy use has been reduced in a given year through changes in maintenance and operating procedures, by not less than 20 percent from a corresponding base period having a degree day variance of less than 10 percent; or

(2)   Recommend appropriate energy conservation maintenance and operating procedures, on the basis of an on-site inspection and review of any scheduled preventive maintenance plan, together with a general estimate or range of energy and cost savings if practical, which may result from—

(i)   Effective operation of ventilation systems and control of infiltration conditions, including—

(A)   Repair of caulking or weatherstripping around windows and doors;

(B)   Reduction of outside air intake, shutting down ventilation systems when the building is not occupied; and

(C)   Assuring central or unitary ventilation controls, or both, are operating properly;

(ii)   Changes in the operation of heating or cooling systems through—

(A)   Lowering or raising indoor temperatures;

(B)   Locking thermostats;

(C)   Adjusting supply or heat transfer medium temperatures; and

(D)   Reducing or eliminating heating or cooling at night or at times when a building or complex is unoccupied;

(iii)   Changes in the operation of lighting systems through—

(A)   Reducing illumination levels;

(B)   Maximizing use of daylight;

(C)   Using higher efficiency lamps; and

(D)   Reducing or eliminating evening cleaning of buildings;

(iv)   Changes in the operation of water systems through—

(A)   Repairing leaks;

(B)   Reducing the quantity of water used, e.g., flow restrictors;

(C)   Lowering settings for hot water temperatures;

(D)   Raising settings for chilled water temperatures; and

Figure 1-3. Detailed Contents of Energy Audits (con't.)

(v) Changes in the maintenance and operating procedures of the utility plant and distribution system through—

(A) Cleaning equipment;

(B) Adjusting air/fuel ratio;

(C) Monitoring combustion;

(D) Adjusting fan, motor, or belt drive systems;

(E) Maintaining steam traps; and

(F) Repairing distribution pipe insulation; and

(vi) Such other actions as the State may determine useful or necessary, consistent with the purposes of the energy audit and acceptable cost constraints of section 450.46.

(c) Based on information gathered under paragraphs (a) and (b) of § 450.42, and paragraphs (a)(1) and (2) of this section, an energy audit shall indicate the need, if any, for the acquisition and installation of energy conservation measures and shall include an evaluation of the need and potential for retrofit based on consideration of one or more of the following—

(1) An energy use index or indices, for example, Btu's per gross square foot per year;

(2) An energy cost index or indices, for example, annual energy costs per gross square foot; or

(3) The physical characteristics of the building envelope and major energy-using systems.

(d) Based on information gathered under paragraph (c) of § 450.42 and subparagraph (a)(4) of this section, an energy audit shall include an indication of whether building conditions or characteristics present an opportunity for use of solar heating and cooling systems or solar hot water systems.

Figure 1-3. Detailed Contents of Energy Audits (concluded)

Technical Assistance Energy Audit– A Technical Assistance Energy Audit is defined in the *Federal Register,* Vol. 44, No. 75, Tuesday, April 17, 1979. The specific content of this audit is illustrated in Figure 1-4.

The criteria for determining who is qualified as a technical assistance analyst generated considerable comment. The final regulations stated

It is the intent of this regulation to establish minimum qualifications for technical assistance analysts to insure that participating institutions select individuals or firms able to perform the very complex and detailed technical assistance program. Accordingly, the final regulation specifies that the technical assistance analyst should be a registered professional engineer or, ideally, an architect and an engineer working as a team. However, the final regulation has been modified to permit a State to specify such alternative qualifications as it may deem appropriate and as are included in its approved State Plan. Such alternative qualifications must insure that the technical assistance analyst has sufficient experience and training to perform all of the minimum requirements of a technical assistance program.

An architect-engineer team provides an especially suitable combination of professional skills to perform the comprehensive analysis of the building or buildings required for a technical assistance program.

---

§ 455.42 Contents of program.

(a) A technical assistance program shall be conducted by a qualified technical assistance analyst, who shall consider all possible energy conservation measures for a building, including solar or other renewable resource measures. A technical assistance program shall include a detailed engineering analysis to identify the estimated costs of, and the energy and cost savings likely to be realized from, implementing each identified energy conservation maintenance and operating procedure. A technical assistance program shall also identify the estimated cost of, and the energy and cost savings likely to be realized from, acquiring and installing each energy conservation measure, including solar and other renewable resource measures, that indicate a significant potential for saving energy based upon the technical assistance analyst's initial consideration.

(b) At the conclusion of a technical assistance program, the technical assistance analyst shall prepare a final report which shall include—

(1) A description of building characteristics and energy data including—

(i) The results of the preliminary energy audit and energy audit (or its equivalent) of the building;

(ii) The operating characteristics of energy using systems; and

(iii) The estimated remaining useful life of the building;

(2) An analysis of the estimated energy consumption of the building, by fuel type (in total Btu's and Btu/sq. ft./yr.), at optimum efficiency (assuming implementation of all energy conservation maintenance and operating procedures);

(3) An evaluation of the building's potential for solar conversion.

(4) A listing of any known local zoning ordinances and building codes which may restrict the installation of solar systems;

(5) A description and analysis of all recommendations, if any, for acquisition and installation of energy conservation measures, including solar and other renewable resource measures, setting forth—

(i) A description of each recommended energy conservation measure;

(ii) An estimate of the cost of design, acquisition and installation of each energy conservation measure;

Figure 1-4. Detailed Contents of a Technical Assistance Energy Audit

(iii) An estimate of the useful life of each energy conservation measure;

(iv) An estimate of increases or decreases in maintenance and operating costs that would result from each energy conservation measure, if any:

(v) An estimate of the salvage value or disposal cost of each energy conservation measure at the end of its useful life, if any;

(vi) An estimate of the annual energy and energy cost savings (using current energy prices) expected from the acquisition and installation of each energy conservation measure. In calculating the potential energy cost savings of each recommended energy conservation measure, including solar or other renewable resource measure, technical assistance analysts shall—

(A) Assume that all energy savings obtained from energy conservation maintenance and operating procedures have been realized;

(B) Calculate the total energy and energy cost savings, by fuel type, expected to result from the acquisition and installation of all recommended energy conservation measures, taking into account the interaction among the various measures; and

(C) Calculate that portion of the total energy and energy cost savings, as determined in (B) above, attributable to each individual energy conservation measure.

(vii) The simple payback period of each recommended energy conservation measure, taking into account the interactions among the various measures. The simple payback period is calculated by dividing the estimated total cost of the measure, as determined pursuant to § 455.42 (b) (5)(ii), by the estimated annual cost saving accruing from the measure, as determined pursuant to § 455.42(b)(5)(vi). For the purposes of ranking applications, the simple payback period shall be calculated using the cost savings resulting from energy savings only, determined on the basis of current energy prices. The estimated cost of the measure shall be the total cost for design and other professional services (excluding costs of a technical assistance program), if any, and acquisition and installation costs. Other economic analyses, such as life-cycle costing, which consider all costs and cost savings, such as maintenance costs and/or savings, resulting from an energy conservation measure, are recommended, but not required, for use by the institution in its decision-making process;

(6) A listing of energy use and cost data for each fuel type used for the prior 12-month period.

(7) A signed and dated certification that the technical assistance program has been conducted in accordance with the requirements of this section and the grant application and that the data presented is accurate to the best of the technical assistance analyst's knowledge.

Figure 1-4. Detailed Contents of a Technical Assistance Energy Audit (concluded)

2

Energy Accounting And Analysis

ENERGY USE PROFILES

The energy audit process for a building emphasizes building envelope, heating and ventilation, air-conditioning, plus lighting functions. For an industrial facility the energy audit approach includes process consideration. Figures 2-1 through 2-3 illustrate how energy is used for a typical industrial plant. It is important to account for total consumption, cost, and how energy is used for each commodity such as steam, water, air and natural gas. This procedure is required to develop the appropriate energy conservation strategy.

The top portion of Figure 2-1 illustrates how much energy is used by fuel type and its relative percentage. The pie chart below shows how much is spent for each fuel type. Using a pie-chart representation or nodal flow diagram can be very helpful in visualizing how energy is being used.

Figure 2-2 on the other hand shows how much of the energy is used for each function such as lighting, process, and building heating and ventilation. Pie charts similar to the right-hand side of the figure should be made for each category such as air, steam, electricity, water and natural gas.

Figure 2-3 illustrates an alternate representation for the steam distribution profile.

Several audits are required to construct the energy use profiles, such as:

Envelope Audit—This audit surveys the building envelope for losses or gains due to leaks, building construction, doors, glass, lack of insulation, etc.

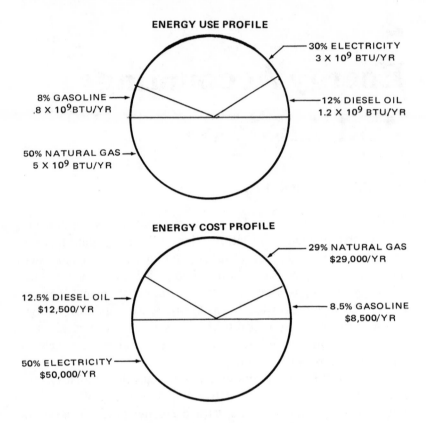

ENERGY USE PROFILE

30% ELECTRICITY
3 X 10⁹ BTU/YR

8% GASOLINE
.8 X 10⁹ BTU/YR

12% DIESEL OIL
1.2 X 10⁹ BTU/YR

50% NATURAL GAS
5 X 10⁹ BTU/YR

ENERGY COST PROFILE

29% NATURAL GAS
$29,000/YR

12.5% DIESEL OIL
$12,500/YR

8.5% GASOLINE
$8,500/YR

50% ELECTRICITY
$50,000/YR

Figure 2-1. Energy Use and Cost Profile

Functional Audit—This audit determines the amount of energy required for a particular function and identifies energy conservation opportunities. Functional audits include:
- Heating, ventilation and air-conditioning
- Building
- Lighting
- Domestic hot water
- Air distribution

Process Audit—This audit determines the amount of energy required for each process function and identifies energy conservation opportunities. Process functional audits include:
- Process machinery

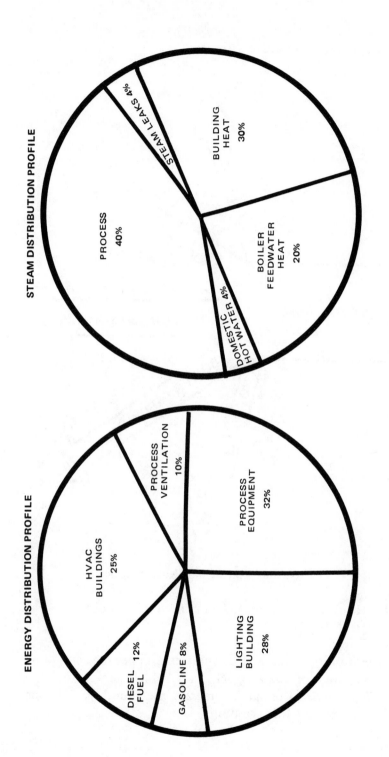

ENERGY DISTRIBUTION PROFILE

PROCESS VENTILATION 10%

HVAC BUILDINGS 25%

PROCESS EQUIPMENT 32%

DIESEL FUEL 12%

GASOLINE 8%

LIGHTING BUILDING 28%

STEAM DISTRIBUTION PROFILE

STEAM LEAKS 4%

BUILDING HEAT 30%

PROCESS 40%

DOMESTIC HOT WATER 4%

BOILER FEEDWATER HEAT 20%

Figure 2-2. Energy Profile by Function

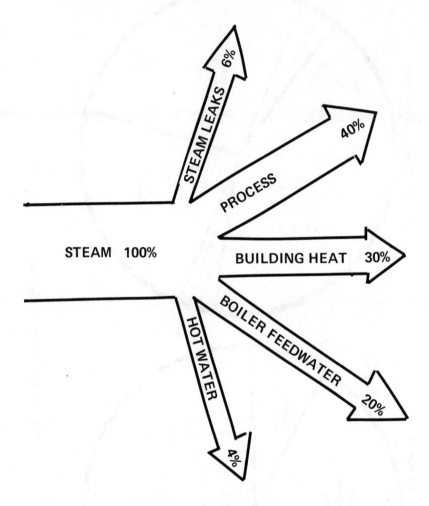

Figure 2-3. Steam Distribution Nodal Diagram

- Heating, ventilation and air-conditioning process
- Heat treatment
- Furnaces

Transportation Audit—This audit determines the amount of energy required for forklift trucks, cars, vehicles, trucks, etc.

Utility Audit—This audit analyzes the monthly, daily or yearly energy usage for each utility.

ENERGY USERS

Energy use profiles for several end-users are summarized in Tables 2-1 through 2-11.

Table 2-1. Energy Use in Apartment Buildings

	Range (%)	Norms (%)
Environmental Control	50 to 80	70
Lighting and Wall Receptacles	10 to 20	15
Hot Water	2 to 5	3
Special Functions		
Laundry, Swimming Pool, Restaurants,		
Parking, Elevators, Security Lighting	5 to 20	10

Source: Federal Energy Commission
Data Estimates, December 24, 1977

Table 2-2. Energy Use in Bakeries

Housekeeping Energy	Percent
Space Heating	21.5
Air Conditioning	1.6
Lighting	1.4
Domestic Hot Water	1.8
TOTAL	26.3
Process Energy	Percent
Baking Ovens	49.0
Pan Washing	10.6
Mixers	4.1
Freezers	3.3
Cooking	2.0
Fryers	1.8
Proof Boxes	1.8
Other Processes	1.1
TOTAL	73.7

Data are for a 27,000-square-foot bakery in Washington, D.C.

Table 2-3. Energy Use in Die Casting Plants

Housekeeping Energy	Percent
Space Heating	24
Air Conditioning	2
Lighting	2
Domestic Hot Water	2
TOTAL	30

Process Energy	Percent
Melting Hearth	30
Quiet Pool	20
Molding Machines	10
Air Compressors	5
Other Processes	5
TOTAL	70

Source: Federal Energy Commission
        Data Estimates, January 11, 1978

Table 2-4. Energy Use in Hospital Buildings

	Range (%)	Norms (%)
Environmental Control	40 to 65	58
Lighting and Wall Receptacles	10 to 20	15
Laundry	8 to 15	12
Food Service, Kitchen Operations	5 to 10	7
Medical Equipment, Sterilization, Incinerator, Parking, Elevators, Security Lighting	5 to 15	8

Source: Federal Energy Commission
        Data Estimates, November 3, 1977

Table 2-5. Energy Use in Hotels and Motels

	Range (%)	Norms (%)
Space Heating	45 to 70	60
Lighting	5 to 15	11
Air Conditioning	3 to 15	10
Refrigeration	0 to 10	4
Special Functions	5 to 20	15
Laundry, Kitchen, Restaurant,		
Swimming Pool, Garage,		
Security Lighting, Hot Water		

Source: Federal Energy Commission
           Data Estimates, December 8, 1977

Table 2-6. Energy Use in Retail Stores

	Range (%)	Norms (%)
HVAC	20 to 50	30
Lighting	40 to 75	60
Special Functions	5 to 20	10
Elevators, General Power, Parking		
Security Lighting, Hot Water		

Source: Federal Energy Commission
           Data Estimates, December 14, 1977

Table 2-7. Energy Use in Restaurants

	Table Restaurant Norms (%)	Fast Food Restaurant Norms (%)
HVAC	32	36
Lighting	8	26
Special Functions		
Food Preparation	45	27
Food Storage	2	6
Sanitation	12	1
Other	1	4

Source: Federal Energy Commission
Data Estimates, December 8, 1977

Table 2-8. Energy Use in Schools

	Range (%)	Norms (%)
Environmental Control	45 to 80	65
Lighting and Wall Receptacles	10 to 20	15
Food Service	5 to 10	7
Hot Water	2 to 5	3
Special Functions	0 to 20	10

Source: Federal Energy Commission
Data Estimates, November 3, 1977

Table 2-9. Energy Use in Transportation Terminals

	Range (%)	Norms (%)
Space Heating	50 to 75	60
Lighting	5 to 25	15
Air Conditioning	5 to 25	15
Special Functions	3 to 20	10
Elevators, General Power, Parking, Security Lighting, Hot Water		

Source: Federal Energy Commission
Data Estimates, December 10, 1977

Table 2-10. Energy Use in Warehouses and Storage Facilities
(Vehicles Not Included)

	Range (%)	Norms (%)*
Space Heating	45 to 80	67
Air Conditioning	3 to 10	6
Lighting	4 to 12	7
Refrigeration	0 to 40	12
Special Functions	5 to 15	8
Elevators, General Power, Parking, Security Lighting, Hot Water		

* Norms for a warehouse or storage facility are strongly dependent on the products and their specific requirements for temperature and humidity control.

Source: Federal Energy Commission
Data Estimates, December 21, 1977

Table 2-11. Comparative Energy Use By System

		Heating & Ventilation	Cooling & Ventilation	Lighting	Power & Process	Domestic Hot Water
Schools	A	4	3	1	5	—
	B	1	4	2	5	3
	C	1	4	2	5	3
Colleges	A	5	2	1	4	3
	B	1	3	2	5	4
	C	1	5	2	4	3
Office Bldg.	A	3	1	2	4	5
	B	1	3	2	4	5
	C	1	3	2	4	5
Commercial Stores	A	3	1	2	4	5
	B	2	3	1	4	5
	C	1	3	2	4	5
Religious Bldg.	A	3	2	1	4	5
	B	1	3	2	4	5
	C	1	3	2	4	5
Hospitals	A	4	1	2	5	3
	B	1	3	4	5	2
	C	1	5	3	4	2

Climatic Zone A: Fewer than 2500 degree days
Climate Zone B: 2500—5500 degree days
Climate Zone C: 5500—9500 degree days

Source: Guidelines For Saving Energy In Existing Buildings ECM—1

Note: Numbers indicate energy consumption relative to each other
  (1) greatest consumption
  (5) least consumption

ENERGY ACCOUNTING

An important part of the overall energy auditing program is to be able to measure where you are, and determine where you are going. It is vital to establish an energy accounting system at the beginning of the program. This section is based on the work of the Carborundum Corporation. The Carborundum Energy Accounting and Analysis System should serve as a useful guide as to how one major energy intensive company established its accounting and analysis procedures.

One of the more important aspects of energy management and conservation is measuring and accounting for energy consumption. At Carborundum an energy accounting and analysis system has been developed which is unique in industry, a simple but powerful analytical, management decision-making tool. The Office of Energy Programs of the U.S. Department of Commerce asked Carborundum to work with them in developing this system into a national system, hopefully to be used in the voluntary industrial conservation program. A number of major U.S. corporations are either using or are considering using the system proposed. The system is offered to those who want to use it.

Most energy accounting systems have been devised and are administered by engineers for engineers. The engineers' principal interest in developing these systems has been the display of energy consumed per unit of production. That ratio has been called "energy efficiency," and changes in energy efficiency are clearly energy conserved or wasted. The engineer focuses all of his attention on reducing energy consumed per unit of production.

An energy efficiency ratio alone, however, cannot answer the kinds of questions asked by business managers and/or government authorities:

- If we are conserving energy, why is our total energy consumption increasing?
- If we are wasting energy, why is our total energy consumption decreasing?
- If we have made no change in energy efficiency, why is our energy consumption changing?

- How much of our energy consumption is due to factors beyond our control, such as weather, legislated environmental controls, etc.?
- How much of our energy consumption is the result of running experiments for saving energy?
- How much of our energy consumption is fixed variable?
- How much of our energy consumption change is due to increased production?

Most energy accounting systems cannot answer such questions because they concentrate solely on energy efficiency. Like the current DOE system, they develop an energy efficiency algorithm. The algorithm begins with total energy consumed divided by the total production in a base period.

The percent conserved numbers are then presented in isolation and the questions suggested earlier are left begging. Of course, as long as the percentages are improving or are above expected levels or goals, few people raise the questions. It is when the trend changes direction or a more detailed analysis is sought that the weakness of the system is recognized. Many explanations can be offered. Adjustments, not being displayed, raise doubts as to their validity.

Clearly, the clerical load of the algorithmic approach is high, as is the editorial load in explaining changes.

The Carborundum System, however, answers just about any question a business manager or a government agency could ask about energy consumption. It does so in a self-explanatory numerical display of all the facts—unadjusted facts; matters of record in any business.

The system can handle any product or service, from foundries to office buildings; sum the changes in diverse situations and present the overall energy impact on a plant, company, city, state or nation. It can express those differences in monetary terms or in energy terms, be they barrels of oil equivalent (BOE), kilowatt hours (KWH), or British thermal units (BTU).

This system requires a minimum of clerical effort for gathering data and can be calculated manually or by computer.

A VARIANCE ANALYSIS

Table 2-12 shows that only 1% more energy was used in 1977 but 14% more was paid for it than in 1976.

Table 2-12. Energy Accounting and Analysis– North America

	1977	1976
Total Energy Used (Billions BTU)	6,847	6,804
Difference 1977/76	43	
% Difference	1%	
Total Energy Cost ($000)	$19,015	$16,721
Difference 1977/76	2,294	
$ Difference	14%	

These differences are caused by a number of factors. Those considered most important are changes in volume and/or mix of products produced, weather, pollution control requirements, alternative fuels (using more or less expensive fuels for the same application than those used in the base period), conservation, and price. The Carborundum System separates all these factors or variances for analysis in both dollars and BTU, as shown in Table 2-13.

Table 2-13. Variance Analysis of Differences Between 1976 and 1977

Contributor	Variance	
	In Thousands of $	Billions of BTU
Volume/Mix	$1,054	418
Weather	(53)	(27)
Pollution	48	23
Other	403	142
Price	1,719	– –
Conservation	(877)	(513)
Alternative Fuels	88*	– –
Net Impact	$2,294	43

*Nonadditive Memo Item

Of the 43 billion BTU and $2,294,000 difference between 1976 and 1977, $1,054,000 and 418 billion BTU are the result of producing more products or a change in product mix. Should we want to separate volume from mix we can do it, but it is not really meaningful at the corporate level since only a handful of plants will have significant mix changes. We do it at the plant level if and when it is useful.

In metallurgy, the quality of the ore or whatever raw material is used can have a significant impact on energy used. The system can reflect this impact as well. At Carborundum, that impact is small and is not shown separately.

The weather was colder in the first quarter of 1977, but milder in the balance of the year, resulting in a reduced weather effect versus the prior year.

Forty-eight thousand dollars and 23 billion BTU were spent for additional pollution control in 1977 than in 1976.

"Other" factors include such things as base loads which represent the fixed versus variable energy load or energy used for experimental processes or start-up of processes with no historical data for comparison. By putting such data into the "other" category, changes in energy efficiency in specific product lines can be isolated for analysis without being distorted by extraneous or extraordinary situations.

An additional $1,719,000 was paid for energy in 1977 because prices were up 13% overall.

Conservation avoided expenditures of $877,000 and 513 billion BTU. This was the result of a 7% reduction in total energy used per unit of production in 1977 versus 1976. Note that the conservation of 513 billion BTU is greater than the volume/ mix increase of 418 billion BTU. *In effect, growth in demand was offset with conservation.*

Being forced to use more expensive alternative forms of energy during curtailments for other reasons cost $88,000 more in 1977. This item is not additive in summing the net impact as it is part of all other factors. It is tracked primarily for information and decision-making purposes, but not as a part of the variance analysis.

The net impact is the algebraic sum of all effects and is the total difference between energy used in this period and last. It is a closed loop which can be as complex or as simple as management wishes it to be. Whether a plant is a woodworking shop or a foundry, the plant manager has the option of making his analysis very deep, or as shallow as he wishes. In any case, all operations are additive to give a total corporate picture.

The analysis in dollars is published each month as part of our corporate operations and financial progress report. The report is subtotaled by division, group and corporate total. Accompanying the numbers is a discussion of the current results and events, along with forecasts of price availability and any other factors subject to change.

Each reporting plant and division receives a computer printout showing complete analysis by product line and by energy type or fuel, allowing plant managers and engineers to make decisions based on simple data analysis in whatever form they wish. A sample analysis is presented later in this chapter.

Data input is a matter of minutes per month in each plant. Corporate clerical work is a matter of two man-days per month using a minicomputer. Printouts are mailed to plants within a week of receipt of input. Data input and printouts are demonstrated and discussed later in this chapter.

Results of the program as of the end of the first half of 1977 indicate savings of 18% over 1972; the objective was 15%. The goal established in 1975 for 1980 was 15%. Having clearly exceeded the long-term goal, it was thought to increase it to 20%, but then decided finally to state the goal in terms mentioned earlier: offset volume change with conservation. Stating the objective in these terms is more realistic because if the volume decreases as a result of an economic recession, it is known that energy conservation will reverse itself if only because a lower capacity utilization results in lower efficiency.

This system, plus conservation-oriented management, does increase energy efficiency and conservation means profit.

The system is so simple that the energy use data of the smallest sales office can be combined with those of the largest foundry for overall analysis. After two years of experience, the system has proven so flexible that it is as applicable to a home, an office building, a hospital or a hotel as to a large factory, powerhouse, or refinery. The system is compatible with the current U.S. Department of Energy (DOE) mandatory energy reporting requirements.

What follows is a description of the workings of the Carborundum System followed by a discussion of analytical methods.

ACCOUNTING INPUT

The data requirements can be as simple or as complex as the user chooses. The data form developed by Carborundum (Figure 2-4) is flexible enough to handle a broad spectrum of complexities.

FUEL USED

The first category of data required is the type of fuel or energy used and its cost. The quantity should be taken directly from utility invoices or inventory differences. One advantage of the Carborundum System is that the units may be metric or imperial or whatever the invoice shows.

The Carborundum System works with five sources of energy: electricity, natural gas, fuel oil, coal and propane. No user need feel restricted to those five or feel that all of them need be used. An "other" category gives the system the flexibility for working with other fuels or forms of energy. In practice, we find that the "other" fuels are an extremely small proportion of our total. Our limited use of the "other" category has prevented distortions and has improved the quality of our analyses.

The conversion factor is the multiplier used to convert the unit of fuel to common thermal units. Carborundum uses British thermal units (BTU), but calories or joules or any other unit could be used.

For a simple energy accounting and analysis, only the fuel used and its cost are required. Each reporting location can stop there or give further data for more thorough analyses.

PRODUCTION

The first category of selection of the total energy distribution is production energy. The production quantity need not be in terms of units produced; it could be number of patrons of a movie theater, customers in a store, passengers in a transportation system, hours or other unit of time in which the facility is used, miles traveled, etc. In any case, the "product" should be clearly defined in the mind of the system's user and should be a common denominator of the business being conducted.

Carborundum Energy Accounting and
Analysis System Data Input Form

Energy Management and Conservation Program

Plant Input Data

Plant _____

Division _____

Group _____

Today's Date _____

Period Covered _____

Description	Elec. kwh (000)*	Gas mcf	Oil gal. (000)*	Coal lbs. (000)*	Propane gal. (000)*	Other (000)*
Total Fuel Used						
Quantity						
Cost ($)						
** Conversion Factor	⨯					
Production						
Product 1 NAME						
Production Unit						
Quant. Prod. (000)						
Fuel Used						
Product 2 NAME						
Production Unit						
Quant. Prod. (000)						
Fuel Used						
Product 3 NAME						
Production Unit						
Quant. Prod. (000)						
Fuel Used						
Product 4 NAME						
Production Unit						
Quant. Prod. (000)						
Fuel Used						
Product 5 NAME						
Production Unit						
Quant. Prod. (000)						
Fuel Used						
Heating						
Degree Days						
Fuel Used						
Cooling						
Degree Days						
Fuel Used						
Pollution Control						
Fuel Used						
Other						
Fuel Used						
** Alternate Fuel						

*All fuels reported in thousands to two decimal places.

Figure 2-4. Carborundum Energy Accounting and Analysis System Data Input Form

A product line may be a process as long as energy and production output are discretely measured.

The production unit should be in physical terms whenever possible—i.e. weight, volume, length, area, or number of items. Nonphysical units such as value, manhours, etc. are subject to distortions. Monetary value suffers from the distortion of inflation and other effects. Manhours worked is a poor energy accounting measure; there will be severe distortions with product mix or productivity changes. That is not to say that nonphysical units may not be used, but rather that the pitfalls of using them must be recognized.

To be useful, the amount of energy specifically used for production should be metered or at least allocated to production from the total. If production is low in energy intensity (energy cost as a per cent of production value), it is sometimes better to attribute all energy to heating and cooling, discussed below. If, on the other hand, energy used for heating and cooling is small compared to the energy used for production, all energy may be allocated to production.

The Carborundum System permits analysis of any number of different product lines for any one location or reporting unit. The input form allows for five product lines as that is the most usually reported. Plants wishing to report more than five may use the extra sheets or may break themselves down into subplants with separate input data for each subplant. Again, to be meaningful, the amount of energy specifically used for each product line must be measured independently or at least allocated from the total.

The amount of fuel or energy used for production is recorded in the same units for each fuel or energy form as the total at the top of the page. No conversion to a common thermal unit is made on the data input sheet.

HEATING AND COOLING

The next two categories of data requirement are heating and cooling. The reporting unit determines if these data are meaningful. The energy used should be discretely metered or allocated to heating and cooling. The amount used should be recorded in the same units for each fuel or energy forms as the total at the top of the input form.

The amount of comfort heating and cooling required is governed by weather conditions as opposed to process heating or cooling which should be considered production energy. For the purpose of this analysis, degree-days are used as the measure of weather intensity. Current and historical degree-day data are easily obtainable from airport or city weather departments, public utilities and other sources of fuel supply. Other factors such as wind, sun, exposure, etc. affect the heating and cooling energy requirements of buildings, but in our experience, degree-days are sufficiently significant and certainly simple enough.

This discussion will not include calculation of degree-days or other factors of weather intensity.

Other variables may affect the amount of heating and cooling energy used. One Carborundum plant varies its manufacturing area significantly as sales volume demands. The production use of energy is insignificant compared to that used for heating and cooling. To compensate for the varying conditions, the heating and cooling energy is treated as production energy and the unit of "production" is square feet of manufacturing space multiplied by degree-days. The use of the Carborundum System is limited only by the user's imagination.

POLLUTION CONTROL

One of the criticisms leveled at most energy reporting systems is the lack of recognition given to changing business conditions. Environmental control requirements are being met, but at the cost of greater energy expenditure to operate the pollution control devices. Many businessmen feel that energy requirements for pollution control diminish the impact of energy conservation efforts. The category of data recognizes pollution control energy requirements by considering it separately. Again, it is up to the reporting unit management to decide if the data are significant and if they will add to the usefulness of energy accounting and analysis. The energy must, of course, be measured or allocated from the total.

OTHER

The final category of data requirement is intended to give the system the flexibility of handling any other category considered useful by reporting unit management. We include in this category, energy consumed in experimental efforts, start-up of a new product line for which there is no history, and base loads of steam plants or process ovens and furnaces which are not variable and are therefore not affected by production volume or weather. Managers who do not want production and weather data analyses distorted by extraneous energy consumption will choose this category. The energy reported should be significant. This energy is not excluded from subsequent analysis, however.

ALTERNATE FUEL

The last line of the form (Figure 2-4) is to indicate those fuels used as alternates for each other anywhere in the reporting unit. In most cases it does not matter if some processes or energy uses have no alternative while others using the same fuel can be switched to another. The alternatives are recognized in the report form so long as they exist anywhere in the reporting unit. This subject will be covered more thoroughly in the discussion of output logic.

BALANCING

Once the input data are complete, one check should be made before treating it. The sum of fuel used for production, heating, cooling, pollution control and "other" should equal the total at the top of the sheet for each fuel used. If the totals do not balance, the error must be found before proceeding. The important thing here is that all energy is accounted for.

ACCOUNTING OUTPUT LOGIC

The output of the Carborundum energy accounting and analysis system is a display of treated data from two time periods and a comparison between them, identifying the nature and magnitude of any changes taking place. The selection of the two time periods is up to the user. The federal government compares current periods against the base year period of 1972. An industry association's reporting to the government would do the same, but for its own purposes it might prefer to compare this quarter vs. last quarter, of this year vs. last year, etc. A company or plant might want to compare this month vs. last month. The Carborundum Company prefers a monthly comparison of this year-to-date vs. last-year-to-date, and keeps a base period data on file for long-range comparisons as well.

The form of the output or display of data treated for analysis is not important but it should contain at least the elements of the Carborundum System output (Figure 2-5) discussed below.

The headings across the top of the form are fuels reported in the input. Each fuel has two columns; data from the current period and data from the period we are comparing against. The last pair of columns on the right are totals.

ENERGY USED "ENERGY (MBTU)"

The first line of data is the result of multiplying the amount of fuel used by the appropriate conversion factor and expressing the result in BTU. The conversion to BTU permits the summing of energy used by the five fuel types plus "other" fuels. The energy shown is the total used in the two time periods compared.

ENERGY COST AND COST PER UNIT OF ENERGY

Energy cost is the year-to-date sums of input data and the sum across the page for each of the two time periods in the comparison. Energy costs per unit are the result of dividing the costs by the energy used in BTU and expressing them in the form of $/BTU. Direct comparisons of the costs of two forms of energy can now be made, either in the same or different periods. The result of the exercise in the totals column is a weighted average cost per BTU. Shifts in the mix of fuels used

SEPTEMBER 1977

PLANT- MIDTOWN
DIVISION- A B C
GROUP- INDUSTRIAL
COMPANY- U.S.INDUSTRY

DESCRIPTION	ELECTRICITY 77~SEP	ELECTRICITY 76~SEP	GAS 77~SEP	GAS 76~SEP	OIL 77~SEP	OIL 76~SEP	COAL 77~SEP	COAL 76~SEP	PROPANE 77~SEP	PROPANE 76~SEP	OTHER 77~SEP	OTHER 76~SEP	TOTAL 77~SEP	TOTAL 76~SEP
ENERGY (MBTU)	2408	2258	1625	2986	4210	5264	0	0	0	0	0	0	8243	10508
ENERGY ($)	15771	14215	3526	4807	10778	12212	0	0	0	0	0	0	30075	31234
COST/UT $/MB	6.55	6.30	2.17	1.61	2.56	2.32	0.00	0.00	0.00	0.00	0.00	0.00	3.65	2.97
PRODUCTION-														
PRODUCT LINE 1:														
QUANTITY	1005	915	1005	915	1005	915	0	0	0	0	0	0		
ENERGY-MBTU	1417	1418	539	1860	1914	548	0	0	0	0	0	0	3870	3826
ENERGY/K-UT	1.410	1.550	.536	2.033	1.905	.599	0.000	0.000	0.000	0.000	0.000	0.000		
EN.COST ($)	9282	8930	1170	2994	4900	1271	0	0	0	0	0	0	15351	13195
EN.EFF-MBTU	141	141	1504	0	-1313	0	0	0	0	0	0	0	332	0
EN.EFF-o/o	9.049	0.000	73.617	0.000	********	0.000	0.000	0.000	0.000	0.000	0.000	0.000	7.911	0.000
PRODUCT LINE 2:														
QUANTITY	31	28	52	47	50	200	0	0	0	0	0	0		
ENERGY-MBTU	763	700	989	939	1216	3628	0	0	0	0	0	0	2968	5267
ENERGY/K-UT	24.613	25.000	19.019	19.979	24.325	18.140	0.000	0.000	0.000	0.000	0.000	0.000		
EN.COST ($)	4998	4407	2446	1512	3113	8417	0	0	0	0	0	0	10257	14335
EN.EFF-MBTU	12	0	50	0	309	0	0	0	0	0	0	0	247	0
EN.EFF-o/o	1.550	0.000	4.803	0.000	-34.100	0.000	0.000	0.000	0.000	0.000	0.000	0.000	9.091	0.000
PRODUCT LINE 3:														
QUANTITY	150	100	0	0	0	0	0	0	0	0	0	0		
ENERGY-MBTU	51	35	0	0	0	0	0	0	0	0	0	0	51	35
ENERGY/K-UT	.340	.350	0.000	0.000	0.000	0.000	0.000	0.000	0.000	0.000	0.000	0.000		
EN.COST ($)	334	221	0	0	0	0	0	0	0	0	0	0	334	221
EN.EFF-MBTU	2	0	0	0	0	0	0	0	0	0	0	0	2	0
EN.EFF-o/o	2.924	0.000	0.000	0.000	0.000	0.000	0.000	0.000	0.000	0.000	0.000	0.000	2.924	0.000
HEATING-														
DEGREE DAYS	393	358	393	358	393	358	393	358	393	358	393	358		
ENERGY-MBTU	0	0	0	0	984	990	0	0	0	0	0	0	984	990
ENERGY/DD	0.000	0.000	0.000	0.000	2.504	2.764	0.000	0.000	0.000	0.000	0.000	0.000		
COOLING-														
DEGREE DAYS	10	44	10	44	10	44	10	44	10	44	10	44		
ENERGY-MBTU	15	67	0	0	0	0	0	0	0	0	0	0	15	67
ENERGY/DD	1.499	1.524	0.000	0.000	0.000	0.000	0.000	0.000	0.000	0.000	0.000	0.000		
POLLUTION CTL ENERGY-MBTU	90	34	0	0	0	0	0	0	0	0	0	0	90	34
OTHER- ENERGY-MBTU	72	0	97	187	96	99	0	0	0	0	0	0	265	286

SEP-76 TO SEP-77 IMPACT --

VOLUME/MIX EFFECT (MBTU)						
PROD.LINE 1	140	183	54	0	0	376
PROD.LINE 2	75	100	2721	0	0	2546
PROD.LINE 3	18			0	0	18
TOTAL-MBTU	232	283	2667	0	0	2152
VOLUME/MIX EFFECT ($)						
PROD.LINE 1	878	295	125	0	0	1298
PROD.LINE 2	472	161	6312	0	0	5679
PROD.LINE 3	110		0	0	0	110
TOTAL-$	1461	455	6187	0	0	4271
WEATHER (MBTU)						
HEATING	0	0	97	0	0	97
COOLING	52	0	0	0	0	52
TOTAL	52	0	97	0	0	45
WEATHER ($)						
HEATING	0	0	224	0	0	224
COOLING	326	0	0	0	0	326
TOTAL	326	0	224	0	0	102
POLLUTION CONTROL-						
MBTU	56	0	0	0	0	56
$	352	0	0	0	0	352
OTHER-						
MBTU	72	90	3	0	0	21
$	452	145	6	0	0	300
ENERGY CONSERVATION-						
MBTU	158	1554	1519	0	0	193
$	996	2502	3525	0	0	27
ALTERNATE FUEL ADJUSTMENT-						
RATIO	0.00	.36	.64	0.00	0.00	0.00
DISTRIBUTION	0	2112	3723	0	0	0
ALTERNATE FUEL IMPACT-						
MBTU	0	487	487	0	0	346
$	0	784	1130	0	0	
PRICE ($)	613	910	1010	0	0	2534
NET IMPACT ($)-						
ACTUAL	1556	1281	1434	0	0	1159
PROGRAM	0	0	0	0	0	0
ENERGY CONSERVATION o/o						
ACTUAL	6.2	48.9	56.5	0.0	0.0	2.3
PROGRAM	0.0	0.0	0.0	0.0	0.0	0.0

Figure 2-5. Energy Management and Conservation Report

will change the weighted average costs/BTU just as any change in individual fuel costs/BTU will affect the weighted averages. Opportunities are identified for overall energy cost reduction through fuel switching.

PRODUCTION

The next series of lines show production data including quantity produced, energy used for that production, energy efficiency, cost of energy used, energy saved (or wasted) as a result of changes in efficiency between time periods in the comparison and percent change in energy efficiency.

Energy used for production is expressed in BTU for each fuel type. Production quantity is not totaled for obvious reasons. Energy efficiency of production is expressed in BTU per thousand units and is the result of dividing the energy used for production by units produced.

The series of production data are repeated for as many product lines as the reporting unit management has chosen.

Obviously, the energy efficiency of different fuels and different product lines can now be compared in the same period or against efficiencies in other periods. Similarly, comparisons can be made of efficiency in one product line versus the efficiency in other periods in the same product line.

HEATING AND COOLING

The next six lines of data in the output show weather intensity in degree-days energy used for heating and cooling and energy efficiency of heating and cooling (energy used per degree-day) in the two time periods under consideration.

Weather intensity and its effects on energy used and energy efficiency can now be compared by fuel and between periods and in total.

POLLUTION CONTROL

The next line of data shows the energy used in BTU for pollution control in each period. If the requirements for pollution control are changing, the effects on energy consumption will be clearly shown.

OTHER

The last line of energy use data in the output shows the energy used in BTU in one period compared to another for such things as experimental efforts, start-up of a new product line for which there is no history and base loads of steam plants which are not weather. As described in the input section, this is a way of pulling these kinds of data out of other effects being isolated for analysis. At the same time, the energy is not excluded from the overall analysis—no energy is excluded.

THIS PERIOD VS. LAST PERIOD IMPACT

Beyond this point in our output, the numbers define the variance analysis which show the impact of changing volume, product mix, weather, pollution control, energy conservation efforts, "Other" effects, and price, on energy usage and cost in the period being analyzed compared to the period used as the basis for analysis. The algebraic sum of all the impacts or variances is the net impact. If it is a valid variance analysis, the net impact is the difference between the total energy used or cost in the period being analyzed and that in the base period. If the net impact is not equal to the difference between totals, there is an error in arithmetic or assumptions.

Also shown among impacts is the effect of using alternative fuels either because of curtailments or cost. This variance is not additive in the variance analysis since the effect cannot be isolated from the other effects without considerable arithmetic. We calculate the impact of alternative fuels only to display it as an economic fact to be taken into consideration for management strategic and decision-making purposes. The energy impact is zero in this system since alternatives are used on a straight BTU exchange basis.

This is not strictly true, of course, as calorific values are not always useful energy values and there are often differences in efficiency of combustion or use. These effects are usually small enough to ignore. If a user feels that they are significant, there is no reason why they cannot be taken into consideration.

VOLUME/MIX IMPACT

The impact of volume and/or product mix changes is the amount of more (or less) energy that is used currently, as opposed to previously, solely as the result of producing more (or less) product or proportionately more (or less) energy intense products.

In mathematical terms, the effect of volume and/or product mix changes on energy is defined as the algebraic sum of the products of the change in volume in the periods under discussion in each product line multiplied by the energy efficiency of production of each product line in the base period. In the Carborundum System this translates into the algebraic sum of the products of the difference in production volume this year-to-date and last year-to-date times the energy used per unit of production last year-to-date for each product line. The monetary impact of volume/mix is the energy impact calculated as above multiplied by the cost per unit of energy last year-to-date. That is to say, the impact of changes in volume/mix on energy use or cost is the difference between this period's volume mix and last period's volume mix times the energy efficiency achieved in the last or base period. The result ignores improvements in efficiency (identified later as energy conservation effects) and inflation (identified later as price effects) and isolates the effects of only volume/mix changes. A more detailed treatment of this effect appears in the analysis section.

WEATHER IMPACT

The effect of weather changes (colder winter or hotter summer) on energy consumption is defined as the change in degree-days in the periods under discussion times the heating or cooling efficiency in the period used as the basis for analysis. In the Carborundum System, this translates into the difference in degree-days this year-to-date and last year-to-date times the energy used per degree-day last year-to-date. The monetary impact of weather is the impact calculated as above times the cost per unit of energy last year-to-date. That is to say, the impact of weather changes on energy use or cost is the difference between this period's weather and last, times the heating/cooling energy efficiency in the last or base period. The result ignores improvements in efficiency (identified later as energy conservation effects) and inflation (identified later as price effects), and isolates the effect of weather.

POLLUTION CONTROL IMPACT

The impact of the energy increase or decrease to control pollution in the current period versus any other time period is simply the difference in the energy used in the two periods. The financial impact is the impact calculated above multiplied by the cost per unit of energy in the last period. The result ignores conservation and price effects as before, and isolates the effect of pollution control.

"OTHER" IMPACTS

The impact of other energy uses, previously defined as experimental, start-up of product lines without history, of base loads, etc., is simply the difference in energy used in the two periods being compared. The economic impact is the impact calculated above multiplied by the cost per unit of energy in the prior period. Again, the result ignores conservation and price effects and isolates the effect of these "other" uses of energy.

ENERGY CONSERVATION

In the Carborundum System, conservation is defined as the reduction in energy consumed in the current period versus that consumed in the comparative period after all other effects (volume/mix, weather, pollution, "other" effects) have been taken into consideration. To arrive at the energy conserved (in BTU) the algebraic sum of all the impacts calculated above is added to the total used in the prior period and that sum subtracted from the total used in the current period. To check the calculation, the sum of all the calculated energy savings in each product line and/or heating and cooling should equal the number derived by subtraction above.

The financial impact of conservation is the product of all the energy conserved multiplied by the costs per unit in the prior period. Some people are concerned about "error" arising from using prior period vs. current period energy unit costs. The magnitude of "error" is not large and if objectives or goals are stated in the same dollars, there should be no problem. In any case, the correction may be made for discussion purposes. Senior management seems to prefer conservation stated in last year's dollars because in the goal-setting process, those are "current dollars" at the time goals are set.

Objective achievement in conservation is thus not distorted by price changes which are more difficult to predict. When comparing performance to a more distant base period, the "error" of using the prior period dollars becomes significant and must be adjusted for. In any case, expressing the conservation impact in the last year's dollars, isolates conservation from price effects.

PRICE IMPACT

The impact of price changes is simply the difference in unit cost in the current period and those in the comparative period multiplied by the energy used in the current period.

NET IMPACT

The net impact, then, is the net effect of all the isolated factors identified. The Carborundum System identifies only the economic net impact in the output format. There is, of course, an energy net impact (in BTU) which would be useful primarily to suppliers, but not really to a user unless he has a limited captive supply. It is certainly of interest to the government.

In either case, the net impact is the algebraic sum of all the isolated factors minus the conservation effect. By definition, the net impact is the difference between the total energy used or its cost in the current period and that of the period being used as a basis for the analysis. In the Carborundum System output format, the differences referred to are those between fuel or total columns in the first two lines of the output. If the net impact by the sum-of-effects method is not equal to the difference between this period and last, there is an error in either the data or the calculations.

At Carborundum, every plant manager, division manager and group vice-president is committed to a net impact for the coming year. This number is tracked versus performance in the output.

ENERGY CONSERVATION PERCENT

The last two lines of the Carborundum energy accounting and analysis system output are the percent energy conserved, actual and programmed. This is an overall conservation percentage change in the current period vs. the prior period. The percentage is arrived at by dividing energy conserved by energy conserved plus the total energy used in the current period.

Commitment by all levels of management at Carborundum to a conservation percentage is made prior to the start of the year and performance is measured against it.

ANALYSIS

An example of a plant accounting and analysis for 1977 vs. 1976 September year-to-date is shown in Figure 2-5. For the most part, data are taken from a combination of real plant situations to illustrate the simplicity and flexibility of the system.

INPUT

Fuel usage data are taken directly from invoices and/or meters. Production data are readily available. Notice the variety of physical units used. Production Line 1 is plastic products and the unit (lbs) is constant for all fuel forms as is quantity produced. In glass products, Product Line 2, the unit is number of items produced with electricity and oil, but the unit is pounds for those produced with gas. Different numbers of items were produced electrically—and oil-fired in the same month. This is not an unusual situation. Gas process production has traditionally been measured in weight of throughput. accounting and analysis. Product Line 3, wooden products, require only electricity.

Plant management could just as easily not have broken products into three lines, but by doing so, we will more properly see the effect of production mix/volume changes. Most energy is metered because we have found that the simple act of metering results in energy awareness which leads to conservation.

September usually has heating degree-days (cold days) and cooling degree-days (warm days). Therefore, both heating and cooling processes took place. It is seen that September '77 was cooler than September '76.

More pollution control equipment was installed in the year between Septembers increasing energy consumption. Plant management chose to study the effect through input of pollution control data.

The plant has three loads of the "other" variety. There are experiments under way to replace gas with electricity in furnacing. Oil-fired equipment has a fixed load which does not vary with production levels. The oil-fired boiler has a fixed load which is unaffected by weather or production.

Since gas and oil are alternate fuels for the plastics line, they are checked in the input data sheet to alert the analyst. It does not matter how much or where the alternates are used for the output logic to be run on the data.

OUTPUT

Using the input data and completing the arithmetic described in the output logic section (Figure 2-6), we produced the numbers shown in Figure 2-5. Analysis results in the following conclusions starting from the top of Figure 2-5:

ARITHMETIC FORMULAE USED IN THE CARBORUNDUM ACCOUNTING AND ANALYSIS SYSTEM
(April 1978)

The numbers (#) used in the following equations refer to the item number at the left margin. MBTU is mega or millions of BTU. YTD is this year to date or this period. LYTD is last year to date or prior period; the period against which comparisons are being made.

1. Energy Used (MBTU) = Invoice or equivalent quantity X input conversion factor to MBTU
2. Energy Dollars = Invoice or equivalent dollars
3. Cost/Unit ($/MBTU) = #2 ÷ #1
4. Production Quantity = Quantity produced from input sheet
5. Production Energy (MBTU) = Input value in invoiced units X input conversion factor to MBTU
6. Energy (MBTU) /Unit of production = #5 ÷ #4
7. Production Energy Cost ($) = #5 X #3
8. Production Energy Saved (MBTU) = (#4 YTD X #6 LYTD) − #5 YTD
9. Production Energy Conservation (%) = (#8 ÷ (#8 + #5 YTD)) X 100
10. Heating Degree Days = Input value
11. Heating Energy (MBTU) = Input value in invoiced units X input conversion factor to MBTU
12. Heating Energy/Degree-Day (MBTU/DD) = #11 ÷ #10
13. Heating Energy Saved (MBTU) = (#10 YTD X #12 LYTD) − #11 YTD
14. Cooling Degree Days = Input value
15. Colling Energy (MBTU) = Input value in invoiced units X input conversion factor to MBTU
16. Cooling Energy/Degree-Day (MBTU/DD) = #15 ÷ #14
17. Cooling Energy Saved (MBTU) = (#14 YTD X #16 LYTD) − #15 YTD
18. Pollution = Input value X input conversion factor to MBTU
19. Other = Input value in invoiced units X input conversion factor to MBTU

A useful check at this point is that the sum of all energy used for production, heating, cooling, pollution and "other" (items 5, 11,

Figure 2-6. Energy Accounting Instructions

15, 18, 19) must equal the total energy used (item 1).

Impacts or Variances

The following is a variance analysis to account for the difference in gross energy used or cost. Cost variance is in terms of last year's dollars, except for price.

20. Volume/Mix effect, Product line 1 (MBTU) = (#4 YTD − #4 LYTD) X #6 LYTD

21. Volume/Mix effect, Product line 1 ($) = #20 X #3 LYTD

22. Weather effect (MBTU) heating = (#10 YTD − #10 LYTD) X #12 LYTD

23. Weather effect (MBTU) cooling = (#14 YTD − #14 LYTD) X #16 LYTD

24. Weather effect ($) heating = #22 X #3 LYTD

25. Weather effect ($) cooling = #23 X #3 LYTD

26. Pollution Control effect (MBTU) = #18 YTD − #18 LYTD

27. Pollution Control effect ($) = #26 X #3 LYTD

28. Other effects (MBTU) = #19 YTD − #19 LYTD

29. Other effects ($) = #28 X #3 LYTD

30. Energy Conservation (MBTU) = #1 LYTD + #20 + #22 + #23 + #26 + #28 − #1 YTD

Energy conservation can be checked by adding items 8, 13, and 17 which must equal item 30.

31. Energy Conservation ($) = #30 X #3 LYTD

32. Alternate fuel ratio = Each alternate fuel LYTD ÷ Total of alternate fuels LYTD

33. Alternate fuel distribution = #32 X Total of alternate fuels YTD

34. Alternate fuel impact (MBTU) = #1 YTD − #33

35. Alternate fuel impact ($) = #34 X #3 LYTD

36. Price ($) = (#3 YTD − #3 LYTD) X #1 YTD

37. Net Impact (MBTU) = #20 + #22 + #23 + #26 + #28 − #30

38. Net Impact ($) = #21 + #24 + #25 + #27 + #29 − #31 + #36

Net impacts can be checked by subtracting item 1, LYTD from item 1, YTD in MBTU and item 2 LYTD from item 2 YTD in dollars which must equal items #37 and #38 respectively.

39. Energy Conservation % = (#30 ÷ (#30 + #1 YTD)) X 100

Figure 2-6. Energy Accounting Instructions (concluded)

1. A 20% drop in total energy use only resulted in a 5% drop in total energy cost. Gas and oil were the major contributors to usage drops and to cost increase.
2. Gas prices ($/MBTU) are up 35%, oil up 10% and electricity up barely 4%. The weighted average energy unit cost is up 22%. If the mix of energy forms had been the same this year as last, the weighted average would only have increased 10%.
3. In spite of the bargain that gas prices still represent over oil (30% cheaper last year, 15% cheaper now), the price gap is closing fast and gas curtailment is forcing us to use proportionately more oil.
4. A small amount of electricity saved is worth a great deal more than the same amount of gas or oil because of the 3:1 cost ratio.
5. Production energy efficiency in plastic products (Product Line 1) is 9.049% improved in electric. Since gas and oil are alternates, the sum of the energy efficiencies for gas and oil for each period divided by each other will yield energy efficiency improvement of the process of 7.257%. The combined effect can be seen in the "total" column where the efficiency improvement is 7.911% for the plastics line and the total saved is 322 MBTU or about 4% of the total energy of the plant. Since the total energy saved is 193 MBTU, the plastics line is clearly the hero of the plant having saved 332 MBTU.

   To calculate MBTU saved by production efficiency, multiply production quantity this period by energy efficiency last period and subtract energy used this period.

   Notice that electricity was saved through efficiencies while gas was saved because of a switch to oil.
6. Increase in production volume of plastic helped conservation efforts but cannot account for it all. The increase in volume was only about 10% vs. the total energy efficiency gain of 7.911%; therefore, whatever effort was made was successful and should be encouraged to continue.
7. Gas curtailment forced Carborundum to switch from

predominantly gas to predominantly oil in the plastics area, which affected the line's use of energy significantly. Since gas is most likely to be curtailed again, efforts to improve combustion practices in oil burners will pay handsome returns. Gas combustion improvement has less leverage since it is not only a lower proportion of the total energy, but a much lower percentage of the total cost.

8. Glass products production was up 10% in electric and gas, but off 75% in oil. The 1.550% efficiency improvement in electric and a 4.803% improvement in gas was shattered by the 34.100% loss of efficiency in oil, which was due to loss of production volume in '77. Apparently September '76 production with oil was a special run because of the disparity of unit production between electric and oil. The result is a loss of 247 MBTU.

The possibility of inventorying and batch processing glass products is being explored in the oil-fired process, since experience of September '76 indicates large potential efficiency gains.

9. Almost half of the energy dollars is spent on the plastic line so our conservation effort is properly directed; that is where we have saved the most. Energy intensity (MBTU/K Unit) is highest, however, in the glass line where a third of our energy dollars is spent. More conservation effort in the glass line would have a greater impact on profit improvement.

10. Wooden products have little energy impact and the insignificant energy improvement shows that little effort has been spent on improving efficiency. In view of the potential impact, this is probably as it should be, but it does show a lack of an energy awareness which would impact all energy use more significantly.

11. In spite of September '77 being 10% colder than September '76, energy used for heating was virtually the same because thermostats were kept down. The energy saved is second only to the 332 MBTU saved in the plastics line which would indicate the desirability of devoting

more effort towards improving insulation and other space heating conservation devices.

12. The requirement for cooling energy was greatly reduced but no significant cooling energy was conserved. Cooling is done by electricity, however, which is two and one-half times the cost of heating oil. Improvements in cooling will yield proportionately more for the dollar than improvements in oil heating.

13. A 10% saving in heating and cooling energy is low. Our experience is that 30% conservation is usually possible in systems over five years old. A 30% improvement would be from ground zero, however, and this output is from last year. Prior conservation efforts are not shown but can be calculated to test for more potential savings.

14. Pollution control energy is a much smaller proportion of the total than most managements believe. That does not mean, however, that its efficiency cannot be improved upon, just that it won't yield very much in savings in proportion to the total plant. In most cases, pollution control devices are electric which is the most expensive energy and from a return on investment point of view, it often is a good savings potential. Maintenance is often all it takes.

15. The use of electricity in the "OTHER" category is for experimental purposes which were not done in 1976. Should the experiments prove fruitful and permanent equipment be installed, the category would be removed from "other" and added to production either in an existing product or process or in a new one as appropriate.

The use of gas under "other" is the fixed load of two tunnel kilns. One was not fired this year; hence the reduction. If the fixed load is reduced through additional insulation it would be reflected.

The use of oil under "other" is the fixed load of a boiler and the same comment applies as with tunnel kilns.

In the "YTD-76 to YTD-77 IMPACT" section the interpretation of the numbers is: "How much more or less energy was used as a result of the variance identified?"

16. The volume/mix effect shows that the plastics line used a total of 376 MBTU more in '77 than in '76 and paid $1298 more for energy only because of the increase in volume. The glass line volume decrease in the oil process cost $5679 less and the loss of efficiency increased the cost by $716.88 (−309 MBTU saved X $2.32/MBTU '76-YTD).

17. The fact that the weather was cooler increased heating costs by $224 but decreased cooling costs by $326 yielding a net reduction in cost of $102 emphasizing the leverage of improving cooling efficiency.

18. The impact of "other" is a reduction in energy (−21 MBTU) but an increase in cost ($300) primarily because of the experimental work in electricity and in spite of the fact that a tunnel kiln was shut down.

19. A most important effect is the fact that energy was conserved (193 MBTU) but dollars were wasted (−$27 saved)! Partly due to the requirement to switch to oil but mostly because of the loss in volume in the oil-fired glass process. Possibly a scheduling problem which could be avoided.

20. The impact of having to switch to oil was $346 which, in view of the total energy cost is not much but a cost nevertheless.

21. Price increases cost more than any other impact other than the loss of volume in the oil-fired glass process.

22. The net impact of the energy situation was a reduction in the total cost of energy of $1159. One conclusion here is that it was pretty cheap energy which was not used. Clearly planning is called for.

23. The net 2.3% conservation is not to be proud of in our experience.

There are other conclusions to be drawn which require standard financial report numbers. Management decisions/ actions based on those already outlined above would include such things as:

- Seek more ways to conserve electricity.
- Find methods of improving efficiency of use of oil in the plastic products line.
- Explore all conservation possibilities in the glass product line.
- Determine economic consequences of inventorying and batch-processing of the oil-fired glass products versus continuous burning.
- Look for more savings potential in the heating and cooling systems.
- Develop an energy awareness in the labor force and at all levels of management.

SUMMARIES

The next level of energy accounting and analysis is the aggregation of data outputs from other locations into division and/or company summaries. Beyond that there can be industry summaries (perhaps by industry associations) ending up finally, in national summaries.

Every number in the right-hand totals column of the output (except cost per BTU and percent conservation) can be added to those in any other output regardless of complexity. Cost per BTU and percent conservation are then calculated from grand totals. Degree-days are not additive as the total would be meaningless. No production quantities are carried forward in combining with other output. To show production quantities in summaries would require an endless number of product lines, needlessly complicating the analysis. Industry production totals would be entered on industry input data forms similar to plant input forms by participants in any industrial energy reporting system. Analysis by product line is carried out at plant levels and summarized verbally at higher levels.

The potential for justification numbers for capital investment should be obvious in the Carborundum System.

The Department of Energy does not need production figures to determine energy consumed or energy saved either in total or in percent. Shifts in consumption are shown as are the reasons for them in the Carborundum System.

AND FINALLY . . .

Experience at Carborundum has been that a location achieves energy conservation and profit improvement very soon after the installation of this system. Whether locations are factories, warehouses, shipping operations or offices; energy and money are saved. In 1977 enough energy was saved to run a major division for a year. The money saved is equivalent to the profits of a major acquisition. The Carborundum Energy Accounting and Analysis System was instrumental in these accomplishments.

3
Survey Instrumentation

To accomplish an energy audit survey it is necessary to clarify energy uses and losses. This chapter illustrates various types of instruments which can aid in the energy audit survey.

MEASURING BUILDING LOSSES

Infrared energy is an invisible part of the electromagnetic spectrum. It exists naturally and can be measured by remote heat-sensing equipment. Within the last four years lightweight portable infrared systems became available to help determine energy losses. Differences in the infrared emissions from the surface of objects cause color variations to appear on the scanner. The hotter the object, the more infrared radiated. With the aid of an isotherm circuit the intensity of these radiation levels can be accurately measured and quantified. In essence the infrared scanning device is a diagnostic tool which can be used to determine building heat losses. Equipment costs range from $400 to $50,000.

An overview energy scan of the plant can be made through an aerial survey using infrared equipment. Several companies offer aerial scan services starting at $1,500. Aerial scans can determine underground stream pipe leaks, hot gas discharges, leaks, etc. Figure 3-1 illustrates typical suppliers in the infrared scanning industry.

Since IR detection and measurement equipment have gained increased importance in the energy audit process, a summary of the fundamentals are reviewed in this section.

In addition to detecting building energy losses IR Thermography has been used for other applications, listed in Table 3-1.

The manufacturers listed should not be considered as a recommendation, but simply as a representative sample of those involved in the field.

For information purposes, the letter (I) or (R) is placed alongside each cited manufacturer to denote that the instruments are of the indicating (I) or recording (R) type or both.

Air Velocity Meter

Alnor Instrument Co.   (I)
7301 N. Caldwell Ave.
Niles, Illinois 60648
(312) 647-7866

Davis Instrument Manufacturing Co.   (I)
513 E. 36 Street
Baltimore, Maryland 21218
(301) 243-4301

Thermonetics Corporation   (I)
P.O. Box 9112
San Diego, California 92109
(714) 488-3077

Edmund Scientific Company   (I)
Edscorp Building
Barrington, New Jersey 08007
(609) 547-3488

Ammeter

Amprobe Instrument   (I,R)
630 Merrick Road
Lynbrook, New York 11563
(516) 593-5600

Gulton Industries, Inc.   (R)
Measurement & Control Systems Division
Gulton Industrial Park
East Greenwich, Rhode Island 02818
(401) 884-6800

Figure 3-1. Manufacturers of Energy Test Equipment

General Electric   (I)
Instrument Products
40 Federal Street
Lynn, Massachusetts 01901
(617) 594-5547

Epic, Inc.   (I)
150 Nassau Street
New York, New York 10038
(212) 349-2470

Combustion Tester

Bacharach Instrument Company   (I)
625 Alpha Drive
Pittsburgh, Pennsylvania 15238
(412) 782-3500

Dwyer Instruments, Inc.   (I)
Highway 212 at 12
P.O. Box 373
Michigan City, Indiana 46360
(219) 872-9141

Milton Ray Company   (I)
Hays-Republic Division
742 E. Eight Street
Michigan City, Indiana 46360
(219) 872-5561

Burrell Corporation   (I)
2223 5th Avenue
Pittsburgh, Pennsylvania 15219
(412) 471-2527

Draft Gauge

Bacharach Instrument Company   (I)
625 Alpha Drive
Pittsburgh, Pennsylvania 15238
(412) 782-3500

Figure 3-1. Manufacturers of Energy Test Equipment (con't.)

Dwyer Instruments, Inc.   (I)
Highway 212 at 12
P.O. Box 373
Michigan City, Indiana 46360
(219) 872-9141

Infrared Pyrometer
William Wahl Corporation   (I,R)
12908 Panama Street
Los Angeles, California 90066
(213) 822-6144

Williamson Corporation   (I)
1152 Main Street
Concord, Massachusetts 01742
(617) 369-9607

Mikron Instrument Company, Inc.   (I)
P.O. Box 211
Ridgewood, New Jersey 07451
(201) 891-7330

Infrared Scanners: (A)—Equipment Supplier; (B)—Service Supplier
Air Image Technology   (B)
Minute Man Airfield
Stowe, Massachusetts 01775

Aero Marine Surveys   (B)
Drawer 1230
New London, Connecticut 06320

A. G. Associates   (B)
P.O. Box 17183
Montgomery, Alabama 36117

AGA Corp.   (A,B)
550 County Ave.
Secaucus, New Jersey 07094

Barnes Engineering Co.   (A,B)
30 Commerce Road
Stamford, Connecticut 06904

Figure 3-1. Manufacturers of Energy Test Equipment (con't.)

Calspan Corp. (B)
4455 Genesee Street
Buffalo, New York 14221

Daedalus Enterprises Inc. (A,B)
Box 1869
Ann Arbor, Michigan 48106

Detroit Diesel Allison (B)
13400 Outer Drive
Detroit, Michigan 48228

Earth Satellite Corp. (B)
7222 47th Street
Washington, D.C. 20015

Earth Science & Consulting Corp. (B)
3001 Red Hill Avenue
Costa Mesa, California 92626

Energy Conservation Consultants (B)
9001 E. Bloomington Freeway
Bloomington, Minnesota 55420

Energy Conservation Consulting Service (B)
1735 K Street NW
Washington, D.C. 20006

Energy Measures Corp. (B)
2808 Longhorn Boulevard
Austin, Texas 78759

Energy Scanners Inc. (B)
550 County Avenue
Secaucus, New Jersey 07094

Engineering Specialists (B)
Box 195
Farmington, Connecticut 06032

Fire Protection System (A)
Division of 3M Co.
Bldg. 223-6SE
St. Paul, Minnesota 55133

Figure 3-1. Manufacturers of Energy Test Equipment (con't.)

Hughes Aircraft Co. (A)
Indistrial Products Division
6155 El Camino Real
Carlsbad, California 92008

Inframetrics Inc. (A)
225 Crescent Street
Waltham, Massachusetts 02154

Infrared Scanning Inc. (B)
8419 Quivira Road
Wichita, Kansas 66215

Ircon Inc. (A)
7555 N. Linden
Skokes, Illinois 60077

ITM Inc. (A)
680 Main Street
Waltham, Massachusetts 02154

Mead Technical Laboratories (B)
3481 Dayton-Xenia Road
Dayton, Ohio 45432

Micron Industrial Co. (A)
P.O. Box 211-T
Ridgewood, New Jersey 07451

Optical Coating Laboratory Inc. (A)
Raytec Division
325 E. Middlefield Road
Mountain View, California 94043

Photo Science Inc. (B)
7840 Airpark Road
Gaithersburg, Maryland 20760

Power Save Co. (B)
P.O. Box 523536
Miami, Florida 33152

Figure 3-1. Manufacturers of Energy Test Equipment (con't.)

Quad Logistics   (B)
3909 Witmer
Niagara Falls, New York 14305

Remote Sensing Institute   (B)
South Dakota State University
Brookings, South Dakota 57007

Texas Instruments Inc.   (A)
P.O. Box 225621, MS949
Dallas, Texas 75265

ThermoTest   (B)
Division of Fuel Savers Inc.
One Elizabeth Town Plaza
Elizabeth, New Jersey 07207

Thermography Of Long Island   (B)
Box 644
Great River, New York 11739

UF Systems Inc.   (A)
1860 Broadway, Suite 612-A
New York, New York 10023

William Wahl Corp.   (A)
Heat Spy Division
12908 Panama Street
Los Angeles, California 90066

Williamson Corp.   (A)
1152 Main Street
Concord, Massachusetts 01742

Footcandle Meter
General Electric   (I)
Lamp Business Division
Nela Park
Cleveland, Ohio 44112
(216) 266-4256

Figure 3-1. Manufacturers of Energy Test Equipment (con't.)

Westinghouse Electric Corporation   (I)
Lamp Division
One Westinghouse Plaza
Bloomfield, New Jersey 07003
(201) 465-0222

Weston Instruments   (I)
614 Frelinghuysen Avenue
Newark, New Jersey
(201) 242-2600

Optical Pyrometer
Pyrometer Instrument Company, Inc.   (I)
234 Industrial Parkway
Northvale, New Jersey 07647
(201) 768-2000

Power Factor Meter
Epic, Inc.   (I)
150 Nassau Street
New York, New York 10038
(212) 349-2470

Psychrometer
Bacharach Instrument Company   (I,R)
625 Alpha Drive
Pittsburgh, Pennsylvania 15238
(412) 782-3500

Weather Measure Corporation   (I,R)
P.O. Box 41257
Sacramento, California 95841
(916) 481-7565

Solar Heat Meter
Metallized Products   (I)
2544 Terminal Drive South
St. Peterburgh, Pennsylvania 33712
(813) 822-9621

Figure 3-1. Manufacturers of Energy Test Equipment (con't.)

Smoke Tester

Bacharach Instrument Company   (I)
625 Alpha Drive
Pittsburgh, Pennsylvania 15238
(412) 782-3500

Dwyer Instruments, Inc.   (I)
Highway 212 at 12
P.O. Box 373
Michigan City, Indiana 46360
(219) 872-9141

Stethoscope

Edmund Scientific Company
Edscorp Building
Barrington, New Jersey 08007
(609) 547-3488

Surface Pyrometer

William Wahl Corporation   (I)
12908 Panama Street
Los Angeles, California 90066
(213) 822-6144

Pyrometer Instrument Company, Inc.   (I)
234 Industrial Parkway
Northvale, New Jersey 07647
(201) 768-2000

Alnor Instrument Company   (I)
7301 N. Caldwell Avenue
Niles, Illinois 60648
(312) 647-7886

Omega Engineering, Inc.   (I)
Box 4047
Stamford, Connecticut 06907
(203) 359-1660

Thermometer

Amprobe Instrument   (I)
630 Merrick Road
Lynbrook, New York 11563
(516) 593-5600

Figure 3-1. Manufacturers of Energy Test Equipment (con't.)

Omega Engineering Inc.   (I,R)
P.O. Box 4047
Stamford, Connecticut 06907
(203) 359-1660

Pacific Transducer Corporation   (R)
2301 Federal Avenue
Los Angeles, California 90064
(213) 478-1134

William Wahl Corporation   (I,R)
12908 Panama Street
Los Angeles, California 90066
(213) 822-6144

Bacharach Instrument Company   (I,R)
625 Alpha Drive
Pittsburgh, Pennsylvania 15238
(412) 782-3500

Brooklyn Thermometer Company, Inc.   (I,R)
90 Verdi Street
Farmingdale, New York 11735
(516) 694-7610

Blue M Electric Company   (I)
Blue Island, Illinois 60406
(312) 468-7755

Voltmeter
Amprobe Instrument   (I,R)
630 Merrick Road
Lynbrook, New York 11563
(516) 593-5600

Gulton Industries, Inc.   (R)
Measurement & Control System Division
Gulton Industrial Park
East Greenwich, Rhode Island 02818
(401) 884-6800

Figure 3-1. Manufacturers of Energy Test Equipment (con't.)

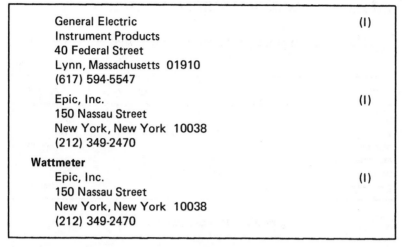

General Electric   (I)
Instrument Products
40 Federal Street
Lynn, Massachusetts 01910
(617) 594-5547

Epic, Inc.   (I)
150 Nassau Street
New York, New York 10038
(212) 349-2470

Wattmeter
Epic, Inc.   (I)
150 Nassau Street
New York, New York 10038
(212) 349-2470

Figure 3-1. Manufacturers of Energy Test Equipment (concluded)

Table 3-1. Applications of IR Thermography

Inspection of power transmission equipment.
Water leakage into building roof insulation.
Checking for poor building insulation.
Detection of thermal pollution in rivers and lakes.
Studying coating uniformity on webs.
Inspecting cooling coils for plugged tubes.
Medical uses involving early detection of malignant tumors.
Spotting plugs and air locks in condenser tubes.
Controlling paper calendaring operations.
Studying the behavior of thermal sealing equipment.
Investigating ultrasonic sealers and sealing operations.
Inspection of electronic circuits.
Hot injection molding problems.
Studying the behavior of heating and cooling devices.
Detection of plugged furnace tubes.
Examination of consumer products for hot spots.
Spotting defects in laminated materials.
Finding leaks in buried steam lines.
Inspection of heavy machinery bearings.
Study of stresses due to thermal gradients in a component.
Detection of defects such as voids and inclusions in castings.

INFRARED RADIATION AND ITS MEASUREMENT

The electromagnetic spectrum is illustrated in Figure 3-2.

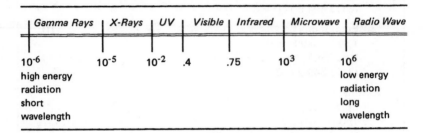

Figure 3-2. Electromagnetic Spectrum

The visible portion of the spectrum runs from .4 to .75 micrometers (μm). The infrared or thermal radiation begins at this point and extends to approximately 1000 μm. Objects such as people, plants, or buildings will emit radiation with wavelengths around 10 μm.

Infrared instruments are required to detect and measure the thermal radiation. To calibrate the instrument a special "black body" radiator is used. A black body radiator absorbs all the radiation that impinges on it and has an absorbing efficiency or emissivity of 1.

The accuracy of temperature measurements by infrared instruments depends on the three processes which are responsible for an object acting like a black body. These processes—absorbed, reflected, and transmitted radiation—are responsible for the total radiation reaching an infrared scanner.

The real temperature of the object is dependent only upon its emitted radiation.

Corrections to apparent temperatures are made by knowing the emissivity of an object at a specified temperature.

The heart of the infrared instrument is the infrared detector. The detector absorbs infrared energy and converts it into electrical voltage or current. The two principal types of detectors are the thermal and photo type. The thermal detector generally requires a given period of time to develop an image on photographic film. The photo detectors are more sensitive and have a higher response time. Television-like displays on a cathode ray tube permit studies of dynamic thermal events on moving objects in real time.

There are various ways of displaying signals produced by infrared detectors. One way is by use of an isotherm contour. The lightest areas of the picture represent the warmest areas of the subject and the darkest areas represent the coolest portions. These instruments can show thermal variations of less than .1°C and can cover a range of −30°C to over 2000°C.

The isotherm can be calibrated by means of a black body radiator so that a specific temperature is known. The scanner can then be moved and the temperatures of the various parts of the subject can be made.

There are many applications of infrared scanning devices as illustrated in Table 3-1.

Figure 3-3 illustrates the use of an aerial thermogram to detect heat losses. Figures 3-4 through 3-8 illustrate typical scanning devices. The information contained in this section should not be construed as a recommendation or complete listing. It simply serves as a sample of the products available.

MEASURING ELECTRICAL SYSTEM PERFORMANCE

The ammeter, voltmeter, wattmeter, power factor meter and footcandle meter are usually required to do an electrical survey. These instruments are described below.

AMMETER AND VOLTMETER

To measure electrical currents, ammeters are used. For most audits alternating currents are measured. Ammeters used in audits are portable and are designed to be easily attached and removed.

Figure 3-9 illustrates two typical types of meters which can be used for current or voltage measurements. Notice the meter illustrated on page 76 can be clamped around the conductors to measure current.

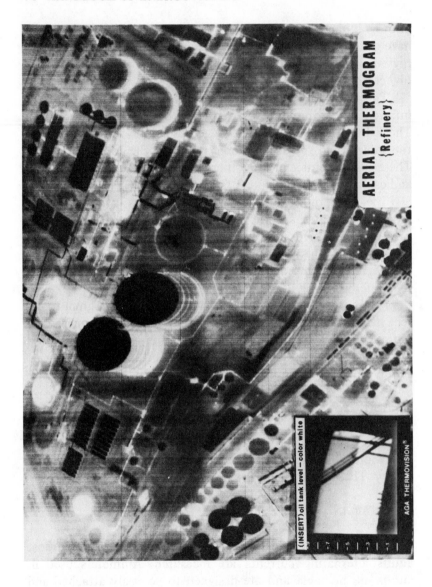

**Figure 3-3.
Aerial
Thermogram**

*(Photograph
courtesy
AGA Co.
Secausus,
New Jersey)*

Figure 3-4. AGA Thermovision® 750 Scanning System
(Photograph courtesy of AGA Company, Secausus, New Jersey)

**Figure 3-5.
Barnes
Thermatrace®**
*(Photograph courtesy of
Barnes Engineering Co.,
Stamford, Connecticut)*

Figure 3-6. Hughes Probeye®
(Photograph courtesy of Hughes Aircraft Company, Carlsbad, California 92008)

Figure 3-7.
Wahl Heatspy®

(Photograph courtesy of William Wahl Corp., Los Angeles, California)

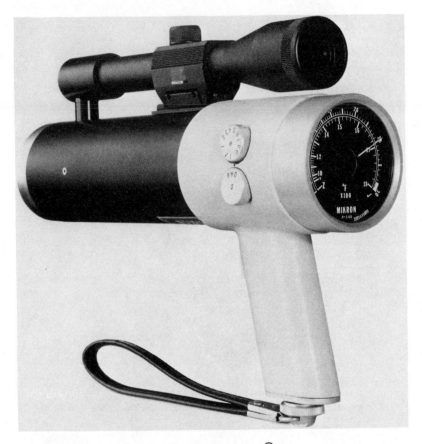

Figure 3-8. Mikron 56®
(Photograph courtesy of Mikron Instrument Company, Ridgewood, New Jersey)

There are many brands and styles of snap-on ammeters commonly available that can read up to 1000 amperes continuously. This range can be extended to 4000 amperes continuously for some models with an accessory step-down current transformer.

The snap-on ammeters can be either indicating or recording with a printout. After attachment, the recording ammeter can keep recording current variations for as long as a full month on one roll of recording paper. This allows studying current variations in a conductor for extended periods without constant operator attention.

Figure 3-9. Meters Used in Electrical Surveys

*(Photographs courtesy of Amprobe Instrument,
Division of Core Industries, Inc.)*

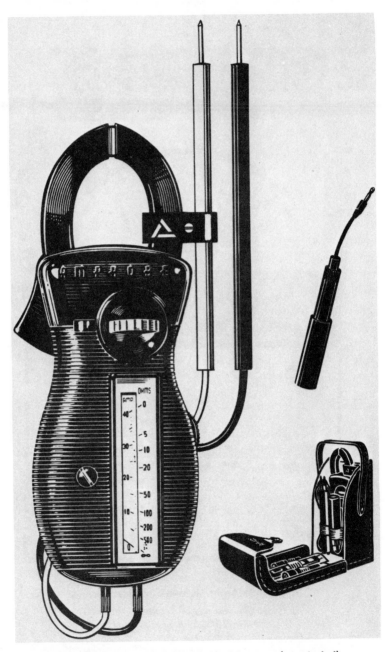

Figure 3-9. Meters Used in Electrical Surveys (concluded)

The ammeter supplies a direct measurement of electrical current which is one of the parameters needed to calculate electrical energy. The second parameter required to calculate energy is voltage, and it is measured by a voltmeter.

Several types of electrical meters can read the voltage or current. A voltmeter measures the difference in electrical potential between two points in an electrical circuit. The meter on page 76 (Figure 3-9) has two voltage probes which can be hand held to the point being measured.

In series with the probes are the galvanometer and a fixed resistance (which determine the voltage scale). The current through this fixed resistance circuit is then proportional to the voltage and the galvanometer deflects in proportion to the voltage.

The voltage drops measured in many instances are fairly constant and need only be performed once. If there are appreciable fluctuations, additional readings or the use of a recording voltmeter may be indicated.

Most voltages measured in practice are under 600 volts and there are many portable voltmeter/ammeter clamp-ons available for this and lower ranges.

WATTMETER AND POWER FACTOR METER

The portable wattmeter can be used to indicate by direct reading electrical energy in watts. It can also be calculated by measuring voltage, current and the angle between them (power factor angle).

The basic wattmeter consists of three voltage probes and a snap-on current coil which feeds the wattmeter movement.

The typical operating limits are 300 kilowatts, 650 volts, and 600 amperes. It can be used on both one- and three-phase circuits.

The portable power factor meter is primarily a three-phase instrument. One of its three voltage probes is attached to each conductor phase and a snap-on jaw is placed about one of the phases. By disconnecting the wattmeter circuitry, it will directly read the power factor of the circuit to which it is attached.

It can measure power factor over a range of 1.0 leading to 1.0 lagging with "ampacities" up to 1500 amperes at 600 volts. This range covers the large bulk of the applications found in light industry and commerce.

The power factor is a basic parameter whose value must be known to calculate electric energy usage. Diagnostically it is a useful instrument to determine the sources of poor power factor in a facility.

Portable digital KWH and KW demand units are now available as indicated in Figure 3-10.

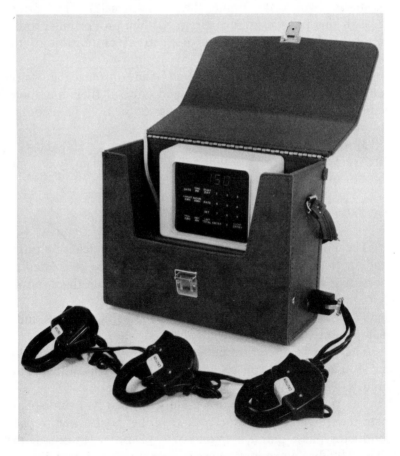

Figure 3-10. Portable Digital KWH and KW Demand Meter
(Photograph courtesy Dupont Energy Management Corp., Dallas, Texas)

Digital read-outs of energy usage in both KWH and KW Demand or in Dollars and Cents, including Instantaneous Usage, Accumulated Usage, Projected Usage for a particular billing period, Alarms when over-target levels desired for usage, and Control-Outputs for load-shedding and cycling are possible.

Continuous displays or intermittent alternating displays are available at the touch of a button of any information needed such as the cost of operating a production machine for one shift, one hour or one week.

Typical manufacturers of these products include:

Dupont Energy Management Corp.
10730 Composite Drive
Dallas, Texas 75220
(214) 351-0544 or 258-0054

The Watt Clock Corporation
P.O. Box 697
Stratford, Connecticut 06497
(203) 378-2500 or (212) 639-9777

FOOTCANDLE METER

Footcandle meters measure illumination in units of footcandles through light-sensitive barrier layer of cells contained within them. They are usually pocket size and portable and are meant to be used as field instruments to survey levels of illumination (illustrated in Figure 3-11). Footcandle meters differ from conventional photographic lightmeters in that they are color and cosine corrected.

TEMPERATURE MEASUREMENTS

To maximize system performance, knowledge of the temperature of a fluid, surface, etc. is essential. Several types of temperature devices are described in this section.

THERMOMETER

There are many types of thermometers that can be used in

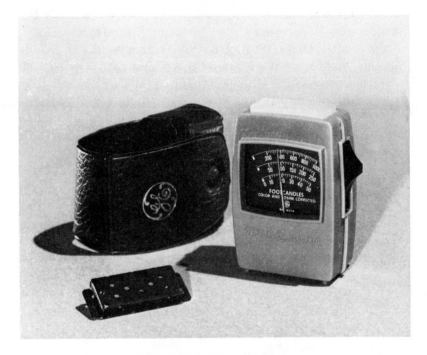

Figure 3-11. Footcandle Meter
(Photograph courtesy of General Electric Company)

an energy audit. The choice of what to use is usually dictated by cost, durability, and application. Figure 3-12 illustrates a common type of temperature measuring device.

For air-conditioning, ventilation and hot-water service applications (temperature ranges 50°F to 250°F) a multipurpose portable battery-operated thermometer is used. Three separate probes are usually provided to measure liquid, air or surface temperatures.

For boiler and oven stacks (1000°F) a dial thermometer is used. Thermocouples are used for measurements above 1000°F.

SURFACE PYROMETER

Surface pyrometers are instruments which measure the temperature of surfaces. They are somewhat more complex than

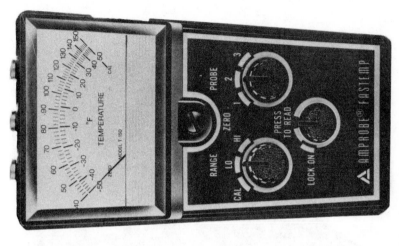

Figure 3-12. Thermometer
(Photograph courtesy of Amprobe Instrument, Division of Core Industries, Inc.)

other temperature instruments because their probe must make intimate contact with the surface being measured. Figure 3-13 illustrates a surface pyrometer.

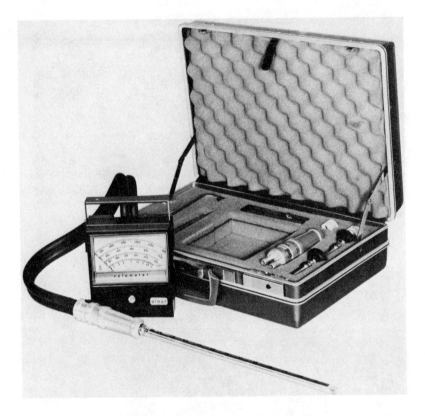

Figure 3-13. Surface Pyrometer
(Photograph courtesy of Alnor Corporation)

Surface pyrometers are of immense help in assessing heat losses through walls and also for testing steam traps.

They may be divided into two classes: low-temperature (up to 250°F) and high-temperature (up to 600-700°F). The low-temperature unit is usually part of the multipurpose thermometer kit. The high-temperature unit is more specialized, but needed for evaluating fired units and general steam service.

There are also noncontact surface pyrometers which measure infrared radiation from surfaces in terms of temperature.

These are suitable for general work and also for measuring surfaces which are visually but not physically accessible.

A more specialized instrument is the optical pyrometer. This is for high-temperature work (above 1500°F) because it measures the temperature of bodies which are incandescent because of their temperature.

PSYCHROMETER

A psychrometer is an instrument which measures relative humidity based on the relation of the dry-bulb temperature and the wet-bulb temperature.

Relative humidity is of prime importance in HVAC and drying operations. Recording psychrometers are also available. Above 200°F humidity studies constitute a specialized field of endeavor.

PORTABLE ELECTRONIC THERMOMETER

The portable electronic thermometer is an adaptable temperature measurement tool. The battery-powered basic instrument, when housed in a carrying case, is suitable for laboratory or industrial use.

A pocket-size digital, battery-operated thermometer is especially convenient for spot checks or where a number of rapid readings of process temperatures need to be taken.

THERMOCOUPLE PROBE

No matter what sort of indicating instrument is employed, the thermocouple used should be carefully selected to match the application and properly positioned if a representative temperature is to be measured. The same care is needed for all sensing devices—thermocouple, bimetals, resistance elements, fluid expansion and vapour pressure bulbs.

SUCTION PYROMETER

Errors arise if a normal sheathed thermocouple is used to measure gas temperatures, especially high ones. The suction pyrometer overcomes these by shielding the thermocouple from wall radiation and drawing gases over it at high velocity to ensure good convective heat transfer. The thermocouple thus produces a reading which approaches the true temperature at the sampling point rather than a temperature between that of the walls and the gases.

MEASURING COMBUSTION SYSTEMS

To maximize combustion efficiency it is necessary to know the composition of the flue gas. By obtaining a good air-fuel ratio substantial energy will be saved.

COMBUSTION TESTER

Combustion testing consists of determining the concentrations of the products of combustion in a stack gas. The products of combustion usually considered are carbon dioxide and carbon monoxide. Oxygen is tested to assure proper excess air levels.

The definitive test for these constituents is an Orsat apparatus. This test consists of taking a measured volume of stack gas and measuring successive volumes after intimate contact with selective absorbing solutions. The reduction in volume after each absorption is the measure of each constituent.

The Orsat has a number of disadvantages. The main ones are that it requires considerable time to set up and use and its operator must have a good degree of dexterity and be in constant practice.

Instead of an Orsat, there are portable and easy to use absorbing instruments which can easily determine the concentrations of the constituents of interest on an individual basis. Set-up and operating times are minimal and just about anyone can learn to use them.

The typical range of concentrations are CO_2:0—20%, O_2:

$0-21\%$ and $CO:0-0.5\%$. The CO_2 or O_2 content along with knowledge of flue gas temperature and fuel type allow the flue gas loss to be determined off standard charts.

BOILER TEST KIT

The boiler test kit illustrated in Figures 3-14 and 3-15 contains the following:

CO_2	Gas Analyzer,
O_2	Gas Analyzer,
	Inclined Monometer,
CO	Gas Analyzer.

The purpose of the components of the kit is to help evaluate fireside boiler operation. Good combustion usually means high carbon dioxide (CO_2), low oxygen (O_2), and little or no trace of carbon monoxide (CO).

GAS ANALYZERS

The gas analyzer illustrated in Figure 3-14 is the Fyrite type. The Fyrite type differs from the Orsat apparatus in that it is more limited in application and less accurate. The chief advantages of the Fyrite are that it is simple and easy to use and is inexpensive. This device is many times used in an energy audit. Three readings using the Fyrite analyzer should be made and the results averaged.

DRAFT GAUGE

The draft gauge is used to measure pressure. It can be the pocket type shown in Figure 3-15, or the inclined monometer type shown with the test kit.

SMOKE TESTER

To measure combustion completeness the smoke detector is used (Figure 3-14). Smoke is unburned carbon which wastes fuel, causes air pollution and fouls heat-exchanger surfaces. To

Gas Analyzer

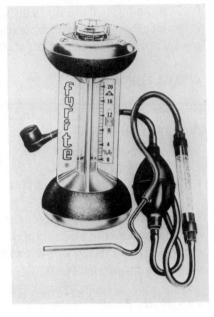

Carbon Monoxide Analyzer

Figure 3-14. Boiler Test Kit

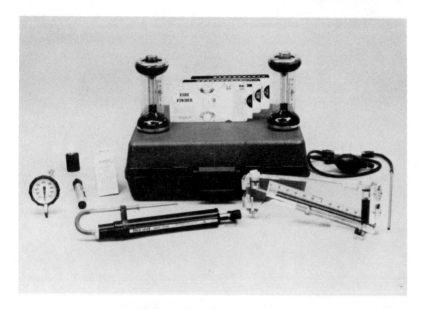

Test Kit *(above)* and Smoke Tester *(below)*

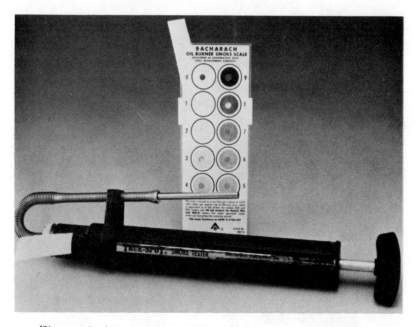

(Photographs these two pages courtesy of Bacharach Instrument Company)

Air Filter Gauge

Hydrogen Sulfide Detector

**Figure 3-15. Components for
Combustion Testing**
*(Photographs courtesy of
Bacharach Instrument Company)*

Draft Gauge

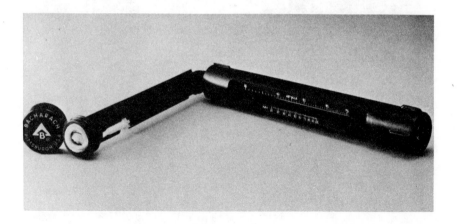

Sling Psychrometer

(Photographs coutrtesy of Bacharach Instrument Company)

use the instrument, a measured volume of flue gas is drawn through filter paper with the probe. The smoke spot is compared visually with a standard scale and a measure of smoke density is determined.

COMBUSTION ANALYZER

The combustion electronic analyzer illustrated in Figure 3-16 permits fast, close adjustments. The unit contains digital displays. A standard sampler assembly with probe (not shown) allows for stack measurements through a single stack or breaching hole.

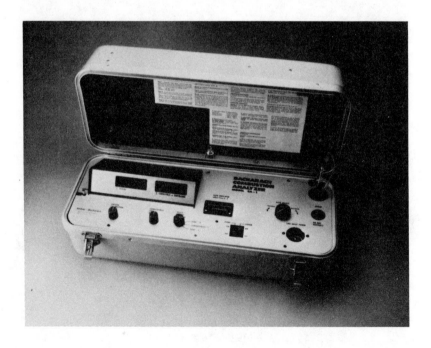

Figure 3-16. Combustion Gas Analyzer with Digital Display

(Photograph courtesy of Bacharach Instrument Company)

MEASURING HEATING, VENTILATION AND AIR-CONDITIONING (HVAC) SYSTEM PERFORMANCE

AIR VELOCITY MEASUREMENT

Table 3-2 summarizes velocity devices commonly used in HVAC applications. The following suggests the preference, suitability, and approximate costs of particular equipment.

- *Smoke pellets*—limited use but very low cost. Considered to be useful if engineering staff has experience in handling.
- *Anemometer* (deflecting vane)—good indication of air movement with acceptable order of accuracy. Considered useful. (Approx. $50).
- *Anemometer* (revolving vane)—good indicator of air movement with acceptable accuracy. However easily subject to damage. Considered useful. (Approx. $100).
- *Pitot tube*—a standard air measurement device with good levels of accuracy. Considered essential. Can be purchased in various lengths—12" about $20, 48" about $35. Must be used with a monometer. These vary considerably in cost but could be in the order of $20 to $60.
- *Impact tube*—usually packaged air flow meter kits, complete with various jets for testing ducts, grills, open areas, etc. These units are convenient to use and of sufficient accuracy. The costs vary around $150 to $300 and therefore this order of cost could only be justified for a large system.
- *Heated thermocouple*— these units are sensitive, accurate, but costly. A typical cost would be about $500 and can only be justified for regular use in a large plant.
- *Hot wire anemometer*- not recommended. Too costly and too complex.

TEMPERATURE MEASUREMENT

Table 3-3 summarizes common devices used for measuring temperature in HVAC applications. The temperature devices most commonly used are as follows:

Table 3-2. Air Velocity Measurement Devices

Device/Meter	Application	Range in FPM	Accuracy	Limitations
Smoke pellet or airborne solid tracer	Low air velocities in room —directional	5 — 50	10% — 20%	Useful in tracing air movement in-directional
Anemometer—deflecting vane type	Air velocities in rooms, grill outlets—directional	30 — 24,000	5%	Not suitable for duct air measurement—requires periodic calibration
Anemometer—revolving vane type	Moderate air velocities in ducts, rooms	100 — 3,000	5% — 20%	Subject to error variations in velocities—easily damaged. Frequent calibration required.
Pitot tube	Standard instrument for duct velocity measurement	180 — 10,000 600 — 10,000 10,000 and up	1% — 5%	Accuracy falls at low air flows.
Impact tube (side wall) meter kits	High velocity—small tube and variable direction	120 — 10,000 600 — 10,000 10,000 and up	1% — 5%	Accuracy related to constant static pressure across stream section
Heated thermocouple anemometer	Air velocities in ducts	10 — 2,000	3% — 20%	Accuracy of some meters bad at low velocities
Hot wire anemometer	(a) Low air velocities in rooms, ducts, etc. (b) High air velocity (c) Transient velocities and turbulences	1 — 1,000 Up to 60,000	1% — 20% 1% — 10%	Requires frequent calibration. Complex to use and very costly.

Table 3-3. Temperature Measurement

Device/Meter	Application	Range in °F	Accuracy °F Less than	Limitation
Glass stem thermometers	Temperature of gas, air, and liquids by contact			In gas and air, glass is affected by radiation. Also liable to break.
Mercury in glass		− 38 to 575	0.1 to 10	
Alcohol in glass		−100 to 1000	0.1 to 10	
Pentane in glass		−200 to 70	0.1 to 10	
Zena or quartz mercury		− 38 to 1000	0.1 to 10	
Resistance thermometers				
Platinum resistance	Precision remote readings	−320 to 1800	0.02 to 5	High cost — accuracy affected by radiation
Nickel resistance	Remote readings	−150 to 300	0.03	
Thermisters	Remote readings	up to 600	0.1	
Thermocouples				
Pt-Pt-Rh thermocouples	Standard for thermocouples	500 to 3000	0.1 to 5	Highest system
Chrome Alumel "	General testing hi-temps	up to 2000	0.1 to 15	Less accurate than above
Iron Constantan "	Same as above but for lower	up to 1500	0.1 to 15	Subject to oxidation
Copper "		"	" "	" " "
Chromel "	readings	up to 700	0.1 to 15	" " "
Bimetallic thermometers	For approximate temperature	0 to 1000	—	Extensive time lag, not for remote use, unreliable
Pressure-bulb thermometers				Usually permanent installations. Requires careful fixing and setting
Gas filled	Suitable for remote reading	−200 to 1000	2	
Vapor filled		20 to 500	2	
Liquid filled		− 50 to 2100	2	
Optical pyrometers	Hi-intensity, narrow spectrum band radiation	1500 and up	15	Limited to combustion setting
Radiation pyrometers	Hi-intensity, total high temperature radiation	Any	—	Relatively costly, easy to use, quite accurate
Indicating Crayons	Approximate surface temp.	125 to 900	+/− 1%	Easy to use, low cost

- *Glass thermometers*—considered to be the most useful of temperature measuring instruments—accurate, convenient, but fragile. Cost runs from $5 each for 12" long mercury in glass. Engineers should have a selection of various ranges.
- *Resistance thermometers*—considered to be very useful for A/C testing. Accuracy is good, reliable and convenient to use. Suitable units can be purchased from $150 up, some with a selection of several temperature ranges.
- *Thermocouples*—similar to resistance thermocouple, but do not require battery power source. Chrome-Alum or iron types are the most useful and have satisfactory accuracy and repeatability. Costs start from $50 and range up.
- *Bimetallic thermometers*— considered unsuitable.
- *Pressure bulb thermometers*—more suitable for permanent installation. Accurate and reasonable in cost—$40 up.
- *Optical pyrometers*—only suitable for furnace settings and therefore limited in use. Cost from $300 up.
- *Radiation pyrometers*—limited in use for A/C work and costs from $500 up.
- *Indicating crayons*—limited in use and not considered suitable for A/C testing—costs around $2/crayon.
- *Thermographs*—use for recording room or space temperature and gives a chart indicating variations over a 12- or 168-hour period. Reasonably accurate. Low cost at around $30 to $60. (Spring wound drive.)

PRESSURE MEASUREMENT (ABSOLUTE AND DIFFERENTIAL)

Table 3-4 illustrates common devices used for measuring pressure in HVAC applications. Accuracy, range, application, and limitations are discussed in relation to HVAC work.
- *Absolute pressure manometer* ⎫   not really suited
- *Diaphragm*   ⎬   to HAVC
- *Barometer (Hg manometer)*   ⎭   test work
- *Micromanometer*—not usually portable, but suitable for

Table 3-4. Pressure Measurement

Device/Meter	Application	Range in FPM	Accuracy	Limitations
Absolute pressure manometer	Moderately low absolute pressure	0 + 30'' Hg	2 – 5%	Not direct reading
Diaphragm gauge	''	0.1 – 70 mm Hg	0.05 mm Hg	Direct reading
Barometer (Hg manometer)	Atmospheric pressure	–	0.001 to 0.01	Not very portable
Micromanometer	Very low pressure differential	0 to 6'' H_2O	0.0005 to 0.0001 H_2O	Not easily portable, hard to use with pulsating pressures
Draft gauges	Moderately low pressure differential	0 to 10'' H_2O	0.05 H_2O	Must be leveled carefully
Manometer	Medium pressure differential	0 to 100 H_2O	0.05 H_2O	Compensation for liquid density
Swing Vane gauge	Moderate low pressure differential	0 to 0.5 H_2O	5%	Generally used at atmospheric pressure only
Bourdon tube	Medium to high pressure differential. Usually to atmospheric	Any	0.05 to 5%	Subject to damage due to overpressure shock
Pressure transducers	Remote reading—responds to rapid change	0.05 to 50,000 psig	0.1 to 0.5%	Require electronic amplified and readout equipment

fixed measurement of pressure differentials across filter, coils, etc. Cost around $30 and up.

- *Draft gauges*– can be portable and used for either direct pressure or pressure differential. From $30 up.
- *Manometers*–can be portable. Used for direct pressure reading and with pitot tubes for air flows. Very useful. Costs from $20 up.
- *Swing Vane gauges*–can be portable. Usually used for air flow. Costs about $30.
- *Bourdon tube gauges*–very useful for measuring all forms of system fluid pressures from 5 psi up. Costs vary greatly from $10 up. Special types for refrigeration plants.

HUMIDITY MEASUREMENT

The data given below indicates the type of instruments available for humidity measurement. The following indicates equipment suitable for HVAC applications.

- *Psychrometers*– basically these are wet and dry bulb thermometers. They can be fixed on a portable stand or mounted in a frame with a handle for revolving in air. Costs are low ($10 to $30) and are convenient to use.
- *Dewpoint Hygrometers*–not considered suitable for HVAC test work.
- *Dimensional change*–device usually consists of a "hair" which changes in length proportionally with humidity changes. Not usually portable, fragile, and only suitable for limited temperature and humidity ranges.
- *Electrical conductivity*–can be compact and portable but of a higher cost (from $200 up). Very convenient to use.
- *Electrolytic*–as above. But for very low temperature ranges. Therefore unsuitable for HVAC test work.
- *Gravemeter*–Not suitable.

4

How To Justify Energy

Utilization Measures

An important aspect of the energy audit is to quantify the cost savings that are likely to be realized through the investment in an energy savings measure. To justify the energy investment cost, a knowledge of life-cycle costing is required.

The life-cycle cost analysis evaluates the total owning and operating cost. It takes into account the "time value" of money and can incorporate fuel cost escalation into the economic model. This approach is also used to evaluate competitive projects. In other words, the life-cycle cost analysis considers the cost over the life of the system rather than just the first cost.

THE TIME VALUE OF MONEY CONCEPT

To compare energy utilization alternatives, it is necessary to convert all cash flow for each measure to an equivalent base. The life-cycle cost analysis takes into account the "time value" of money, thus a dollar in hand today is more valuable than one received at some time in the future. This is why a time value must be placed on all cash flows into and out of the company.

To convert cash from one time to another, any one of the six standard interest factors can be used, as illustrated in Figure 4-1. The seventh factor in the table takes into account escalation. Each factor is described in detail in Figures 4-2 through 4-8.

Single Payment Compound Amount—SPCA

The SPCA factor is the future value of one dollar in "n" periods at interest of "i" percent.

$$S = P \times (SPCA)^n_i \qquad \text{Formula (4-1)}$$

$$SPCA = (1 + i)^n$$

Single Payment Present Worth—SPPW

The SPPW factor is the present worth of one dollar, "n" periods from now at interest of "i" percent.

$$P = S \times (SPPW)_i^n \qquad \text{Formula (4-2)}$$

$$SPPW = {1}/{(1 + i)^n}$$

Uniform Series Compound Amount—USCA

The USCA factor is the future value of a uniform series of one dollar deposits.

$$S = R \times (USCA)_i^n \qquad \text{Formula (4-3)}$$

$$USCA = \frac{(1 + i)^n - 1}{i}$$

Sinking Fund Payment—SFP

The SFP factor is the uniform series of deposits whose future value is one dollar.

$$R = S \times (SFP)_i^n \qquad \text{Formula (4-4)}$$

$$SFP = {i}/{(1 + i)^n - 1}$$

Uniform Series Present Worth—(USPW)

The USPW factor is the present value of uniform series of one dollar deposits.

$$P = R \times (USPW)_i^n \qquad \text{Formula (4-5)}$$

Capital Recovery—CR

The CR factor is the uniform series of deposits whose present value is one dollar.

$$R = P \times (CR)_{i}^{n} \qquad \text{Formula (4-6)}$$

$$USPW = \frac{(1+i)^n - 1}{i(1+i)^n}$$

$$CR = \frac{i(1+i)^n}{(1+i)^n - 1}$$

Gradient Present Worth—GPW

The GPW factor is the present value of a gradient series.

$$P = R \times (GPW)_{i}^{n} \qquad \text{Formula (4-7)}$$

$$GPW = \frac{1+e}{i-e}\left[1 - \left(\frac{1+e}{1+i}\right)^n\right]$$

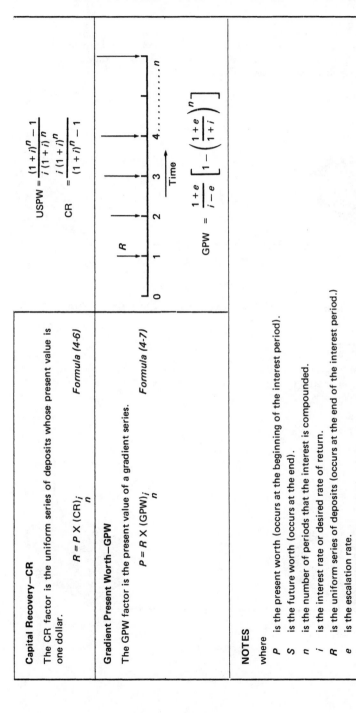

NOTES

where

P is the present worth (occurs at the beginning of the interest period).

S is the future worth (occurs at the end).

n is the number of periods that the interest is compounded.

i is the interest rate or desired rate of return.

R is the uniform series of deposits (occurs at the end of the interest period).

e is the escalation rate.

Figure 4-1. Interest Factors

$SPCA = (1 + i)^n$

This factor is used to determine the future amount S that a present sum P will accumulate at i-percent interest, in n years. If P (present worth) is known and S (future worth) is to be determined, then Formula 4-1 is used.

$$S = P \times (SPCA)_{n \atop i}$$ *Formula (4-1)*

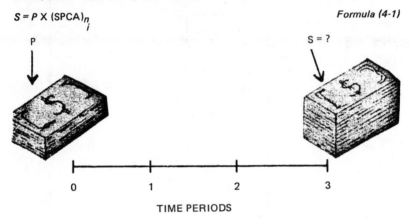

Figure 4-2. Single Payment Compound Amount (SPCA)

$$SPPW = \frac{1}{(1 + i)^n}$$

This factor is used to determine the present worth, P, that a future amount, S, will be at interest of i-percent, in n years. If S is known, and P is to be determined, then Formula 4-2 is used.

$$P = S \times (SPPW)_{i \atop n}$$ *Formula (4-2)*

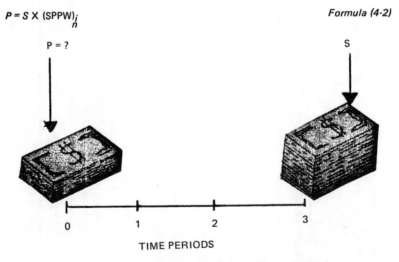

Figure 4-3. Single Payment Present Worth (SPPW)

$$\text{USCA} = \frac{(1 + i)^n - 1}{i}$$

This factor is used to determine the amount S that an equal annual payment R will accumulate to in n years at i-percent interest. If R (uniform annual payment) is known, S (the future worth of these payments), is required, then Formula 4-3 is used.

$S = R \times (\text{USCA})_i^n$ *Formula (4-3)*

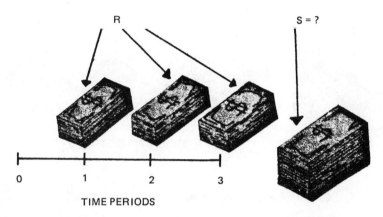

Figure 4-4. Uniform Series Compound Amount (USCA)

$$\text{SFP} = \frac{i}{(1 + i)^n - 1}$$

This factor is used to determine the equal annual amount R that must be invested for n years at i-percent interest in order to accumulate a specified future amount. If S (the future worth of a series of annual payments) is known, R (value of those annual payments), is required, then Formula 4-4 is used.

$R = S \times (\text{SFP})_i^n$ *Formula (4-4)*

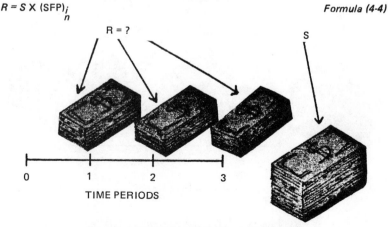

Figure 4-5. Sinking Fund Payment (SFP)

$$USPW = \frac{(1 + i)^n - 1}{i(1 + i)^n}$$

This factor is used to determine the present amount P that can be paid by equal payments of R (uniform annual payment) at i-percent interest, for n years. If R is known P is required, then Formula 4-5 is used.

$P = R \times (USPW)_{i \atop n}$ *Formula (4-5)*

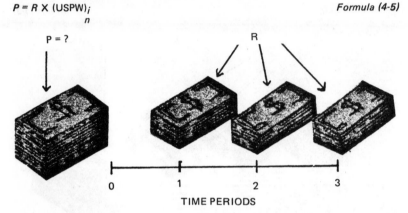

Figure 4-6. Uniform Series Present Worth (USPW)

$$CR = \frac{i(1 + i)^n}{(1 + i)^n - 1}$$

This factor is used to determine an annual payment R required to pay off a present amount P at i-percent interest, for n years. If the present sum of money, P spent today, and uniform payment R needed to pay back P over a stated period of time is required, then Formula 4-6 is used.

$R = P \times (CR)_{i \atop n}$ *Formula (4-6)*

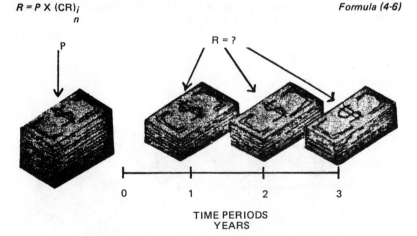

Figure 4-7. Capital Recovery (CR)

$$GPW = \frac{1+e}{i-e} \left[1 - \left(\frac{1+e}{1+i} \right)^{n} \right]$$

This factor is used to determine the present amount P that can be paid by annual amounts R which escalate at $e\%$, at $i\%$ interest for n years. If R is known and P is required, then Formula 4-7 is used.

$P = R \times (GPW)_{i \atop n}$ *Formula (4-7)*

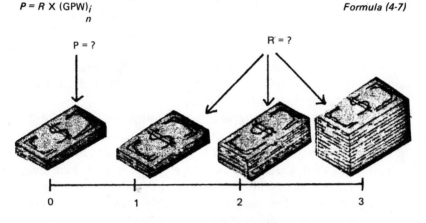

P = ?   R = ?

0   1   2   3

Figure 4-8. Gradient Present Worth (CPW)

Interest factors are seldom calculated. They can be determined from computer programs, and interest tables included in Chapter 15, Tables 15-1 through 15-13. Each factor is defined when the number of periods *(n)* and interest rate *(i)* are specified. In the case of the Gradient Present Worth Factor the escalation rate must also be stated.

The three most commonly used methods in life-cycle costing are the annual cost, present worth and rate-of-return analysis.

In the present worth method a minimum rate of return *(i)* is stipulated. All future expenditures are converted to present values using the interest factors. The alternative with lowest effective first cost is the most desirable.

A similar procedure is implemented in the annual cost method. The difference is that the first cost is converted to an annual expenditure. The alternative with lowest effective annual cost is the most desirable.

In the rate-of-return method, a trial-and-error procedure is usually required. Interpolation from the interest tables can determine what rate of return *(i)* will give an interest factor which will make the overall cash flow balance. The rate-of-return analysis gives a good indication of the overall ranking of independent alternates.

The effect of escalation in fuel costs can influence greatly the final decision. When an annual cost grows at a steady rate it may be treated as a gradient and the Gradient Present Worth Factor can be used.

Special appreciation is given to Rudolph R. Yaneck and Dr. Robert Brown for use of their specially designed interest and escalation tables used in this text.

When life-cycle costing is used to compare several alternatives the differences between costs are important. For example, if one alternate forces additional maintenance or an operating expense to occur, then these factors as well as energy costs need to be included. Remember, what was previously spent for the item to be replaced is irrelevant. The only factor to be considered is whether the new cost can be justified based on projected savings over its useful life.

EQUIPMENT LIFE

To estimate equipment life, Table 4-1 can be used. This table is extracted with permission from *ASHRAE Journal,* October 1978, Vol. 20(10) page 42.

PAYBACK ANALYSIS

The simple payback analysis is sometimes used instead of the methods previously outlined. The simple payback is defined as initial investment divided by annual savings after taxes. The simple payback method does not take into account the effect of interest or escalation rate.

Since the payback period is relatively simple to calculate and due to the fact managers wish to recover their investment as rapidly as possible the payback method is frequently used.

It should be used in conjunction with other decision-making tools. When used by itself as the principal criterion it may re-

Table 4-1. Equipment Service Life Statistics

Equipment Item	Mean	Median	Mode(s)	Percentiles 25%	75%	N
UNITARY EQUIPMENT						
Room Air Conditioners						
(window or through-the-wall)	10	10	10	5	10	38
Unitary Air Conditioners						
1. Air cooled—residential	14	15	15	8	20	29
(single package or aplit system)						
2. Air cooled—commercial/industrial	15	15	15	10	20	40
(single package—through-the-wall						
or split system)						
3. Water cooled—electric	16	15	15-20	10	20	17
Unitary Heat Pumps						
1. Air source—residential	11	10	10	10	12.5	12
2. Air source—commercial/industrial	15	15	15	11	15	13
(single package or aplit system)						
3. Water source—comm./industrial	13	13	10	10	20	8
Computer Room Conditioners	18	15	15	15	20	23
ROOF TOP HVAC SYSTEMS						
Single Zone	15	15	15	10	20	30
Heating, ventilating and cooling or						
cooling only						
Multizone	16	15	15	10	20	25
Heating, ventilating and cooling or						
cooling only						
HEATING EQUIPMENT						
Boilers						
1. Steam—steel watertube	30	26	40	20	40	30
—steel firetube	24	25	25	20	30	14
—cast iron	30	30	30	20	35	12
2. Hot water—steel watertube	24	23	20	20	27	12
—steel firetube	23	24	30	17	30	16
—cast iron	30	30	30	20	40	13
3. Electric	14	15	15	7	17	9
Burners						
Gas—forced and natural and oil-forced	22	20	20	17	27	58
Furnaces						
Gas or oil	18	20	20	12	20	35

Table 4-1. Equipment Service Life Statistics (con't.)

Equipment Item	Mean	Median	Mode(s)	Percentiles		
				25%	75%	N
Unit Heaters						
Gas or electric	14	13	10	10	20	28
Hot water or steam	23	20	20	20	30	30
Radiant Heaters and Panels						
Electric heaters	11	10	10	5	25	6
Hot water or steam panels	26	25	20-25	20	30	7
AIR HANDLING AND TREATING EQUIPMENT						
Terminal Units						
1. Induction units	26	20	20	20	30	16
2. Fan coil	21	20	20	16	22	28
3. Diffusers, grilles and registers	35	27	20	20	50	26
4. Double duct mixing boxes—constant or variable air volume	21	20	20	15	30	20
5. Variable air volume (VAV) boxes single duct	24	20	20	20	30	7
Air Washers	20	17	30	10	30	6
Humidifiers	18	15	10	10	20	23
Ductwork	35	30	50	24	50	31
Dampers including actuators	15	20	20	15	30	20
Fans (supply or exhaust)						
1. Centrifugal—forward curve or backward inclined	27	25	20	20	40	43
2. Axial flow	23	20	20	10	30	16
3. Wall-mounted—propeller type	17	15	20	10	20	15
4. Ventilating—roof mounted	17	20	20	10	20	22
HEAT EXCHANGERS						
Coils						
1. DX	22	20	20	15	27	21
2. Water or steam	24	20	20	20	30	49
3. Electric	15	15	10-15-20	10	20	9
Shell and Tube	25	24	20	20	30	20
COOLING EQUIPMENT						
Reciprocating Compressors	18	20	20	12	20	7
Chillers—packaged—reciprocating	19	20	20	15	20	34
—centrifugal	25	23	20	20	30	28
—absorption	24	23	20	20	30	16
HEAT REJECTION EQUIPMENT						
Cooling Tower—metal—galvanized	18	20	20	10	20	33
—wood	22	20	20	15	27	25
—ceramic	33	34	20	20	5	6

Table 4-1. Equipment Service Life Statistics (concluded)

Equipment Item	Mean	Median	Mode(s)	Percentiles 25%	75%	N
Air-cooled Condenser	20	20	20	15	25	27
Evaporative Condenser	18	20	20	15	20	13
GENERAL COMPONENTS						
Insulation						
1. Preformed—block, molded, etc.	27	20	20	20	30	43
2. Blankets, batts	29	24	20	20	40	23
Pumps						
1. Circulating, base-mounted	19	20	20	13	24	37
2. Circulating, pipe-mounted	12	10	10-15	6	15	28
3. Sump and well	15	10	30	6	30	25
4. Condensate and receiver	18	15	15	10	25	25
Engines, Turbines, Motors						
1. Reciprocating engine	19	20	20	20	20	12
2. Turbines—steam	30	30	40	24	30	13
3. Electric motors	18	18	20	13	20	24
Motor Starters—across line or magnetic	19	17	20	10	30	34
Transformers						
Dry type or oil-filled	31	30	30	20	40	49
Controls and instrumentation						
1. Pneumatic	21	20	20	15	24	34
2. Electrical	17	16	20	10	20	24
3. Electronic	15	15	10-15	10	20	16
4. Automated (computer) building control systems	22	20	20-25	10	25	8
Valve Actuators						
1. Electric	16	14	10-20-30	5	25	18
2. Hydraulic	15	15	20	5	24	8
3. Pneumatic	18	20	20	10	25	26
4. Self-contained	14	10	5-20	5	24	9

sult in choosing less profitable investments which yield high initial returns for short periods as compared with more profitable investments which provide profits over longer periods of time.

JOB SIMULATION EXPERIENCE®

Throughout the text you will experience job situations and problems. Each simulation experience is denoted by SIM. The answer will be given below the problem. Cover the answer, then you can "play the game."

SIM 4-1

An electrical energy audit indicates electrical motor consumption is 4×10^{12} KWH per year. By upgrading the motor spares with high efficiency motors a 10% savings can be realized. The additional cost for these motors is estimated at $30,000. Assuming a 3¢ per KWH energy charge and 20-year life, is the expenditure justified based on a minimum rate of return of 20% before taxes? Solve the problem using the present worth, annual cost, and rate of return methods.

ANALYSIS

Present Worth Method

	Alternate 1 Present Method	*Alternate 2 Use High Efficiency Motor Spares*
(1) First Cost (P)	–	$30,000
Annual Cost (R)	$4 \times 10^{12} \times .03$ = $120,000	$.9 \times$ $120,000 = $108,000
USPW (Table 15-4)	4.86	4.86
(2) RX USPW =	$583,200	$524,880
Present Worth (1) + (2)	$583,200	$554,880 ← Choose Alternate with Lowest First Cost

Annual Cost Method

	Alternate 1	*Alternate 2*
(1) First Cost (P)	–	$30,000
Annual Cost (R)	$120,000	$108,000
CR (Table 15-4)	.2	.2
(2) P X CR	–	6000
Annual Cost (1) + (2)	$120,000	$114,000 ← Choose Alternate with Lowest First Cost

Rate of Return Method

$$P = R \text{ (USPW)} = (\$120,000 - \$108,000) \times \text{USPW}$$

$$\text{USPW} = \frac{30,000}{12,000} = 2.5$$

What value of i will make USPW = 2.5?
i = 40% from Table 15-7.

SIM 4-2

Show the effect of 10% escalation on the rate of return analysis given the

Energy equipment investment = $20,000
After tax savings   = $ 2,600
Equipment life (n)   = 15 years

ANALYSIS

Without escalation

$$CR = \frac{R}{P} = \frac{2,600}{20,000} = .13$$

From Table 15-1
The rate of return is 10%
With 10% escalation assumed:

$$GPW = \frac{P}{G} = \frac{20,000}{2,600} = 7.69$$

From Table 15-1
The rate of return is 21%

Thus we see that taking into account a modest escalation rate can dramatically affect the justification of the project.

DEPRECIATION, TAXES, AND THE TAX CREDIT

DEPRECIATION

Depreciation affects the "accounting procedure" for determining profits and losses and the income tax of a company. In other words, for tax purposes the expenditure for an asset such as a pump or motor can not be fully expensed in its first year. The original investment must be charged off for tax purposes over the useful life of the asset. A company usually wishes to expense an item as quickly as possible.

The Internal Revenue Service allows several methods for determining the annual depreciation rate.

*Straight-Line Depreciation—*The simplest method is referred to as a straight-line depreciation and is defined as:

$$D = \frac{P - L}{n}$$ *Formula (4-8)*

Where:

D   is the annual depreciation rate

L   is the value of equipment at the end of its useful life, commonly referred to as salvage value

n   is the life of the equipment which is determined by Internal Revenue Service Guidelines

P   is the initial expenditure.

*Sum-of-Years Digits—*Another method is referred to as the sum-of-years digits. In this method the depreciation rate is determined by finding the sum of digits using the following formula:

$$N = n \frac{(n + 1)}{2}$$ *Formula (4-9)*

Where n is the life of equipment.

Each year's depreciation rate is determined as follows:

First year $\qquad D = \frac{n}{N} (P - L)$ *Formula (4-10)*

Second year $\qquad D = \frac{n - 1}{N} (P - L)$ *Formula (4-11)*

n year $\qquad D = \frac{1}{N} (P - L)$ *Formula (4-12)*

*Declining-Balance Depreciation—*The declining-balance method allows for larger depreciation charges in the early years which is sometimes referred to as fast write-off.

The rate is calculated by taking a constant percentage of the declining undepreciated balance. The most common method used to calculate the declining balance is to predetermine the depreciation rate. Under certain circumstances a rate equal to 200 per cent of the straight-line depreciation rate may be used. Under other circumstances the rate is limited to 1½ or ¼ times as great as straight-line depreciation. In this method the salvage value or undepreciated book value is established once the depreciation rate is preestablished.

To calculate the undepreciated book value Formula 4-13 is used:

$$D = 1 - \left(\frac{L}{P}\right)^{1/N} \qquad\qquad Formula\ (4\text{-}13)$$

Where

D   is the annual depreciation rate
L   is the salvage value
P   is the first cost.

SIM 4-3

Calculate the depreciation rate using the straight-line, sum-of-years digit, and declining-balance methods.

Salvage value is 0
n = 5 years
P = 150,000
For declining balance use a 200% rate.

Straight-Line Method

$$D = \frac{P - L}{n} = \frac{150,000}{5} = \$30,000 \text{ per year}$$

Sum-of-Years Digits

$$N = \frac{n(n+1)}{2} = \frac{5(6)}{2} = 15$$

$$D_1 = \frac{n}{N}(P) = \frac{5}{15}(150,000) = 50,000$$

N		P
1	=	$50,000
2	=	40,000
3	=	30,000
4	=	20,000
5	=	10,000

Declining-Balance Method

$D = 2 \times 20\% = 40\%$ (Straight Line Depreciation Rate = 20%)

Year	Undepreciated Balance at Beginning of Year	Depreciation Charge
1	150,000	60,000
2	90,000	36,000
3	54,000	21,600
4	32,400	12,960
5	19,440	7,776
TOTAL		138,336

Undepreciated Book Value (150,000 − 138,336) = $11,664

TAX CONSIDERATIONS

Tax-deductible expenses such as maintenance, energy, operating costs, insurance and property taxes reduce the income subject to taxes.

For the after tax life-cycle cost analysis and payback analysis the actual incurred annual savings is given as follows:

$$AS = (1-I)\ E + ID \qquad \textit{Formula (4-14)}$$

Where:

AS = yearly annual after tax savings (excluding effect of tax credit)

E = Yearly annual energy savings (difference between original expenses and expenses after modification)

D   =   annual depreciation rate

I   =   income tax bracket

Formula 4-14 takes into account that the yearly annual energy savings is partially offset by additional taxes which must be paid due to reduced operating expenses. On the other hand, the depreciation allowance reduces taxes directly.

TAX CREDIT

A tax credit encourages capital investment. Essentially the tax credit lowers the income tax paid by the tax credit to an upper limit.

In addition to the investment tax credit, the Business Energy Tax Credit as a result of the National Energy Plan, can also be taken. The Business Energy Tax Credit applies to industrial investment in alternative energy property such as boilers for coal, heat conservation, and recycling equipment. The tax credit substantially increases the investment merit of the investment since it lowers the **bottom** line on the tax form.

ENERGY TAX ACT

The Energy Tax Act of 1978 provides for:

(1) Business Energy Tax Credits:
- Business tax credits for industrial investment in alternative energy property (such as boilers for coal, nonboiler burners for alternate fuels, heat-conservation equipment and recycling equipment).
- Denial of tax benefits for new oil and gas-fired boilers.
- Denial of investment tax credit and accelerated depreciation for new gas and oil boilers.

(2) An additional 10 percent investment tax credit (nonrefundable except for solar equipment) is provided for investment in:
- Alternative Energy Property: This applies to boilers and other combustors which use coal or an alternative fuel, equipment to produce alternative fuels, pollution control equipment, equipment for handling and stor-

age of alternate fuels, and geothermal equipment. The
credit is not available to utilities.
- Solar or Wind Energy Property: A refundable credit
for investments in equipment to use renewable energy
to generate electricity or to heat or cool, or provide
hot water. This credit is not available to utilities.
- Specially Defined Energy Property: This applies to
equipment to improve the heat efficiency of existing
industrial processes, including heat exchangers and
recuperators.

AFTER-TAX ANALYSIS

To compute a rate of return which accounts for taxes, depreciation, escalation, and tax credits a cash-flow analysis is
usually required. This method analyzes all transactions including first and operating costs. To determine the after-tax rate of
return a trial and error or computer analysis is required.

The Present Worth Factors summarized in Table 4-2 can be
used for this analysis. All money is converted to the present
assuming an interest rate. The summation of all present dollars
should equal zero when the correct interest rate is selected, as
illustrated in Figure 4-9.

This analysis can be made assuming a fuel escalation rate by
using the Gradient Present Worth interest of the Present Worth
Factor.

SIM 4-4

Comment on the after-tax rate of return for the installation
of a heat-recovery system with and without tax credit given the
following:
- First Cost $100,000
- Year Savings   40,000
- Straight-line depreciation life and equipment life of 5
years
- Income tax bracket 46%

Table 4-2. Present Worth Interest Factors

Period n	Single-payment present-worth (SPPW)	Single-payment present-worth (SPPW)	Single-payment present-worth (SPPW)	Single-payment present-worth (SPPW)	Single payment present-worth (SPPW)	Single-payment present-worth (SPPW)	Single-payment present-worth (SPPW)
	Present value of $1 $\dfrac{1}{(1+i)^n}$ 12%	Present value of $1 $\dfrac{1}{(1+i)^n}$ 15%	Present value of $1 $\dfrac{1}{(1+i)^n}$ 20%	Present value of $1 $\dfrac{1}{(1+i)^n}$ 25%	Present value of $1 $\dfrac{1}{(1+i)^n}$ 30%	Present value of $1 $\dfrac{1}{(1+i)^n}$ 40%	Present value of $1 $\dfrac{1}{(1+i)^n}$ 50%
1	0.8929	0.8696	0.8333	0.8000	0.7692	0.7143	0.6667
2	0.7972	0.7561	0.6944	0.6400	0.5917	0.5102	0.4444
3	0.7118	0.6575	0.5787	0.5120	0.4552	0.3644	0.2963
4	0.6355	0.5718	0.4823	0.4096	0.3501	0.2603	0.1975
5	0.5674	0.4972	0.4019	0.3277	0.2693	0.1859	0.1317
6	0.5066	0.4323	0.3349	0.2621	0.2072	0.1328	0.0878
7	0.4523	0.3759	0.2791	0.2097	0.1594	0.0949	0.0585
8	0.4039	0.3269	0.2326	0.1678	0.1226	0.0678	0.0390
9	0.3606	0.2843	0.1938	0.1342	0.0943	0.0484	0.0260
10	0.3220	0.2472	0.1615	0.1074	0.0725	0.0346	0.0173
11	0.2875	0.2149	0.1346	0.0859	0.0558	0.0247	0.0116
12	0.2567	0.1869	0.1122	0.0687	0.0429	0.0176	0.0077
13	0.2292	0.1625	0.0935	0.0550	0.0330	0.0126	0.0051
14	0.2046	0.1413	0.0779	0.0440	0.0254	0.0090	0.0034
15	0.1827	0.1229	0.0649	0.0352	0.0195	0.0064	0.0023
16	0.1631	0.1069	0.0541	0.0281	0.0150	0.0046	0.0015
17	0.1456	0.0929	0.0451	0.0225	0.0116	0.0033	0.0010
18	0.1300	0.0808	0.0376	0.0180	0.0089	0.0023	0.0007
19	0.1161	0.0703	0.0313	0.0144	0.0068	0.0017	0.0005
20	0.1037	0.0611	0.0261	0.0115	0.0053	0.0012	0.0003
21	0.0926	0.0531	0.0217	0.0092	0.0040	0.0009	0.0002
22	0.0826	0.0462	0.0181	0.0074	0.0031	0.0006	0.0001
23	0.0738	0.0402	0.0151	0.0059	0.0024	0.0004	—
24	0.0659	0.0349	0.0126	0.0047	0.0018	0.0003	—
25	0.0588	0.0304	0.0105	0.0038	0.0014	0.0002	—

Year	1 Investment	2 Tax Credit	3 After Tax Savings (AS)	4 (Table 4-1) Single Payment Present Worth Factor	(2 + 3) X 4 Present Worth
0	--P				--P
1		+TC	AS	$SPPW_1$	$+P_1$
2			AS	$SPPW_2$	P_2
3			AS	$SPPW_3$	P_3
4			AS	$SPPW_4$	P_4
Total					ΣP

$$AS = (1 - I) E + ID$$

Trial & Error Solution:

Correct i when $\Sigma P = 0$

Figure 4-9. Cash Flow Rate of Return Analysis

ANALYSIS

$$D = 100{,}000/5 = 20{,}000$$
$$AS = (1-I) E + ID = .54(40{,}000) + .46(20{,}000)$$
$$= 21{,}600 + 9{,}200 = 30{,}800$$

Without Tax Credit

First Trial $i = 20\%$

Investment	After Tax Savings	SPPW 20%	PW
0 – 100,000			−100,000
1	30,800	.833	25,656
2	30,800	.694	21,375
3	30,800	.578	17,802
4	30,800	.482	14,845
5	30,800	.401	12,350
		Σ −	7,972

Since summation is negative a higher present worth factor is required. Next try is 15%.

Investment	After Tax Savings	SPPW 15%	PW
0 – 100,000			−100,000
1	30,800	.869	+ 26,765
2	30,800	.756	+ 23,284
3	30,800	.657	+ 20,235
4	30,800	.571	+ 17,586
5	30,800	.497	+ 15,307
			+ 3,177

Since rate of return is bracketed, linear interpolation will be used.

$$\frac{3177 + 7971}{-5} = \frac{3177 - 0}{15 - i\%}$$

$$i = \frac{3177}{2229.6} + 15 = 16.4\%$$

With Tax Credit

Tax Credit = 10% (Investment) + 10% (Energy) = 20%

Investment	Tax Credit	After Tax Savings	SPPW 20%	PW
0 – 100,000				−100,000
1	20,000	30,800	.833	45,656
2		30,800	.694	21,375
3		30,800	.578	17,802
4		30,800	.482	14,845
5		30,800	.401	12,350
				+ 12,028

Next Try, 25%

$$PW$$

$$
\begin{array}{r}
-100,000 \\
44,640 \\
19,712 \\
15,769 \\
\underline{10,093} \\
-\ \ 9,786
\end{array}
$$

$$\frac{12,028 + 9,786}{-5} = \frac{12,028}{20 - i}$$

$$i = 22.75\%$$

COMPUTER PROGRAMS

To readily do life-cycle cost analysis several computer programs are available. Prerecorded magnetic cards, as illustrated in Figure 4-10, can be used with programmable calculators.

For further information contact:

Scotch Programs
Box 430734
Miami, Florida 33143

Andrew Susemichael
Hughes & Susemichel, Inc.
2420 Frankfort Avenue
Louisville, Kentucky 40206

**Figure 4-10. Prerecorded Magnetic Card Programs
For Use with Programmable Calculators**
(Photograph courtesy of Scotch Programs)

5

The Heating,

Ventilation And

Air-Conditioning Audit

Energy audits of Heating, Ventilation and Air-Conditioning (HVAC) Systems is a very important portion of the overall program. HVAC standards such as ASHRAE 90-75 exist for defining energy-efficient systems in new construction. On the other hand, as of this writing no standards exist to define HVAC-efficient systems for existing buildings.

The purpose of this chapter is to highlight "low cost-no cost" areas that should be investigated in the HVAC Energy Audit. Portions of material used in this section and audit forms appearing in Chapter 15 are based upon two publications: "Guidelines for Saving Energy in Existing Buildings—Building Owners and Operators Manual," ECM-1; and "Engineers, Architects and Operators Manual," ECM-2. Both manuals were prepared for the government by Fred S. Dubin, Harold L. Mindell and Selwyn Bloome. The volumes were originally published by the U.S. Department of Commerce National Technical Information Service PB-249928 and PB-249929 and are available from Superintendent of Documents, U.S. Government Printing Office, Washington, D.C. 20402. Reference to ECM-1 and ECM-2 in the text refer to the original publication. The original document published is one of the most extensive works on energy conservation in existing buildings. The author expresses appreciation and credit to this work as one of the outstanding contributions in the energy audit field.

To use the short-cut methods described in this chapter and the chapter on building energy audits (Chapter 6), knowledge of local weather data is required. Chapter 15, Table 15-14 and Figures 15-1 through 15-5 should prove helpful.

In addition Chapter 15 contains various audit forms which can be modified to fit particular needs, such as those shown in Figures 15-6 through 15-24.

A more detailed engineering approach is sometimes required utilizing computer programs, discussed at the end of this chapter, or detailed manual calculations. For manual engineering calculations reference is made to "Cooling and Heating Load Calculations," ASHRAE GRP 158 available from: American Society of Heating, Refrigeration and Airconditioning Engineers, Inc., 345 East 47th Street, New York, NY 10017.

Complete engineering weather data can be found in Air Force Manual, AFM 88-29, "Facility Design and Planning in Engineering Weather Data," available from the Superintendent of Documents, Washington, D.C. 20402.

THE VENTILATION AUDIT

Several existing codes require outside air requirements in excess of those required to dilute carbon dioxide and odors. Some localities have adopted ASHRAE Standard 62-73 for outside air and exhaust requirements. This standard establishes a basic SCFM per person outside air requirement. The meaning of the word ventilation has also changed as a result of this standard. Ventilation in effect means "an outside (outdoor) air supply plus any recirculated air that has been treated to maintain the desired quality of air within a designated space."

To accomplish an Energy Audit of the ventilation system the following steps can be followed:

1. Measure volume of air at the outdoor air intakes of the ventilation system. Record ventilation and fan motor nameplate data.

2. Determine local code requirements and compare against measurements.
3. Check if code requirements exceed "Recommended Ventilation Standards," Figure 5-1.
4. Apply for Code Variance if it is determined that existing standards are higher than required.

To decrease CFM, the fan pulley can be changed. Two savings are derived from this change, namely:

- Brake horsepower of fan motor is reduced.
- Reduced heat loss during heating season.

To compute the savings Formulas 5-1 and 5-2 are used. Figure 5-2 can also be used to compute fan power savings as a result of air flow reduction.

$$\text{HP (Reduction)} = \text{HP} \times \left(\frac{\text{CFM (New)}}{\text{CFM (Old)}} \right)^3 \qquad \textit{Formula (5-1)}$$

$$\text{Q (Saved)} = \frac{1.08 \text{ BTU}}{\text{HR}-\text{CFM}-°\text{F}} \times \text{CFM (Saved)} \times \Delta\text{T} \quad \textit{Formula (5-2)}$$

$$\text{KW} = \text{HP} \times .746/\eta \qquad\qquad \textit{Formula (5-3)}$$

Where
  HP = Motor Horsepower
  CFM = Cubic feet per minute
  ΔT = Average temperature gradient
  KW = Motor Kilowatts (K = 1000)
  η = Motor efficiency

In addition to reducing air flow during occupied periods, consideration should be given to shutting the system down during unoccupied hours.

If the space was cooled, additional savings will be achieved. The quantity of energy required to cool and dehumidify the ventilated air to indoor conditions is determined by the enthalpy difference between outdoor and indoor air. To compute the energy savings for the cooling season Figure 5-3 can be used.

SIM 5-1

An energy audit indicates ventilation in a storage area can be reduced from four to two changes per hour during the winter months—240 days, 4200 degree-days.

1. *Office Buildings* (1)
   Work Space . . . . 5 CFM/person
   Heavy Smoking Areas. . . . . . . .15 CFM/person
   Lounges. . . . . 5 CFM/person
   Cafeteria . . . . 5 CFM/person
   Conference Rooms . . . . .15 CFM/person
   Doctor Offices . . . . 5 CFM/person
   Toilet Rooms . . . . .10 air changes/hour
   Lobbies. 0
   Unoccupied Spaces 0

2. *Retail Stores* (1)
   Trade Areas . . . . 6 CFM/customer
   Street level with heavy use
   (less than 5,000 sq ft with
   single or double outside door) . . 0
   Unoccupied Spaces 0

3. *Religious Buildings* (1)
   Halls of Worship . . . . 5 CFM/person
   Meeting Rooms. . . . . .10 CFM/person
   Unoccupied Spaces 0

4. *Maintenance* (2) . . . . 2 air changes/hour (winter)
                                          6 air changes/hour (summer)

5. *Warehouse* (2). . . . . 1½–2 air changes/hour (winter)
                                          5 air changes/hour (summer)

6. *Waste Treatment* (2) . . . . 4 air changes/hour (winter)
                                          15 air changes/hour (summer)

Source:
   (1) Guidelines For Saving Energy in Existing Buildings—Building
       Owners and Operators Manual, ECM-1.
   (2) Instructions For Energy Auditors — Vol. II, DOE/CS-00 41/13

NOTE: Air changes/hour based on non-airconditioned space.

Figure 5-1. Ventilation Recommendations

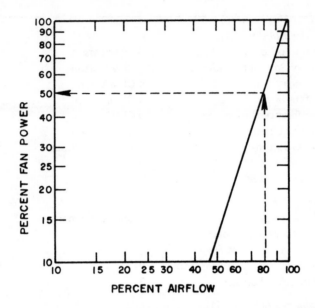

Figure 5-2. Decrease in Horsepower Accomplished By Reducing Fan Speed (Based on Laws of Fan Performance)
(Source: NBS Handbook 115 Supplement 1)

Comment on the energy savings based on the following audit data:

- Building size: 20H X 150W X 100L
- Inside temperature: 70°F
- Motor Horsepower: 20 HP
- Nameplate Electrical Efficiency: .8
- Utility Costs: $4/10^6 BTU, 5¢ per KWH
- Hours of Operation 5760
- Boiler Efficiency = .65

ANALYSIS

Volume of Warehouse Area = 20 X 150 X 100 = 300,000 ft³
Present Rate: 4 X 300,000 X 1/60 = 20,000 CFM
Reduced Rate = 2 X 300,000 X 1/60 = 10,000 CFM

Savings Due to Reduced Horsepower

Reduced Horsepower = 20 HP X (2/4)³ = 2.5 HP

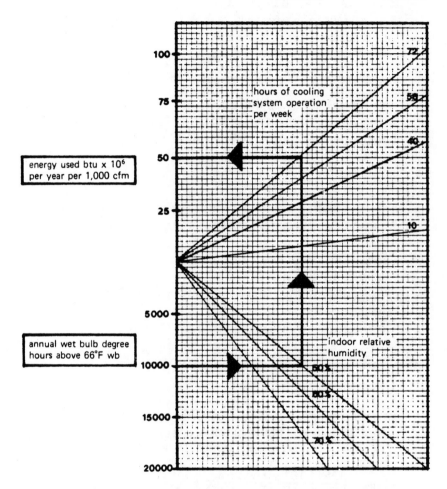

Figure 5-3. Yearly Energy Used Per 1,000 CFM to Maintain Various
Humidity Conditions
*(Source: Guidelines For Saving Energy in Existing Buildings—Building Owners
and Operating Manual, ECM-1)*

Savings Electricity = (20—2.5) X .746/.8 X 5¢ KW X 5760
           = $4,699.80

Savings Due to Reduced Heat Loss

Average ΔT = 4200 degree-days/240 days = 17.5°F
Average Outdoor = 65 − 17.5 = 47.5
Temperature during Heating Seasons

$$\text{Heat Removed} = \frac{1.08 \text{ BTU}}{\text{HR}-\text{CFM}-°\text{F}} \text{ X CFM } \Delta T =$$

1.08 (20,000 − 10,000) X 17.5 = 189,000 BTUH
Savings = 189,000 X \$4/10^6 BTU/.65 X 5760 = \$6698
Total Annual Savings = \$4699 + 6698 = \$11,397

SIM 5-2

For the building of SIM 5-1, compute the cooling savings resulting from reducing air changes per hour from 4 to 2.
   Audit Data:
   Annual Wet Bulb Degree-Hours above 66°F = 8,000
   Relative Humidity = 50%
   Hours of Cooling System Operation per Week = 40
   Electricity Rate = 5¢ per KWH
   Refrigeration Consumption = .8 KW/Ton-Hr.

ANALYSIS

From Figure 5-3
Energy Used per year per 1000 CFM is 22.5 X 10^6 BTU
Energy Saved = (20,000−10,000 CFM) X 22.5 X 10^6 BTU
             = 225 X 10^6 BTU/Yr.

$$\text{Savings} = \frac{225 \text{ X } 10^6 \text{ BTU/Yr}}{12,000 \text{ BTU/Ton-Hr}} \text{ X .8 KW/Ton-Hr X 5¢/KWH}$$

= \$750/Yr

THE TEMPERATURE AUDIT

As a result of President Carter's Directive to Federal Agencies and Executive Departments energy consumption is to be reduced by 5% for the 12-month period beginning April 1, 1979. As a result the following temperature standards were mandated:

Winter Heating—Thermostats will be set at not more than 65 degrees during the day and 55 degrees during the night. The use of portable electric heaters will be permitted only to the extent necessary to maintain these standards.

Summer Cooling—Air-conditioning systems, whether centrally or individually controlled, will be operated at not less than 80 degrees. Care should also be taken to assure that doors to air-conditioned rooms are not left open, and that cooling units are turned off when not in use.

The temperature audit should include the following:
- Determine indoor temperature settings for each space and season.
- Determine spaces which are unoccupied.
- Check if temperatures exceed "Recommended Temperature Standards," Figures 5-4 and 5-5.
- Implement setbacks by resetting thermostats manually, installing clocks or adjusting controls.
- Turn off cooling systems operated in summer during unoccupied hours.
- Experiment to determine optimum setback temperature.
- Lower temperature settings of occupied spaces based on "Recommended Ventilation Standards," Figures 5-4 and 5-5.

Public mandatory state and federal standards should be followed. Check that temperature requirements specified in OSHA are not violated. Changing temperatures in occupied periods could cause labor relations problems. It is suggested that where code dictates otherwise, variances should be obtained. Agreement by Labor Relations Department is also important.

Other considerations in setting back temperatures during occupied hours include:
1. In spaces used for storage and which are mostly unoccupied, equipment and piping freeze protection is the main consideration.

	A Dry Bulb °F occupied hours maximum	B Dry Bulb °F unoccupied hours (set-back)	
1. OFFICE BUILDINGS, RESIDENCIES, SCHOOLS			
Offices, school rooms, residential spaces	68°	55°	
Corridors	62°	52°	
Dead Storage Closets	50°	50°	
Cafeterias	68°	50°	
Mechanical Equipment Rooms	55°	50°	
Occupied Storage Areas, Gymnasiums	55°	50°	
Auditoriums	68°	50°	
Computer Rooms	65°	As required	
Lobbies	65°	50°	
Doctor Offices	68°	58°	
Toilet Rooms	65°	55°	
Garages	Do not heat	Do not heat	
2. RETAIL STORES			
Department Stores	65°	55°	
Supermarkets	60°	50°	
Drug Stores	65°	55°	
Meat Markets	60°	50°	
Apparel (except dressing rms)	65°	55°	
Jewelry, Hardware, etc.	65°	55°	
Warehouses	55°	50°	
Docks and platforms	Do not heat	Do not heat	
3. RELIGIOUS BUILDINGS		24 Hrs or less	Greater than 24 Hrs
Meeting Rooms	68°	55°	50°
Halls of Worship	65°	55°	50°
All other spaces	As noted for office buildings	50°	40°

Source: Guidelines For Saving Energy in Existing Buildings—Building Owners
and Operators Manual, ECM-1

Figure 5-4. Suggested Heating Season Indoor Temperatures

I. COMMERCIAL BUILDINGS	Occupied Periods	
	Dry Bulb Temperature*	Minimum Relative Humidity
Offices	78°	55%
Corridors	Uncontrolled	Uncontrolled
Cafeterias	75°	55%
Auditoriums	78°	50%
Computer Rooms	75°	As needed
Lobbies	82°	60%
Doctor Offices	78°	55%
Toilet Rooms	80°	
Storage, Equipment Rooms	Uncontrolled	
Garages	Do Not Cool or Dehumidify.	

II. RETAIL STORES	Occupied Periods	
	Dry Bulb Temperature	Relative Humidity
Department Stores	80°	55%
Supermarkets	78°	55%
Drug Stores	80°	55%
Meat Markets	78°	55%
Apparel	80°	55%
Jewelry	80°	55%
Garages	Do Not Cool.	

* Except where terminal reheat systems are used. With terminal reheat systems the indoor space conditions should be maintained at lower levels to reduce the amount of reheat. If cooling energy is not required to maintain temperatures, 74°F would be recommended instead of 78°F.

Source: Guidelines For Saving Energy In Existing Buildings—Building Owners and Operators Manual, ECM-1

Figure 5-5. Suggested Indoor Temperature and Humidity Levels in the Cooling Season

2. Consider maintaining stairwell temperatures around 55°F in winter.
3. For areas where individuals commonly wear outdoor clothing such as stores, lower temperatures in winter.

SAVINGS AS A RESULT OF SETBACK

Figures 5-6 and 5-7 can be used to estimate savings as a result of setbacks for winter and summer respectively.

To use Figure 5-6:
1. Determine degree-days for location.
2. Calculate BTU/square foot/year used for heating.
3. Draw a line horizontally from specified degree-days to intersection of setback temperature. Extend line vertically and proceed along sloped lines as illustrated in the figure.
4. Draw a line horizontally from BTU/square foot/year until it intersects sloped line. Proceed vertically and read BTU/square foot/year savings on upper horizontal axis.

To use Figure 5-7:
1. Add the BTU/hour/1000 CFM for each temperature starting.
2. Start with one temperature above original set point.
3. Add contributions for each set point temperature until new setting is reached.

SIM 5-3

An energy audit indicates that the temperature of the building can be set back 20°F during unoccupied hours.

Comment on the energy savings based on the following audit data:

Heating Degree-Days = 6,000
Present Heating Consumption =
    60,000 BTU/square foot/year
Floor Area = 100,000 square feet
Utility Cost = $4/10^6 BTU
Boiler Efficiency = .65

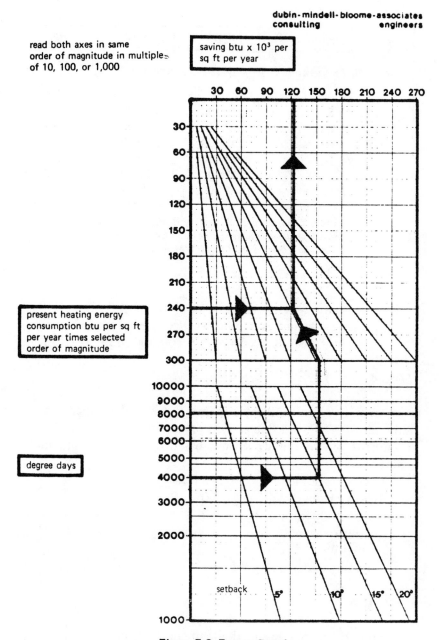

Figure 5-6. Energy Saved
(Source: Guidelines For Saving Energy In Existing Buildings—
Building Owners and Operators Manual, ECM-1)

Relative Humidity	50%	60%	70%
Dry Bulb Temperature	BTU/Hour/1000 CFM		
72°F	0	0	0
73°F	2,700	2,433	3,000
74°F	2,657	2,400	3,257
75°F	3,000	2,572	3,000
76°F	3,000	2,572	3,000
77°F	3,000	2,572	3,429
78°F	3,000	2,572	3,429

Figure 5-7. Effect of Raising Dry Bulb Temperature
(Source: Guidelines For Saving Energy In Existing Buildings--
Building Owners and Operators Manual, ECM-1)

ANALYSIS

From Figure 5-6:
Energy Savings is 36,000 BTU/square foot/year
Savings = 36,000 X $4/$10^6$ X 100,000/.65 = $22,153

SIM 5-4

An energy audit indicates an indoor dry bulb temperature in summer of 73°F. It is determined to raise the set point to 78°F. Comment on the energy savings based on the following audit data:

Total outdoor air	15,000 CFM
Relative Humidity	50%
Hours of Operation	40
Cooling Season	20 weeks/year
Annual W B degree- hours above 66°F, WB	6,000

ANALYSIS

From Figure 5-7, raising the temperature from 73°F to 78°F, a total savings of the following will occur:

74	2,656
75	3,000
76	3,000
77	3,000
78	3,000

Total.................14,656 BTU/Hour/1000 CFM
Savings: 14,656 BTU/Hour/1000 CFM X 15,000 CFM X
$4/10^6$ BTU/.65 X 40 Hours/Week X 20 Weeks/
Year = $1,082 per year.

THE HUMIDITY AUDIT

Desired relative humidity requirements are achieved by va-
porizing water into the dry ventilating air. Approximately 1000
BTUs are required to vaporize each pound of water. To save energy, humidification systems should not be used during unoccupied hours. Most humidification systems are used to maintain
the comfort and health of occupants, to prevent cracking of
wood, and to preserve materials. In lieu of specific standards it
is suggested that 20% relative humidity be maintained in all
spaces occupied more than four hours per day. If static shocks
or complaints arise, increase the humidity levels in 5% increments until the appropriate level for each area is determined.
Figure 5-8 can be used to estimate the savings in winter as a result of lowering the relative humidity requirements.

SIM 5-4

An energy audit of the humidification requirements indicated the following data:

Outdoor air rate plus infiltration	10,000 CFM
Annual Wet Bulb Degree-Hours	
Below 54°WB and 68°F	65,000
Cost of Fuel	$4 per million BTU
Boiler Efficiency	.65
Type	Department Store
	112 hours occupancy/
	week

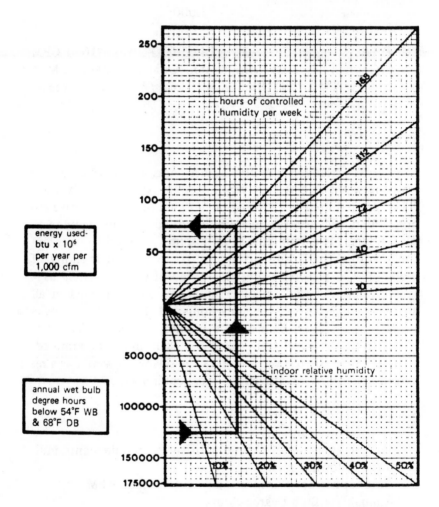

Figure 5-8. Yearly Energy Used Per 1,000 CFM to Maintain Various Humidity Conditions
(Source: Guidelines For Saving Energy In Existing Buildings—Building Owners and Operators Manual, ECM-1)

Determine the savings as a result of lowering the relative humidity of the building from 50% to 30% during the heating season.

ANALYSIS

From Figure 5-8:

Energy used at 50 RH = 65 X 10^6 BTU/Yr per 1000 CFM
Energy used at 30 RH = 35 X 10^6 BTU/Yr per 1000 CFM
Energy saved = (65−35) X 10^6 X 10 = 300 X 10^6 BTU/Yr
Savings = 300 X 10^6 X $4/$10^6$/.65 = $1,846

In the case of the cooling season check to determine if levels are consistent with Figure 5-5. Higher levels of humidification than required during the cooling season waste energy. Figure 5-9 should be used to estimate savings as a result of maintaining a higher RH level.

SIM 5-5

Determine the savings based on increasing the relative humidity from 50% to 70% based on the audit data:

Annual Wet Bulb Degree-Hours above 66°F	8,000
Operation per week	40 hours
Outside CFM	20,000
Refrigeration consumptions	.8 KW/Ton Hour
Electric rate	5¢ per KWH

ANALYSIS

From Figure 5-9:

Energy used at 50% RH   22.5 X 10^6 BTU/Yr per 1000 CFM
Energy used at 70% RH   16 X 10^6 BTU/Yr per 1000 CFM
Energy saved = (22.5−16) X 10^6 X 20 = 130 X 10^6 BTU/Yr

$$\text{Savings} = \frac{130 \times 10^6}{12,000 \text{ BTU/Ton-Hr}} \times .8 \text{ KW/Ton-Hr} \times 5¢/\text{KWH}$$
$$= \$433/\text{Yr}$$

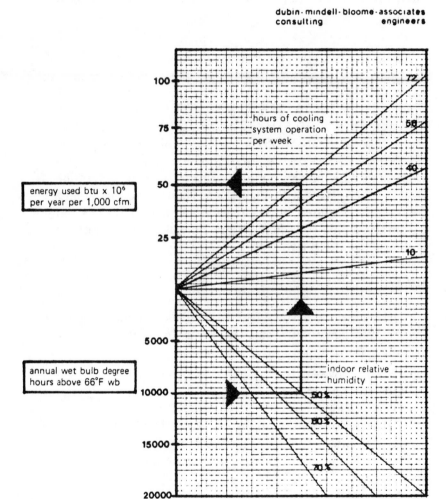

**Figure 5-9. Yearly Energy Used Per 1,000 CFM to Maintain
Various Humidity Conditions**
*(Source: Guidelines For Saving Energy In Existing Buildings—
Building Owners and Operators Manual, ECM-1)*

COMPUTER PROGRAM ANALYSIS

Computer program analysis is a very important design tool in the energy audit process. Manual load calculations are based on steady-state conditions. These calculations are usually based on maximum or minimum conditions and give reasonable indications of equipment size. They do not however indicate how the system will perform. Probably the greatest opportunity for savings exists under part-load conditions.

Computer programs simulate energy consumption based on stored weather data; this enables a comprehensive month-by-month energy report to determine the optimum system performance. The total system can be analyzed including lighting, HVAC, and building envelope. Thus alternatives may be investigated with all parameters considered.

Figure 5-10 describes in detail several programs available from: Professional Services Division, Control Data Corporation, P.O. Box 7090, Sunnyvale, CA 94086.

"Energy Analysis" Computer program is licensed by the Canadian Government and made free of charge. This program system has gained widespread acceptance and is available from Ross F. Meriwether & Associates, San Antonio, Texas.

Another widely used program, "Trace," is available from Thane Co., La Crosse, WI.

It should be noted that in several instances the same program is available from several sources such as the NBSLD program which may be purchased directly from the National Bureau of Standards for under $5.00.

Figure 5-11 lists computer programs according to type of program, with a brief description (or name) of the program, and the author of the program.

ENERGY RECOVERY SYSTEMS

The HVAC Energy Audit should analyze opportunities for recovering energy. To recover heat from exhausts, several

BLAST
Building Loads Analysis and System Thermodynamics

BLAST is a comprehensive energy-analysis computer program for estimating hourly space heating and cooling requirements; hourly performance of fan systems; and hourly performance of conventional heating and cooling plants, total energy plants and/or solar energy systems. It was developed by the U.S. Army Construction Engineering Research Laboratory at Champaign, Illinois.

CCB/CALERDA

CCB/CALERDA is a building energy analysis program developed by Consultants Computation Bureau of Oakland, California, to assist the building design, construction, and code-enforcement community in planning for and practicing energy conservation. Available in the United States and Canada through Control Data Corporation's CYBERNET Services network, CALERDA allows architects and engineers to compute energy consumption in buildings.

CALERDA has advanced the state of the art in energy analysis with several unique features: a Building Description Language (BDL) which simplifies input, the ability to simulate a large variety of conventional and solar energy systems that can be operated optimally or by user-specified rules, and a program architecture making efficient use of computer resources. The program performs an hour-by-hour simulation of the heating, ventilating, and air-conditioning systems as they respond to changing weather and internal heat loads. The calculations incorporate thermal lag due to the construction of the building envelope.

EP – ENERGY PROGRAMS

Energy Programs (EP) analyze energy consumption in new or existing buildings. EP is made up of two sections, loads and energy analysis. The loads section of the program allows the mechanical engineer to calculate heating and cooling building loads and the energy analysis section calculates the building energy consumption through a full year's operation.

Starting from initial design concepts, the engineer may calculate the building heating and cooling loads and then, by adding to this data base, build a data file for a system simulation energy analysis. Building modeling is achieved through the flexibility of the program. Computer calculations may be verified by requesting sample calculations for selected periods. The user and program communicate interactively; the user responds to program requests for unit system, material selection, parameter values and output options. EP is available in batch and interactive versions through Control Data's CYBERNET Services worldwide data services network.

Figure 5-10. Computer Programs

NBSLD
National Bureau of Standards Load Determination Program

The National Bureau of Standards Load Determination computer program (NBSLD) estimates the amount of energy used in heating and cooling buildings. The program uses new algorithms recommended by the American Society of Heating, Refrigerating and Air-Conditioning Engineers (ASHRAE) Task Group on Energy Requirements.

NBSLD computes energy consumption by solving simultaneous heat balance equations for the interior surface of a room or space. Conduction transfer functions are used to calculate transient heat conduction through exterior walls and the interior of structures. Although heat balance equation calculations are more time consuming than the weighting factor approach, they are more precise.

Batch and interactive versions of NBSLD are available in the United States and Canada through Control Data's CYBERNET Services data services networks.

ENERGY ANALYST

ENERGY ANALYST is a building model designed by American Energy Services, Inc. expressly for energy audits. ENERGY ANALYST allows a user to quickly and efficiently model a building's energy consumption characteristics and compare the savings which would result from various energy conservation alternatives. It is designed to model the majority of building types—commercial structures, schools, apartments.

ENERGY ANALYST separates energy consumption into a number of components such as window infiltration, fan operation, outside air ventilation, and domestic hot water consumption. It prints a comparison of energy conservation alternatives with the base model. Finally, it computes life-cycle costs for the selected alternatives.

ECUBE 75
Energy Conservation Using Better Engineering

ECUBE 75 is an integrated series of energy analysis computer programs. It evaluates energy systems to determine which equipment most economically satisfies the energy requirements of a particular structure. ECUBE 75 provides energy decision-makers with an efficient, affordable tool during the early stages of building construction planning, as well as a means to make a realistic evaluation of proposed conservation measures on existing buildings. The program weighs the effects of weather, orientation, usage profiles, lights, motors and varying ventilation requirements on the system and generates reports which indicate the amounts of energy the site will consume with alternative types of equipment. It also provides data on economic comparison, based on factors such as equipment characteristics, local weather profiles, in-

Figure 5-10. Computer Programs (con't.)

terest charges, and fuel and electrical costs. It has recently been enhanced through the addition of a solar load calculating program module which includes the effects of building shading features and now hosts an improved airside simulation module.

ECUBE 75 is a batch program, operational on Control Data CYBER 70 and 6000-series computer systems. It is available exclusively through the CYBER-NET nationwide computer services network. Although ECUBE 75 usage was formerly restricted to an authorized membership list, it may now be used by anyone registering with the American Gas Association.

FCHART
Interactive Solar Heating Design Program

FCHART (Interactive Solar Heating Design Program) offers a fast and efficient method of designing solar heating systems. The method, developed at the Solar Energy Laboratory of the University of Wisconsin, is based on standard system configurations using either liquid or air as the heat transfer medium. It treats the collector area as the main design variable; secondary design variables are also included, such as storage unit capacity.

The f-chart method derives its name from charts based on correlating hundreds of detailed simulations of solar heating systems. For standard configurations, the f-charts eliminate the need for detailed simulations requiring hourly meteorological data.

Meteorological data required to use the f-chart method include the long-term monthly average of:
- Daily total solar radiation on a horizontal surface
- Ambient temperature
- Heating degree days (65°F base)

SOLCOST
Solar Energy Design Program

SOLCOST (Solar Energy Design Program) assists in the design of residential and light commercial solar-heating and solar-service hot-water systems. This program estimates thermal performance and the resulting payback and rate of return from a solar energy project. SOLCOST performs solar system sizing based on solar-versus-conventional cost comparisons.

An effective aid for designers without previous thermal engineering experience, SOLCOST was developed by Martin Marietta for the U.S. Department of Energy (DOE). It is an interactive system, available through Control Data's CYBERNET Services in the United States and Canada.

Figure 5-10. Computer Programs (concluded)

DESIGN PROGRAMS

TYPE	NAME	AUTHOR
Building Form		
Form Generation	Form Generation	University of Southern California
Shading Analysis	SHADOW	University of Texas
	SUNNY	University of Texas
Solar Gain Analysis	SUNSET	Dubin-Mindell-Bloome Associates
Building Exterior Envelope		
Glass Comparison	Glass Comparison	Libbey-Owens-Ford
Building Interior Planning		
Optimization	ARK-2	Perry, Dean & Stewart
	B.O.P.	Skidmore, Owings & Merrill
Lighting		
Conventional	Lighting II	APEC
	Lighting	Dalton, Dalton, Little & Newport
	Interior Lighting	
	Analysis & Design	Giffels Associates, Inc.
ESI	Lighting Program	Isaac Goodbar
	Lighting Program	Illumination Computing Service
	Lighting Program	Ian Lewen
	Lumen II	Smith, Hinchman & Grylls
Daylighting	Daylighting	Libbey-Owens-Ford
Power		
Distribution Network	Electrical Feeder II	APEC
	Electrical Feeder	
	Sizing	Dalton, Dalton, Little & Newport
	Three Phase Fault	
	Analysis	Giffels Associates, Inc.
Demand Study	Electrical Demand	
	Load Study	Giffels Associates, Inc.
HVAC		
Equipment Selection	HCC-III (Mini-Deck)	APEC
	Equipment Selection	Carrier Air Conditioning Co.
	Equipment Selection	Trane Co.
Duct Design	Duct Program	APEC
	Several	Dalton, Dalton, Little & Newport
	Several	Giffels Associates, Inc.
Air Handing Unit Design	Fan Static	
	Calculations	Giffels Associates, Inc.
Domestic Water		
Piping Design	Piping Program	APEC
	Several	Dalton, Dalton, Little & Newport
	Several	Giffels Associates, Inc.

Figure 5-11. A Sampling of Available Computer Programs

TYPE	NAME	AUTHOR
Vertical Transportation		
Elevator Design	Elevator Design	Dover Corporation
	Elevator Design	Otis Elevator
Operation & Maintenance		
Automated Control Systems		Honeywell, Inc.
		Johnson Control Service
		Powers Regulator Company
		Robertshaw Controls
Solar Energy Systems		
Solar Collector Models	Flat Plate Collector	Honeywell, Inc.
	Parabolic Trough	
	Collector	Honeywell, Inc.
	Flat Plate Collector	Westinghouse

ENERGY PROGRAMS

Commercial Programs

ECUBE	American Gas Association
HCC-III	APEC
Energy Analysis	Caudill Rowlett Scott
AXCESS	Electric Energy Association
Glass Comparison	Libbey-Owens-Ford
Energy Program	MEDSI
Energy Analysis	Meriwether & Associates
Building Cost Analysis	PPG Industries
TRACE	TRANE Company
Energy Program	Westinghouse Corp.
HACE	WTA Computer Services, Inc.

Research Programs/Negotiable

CADS	UCLA
SIMSHAC	Colorado State University
FINAL	Dalton, Dalton, Little & Newport
HVAC Load	Giffels Associates, Inc.
Energy Program	Honeywell, Inc.
NBSLD (Honeywell)	Honeywell, Inc.
Energy Program	University of Michigan
NBSLD	National Bureau of Standards
B.E.A.P.	Pennsylvania State University
Post Office Program	
DEROB	University of Texas
TRANSYS	University of Wisconsin

In-House Program/Proprietary

Energy Program	General Electric Company
Residential & Small Commercial	Honeywell, Inc.
Energy Program	IBM

Figure 5-11. A Sampling of Available Computer Programs (concluded)
(Source: Guidelines For Saving Energy in Existing Buildings—
Building Owners and Operators Manual—ECM-1)

devices can be used including the heat wheel, air-to-air heat exchanger, heat pipe and coil run-around cycle. Examples of these systems and devices are illustrated in Figure 5-12.

HEAT WHEELS

Heat wheels are motor-driven devices packed with heat-absorbing material such as a ceramic. As the device turns by means of a motor, heat is transferred from one duct to another.

AIR-TO-AIR HEAT EXCHANGER

The air-to-air heat exchanger consists of an open-ended steel box which is compartmentalized into multiple narrow channels. Each passage carries exhaust air alternating with make-up air. Energy is transmitted by means of conduction through the walls.

HEAT PIPES

A heat pipe is installed through adjacent walls of inlet and outlet ducts; it consists of a short length of copper tubing sealed at both ends. Inside is a porous cylindrical wick and a charge of refrigerant. Its operation is based on a temperature difference between the ends of the pipe, which causes the liquid in the wick to migrate to the warmer end to evaporate and absorb heat. When the refrigerant vapor returns through the hollow center of the wick to the cooler end, it gives up heat, condenses, and the cycle is repeated.

COIL RUN-AROUND CYCLE

The coil run-around cycle transfers energy from the exhaust stream to the make-up stream continuously circulating a heat transfer medium, such as ethylene glycol fluid, between the two coils in the ducts.

In winter, the warm exhaust air passes through the exhaust coils and transfers heat to the ethylene glycol fluid. The fluid is

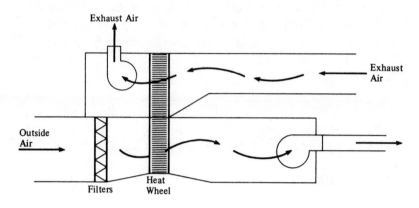

HEAT WHEELS

Air to Air Heat Exchanger

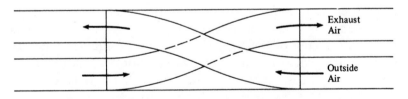

AIR-TO-AIR HEAT PIPES AND EXCHANGERS

Figure 5-12. HVAC Heat Recovery

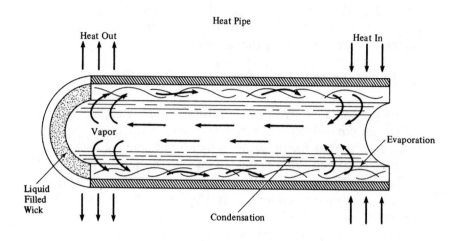

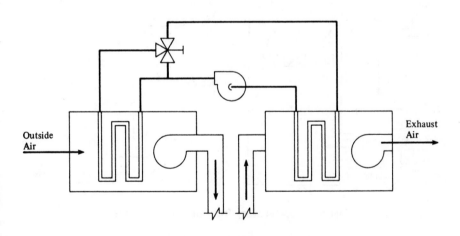

Figure 5-12. HVAC Heat Recovery (concluded)

pumped to the make-up air coil where it preheats the incoming air. The system is most efficient in winter operation, but some recovery is possible during the summer.

HEAT FROM LIGHTING SYSTEMS

Heat dissipated by lighting fixtures which is recovered will reduce air-conditioning loads, will produce up to 13 percent more light output for the same energy input, and can be used as a source of hot air. Two typical recovery schemes are illustrated in Figure 5-13. In the total return system, all of the air is returned through the luminaires. In the bleed-off system, only a portion is drawn through the lighting fixtures. The system is usually used in applications requiring high ventilation rates.

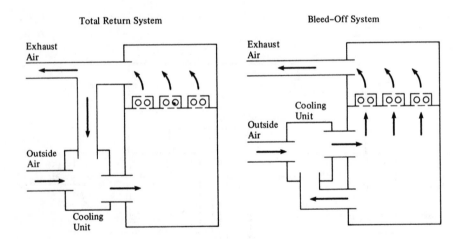

Figure 5-13. Recovery from Lighting Fixtures

SIM 5-6

Roof-mounted, air-cooled condensers are traditionally used to cool the gas from refrigeration equipment. Comment on how the system diagrammed below can be made more efficiently.

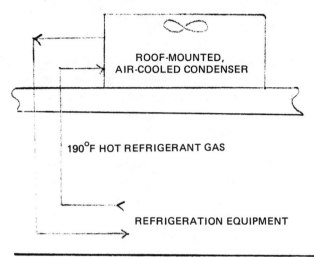

ROOF-MOUNTED,
AIR-COOLED CONDENSER

190°F HOT REFRIGERANT GAS

REFRIGERATION EQUIPMENT

ANALYSIS

This example illustrates a retrofit installation where heat is recovered by the addition of a heat exchanger to recapture the energy which was previously dissipated to the atmosphere. This energy can be used to preheat the domestic water supply for various processes.

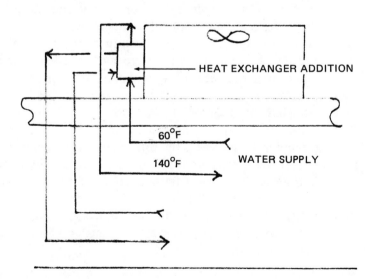

HEAT EXCHANGER ADDITION

60°F

140°F   WATER SUPPLY

ECONOMIZER CYCLE

In addition to heat recovery opportunities, the audit should uncover system modifications which will save energy such as the economizer cycle. The economizer cycle uses outside air as the cooling source when it is cold enough. There are two suitable economizer systems:

1. System monitors and responds to dry-bulb temperature only. It is suitable where wet-bulb degree-hours are less than 8000 per year.
2. System monitors and responds to the WB and DB temperatures (enthalpy), and is most effective and economic in locations which experience more than 8000 WB degree-hours.

SYSTEM 1 – ECONOMIZER CYCLE COOLING

Provide controls, dampers and interlocks to achieve the following control sequence:

a) When the outdoor air DB temperature is lower than the supply air DB temperature required to meet the cooling load, turn off the compressor and chilled water pumps, and position outdoor air—return air—exhaust air dampers to attain the required supply air temperature.
b) When the outdoor air DB temperature is higher than the supply air temperature required to meet the loads, but is lower than the return air temperature, energize the compressors and chilled water pumps and position dampers for 100% outdoor air.
c) Use minimum outdoor air whenever the outdoor dry-bulb temperature exceeds the return air DB temperature.
d) Whenever the relative humidity in the space drops below desired levels and more energy is consumed to raise the RH than is saved by the economizer system, consider using refrigeration in place of economizer cooling. This condition may exist in very cold climates and must be analyzed in detail.

SYSTEM 2 – ENTHALPY CYCLE COOLING

Provide the equipment, controls, dampers and interlocks to achieve the following control sequence:

The four conditions listed for system 1 above are similar for this system with the exception that enthalpy conditions are measured rather than dry-bulb conditions.

If changes to outside air intake are contemplated, take careful note of all codes bearing on ventilation requirements. Fire and safety codes must also be observed.

APPLICATIONS OF SYSTEMS 1 AND 2

- Single duct, constant volume systems
- Variable volume air systems
- Induction systems
- Terminal reheat systems, dual duct systems, and multi-zone systems.

Economizer and Enthalpy systems are less effective if used in conjunction with heat-recovery systems. Trade-offs should be analyzed.

TEST AND BALANCE CONSIDERATIONS

Probably the biggest overlooked low-cost energy audit requirement is a thorough Test, Balance and Adjust Program. In essence the audit should include the following steps:

1. *Test*—Quantitative determination of conditions within the system boundary, including flow rates, temperature and humidity measurements, pressures, etc.
2. *Balance*—Balance the system for required distribution of flows by manipulation of dampers and valves.
3. *Adjust*—Control instrument settings, regulating devices, control sequences should be adjusted for required flow patterns.

In essence the above program checks the designer's intent against actual performance and balances and adjusts the system for peak performance.

Several sources outlining Test and Balance Procedures are:
- Construction Specifications Institute (CSI), which offers a specification series that includes a guide specification Document 15050 entitled "Testing and Balancing of Environmental Systems." Reprints of this paper are available. It explains factors to be considered in using the guide specification for project specifications.
- Associated Air Balance Council (AABC), the certifying body of independent agencies.
- National Environmental Balancing Bureau (NEBB), sponsored jointly by the Mechanical Contractors Association of America and the Sheet Metal and Air Conditioning Contractors National Association as the certifying body of the installing contractors' subsidiaries.

6

The Building System Energy Audit

The Building System Energy Audit (BSEA) requires gathering the following data:
1. Building characteristics and construction
   a. Window characteristics
   b. Openings and major leaks
2. Insulation status

BUILDING DYNAMICS

The building experiences heat gains and heat losses depending on whether the cooling or heating system is present, as illustrated in Figures 6-1 and 6-2. Only when the total season is considered in conjunction with lighting and heating, ventilation and air-conditioning (HVAC) can the energy choice be decided.

Many of the audits discussed in this chapter apply the principle of reducing the heat load or gain of the building. Thus the internal HVAC load would decrease. A caution should be made that without a detailed engineering analysis, a computer simulation, an oversimplification may lead to a wrong conclusion. The weather data for your area and the effect of the total system should not be overlooked.

In order to use the methods described in this chapter, weather data in Chapter 15, Table 15-14 and Figures 15-1 through 15-5 can be used. Figure 15-14 illustrates an energy audit form for a building that may be modified to suit your particular needs.

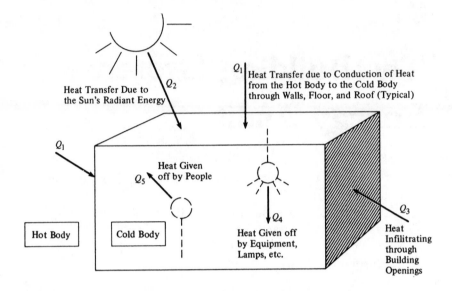

Heat Gain = $Q_1 + Q_2 + Q_3 + Q_4 + Q_5$

Figure 6-1. Heat Gain of a Building

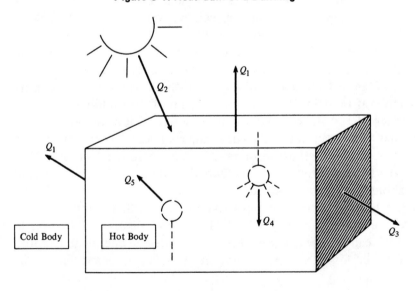

Heat Loss = $Q_1 + Q_3 - Q_2 - Q_4 - Q_5$

Figure 6-2. Heat Loss of a Building

SIM 6-1

Comment on the effect to the overall heat balance by adding skylights to the roof.

ANALYSIS

The effect of adding skylights will influence the overall energy balance in several ways.
1. The illumination from skylights will decrease the need for lighting systems. As an example a building with 6% coverage with skylights may receive ample illumination to turn off the lighting systems most daylight hours.
2. The solar heat gain factor is increased and if the building is air-conditioned more tons and more energy are required.
3. The excess solar heat gain during the winter months may decrease heating loads.

A detailed analysis is available from: Architectural Aluminum Manufacturers Association, 35 East Wacker Drive, Chicago, Illinois 60601 (312) 782-8256—"Voluntary Standard Procedure for Calculating Skylite Annual Energy Balance."

BUILDING CHARACTERISTICS
AND CONSTRUCTION

The BSEA should record for each space the size, physical characteristics, hours of operation and function. The assorted materials of construction, windows, doors, holes, percentage glass, etc. should also be recorded.

INFILTRATION

Leakage or infiltration of air into a building is similar to the effect of additional ventilation. Unlike ventilation it cannot be controlled or turned off at night. It is the result of cracks, openings around windows and doors, and access openings. Infiltration is also induced into the building to replace exhaust air unless the

HVAC balances the exhaust. Wind velocity increases infiltration and stack effects are potential problems.

A handy formula which relates ventilation or infiltration rates to heat flow is Formula 6-1.

$$Q = 1.08 \times CFM \times \Delta T \qquad \qquad Formula\ (6\text{-}1)$$

Where:

Q is heat removal, BTU/Hr
CFM is ventilation or infiltration rate, cubic feet per minute
ΔT is the allowable heat rise.

Heat losses and gains from openings can significantly waste energy. All openings should be noted in the BSEA. Figure 6-3 illustrates the effect of the door size and time opened on the average annual heat loss. The graph is based upon a six-month heating season (mid-October to mid-April) and an average wind velocity of 4 mph. It is assumed that the heated building is maintained at 65°F. To adjust Figure 6-3 for different conditions use Formula 6-2.

$$Q = Q_1 \times \frac{d}{5} \times \frac{65 - T}{13} \qquad \qquad Formula\ (6\text{-}2)$$

Where:

Q is the adjusted heat loss, BTU/year
Q is the heat loss from Figure 6-3
d is the days of operation
T is the average ambient temperature during the heating season, °F.

If the space was air-conditioned there would be an additional savings during the cooling season.

To reduce heat loss for operating doors, the installation of vinyl strips (see Figure 6-4) is sometimes used. This type of strip is approximately 90% efficient in reducing heat losses. The problem in using the strip is obtaining operator acceptance. Operators may feel these strips interfere with operations or cause a safety problem since vision through the access way is reduced.

An alternate method to reduce infiltration losses through access doors is to provide an air curtain.

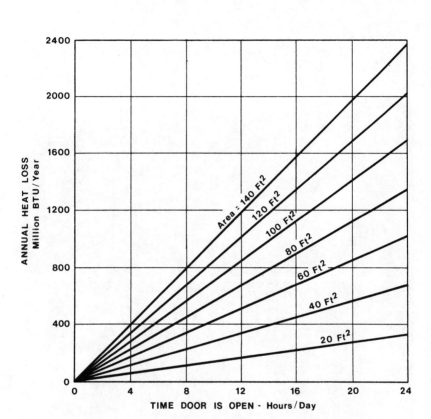

Figure 6-3. Annual Heat Loss from Doors
(Source: Georgia Tech Experiment Station)

SIM 6-2

An energy audit of a building indicated that the warehouse is maintained at 65°F during winter and has three 10 ft X 10 ft forklift doors. The warehouse is used 24 hours, 6 days per week, and the doors are open 8 hours per day. The average ambient temperature during the heating season is 48°F. Comment on adding vinyl strips (installed cost $2,000) which are 90% efficient, given the cost of heating fuel is $4/million BTU.

Figure 6-4. Installation of Vinyl Strips on Forklift Door

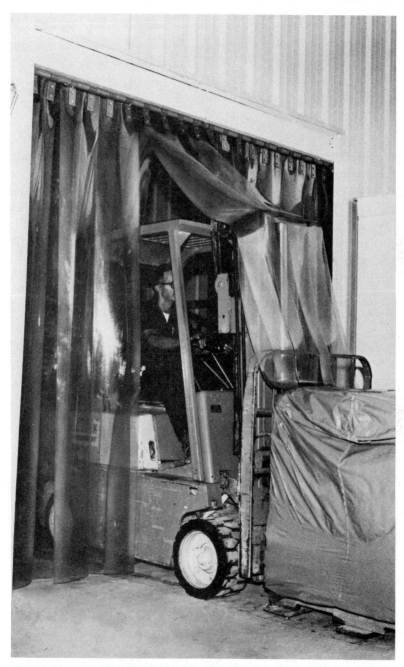

(Photographs courtesy of MetalGlas Products, Inc.)

ANALYSIS

From Figure 6-3, Q = 600 X 10^{12} BTU/Year

Therefore Q = 600 X 10^6 X $\frac{6}{5}$ X $\frac{65-48}{13}$ =

941 million BTU/Yr per door

Q = 3 X .9 X 941 X $4/million BTU .65 = $15,635

Since the payback period before taxes is less than one year, the investment seems justified.

To estimate infiltration through windows Table 6-1 and Figure 6-5 may be used. This data also includes another estimating tool for determining infiltration through doors.

To compute the energy saved based on reducing the infiltration rates, Figure 6-6 and 6-7 are used for the heating and cooling seasons respectively.

SIM 6-3

An energy audit survey indicates 300 windows, poorly fitted wood sash, in a building which are not weatherstripped. Comment on the savings for weatherstripping given the following:

Data: Window size 54″ X 96″
Degree-days = 8,000
Cost of heating = $4/10^6 BTU
One-half the windows face the wind at any one time
Hours of occupation = 5760
Wet-Bulb Degree-hours = 2,000 greater than 66°F
Wind velocity summer 10 MPH
Refrigeration consumption = .8 KW/Ton-Hr
Electric rate = 5¢ KWH
Hours of operation = 72
Indoor temperature winter 68°F
RH summer 50%
Boiler efficiency = .65

ANALYSIS

Area of windows = $\frac{54 \times 96}{144}$ = 36 ft^2 per window

Coefficients from Table 6-1
With No Weatherstripping 1.52
With Weatherstripping   .47
Infiltration before = 36 X 300/2 X 1.52 = 8208 CFM
Infiltration after weatherstripping = 36 X 300/2 X .47 =
$$2538 \text{ CFM}$$
Savings with weatherstripping = 8208 – 2538 = 5670
From Figure 6-6 Q = 100 X 10^6 BTU/Year/1000 CFM
Savings during winter = 5.67 X 100 X 10^6 X $4/$10^6$/.65 =
$$\$3489$$
From Figure 6-7 Q = 10 X 10^6 BTU/Year/1000 CFM

Savings during summer (at 10 MPH wind velocity)
Savings summer = 5.67 X 10 X 10^6/12,000 X .8 X .05 X
$$10/15 = \$125.00$$

Total savings = $3614 per year

REDUCING INFILTRATION

In addition to weatherstripping, several key areas should not be overlooked in reducing infiltration losses.

Vertical shafts, such as stairwells, should be isolated as illustrated in Figure 6-8. Always check with fire codes before modifying building egress.

Poor quality outdoor air dampers are another source of excess infiltration. Dampers of this nature do not allow for accurate control and positive closure. Replacement with good quality opposed-blade dampers with seals at the blade edges and ends will reduce infiltration losses. (See Figure 6-9.)

The third area is to check exhaust hoods such as those used in kitchens and process equipment. Large open hoods are usually required to maintain a satisfactory capture velocity to remove fumes, smoke, etc. These hoods remove large volumes of air. The air is made up through the HVAC system which heats it up in winter and cools and dehumidifies it in summer. Several areas should be checked to reduce infiltration from hoods.

• Minimum capture velocity to remove contaminants.

Table 6-1. Infiltration Through Windows and Doors — Winter*

15 MPH Wind Velocity†

DOUBLE HUNG WINDOWS ON WINDWARD SIDE‡

	CFM PER SQ FT AREA					
	Small — 30" X 72"			Large — 54" X 96"		
DESCRIPTION	No W-Strip	W-Strip	Storm Sash	No W-Strip	W-Strip	Storm Sash
Average Wood Sash	.85	.52	.42	.53	.33	.26
Poorly Fitted Wood Sash	2.4	.74	1.2	1.52	.47	.74
Metal Sash	1.60	.69	.80	1.01	.44	.50

NOTE: W-Strip denotes weatherstrip.

CASEMENT TYPE WINDOWS ON WINDWARD SIDE‡

	CFM PER SQ FT AREA									
	Percent Ventilated Area									
DESCRIPTION	0%	25%	33%	40%	45%	50%	60%	66%	75%	100%
Rolled Section—Steel Sash										
Industrial Pivoted	.65	1.44	—	1.98	—	—	—	2.9	—	5.2
Architectural Projected	—	.78	—	—	—	1.1	1.48	—	—	—
Residential	—	—	.56	—	—	.98	—	.63	.78	1.26
Heavy Projected	—	—	—	—	.45	—	—	—	—	—
Hollow Metal—Vertically Pivoted	.54	1.19	—	1.64	—	—	—	2.4	—	4.3

DOORS ON ONE OR ADJACENT WINDWARD SIDES‡

DESCRIPTION	Infrequent Use	Average Use			
		1 & 2 Story Building	Tall Building (ft)		
			50	100	200
Revolving Door	1.6	10.5	12.6	14.2	17.3
Glass Door—(3/16" Crack)	9.0	30.0	36.0	40.5	49.5
Wood Door 3'7"	2.0	13.0	15.5	17.5	21.5
Small Factory Door	1.5	13.0			
Garage & Shipping Room Door	4.0	9.0			
Ramp Garage Door	4.0	13.5			

CFM PER SQ FT AREA**

* All values are based on the wind blowing directly at the wind or door. When the prevailing wind direction is oblique to the window or doors, multiply the above values by 0.60 and use the total window and door area on the windward side(s).

† Based on a wind velocity at 15 mph. For design wind velocities different from the base, multiply the table values by the ratio of velocities.

‡ Stack effect in tall buildings may also cause infiltration on the leeward side. To evaluate this, determine the equivalent velocity (V_e) and subtract the design velocity (V). The equivalent velocity is:

$$V_e = \sqrt{V^2 - 1.75a} \quad \text{(upper section)}$$
$$V_e = \sqrt{V^2 - 1.75b} \quad \text{(lower section)}$$

Where a and b are the distances above and below the mid-height of the building, respectively, in ft.
Multiply the table values by the ratio ($V_e - V$)/15 for doors and one-half of the windows on the leeward side of the building. (Use values under "1 & 2 Story Building" for doors on leeward side of tall buildings.)

** Doors on opposite sides increase the above values 25%. Vestibules may decrease the infiltration as much as 30% when door usage is light. If door usage is heavy, the vestibule is of little value in reducing infiltration. Heat added to the vestibule will help maintain room temperature near the door.

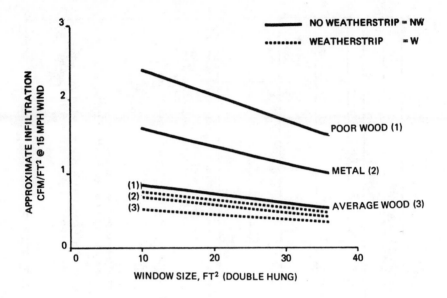

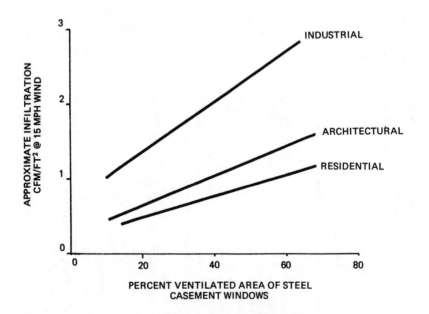

Figure 6-5. Infiltration Through Windows and Door — Winter
(Source: Instructions For Energy Auditors, Vol. II)

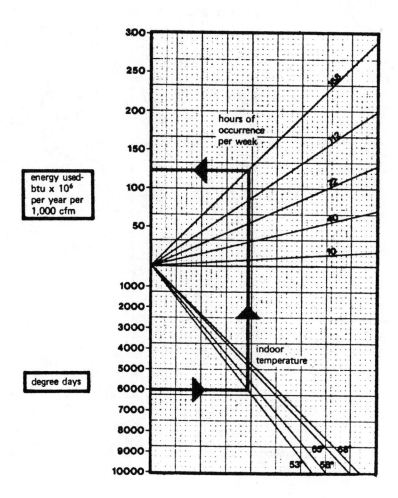

Figure 6-6. Yearly Energy Used Per 1,000 CFM Outdoor air
(Source: Guidelines For Saving Energy In Existing Buildings—
Building Owners and Operators Manual, ECM-1)

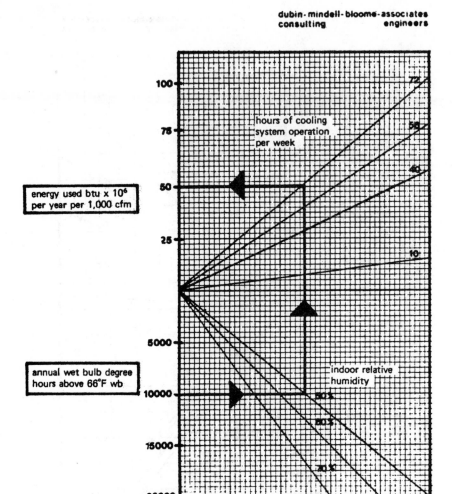

**Figure 6-7. Yearly Energy Used Per 1,000 CFM to Maintain
Various Humidity Conditions**
*(Source: Guidelines For Saving Energy in Existing Buildings—
Building Owners and Operators Manual, ECM-1)*

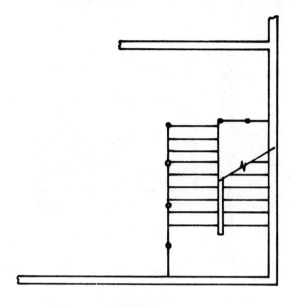

BEFORE

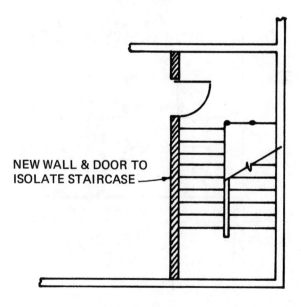

NEW WALL & DOOR TO
ISOLATE STAIRCASE

AFTER

Figure 6-8

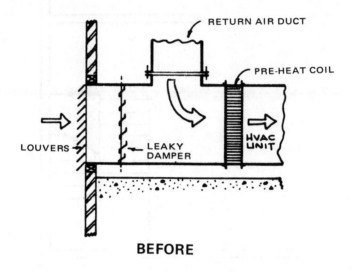

BEFORE

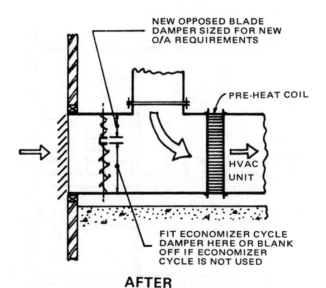

AFTER

Figure 6-9

- Reducing exhaust air by filterizing fitting baffles or a false hood inside existing hood. (See Figure 6-10.)
- Installing a separate make-up air system for hoods. The hood make-up air system would consist of a fan drawing in outdoor air and passing through a heating coil to temper air.

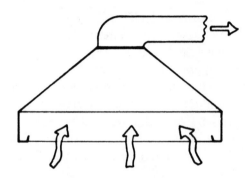

LOW VELOCITY EXHAUST
(HIGH VOLUME)

BEFORE

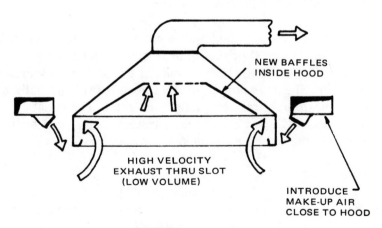

NEW BAFFLES
INSIDE HOOD

HIGH VELOCITY
EXHAUST THRU SLOT
(LOW VOLUME)

INTRODUCE
MAKE-UP AIR
CLOSE TO HOOD

AFTER

Figure 6-10

HEAT FLOW DUE TO CONDUCTION

When a temperature gradient exists on either side of a wall, a flow of heat from hot side to cold side occurs. The flow of heat is defined by Formula 6-3.

$$Q = k/d \cdot A \cdot \Delta T \qquad \text{\textit{Formula (6-3)}}$$
$$U = k/d = 1/R$$

Where:

   Q   is the rate of flow BTUH
   d   is the thickness of the material in inches
   A   is the area of the wall, ft^2
   ΔT is the temperature difference, °F
   U   is the conductance of the material—BTU/hr/sq ft/F
   k   is the conductivity of the material
   R   is the resistance of the material.

Resistance of material in series are additive. Thus the importance of insulation is that it increases the R factor, which in turn reduces the heat flow.

Complete tables for conductors and resistances of various building materials can be found in the ASHRAE Guide and Data Book.

HEAT FLOW DUE TO RADIATION

When analyzing a building the conductive portion and radiant portion of heat flow should be treated independently.

Radiation is the transfer of radiant energy from a source to a receiver. The radiation from the source (sun) is partially absorbed by the receiver and partially reflected. The radiation absorbed depends upon its surface emissivity, area, and temperature, as expressed by Formula 6-4.

$$Q = \epsilon \, \sigma \, A \, T^4 \qquad \text{\textit{Formula (6-4)}}$$

Where:

   Q = rate of heat, flow by radiation, BTU/hr
   ϵ = emissivity of a body, which is defined as the rate of energy radiated by the actual body. $\epsilon = 1$ for a block body.
   σ = Stephen Boltzman's Constant, 1.71×10^{-9} BTU/ft$^2 \cdot$ hr $\cdot T^4$
   A = surface area of body in square feet.

In addition the radiant energy causes a greater skin temperature to exist on horizontal surfaces such as the roof. The effect is to cause a greater equivalent ΔT which increases the conductive heat flow. Radiant energy flow through roofs and glass should be investigated since it can significantly increase the heat gain of the building. Radiant energy, on the other hand, reduces HVAC requirements during the heating season.

ENERGY AUDITS OF ROOFS

The handy tables and graphs presented in this section are based on the "sunset" program developed for the ECM-2 Manual. The program was based on internal heat gains of 12 BTU/square feet/hour when occupied, 10% average outdoor air ventilation when occupied, and one-half air change per hour continuous infiltration. For significantly different conditions an individual computer run should be made using one of the programs listed in Chapter 5.

A summary of heat losses and heat gains for twelve cities is illustrated in Figures 6-11 and 6-12 respectively. The cumulative values shown take into account both conductive and radiant contributions. Thus a dark covered roof will reduce the heat loss during the winter but increases the heat gain in the summer. Usually the cooling load dictates the color of the roof.

To reduce the HVAC load the U-Factor of the roof is increased by adding insulation.

Estimates of savings can be made by using Figures 6-13, 6-14, and 6-15. The figures take into account both radiant effect and the greater ΔT which occurs due to radiant energy. For cooling load considerations the color of the roof is important. Light color roofs, or adding a surface layer of white pebbles or gravel, are sometimes used. (Care should be taken on existing buildings that structural bearing capacity is not exceeded.)

In addition the roof temperature can be lowered by utilizing a roof spray. (Care should be taken that proper drainage and structural considerations are taken into account.)

Solar radiation data is illustrated in Figure 15-1, Chapter 15.

dubin-mindell-bloome-associates
consulting engineers

YEARLY HEAT LOSS/SQUARE FOOT THROUGH ROOF

City	Latitude	Solar Radiation Langley's	Degree-Days	Heat Loss Through Roof BTU/Ft² Year			
				U=0.19		U=0.12	
				a=0.3	a=0.8	a=0.3	a=0.8
Minneapolis	45°N	325	8,382	35,250	30,967	21,330	18,642
Denver	40°N	425	6,283	26,794	22,483	16,226	13,496
Concord, N.H.	43°N	300	7,000	32,462	27,678	19,649	16,625
Chicago	42°N	350	6,155	27,489	23,590	16,633	14,190
St. Louis	39°N	375	4,900	20,975	17,438	12,692	10,457
New York	41°N	350	4,871	21,325	17,325	12,911	10,416
San Francisco	38°N	410	3,015	10,551	8,091	6,381	4,784
Atlanta	34°N	390	2,983	12,601	9,841	7,619	5,832
Los Angeles	34°N	470	2,061	4,632	3,696	2,790	2,142
Phoenix	33°N	520	1,765	5,791	4,723	3,487	2,756
Houston	30°N	430	1,600	6,045	4,796	3,616	2,778
Miami	26°N	451	141	259	130	139	55

a is the absorption coefficient of the building material

a = .3 (White)
a = .5 (Light colors such as yellow, green, etc.)
a = .8 (Dark colors)

Figure 6-11. Heat Losses for Roofs

(Source: Guidelines For Saving Energy in Existing Buildings—Engineers, Architects and Operators Manual, ECM-2)

dubin-mindell-bloome-associates
consulting engineers

YEARLY HEAT GAIN/SQUARE FOOT THROUGH ROOF

City	Latitude	Solar Radiation Langley's	D.B. Degree-Hours Above 78°F	Heat Gain Through Roof BTU/Ft² Year			
				U=0.19		U=0.12	
				a=0.3	a=0.8	a=0.3	a=0.8
Minneapolis	45°N	325	2,500	2,008	8,139	1,119	4,728
Concord, N.H.	43°N	300	1,750	1,892	7,379	1,043	4,257
Denver	40°N	425	4,055	2,458	9,859	1,348	5,680
Chicago	42°N	350	3,100	2,104	7,918	1,185	4,620
St. Louis	39°N	375	6,400	4,059	12,075	2,326	7,131
New York	41°N	350	3,000	2,696	9,274	1,534	5,465
San Francisco	38°N	410	3,000	566	5,914	265	3,354
Atlanta	34°N	390	9,400	4,354	14,060	2,482	8,276
Los Angeles	34°N	470	2,000	1,733	10,025	921	5,759
Phoenix	33°N	520	24,448	12,149	24,385	7,258	14,649
Houston	30°N	430	11,500	7,255	20,931	4,176	12,369
Miami	26°N	451	10,771	9,009	24,594	5,315	14,716

a is the absorption coefficient of the building material

a = .3 (White)

a = .5 (Light colors such as yellow, green, etc.)

a = .8 (Dark colors)

Figure 6-12. Heat Gains for Roofs

(Source: Guidelines For Saving Energy in Existing Buildings—Engineers, Architects and Operators Manual, ECM-2)

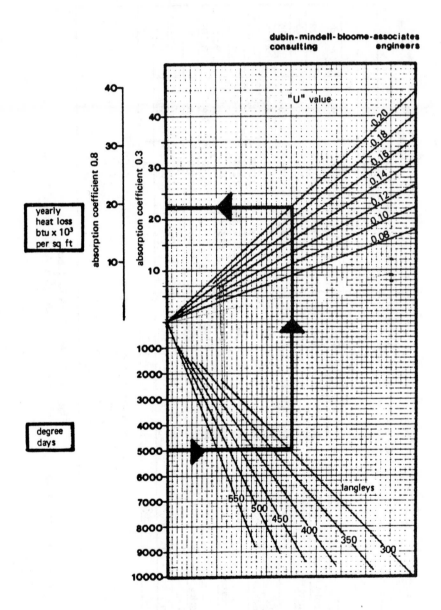

Figure 6-13. Yearly Heat Loss Through Roof
*(Source: Guidelines For Saving Energy in Existing Buildings—
Engineers, Architects and Operators Manual, ECM-2)*

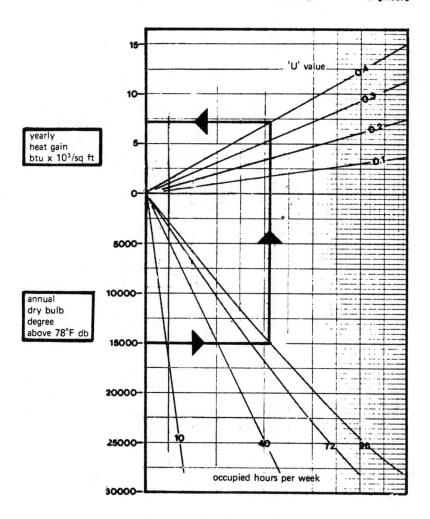

Figure 6-14. Yearly Conduction Heat Gain Through Walls,
Roofs and Floors
(Source: Guidelines For Saving Energy in Existing Buildings—
Engineers, Architects and Operators Manual, ECM-2)

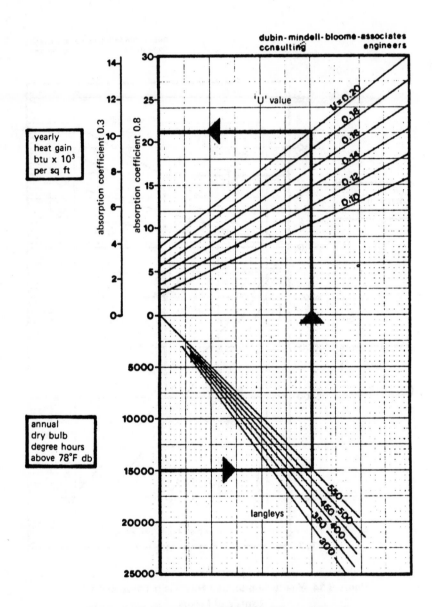

Figure 6-15. Yearly Solar Heat Gain Through Roof
(Source: Guidelines For Saving Energy in Existing Buildings—
Engineers, Architects and Operators Manual, ECM-2)

COMPUTER SERVICES

Most manufacturers of roof insulation and window treatments offer computer simulations to estimate savings as a result of using their products. These programs are usually available at no cost through authorized distributors and contractors.

For information concerning insulation products and services call the nearest authorized distributor or contact:

> Thermal Insulation Manufacturers' Association (TIMA)
> 7 Kirby Plaza
> Mt. Kisco, New York 10549

Manufacturers such as Koolshade and 3M offer computer load simulations for their products. For information concerning window treatments contact the manufacturers listed in the next section.

SIM 6-4

An energy audit of the roof indicates the following:

Area	20,000 square feet
Present "R" value =	8
(Estimation based on insulation thickness and type)	
Degree-Days (winter)	3,000
Occupied hrs/week	40
D.B. Degree-Hours above 78°F	9,400
Fuel cost	$5/10^6$ BTU
Boiler efficiency	.65
Electric rate	6¢ per KWH
Air-condition requirement	.8 KW/Ton-Hr
Roof Absorption	.3
Solar radiation	390 Langleys

It is proposed that additional insulation of R=13 should be installed.

Comment on the potential savings.

ANALYSIS

$R_T = R_1 + R_2 = 8 + 13 = 21$
$U_{Before} = 1/8 = .125$
$U_{After} = 1/21 = .047$

Savings
　Winter
　　From Figure 6-13
　　$Q_{Before} = 7$ BTU $\times 10^3$ per square feet
　　$Q_{After} = 2$ BTU $\times 10^3$ per square feet
　　Savings = $(7-2) \times 10^3 \times 20 \times 10^3 \times 5/10^6 /.65 = \$769$

　Summer
　　Conduction
　　From Figure 6-14
　　$Q_{Before} = 1 \times 10^3$ BTU/sq ft/yr
　　$Q_{After} = .4 \times 10^3$ BTU/sq ft/yr
　　Savings = $(1-.4) \times 10^3 \times 20,000 = 12,000 \times 10^3$ BTU/Yr

　　Radiation
　　From Figure 6-15
　　$Q_{Before} = 8.5 \times 10^3$ BTU/sq ft/yr
　　$Q_{After} = 2.5 \times 10^3$ BTU/sq ft/yr
　　Savings = $(8.5-2.5) \times 10^3$ BTU/sq ft/yr $\times 20,000 =$
　　　　　　120,000 $\times 10^3$ BTU/yr

　　Savings $= \dfrac{(120,000 + 12,000)}{12,000} \times 10^3 \times .8 \times .06 = \$528/yr$

　Total Savings = \$1297/year.

Figure 6-16 illustrates typical insulation conductance values recommended based on degree-day data.

**INSULATION VALUE FOR HEAT FLOW THROUGH
OPAQUE AREAS OF ROOFS AND CEILINGS**

Heating Season Degree-Days	U value (Btu/hr/sq ft/°F)
1 - 1000	0.12
1001 - 2000	0.08
2001 and above	0.05

**INSULATION VALUE FOR HEAT FLOW THROUGH
OPAQUE EXTERIOR WALLS FOR HEATED AREAS**

Heating Seasons Degree-Days	U value (Btu/hr/sq ft/°F)
0 - 1000	0.30
1001 - 2500	0.25
2500 - 5000	0.20
5000 - 8000	0.15

Cooling Season — The recommended U value of insulation for heat flow through exterior roofs, ceilings, and walls should be less than 0.15 Btu/hr/sq ft/ °F.

Figure 6-16. Insulation Conductance Values for Roofs and Walls
(Source: Instructions For Energy Auditors)

THE GLASS AUDIT

CONDUCTION CONSIDERATIONS

Glass traditionally has poor conductance qualities and accounts for significant heat gains due to radiant energy.

To estimate savings as a result of changing glass types, Figures 6-17 through 6-22 can be used. Figures 6-19 and 6-20 illustrate the heat loss and gain due to conduction for winter and summer respectively. Figures 6-21 and 6-22 can be used to calculate the radiant heat gain during summer.

To decrease losses due to conductance either the glass needs to be replaced, modified, or an external thermal blanket added. Descriptions of window treatments are discussed at the end of the chapter.

dubin-mindell-bloome-associates
consulting   engineers

| City | Latitude | Solar Radiation Langleys | Degree-Days | Heat Loss Through Window BTU/ft² Year | | | | | |
| | | | | North | | East & West | | South | |
				Single	Double	Single	Double	Single	Double
Minneapolis	45°N	325	8,382	187,362	94,419	161,707	84,936	140,428	74,865
Concord, N.H.	43°N	300	7,000	158,770	83,861	136,073	73,303	122,144	67,586
Denver	40°N	425	6,283	136,452	70,449	117,487	62,437	109,365	59,481
Chicago	42°N	350	6,155	147,252	75,196	126,838	65,810	110,035	58,632
St. Louis	39°N	375	4,900	109,915	56,054	94,205	49,355	84,399	45,398
New York	41°N	350	4,871	109,672	54,986	93,700	48,611	82,769	44,580
San Francisco	38°N	410	3,015	49,600	25,649	43,866	23,704	41,691	23,239
Atlanta	34°N	390	2,983	63,509	31,992	55,155	28,801	51,837	28,092
Los Angeles	34°N	470	2,061	21,059	11,532	19,487	10,954	19,485	10,989
Phoenix	33°N	520	1,765	25,951	14,381	22,381	12,885	22,488	12,810
Houston	30°N	430	1,600	33,599	17,939	30,744	17,053	30,200	16,861
Miami	26°N	451	141	1,404	742	1,345	742	1,345	742

Figure 6-17. Yearly Heat Loss/Square Foot of Single Glazing and Double Glazing
(Source: Guideline For Saving Energy in Existing Buildings—Engineers, Architects and Operators Manual, ECM-2)

dubin-mindell-bloome-associates
consulting
engineers

| City | Latitude | Solar Radiation Langleys | D.B. Degree-Hours Above 78°F | Heat Gain Through Window BTU/ft² Year | | | | | |
| | | | | North | | East & West | | South | |
				Single	Double	Single	Double	Single	Double
Minneapolis	45°N	325	2,500	36,579	33,089	98,158	88,200	82,597	70,729
Concord, N.H.	43°N	300	1,750	33,481	30,080	91,684	82,263	88,609	76,517
Denver	40°N	425	4,055	44,764	39,762	122,038	108,918	100,594	85,571
Chicago	42°N	350	3,100	35,595	31,303	93,692	83,199	87,017	74,497
St. Louis	39°N	375	6,400	55,242	45,648	130,018	112,368	103,606	85,221
New York	41°N	350	3,000	40,883	35,645	109,750	97,253	118,454	102,435
San Francisco	38°N	410	3,000	29,373	28,375	88,699	81,514	73,087	64,169
Atlanta	34°N	390	9,400	59,559	50,580	147,654	129,391	106,163	87,991
Los Angeles	34°N	470	2,000	47,912	43,264	126,055	112,869	112,234	97,284
Phoenix	33°N	520	24,448	137,771	97,565	242,586	191,040	211,603	131,558
Houston	30°N	430	11,500	88,334	72,474	213,739	184,459	188,718	156,842
Miami	26°N	451	10,771	98,496	79,392	237,763	203,356	215,382	179,376

Figure 6-18. Yearly Heat Gain/Square Foot of Single Glazing and Double Glazing
(Source: Guidelines For Saving Energy in Existing Buildings—Engineers, Architects and Operators Manual, ECM-2)

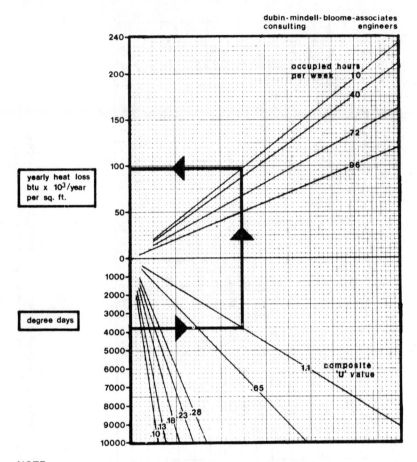

NOTE

The development of this figure was based on the assumptions that

1. Thermal barriers are closed only when the building is unoccupied
2. The average degree-day distribution is 25% during the daytime and 75% during nighttime.

The number of degree days occurring when the thermal barriers are closed (adjusted degree-days — DD_A) were determined from the characteristic occupancy periods shown in the figure. This can be expressed as a fraction of the total degree-days (DD_T) by the relationship:

$$DD_A = 0.25 \; DD_T \left(\frac{\text{unoccupied daytime hours/week}}{\text{total daytime hours/week}} \right) + 0.75 \; DD_T \left(\frac{\text{unoccupied nighttime hours/week}}{\text{total nighttime hours/week}} \right)$$

Yearly heat losses can then be determined by: Q (heat loss/yr) = DD_A X U value X 24

Figure 6-19. Yearly Heat Loss for Windows with Thermal Barriers
(Source: Guidelines For Saving Energy in Existing Buildings—Engineers, Architects and Operators Manual, ECM-2)

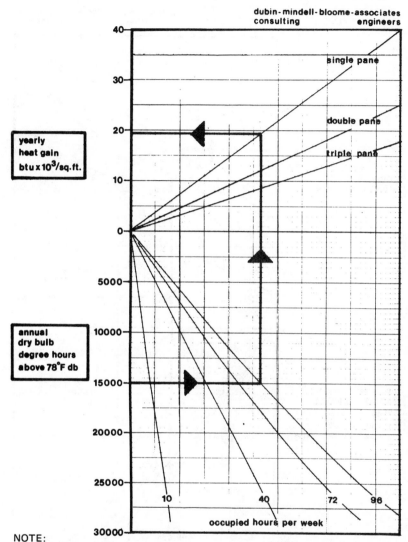

NOTE:
     The figure is based on the formula: Q (heat gain)/yr = degree hours/yr X U value.
U values assumed were 1.1 for single pane, 0.65 for double pane and 0.47 for triple
pane. The major portion of degree hours occur between 10 a.m. and 3 p.m. Hence,
for occupancies between 10 and 56 hours/week, the degree hour distribution can be
assumed to be linear. However, for occupancies greater than 56 hours/week the degree hour distribution becomes nonlinear, particularly in locations with greater than
15,000 degree hours. This is reflected by the curves for 72 and 96 hour/week occupancies.

Figure 6-20. Yearly Conduction Heat Gain Through Windows
*(Source: Guidelines For Saving Energy in Existing Buildings—Engineers, Architects
and Operators Manual, ECM-2)*

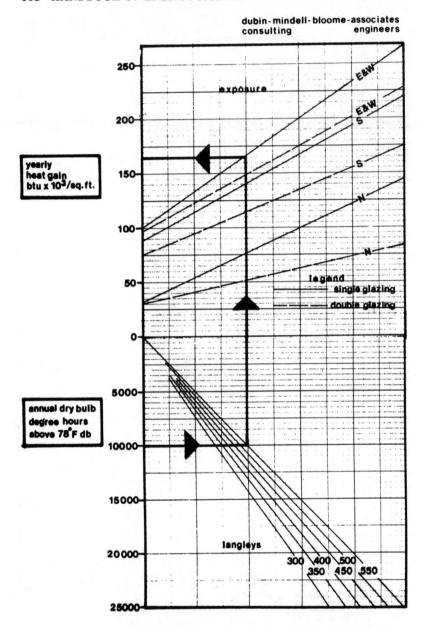

(See page 184 for notes on this figure)

Figure 6-21. Yearly Solar Heat Gain Through Windows
Latitude 25°N — 35°N

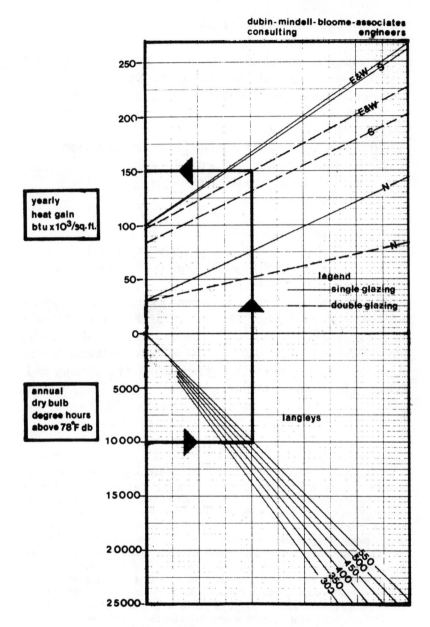

(See page 184 for notes on this figure)

Figure 6-22. Yearly Solar Heat Gain Through Windows
Latitude 35°N — 45°N

SOLAR RADIATION CONSIDERATIONS

In addition to heat flow due to conduction, a significant heat flow occurs through glass due to the sun's radiant energy. The radiant energy will decrease heating requirements during the winter time but greatly increase the air-conditioning load during the cooling season.

To reduce solar loads, several common devices are used.

- Roller shades (least expensive)
- Reflective polyester film
- Venetion blinds
- Vertical louver blinds
- External louvered screens
- Tinted or reflective glass (most expensive)

Descriptions of window treatments are discussed at the end of this chapter.

To determine the energy saved from shading devices, Figures 6-21 and 6-22 can be used. Occupancy for these figures is based on 5 days/week, 12 hours/day. If space is occupied differently, prorate the results. The savings for window treatments is estimated by multiplying the annual heat gain by the shading coefficient of the window treatment.

NOTES FOR FIGURES 6-21 AND 6-22

These figures are based on the "Sunset" Computer program which was used to calculate solar effect on windows for 12 locations. The program calculates hourly solar angles and intensities for the 21st day of each month. Radiation intensity values were modified by the average percentage of cloud cover taken from weather records on an hourly basis. Heat gains are based on a 78°F indoor temperature. During the cooling season, internal gains, ventilation, infiltration and conduction through the building can create a cooling load. The additional load caused by heat gain through the windows was calculated for each day. Daily totals were then summed for the number of days in each month to arrive at monthly heat gains. The length of the cooling season for each location considered was determined from weather data and characteristic operating periods. Yearly heat gains were derived by summing monthly totals for the length of the cooling season. Gains are based purely on the solar component. The solar component was then plotted and extrapolated to include the entire range of degree hours. The heat gains assume that the windows are subjected to direct sunshine. If shaded, gains should be read from the north exposure line. The accuracy of the graph diminishes for location with less than 5,000 degree hours.

WINDOW TREATMENTS

Several types of window treatments to reduce losses have become available. This section describes some of the products on the market based on information supplied by manufacturers. No claims are made concerning the validity or completeness described. The summary is based on "Windows For Energy Efficient Buildings" as prepared by the Lawrence Berkeley Laboratory for U.S. DOE under contract W-7405-ENG-48.

In addition to the computer programs indicated in Chapter 5, window treatment manufacturers offer a wide variety of "free programs" to help in evaluation of their products. For example 3M Company and Koolshade Corp. offer programs that indicate potential savings with window treatments.

Solar Control

Solar Control Films—A range of tinted and reflective polyester films are available to adhere to inner window surfaces to provide solar control for existing clear glazing. Films are typically two- or three-layer laminates composed of metalized, transparent and/or tinted layers. Films are available with a wide range of solar and visible light transmittance values, resulting in shading coefficients as low as 0.24. Most films are adhered with precoated pressure sensitive adhesives. Reflective films will reduce winter U values by about 20%. (Note that a new solar control film, which provides a U value of 0.68, is described in the Thermal Barriers section below. Films adhered to glass improve the shatter resistance of glazing and reduce transmission, thus reducing fading of furnishings. Major manufacturers of solar control films are listed below.

3M Company, Energy Control Products, 3M Center, Saint Paul, Minnesota 55101, (612) 733-1110

Madico, 64 New Industrial Parkway, Woburn, Massachusetts 01801, (617) 935-7850

Solar-X Corporation, 25 Needham Street, Newton, Massachusetts 02161, (617) 244-8686

National Metallizing Division, Solar Control Products,

**Figure 6-23
Application of Films
to Windows**

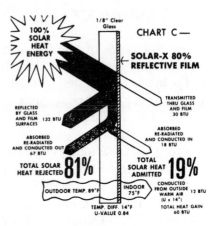

Figure 6-24. Application of Window Film
(Photograph courtesy of 3M Company)

Standard Packaging Corporation, Cranbury, New Jersey 08512, (609) 655-4000

Fiber Glass Solar Control Screens—Solar control screen provides sun and glare control as well as some reduction in winter heat loss. Screens are woven from vinyl-coated glass strands and are available in a variety of colors. Depending on color and weave, shading coefficients of 0.3-0.5 are achieved. Screens are durable, maintenance free, and provide impact resistance. They are usually applied on the exterior of windows and may (1) be attached to mounting rails and stretched over windows, (2) mounted in rigid frames and installed over windows, or (3) made into roller shades which can be retracted and stored as desired. Names of local distributors, installers, and retailers may be obtained by writing to major fabric manufacturers.

Phifer Wire Products Company, Box 1700, Tuscaloosa, Alabama 35401, (205) 345-2120

J. P. Stevens & Co., Inc., Box 1138, Walterboro, South Carolina 29488, (803) 538-8041

Chicopee Manufacturing Co., Box 47520, Atlanta, Georgia 30362, (404) 455-3754

Motorized Window Shading System—A variety of plastic and fabric shades is available for use with a motorized window shading system. Reversible motor is located within the shade tube roller and contains a brake mechanism to stop and hold in any position. Motor controls may be gauged and operated locally or from a master station. Automatic photoelectric controls are available that (1) monitor sun intensity and angle and adjust shade position to provide solar control and (2) employ an internal light sensor and provide a preset level of internal ambient light.

Exterior Sun Control Louvers—Operable external horizontal and vertical louver systems are offered for a variety of building sun control applications. Louvers are hinged together and can be rotated in unison to provide the desired degree of shading for any sun position. Operation may be manual or electric; electrical operation may be initiated by manual switches, time clock, or sun sensors. Louvers may be closed to reduce night thermal losses. Sun control elements are available in several basic shapes and in a wide range of sizes.

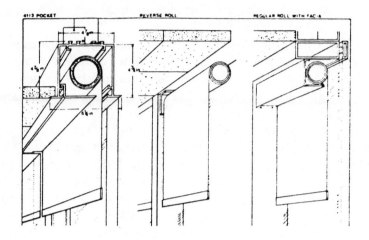

Figure 6-25. Motorized Shade System
(Courtesy Joel Berman Associates, Inc., 102 Prince Street, New York,
New York 10012, (212) 226-2050)

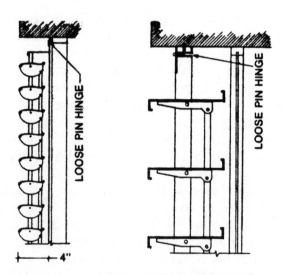

Figure 6-26. Mounting of External Louvers
Courtesy Brown Manufacturing Company, P.O. Box 14546,
Oklahoma City, Oklahoma 73114, (405) 751-1323

Figure 6-27. Installation of Louvered Solar Screens

Greenwich Harbor, Greenwich, Connecticut is seen through 1316 KoolShade louvers at left and through 34 conventional venetion blind louvers on the right. The two panels are otherwise identical, having the same slat angle and ratio of louver width to louver spacing.

External Venetian Blinds—Externally mounted, all weather, venetian blinds may be manually operated from within a building or electrically operated and controlled by means of automatic sun sensors, time controls, manual switches, etc. Aluminum slats are held in position with side guides and controlled by weatherproof lifting tapes. Slats can be tilted to modulate solar gain, closed completely, or restricted to admit full light and heat. Blinds have been in use in Europe for many years and have been tested for resistance to storms and high winds.

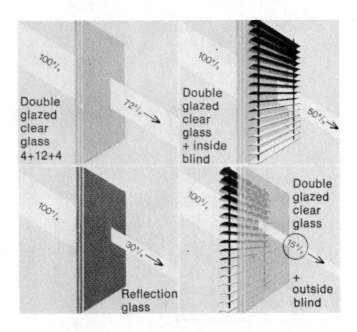

Figure 6-28. Exterior "L"-Type Venetian Blind
(Courtesy Lamellenstoren, Swiss Blinds Division, Richard Goder Associates, Inc., Box 1264, Rosemount, Illinois 60018, (312) 297-6420)

Adjustable Louvered Windows—Windows incorporating adjustable external louvered shading devices. Louvers are extruded aluminum or redwood, 3 to 5 inches wide, and are manually controlled. Louvers may be specified on double-hung, hinged, or louvered-glass windows. When open, the louvers provide control of solar gain and glare; when closed, they provide privacy and security.

Solar Shade Windows, Clearview Corporation, 3987 Pacific Boulevard, San Mateo, California 94403.

*Solar Shutters—*The shutter is composed of an array of aluminum slats set at 45° or 22½° from the vertical to block direct sunlight. Shutters are designed for external application and may be mounted vertically in front of window or projected outward from the bottom of the window. Other rolling and hinged shutters are stored beside the window and roll or swing into place for sun control, privacy, or security.

Thermal Barriers

*Multilayer, Roll-Up Insulating Window Shade—*A multilayer window shade which stores in compact roll and utilizes spacers to separate the aluminized plastic layers in the deployed position, thereby creating a series of dead air spaces. Five-layer shade combined with insulated glass provides R8 thermal resistance. Figure 6-29 illustrates a thermal window shade.

High "R" Shade Insulating Shade Company, 17 Water Street, Guilford, Connecticut 06437, (203) 453-9334.

*Insulating Window Shade—*ThermoShade thermal barrier is a roll-up shade composed of hollow, lens-shaped, rigid white PVC slats with virtually no air leakage through connecting joints. Side tracking system reduces window infiltration. Designed for interior installation and manual or automatic operation.

*Insulating Window Shade—*When added to a window, the roll-up insulating shade provides R4.5 for single-glazed window or R5.5 for double-glazed window. Quilt is composed of fabric outer surfaces and two polyester fiberfill layers sandwiched around a reflective vapor barrier. Quilt layers are ultrasonically welded. Shade edges are enclosed in a side track to reduce infiltration.

Window Quilt, Appropriate Technology Corporation, P.O. Box 975, Brattleboro, Vermont 05301.

*Reflective, Perforated Solar Control Laminate—*Laminate of metalized weatherable polyester film and black vinyl which

Figure 6-29. Thermal Window Shade Installation
(Photograph courtesy of High "R" Shade Company)

is then perforated with 225 holes/in^2, providing 36% open area. Available in a variety of metallized and nonmetallized colors, the shading coefficients vary from 0.30 to 0.35 for exter-

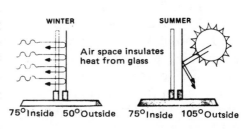

WINTER   SUMMER

Air space insulates heat from glass

75°Inside   50°Outside   75°Inside   105°Outside

nally mounted screens and 0.37 to 0.45 for the material adhered to the inner glass surface. The laminate is typically mounted in aluminum screen frames which are hung externally, several inches from the window; it can also be utilized in a roll-up form. Some reduction in winter U value can be expected with external applications.

Reflect-O-Screen Incorporated, 7521 East Second Street, P.O. Box 147, Scottsdale, Arizona 85252, (602) 994-0317.

Semi-Transparent Window Shades—Roll-up window shades made from a variety of tinted or reflective solar control film laminates. These shades provide most of the benefits of solar control film applied directly to glass but provide additional flexibility and may be retracted on overcast days or when solar heat gain is desired. Shades available with spring operated and gravity (cord and reel) operated rollers as well as motorized options. Shading coefficients as low as 0.13 are achieved and a tight fitting shade provides an additional air space and thus reduced U-value.

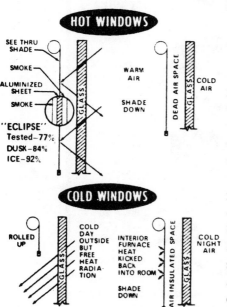

Plastic View Transparent Shades, Incorporated, 15468 Cabrito Road, Van Nuys, California 91408, (213) 786-2801.

Louvered Metal Solar Screens—Solar screen consists of an array of tiny louvers which are formed from a sheet of thin aluminum. The louvered aluminum sheet is then installed in conventional screen frames and may be mounted against a window in place of a regular insect screen or mounted away from the building to provide free air circulation around the window. View to the outside is maintained while substantially reducing solar gain. Available in a light green or black finish with shading coefficients of 0.21 or 0.15, respectively.

ShadeScreen, Kaiser Aluminum, 300 Lakeshore Drive, Oakland, California 94643.

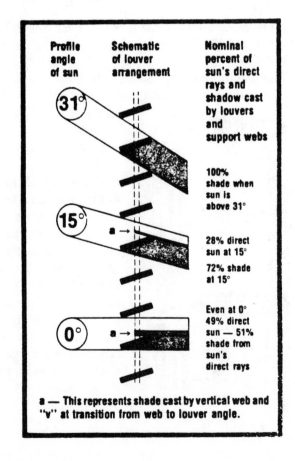

Profile angle of sun | Schematic of louver arrangement | Nominal percent of sun's direct rays and shadow cast by louvers and support webs

31°

100% shade when sun is above 31°

15°

28% direct sun at 15°

72% shade at 15°

0°

Even at 0° 49% direct sun — 51% shade from sun's direct rays

a — This represents shade cast by vertical web and "v" at transition from web to louver angle.

Operable External Louvre Blinds—Solar control louvre
blinds, mounted on the building exterior, can be controlled
manually or automatically by sun and wind sensors. Slats can
be tilted to modulate light, closed completely, or retracted to
admit full light and heat. Developed and used extensively in
Europe, they provide summer sun control, control of natural
light, and reduction of winter heat loss.

Louvered Metal Solar Screens—Solar screen consists of an
array of tiny fixed horizontal louvers which are woven in place.
Louvers are tilted at 17° to provide sun control. Screen material
is set in metal frames which may be permanently installed in a
variety of configurations or designed for removal. Installed
screens have considerable wind and impact resistance. Standard
product (17 louvers/inch) has a shading coefficient of 0.23; low
sun angle variant (23 louvers/inch) has a shading coefficient of
0.15. Modest reductions in winter U value have been measured.

(MAGNIFIED VIEW)

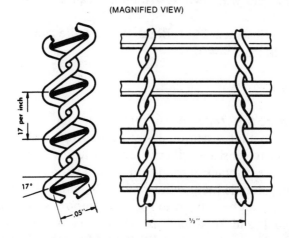

Koolshade Corporation, 722 Genevieve Street, P.O. Box 210,
Solana Beach, California 92075, (714) 755-5126.

A comparison of visibility with the louvered screens against
conventional venetion blinds is illustrated in Figure 6-27.

Insulating Solar Control Film—A modified solar control
film designed to be adhered to the interior of windows provides
conventional solar control function and has greatly improved
insulating properties. Film emissivity is 0.23-0.25 resulting in

a U value of 0.68 Btu/ft^2 hr-$^\circ$F under winter conditions, compared to 0.87 for conventional solar control films and 1.1 for typical single-glazed windows.

Energy Control Products, 3M Company, 3M Center, Building 207, St. Paul, Minnesota 55101.

Interior Storm Window—Low cost, do-it-yourself interior storm window with a rigid plastic glazing panel. Glazing panel may be removed for cleaning or summer storage. Reduces infiltration losses as well as conductive/convective heat transfer.

The In-Sider, Plaskolite Incorporated, 1770 Joyce Avenue, Columbus, Ohio 43216, (215) 563-7600.

Retrofit Insulating Glass System—Single glazing is converted to double glazing by attaching an extra pane of glass with neoprene sealant. A dessicant-filled aluminum spacer absorbs moisture between the panes. An electric resistance wire embedded in the neoprene is heated with a special power source. This hermetically seals the window. New molding can then be applied if desired.

Energy Sealants, 1611 Borel Place, Suite 240, San Mateo, California 94402.

Infiltration

Weather-Strip Tape—A polypropylene film scored along its centerline so that it can be easily formed into a "V" shape. It has a pressure sensitive adhesive on one leg of the "V" for application to seal cracks around doors and windows. On an average fitting, double-hung window it will reduce infiltration by over 70%. It can be applied to rough or smooth surfaces.

Scotch Brand Weatherstrip, 3M Company, Energy Control Products, 3M Center, St. Paul, Minnesota 55101, (612) 733-1110.

PASSIVE SOLAR BUILDING DESIGNS

A passive solar system is defined as one in which thermal energy flows by natural means. Examples of solar building design include:

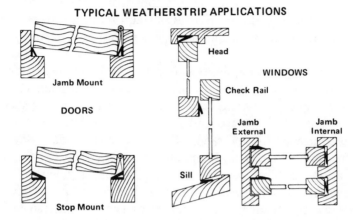

TYPICAL WEATHERSTRIP APPLICATIONS

- Solar greenhouses which are built on the south side of buildings. These can produce 60-100% of heating and cooling requirements.
- Underground buildings which use ground temperature to provide year-round temperature requirements.
- Enhanced natural ventilation through solar chimneys or use of "Trombe wall."

In these examples and others passive systems accomplish work (heating and cooling) by natural means such as gravity flows, thermosiphons, etc.

To study how the building reacts to loads, its storage effect, etc. computer simulations are many times used. One such system is described below:

PEGFIX—predicts auxiliary heat demand and excess heat available in a space with user-defined maximum and minimum air temperatures. The program is directly useful in sizing and specifying system components and auxiliary equipment. Results stored by PEGFIX are: total auxiliary heating load, excess heat available, maximum fan rate required to remove excess heat, and maximum hourly auxiliary load.

PEGFLOAT—predicts hourly temperatures of air and storage mass in a space without auxiliary heat input or removal of excess heat. Its purpose is to evaluate temperature excursions in a 100% solar-dependent operating mode. This program can examine non-south glazing orientations with user-specified hourly values for insolation. PEGFLOAT automatically stores maximum and minimum air and storage temperatures of the system modelled.

Both programs require few user-defined inputs regarding the building design and local weather: heat loss coefficients; effective thermal capacity and storage surface area; solar energy available, fraction to storage and fraction to air; average outdoor temperature and daily range. Programs differentiate day and night heat loss values, and can automatically proportion daylong insolation. Each can be run through a 24-hour day, without user interaction, in five to nine minutes. Hourly values of air and storage temperatures, and auxiliary or excess heat, can be displayed without interrupting program execution. Optional hourly display does not affect data storage. Available from: Princeton Energy Group, 729 Alexander Road, Princeton, New Jersey 08540.

REDUCING STRATIFIED AIR

As indicated in this chapter both the HVAC and building envelope considerations must be considered. An example of this system approach occurs when heat stratification near ceilings is reduced.

One way of reducing air temperatures near ceilings during the heating season is to use a circulation fan with connected ductwork, as illustrated in Figure 6-30.

The result of reducing ceiling temperature is a reduction in conduction and exhaust losses.

SIM 6-5

Comment on reducing the stratified air temperature from 90°F to 75°F during the heating season.

U = .1

Area = 20,000 square feet

Assume an outside temperature of 15°F and exhaust CFM of 20,000.

ANALYSIS

A handy formula to relate heat loss from CFM exhausts is:

$Q = 1.08$ BTU Min./Hr, Ft^3, F $\times \Delta T$

Before change

$Q_{conduction} = U\ A\Delta T = .1 \times 20,000 \times 75 = 150,000$ BTU/H

$Q_{CFM} = 1.08 \times 20,000 \times 75$
$\quad = 1,620,000$ BTU/H

$Q_T \quad = 1,770,000$ BTU/H

After change in stratification temperature

$Q_c = .1 \times 20,000 \times 60 = 120,000$ BTU/H

$Q_{CFM} = 1.08 \times 20,000 \times 60$
$\quad = 1,296,000$ BTU/H

$Q_T \quad = 1,416,000$ BTU/H

% savings — heating season
$= 100 - 1,416,000/1,770,000 \times 100 = 20\%$

Figure 6-30
Reducing Air Stratification
Temperatures
(Photograph courtesy of Rusth Industries, Beaverton, Oregon)

7

The Electrical System Energy Audit

The Electrical System Energy Audit (ESEA) requires gathering the following data:
1. Electrical Rate Tariff
2. Existing Lighting System Survey
3. Distribution System Characteristics
   a. Motor Loads
   b. Power Factor and Demand

Typical information gathering forms are illustrated in Chapter 15, Figures 15-15 through 15-18.

Before an ESEA can be analyzed, a thorough knowledge of how electricity is billed needs to be known. The ESEA should uncover what items should be implemented and the effective cost benefit analysis.

Each component of the ESEA is discussed in this section.

ELECTRICAL RATE TARIFF

The basic electrical rate charges contain the following elements:

Billing Demand—The maximum kilowatt requirement over a 15-, 30-, or 60-minute interval.

Load Factor—The ratio of the average load over a designated period to the peak demand load occurring in that period.

Power Factor—The ratio of reactive power to resistive power. Traditionally electrical rate tariffs have a decreasing kilowatt hour (KWH) charge with usage. This practice is likely to gradually phase out. New tariffs are containing the following elements:

Time of Day—Discounts are allowed for electrical usage during off-peak hours.

Ratchet Rate—The billing demand is based on 80-90% of peak demand for any one month. The billing demand will remain at that ratchet for 12 months even though the actual demand for the succeeding months may be less.

The effect of changes in electrical rate tariffs can be significant as illustrated in SIM 7-1.

SIM 7-1

The existing rate structure is as follows:

Demand Charge:

First 25 KW of billing demand	$4.00 per KW per month
Next 475 KW of billing demand	$3.50 per KW per month
Next 1000 KW	$3.25 per KW per month

Energy Charge:

First 2,000 KW-Hrs per month	4¢ per KWH
Next 18,000 KW-Hrs per month	3¢ per KWH
Next 180,000 KW-Hrs per month	2.2¢ per KWH
Etc.	

The new proposed schedule deletes price breaks for usage.

	Billing Months June—September	Billing Months October—May
Demand Charge	$13.00 per KW/Month	$5.00 per KW/Month
Energy Charge	2.5¢ per KWH	1.5¢ per KWH

Demand charge based on greatest billing demand month.

Comment on the proposed billing as it would affect an industrial customer who uses 475 KW per month, 330 hours, 900 KW winter (8 months) demand, 1200 KW summer (4 months) demand.

ANALYSIS

The proposed rate schedule has two major changes. First, billing demand is on a ratchet basis and discourages peak demand during summer months. The high demand charge encourages the plant to improve the overall load factor. The increased demand charge is partially offset with a lower energy usage rate.

Original Billing
```
Winter: First   25 KW       $   100
Demand Next 475 KW            1,660
        Next 400 KW          1,300
                            $3,060
```
Summer: $4,035
Total Demand: 8 X 3060 +4 X 4035 = $40,620
Usage Charge: 475 KW X 330 Hours = 156,750 KWH
```
First    2,000 KWH @ 4¢ =  $    80
Next   18,000 KWH @ 3¢ =       540
Next  136,750 KWH @ 2.2¢ =  3,008
                           $3,628
```
Total Usage: 3628 X 12 + $43,536
    Total Charge = $84,156 or 5.3¢ per KWH

Proposed Billing
Demand: 1200 X $13.00 X 4 months = $ 62,000
        1200 X $ 5.00 X 8 months = $ 48,000
Total Demand: $110,400
Usage: 500 KW X 330 X 2.5¢ X 4 = $16,500
        500 KW X 330 X 1.5¢ X 8 = $19,800
Total Usage: $36,300
    Total Charge = $146,700 or 9.3¢ per KWH or a 75% increase

LIGHTING SYSTEM AUDIT

To perform a lighting audit the following information is required:

Room Classification—office, storage, etc.

Room Characteristics—height, width, length, and color

Fixture Characteristics—type of lamp, fixture mounting height, ballast and lamp wattage, plus measured foot-candle level.

This information will not only give crude measurements of performance such as watts/square foot, but will also provide sufficient data for a technical analysis. The most common method used to calculate illumination requirements is referred to as the lumen method.

LUMEN METHOD

$$N = \frac{F_1 \times A}{Lu \times L_1 \times L_2 \times Cu}$$ *Formula (7-1)*

where

N is the number of lamps required.

F_1 is the required footcandle level at the task. A footcandle is a measure of illumination; one standard candle power measured one foot away.

A is the area of the room in square feet.

Lu is the Lumen output per lamp. A Lumen is a measure of lamp intensity: its value is found in the manufacturer's catalogue.

Cu is the coefficient of utilization. It represents the ratio of the Lumens reaching the working plane to the total Lumens generated by the lamp. The coefficient of utilization makes allowances for light absorbed or reflected by walls, ceilings, and the fixture itself. Its values are found in the manufacturer's catalogue.

L_1 is the lamp depreciation factor. It takes into account that the lamp Lumen depreciates with time. Its value is found in the manufacturer's catalogue.

L_2 is the luminaire (fixture) dirt depreciation factor. It takes into account the effect of dirt on a luminaire, and varies with type of luminaire and the atmosphere in which it is operated.

The lumen method formula illustrates several ways lighting efficiency can be improved. First, the type of lamp which directly affects the lumen output should be analyzed. Figure 7-1 illustrates lumen outputs of various types of lamp.

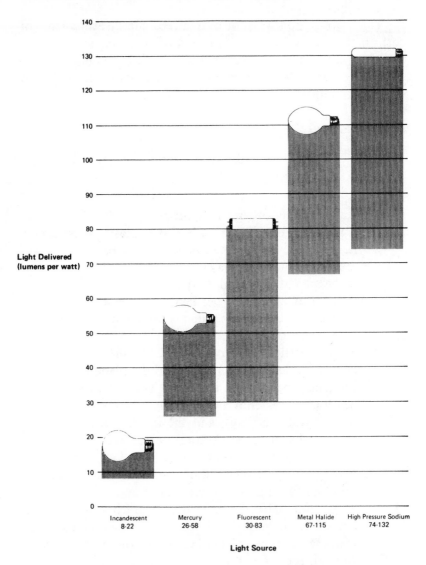

Figure 7-1. Efficiency of Various Light Sources

Many manufacturers are producing highly efficient lamp substitutes for existing lighting systems. For example, for a premium of less than 15%, highly efficient 40-watt fluorescent lamps can replace existing lamps. The end result is a 3-5% reduction in illumination with a 12% reduction in energy usage. Thus there is usually a trade-off in increased first cost coupled with a reduction in illumination and energy usage.

Lamp characteristics of several widely used types are described in this section.

EFFICIENT USE OF INCANDESCENTS

Even though incandescent lighting is not the most energy-efficient per se, efficiencies can be achieved by choosing the right type and wattage of bulb.

An important rule of thumb in determining efficiencies of incandescents is that efficiency increases as the wattage increases. For example, one 100-watt incandescent bulb has an output of 18 lumens per watt, while a 60-watt bulb produces only 14 lumens per watt. Thus, the substitution of one 100-watt bulb (1800 lumens) for two 60-watt bulbs (1680 lumens) produces more light and uses less electricity. This type of substitution saves energy, reduces maintenance, frees circuitry, and therefore should be made wherever possible.

A factor that has a significant impact on the efficiency of incandescents is the *life span* of the bulb, which is measured in hours. Not only do incandescents have the shortest life span of all available lamps, but near the end of the bulb lifetime the light output has depreciated by 20 percent of its original output. Light output is reduced because, as the coiled tungsten filament in incandescent bulbs emits light, molecules of the metal burn off. These molecules become deposited on the surface of the bulb, and slowly cause the bulb to darken. As it darkens, the bulb consumes the same amount of energy as it did when new, yet it produces less light. The bulb eventually burns out when the filament ruptures. Energy and, in the long run, money can be saved by replacing darkened bulbs before they burn out. *Long-life* bulbs (which last from 2500 to 3500 hours) are the least efficient incandescents of all, because light output is sacrificed in favor of long life.

A tinted bulb has a lower light output than a standard incandescent bulb of the same wattage. This is because the coating on the bulb inhibits the transmission of light. And the higher prices of tinted bulbs further illustrate that energy efficiency is often less expensive from the start.

EFFICIENT TYPES OF INCANDESCENTS
FOR LIMITED USE

Attempts to increase the efficiency of incandescent lighting while maintaining good color rendition have led to the manufacture of a number of energy-saving incandescent lamps for limited residential use.

Tungsten Halogen—These lamps vary from the standard incandescent by the addition of halogen gases to the bulb. Halogen gases keep the glass bulb from darkening by preventing the filament from evaporating, and thereby increase lifetime up to four times that of a standard bulb. The lumen-per-watt rating is approximately the same for both types of incandescents, but tungsten halogen lamps average 94-percent efficiency throughout their extended lifetime, offering significant energy and operating cost savings. However, tungsten halogen lamps require special fixtures, and during operation, the surface of the bulb reaches very high temperatures, so they are not commonly used in the home.

Reflector or R-Lamps—Reflector lamps (R-lamps) are incandescents with an interior coating of aluminum that directs the light to the front of the bulb. Certain incandescent light fixtures, such as recessed or directional fixtures, trap light inside. Reflector lamps project a cone of light out of the fixture and into the room, so that more light is delivered where it is needed. In these fixtures, a 50-watt reflector bulb will provide better lighting and use less energy when substituted for a 100-watt standard incandescent bulb.

Reflector lamps are an appropriate choice for task lighting, because they directly illuminate a work area, and for accent lighting. Reflector lamps are available in 25, 30, 50, 75, and 150 watts. While they have a lower initial efficiency (lumens per watt) than regular incandescents, they direct light more effectively, so that more light is actually delivered than with regular incandescents. Refer to Figure 7-2.

Standard Incandescent

R-Lamp

A high percentage
of light output
is trapped in fixture

An aluminum
coating directs light
out of the fixture

ER Lamp

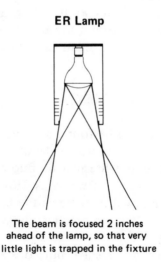

The beam is focused 2 inches
ahead of the lamp, so that very
little light is trapped in the fixture

Figure 7-2. Comparison of Incandescent Lamps

PAR Lamps—Parabolic aluminized reflector (PAR) lamps are reflector lamps with a lens of heavy, durable glass, which makes them an appropriate choice for outdoor flood and spot lighting. They are available in 75, 150, and 250 watts; they have longer lifetimes with less depreciation than standard incandescents.

ER Lamps—Ellipsoidal reflector (ER) lamps are ideally suited for recessed fixtures, because the beam of light produced is focused two inches ahead of the lamp to reduce the amount of light trapped in the fixture. In a directional fixture, a 75-watt ellipsoidal reflector lamp delivers more light than a 150-watt R-lamp. Refer to Figure 7-2.

FLUORESCENT LIGHTING

Unlike incandescent bulbs, fluorescent lamps do not depend on the buildup of heat for light; rather, they convert energy to light by using an electric charge to "excite" gaseous atoms within the fluorescent tube. The charge is sparked in the ballast and flows through cathodes in either end of the tube. The resulting gaseous discharge causes the phosphor coating on the inside of the tube to "fluoresce," and emit strong visible light. Because the buildup of heat is not requisite to the creation of the light, the energy wasted as heat is significantly less than is wasted by incandescent lighting.

EFFICIENT USE OF FLUORESCENTS

Energy savings are to be found simply in the use of fluorescents rather than in the choice of lamps or wattages, because the efficiency rating and lifespan of fluorescents remain consistently high over a range of wattages. However, the efficiency of a fluorescent lamp will increase as the length of the tube increases. Therefore, wherever practical, large fixtures should be used to save energy.

The ballast consumes a small but constant amount of energy, even when a tube has been removed. Disconnecting the ballast or unplugging a fixture not in use is a good way to conserve electricity. As one ballast is often shared by two or more lamps where fluorescent lights are arranged in strips, removing one lamp will cause the others activated by the same ballast to go out. An electrician can make the simple adjustments required to prevent this.

While turning off incandescent lamps not in use is a commonly recognized way to achieve energy savings, misunderstandings abound as to the efficiencies of turning fluorescent lamps on and off. Like incandescents, fluorescent lamps should be turned off when not in use, even if only for a few minutes. No energy is required to turn a light off, and the initial charge requited to turn a fluorescent back on does not use a significant amount of energy unless the switch is flipped back and forth in rapid succession. Fluorescent lamp life is rated according to the number of hours of operation per start, and while it was once true that the greater the number of hours operated per start, the longer the lamp life, recent technology has increased lamp life ratings to an extent that makes the number of starts far less important than they were 10 or 20 years ago. As a rule, if a space is to remain unoccupied for more than 15 minutes, fluorescent lamps should be turned off.

OUTDOOR HID LIGHTING

Because outdoor security and safety lights burn for long hours—sometimes from dusk to dawn—the potential for energy savings is great. This is especially true for outdoor home lighting, which commonly uses incandescent floodlights instead of more energy-efficient High Intensity Discharge (HID) lamps.

The greater efficiency of HID lamps can be seen from the lumen-per-watt information given in Figure 7-1. Considering the higher wattages needed for outdoor security lamps and the long hours they burn, the higher initial investment required for energy-efficient HID lamps makes sense.

Three types of HID lamps are on the market: mercury, metal halide, and high-pressure sodium. All three are more energy-efficient than the standard incandescent bulbs, and are commonly used in business and industry for lighting large areas, such as parking lots, arenas, and lobbies. Each type requires a ballast designed specifically for it.

Mercury—Of the three, mercury lamps are the most commonly used outdoor lighting source. They have the lowest installation cost and a very long life. They are available in 40, 50, 75, 100, and 250 watts, and while comparable in size to incandescent lamps of the same wattage, produce twice as much light. Clear mercury lamps have poor color rendition—they accentuate blue tones—but color-corrected deluxe cool white or deluxe warm white lamps give objects a more familiar appearance. For long-burning outdoor safety lighting, where efficiency is generally more important than color rendition, mercury lamps are a good choice.

Metal Halide—Metal halide lamps are more efficient and have a better color rendition than mercury lamps. They are widely used for general commercial interior and exterior lighting, but because the lowest wattage available is 175 watts, they provide greater levels of illumination than ordinarily required by a homeowner.

High Pressure Sodium—These are the most energy-efficient light source currently on the market. Homeowners generally would use them only for outdoor lighting, however, because the lowest wattage is 70 watts, and its high lumen output is generally too bright for interior home use. In addition, the color produced by these lamps is golden-white, which grays the color red and blue objects. However, they are excellent sources for lighting large outdoor areas.

Apart from color rendition, HID lamps pose one potential drawback—a start-up delay of from 1 to 7 minutes from the time they are switched on until they fully illuminate. However, the continued refinement of HID lamps, particularly the metal halide and the high pressure sodium lamps, is expected to make them practical alternatives.

OTHER EFFICIENCY CRITERIA

Other lighting efficiency criteria are illustrated by Formula (7-1).

Footcandle Level—The footcandle level required is that at the task. Footcandle levels can be lowered to one-third of the levels for surrounding areas such as aisles. (A minimum 20-footcandle level should be maintained.)

The placement of the lamp is also important. If the luminaire can be lowered or placed at a better location the lamp wattage may be reduced.

Coefficient of Utilization (Cu)—The color of the walls, ceiling, and floors, the type of luminaire, and the characteristics of the room determine the Cu. This value is determined based on manufacturer's literature. The Cu can be improved by analyzing components such as lighter colored walls and more efficient luminaires for the space.

Lamp Depreciation Factor and *Dirt Depreciation Factor*— These two factors are involved in the maintenance program. Choosing a luminaire which resists dirt build-up, group relamping and cleaning the luminaire, will keep the system in optimum performance. Taking these factors into account can reduce the number of lamps initially required.

In addition to these items consideration should be given to the following:

Operation—Significant energy savings can be achieved simply by using light sources efficiently. The following checklist suggests ways to increase lighting efficiency.

- Lower wattages, eliminate unnecessary light, and rely on daylight whenever possible.
- Replace two bulbs with one having a comparable number of lumens.
- Place fixtures on separate switches so they can be operated independently of each other.
- Convert decorative outdoor gas lamps to standard incandescent or mercury lamps. If the lamp cannot be converted, limit its use but maintain safety and security by using other sources to light the area.

Timing Devices, Photocells, and Dimmers—The practice of inadvertently leaving lights burning when they are not needed can be eliminated by installing small timing devices or photocells to indoor and outdoor lighting. Timing devices can be set to automatically turn lights off and on at predetermined times, for example, on at dusk and off at dawn. Timers can be purchased in most hardware or department stores for prices ranging from $10.00 to $20.00.

Photocells offer an automatic way to turn lights on and off in direct response to the amount of natural light available. Photocells are small photoelectric cells, sometimes less than an inch in diameter, that are sensitive to sunlight. When light strikes a photocell, it is converted to electrical energy. The brighter the light, the stronger the resulting electrical charge. Photocells are designed so that when a certain amount of natural daylight strikes them, the electrical charge created by the light triggers a mechanism that switches lights off; when daylight wanes, on stormy days, or when clouds temporarily decrease the amount of natural light available, the photocell switches lights on again. The reliability and low initial cost of photocells make them an excellent tool for conserving energy.

Nearly all types of light sources can be dimmed by controlling the amount of power applied to them. Dimmer controls permit the occupant to adjust the level of light in a room over the full range, from off to the highest illumination level, in response to the varying light levels required at different times of the day, in different rooms of a building, and by different activities in a room. Dimmers can achieve energy savings if they are used regularly.

Two types of energy-saving dimmer controls are currently on the market: solid-state and variable-automatic transformers. Both save energy by reducing the amount of electricity delivered to the light. In addition, because bulbs are operating on reduced voltage, the life of the bulb is extended. Dimmer fixtures replace standard light switches, and are inexpensive and easy to install. New models on the market can be attached to table lamps as well.

Dimmers for fluorescent lamps must be used with a special dimmer ballast, which replaces the standard ballast. Because the use of fluorescent lamps in itself provides energy savings, the use of dimmers with fluorescent lamps is not as widespread as with incandescent bulbs. Currently, dimming equipment is available for only 30-watt and 40-watt rapid-start fluorescent lamps.

The precursor of photocells and dimmers is a dimming mechanism still sold occasionally, called a rheostat. Because it works by transforming into heat that portion of the electrical energy not used for light, it does not save energy and thus is not recommended for use.

As an alternative to full-range dimmers, there are "hi-lo" switches on the market that provide two settings for overhead lamps. While they do not provide the flexibility of a full-range dimmer, they do achieve energy savings, and are comparable to the three-way bulbs used in table lamps.

When used regularly, the costs of these lighting controls are more than offset by the electricity saved from the lower levels of illumination they make possible.

SIM 7-2

An evaluation needs to be made to replace all 40-watt fluorescent lamps with a new lamp which saves 12% or 4.8 watts and gives the same output. The cost of each lamp is $1.40.

Assuming a rate of return before taxes of 25% is required, can the immediate replacement be justified. Hours of operation are 5800 and the lamp life is two years. Electricity cost is 3.5¢ per KWH.

ANALYSIS

$R = P \times CR$
$R = 5800 \times 4.8 \times .035/1000 = \$.97$
$CR = .97/1.4 = .69$

From Table 15-5 a rate of return of 25% is obtained when analyzing energy conservation measures. Never look at what was previously spent or the life remaining. Just determine if the new expenditure will pay for itself.

ELECTRICAL SYSTEM DISTRIBUTION AUDIT

The total power requirement of a load is made up of two components: namely, the resistive part and the reactive part.

The resistive portion of a load can not be added directly to the reactive component since it is essentially ninety degrees out of phase with the other. The pure resistive power is known as the watt, while the reactive power is referred to as the reactive volt amperes. To compute the total volt ampere load it is necessary to analyze the power triangle indicated below:

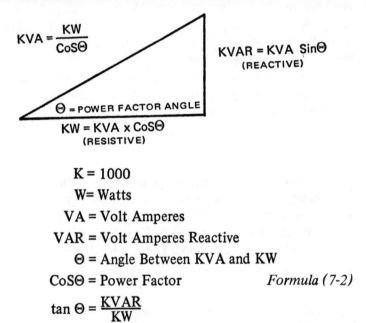

$$K = 1000$$
$$W = Watts$$
$$VA = Volt\ Amperes$$
$$VAR = Volt\ Amperes\ Reactive$$
$$\Theta = Angle\ Between\ KVA\ and\ KW$$

$$Cos\Theta = Power\ Factor \qquad \qquad \textit{Formula (7-2)}$$

$$\tan \Theta = \frac{KVAR}{KW}$$

For a balanced 3-phase load

$$Power = \underbrace{\sqrt{3}\ V_L\ I_L}\ Cos\Theta \qquad \textit{Formula (7-3)}$$

Watts	Volt	Power
	Amperes	Factor

For a balanced 1-phase load

$$P = V_L\ I_L\ Cos\Theta \qquad \textit{Formula (7-4)}$$

The standard power rating of a motor is referred to as a horsepower. In order to relate the motor horsepower to a kilowatt (KW) multiply the horsepower by .746 (Conversion Factor) and divide by the motor efficiency.

$$KVA = \frac{HP \times .746}{\eta \times P.F.} \qquad \textit{Formula (7-5)}$$

HP = Motor Horsepower
η = Efficiency of Motor
P.F. = Power Factor of Motor

Motor efficiencies and power factors vary with load. Typical values are shown in Table 7-1. Values are based on totally enclosed fan-cooled motors (TEFC) running at 1800 RPM "T" frame.

Table 7-1.

HP RANGE	3-30	40-100
η% at		
½ Load	83.3	89.2
¾ Load	85.8	90.7
Full Load	86.2	90.9
P.F. at		
½ Load	70.1	79.2
¾ Load	79.2	85.4
Full Load	83.5	87.4

POWER FACTOR EFFICIENCY IMPROVEMENT

The ESEA should collect the following data:
• Plant Power Factor
• Motor nameplate date, type, horsepower, speed, full-load and part-load amperage.
• Nameplate data should be compared to actual running motor amperage.

As indicated in Table 7-1 small, partially-loaded motors contribute to poor power factors and electrical efficiency for buildings and plants.

The ESEA should determine which motors are oversized and may be replaced with a smaller frame size.

A second method to improve the plant or building power factor is to use energy efficient motors. Energy efficient motors are available from manufacturers such as Gould, Inc. and Baldor. Energy efficient motors are approximately 30 percent more expensive than their standard counterpart. Based on the energy cost it can be determined if the added investment is justified. With the emphasis on energy conservation, new lines of energy efficient motors are being introduced. Figures 7-3 and 7-4 illustrate a typical comparison between energy efficient and standard motors.

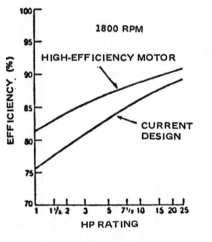

Figure 7-3
Efficiency vs Horsepower
Rating (Dripproof Motors)

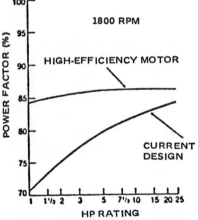

Figure 7-4
Power Factor vs Horsepower
Rating (Dripproof Motors)

A third method to improve the power factor is to add capacitor banks to lower the total reactive KVAR. The line current will also be reduced, thus the corresponding $I^2 R$ loss through cables will also be lowered. Table 7-2 can be used to estimate the connective capacitance required.

Table 7-2. Shortcut Method—Power Factor Correction

KW MULTIPLIERS FOR DETERMINING CAPACITOR KILOVARS

ORIGINAL POWER FACTOR IN PERCENTAGE	DESIRED POWER-FACTOR IN PERCENTAGE																				
	80	81	82	83	84	85	86	87	88	89	90	91	92	93	94	95	96	97	98	99	100
50	.982	1.008	1.034	1.060	1.086	1.112	1.139	1.165	1.192	1.220	1.248	1.276	1.303	1.337	1.369	1.403	1.441	1.481	1.529	1.590	1.732
51	.936	.962	.988	1.014	1.040	1.066	1.093	1.119	1.146	1.174	1.202	1.230	1.257	1.291	1.323	1.357	1.395	1.435	1.483	1.544	1.688
52	.894	.920	.946	.972	.998	1.024	1.051	1.077	1.104	1.132	1.160	1.188	1.215	1.249	1.281	1.315	1.353	1.393	1.441	1.502	1.644
53	.850	.876	.902	.928	.954	.980	1.007	1.033	1.060	1.088	1.116	1.144	1.171	1.205	1.237	1.271	1.309	1.349	1.397	1.458	1.600
54	.809	.835	.861	.887	.913	.939	.966	.992	1.019	1.047	1.075	1.103	1.130	1.164	1.196	1.230	1.268	1.308	1.356	1.417	1.559
55	.769	.795	.821	.847	.873	.899	.926	.952	.979	1.007	1.035	1.063	1.090	1.124	1.156	1.190	1.228	1.268	1.316	1.377	1.519
56	.730	.756	.782	.808	.834	.860	.887	.913	.940	.968	.996	1.024	1.051	1.085	1.117	1.151	1.189	1.229	1.277	1.338	1.480
57	.692	.718	.744	.770	.796	.822	.849	.875	.902	.930	.958	.986	1.013	1.047	1.079	1.113	1.151	1.191	1.239	1.300	1.442
58	.655	.681	.707	.733	.759	.785	.812	.838	.865	.893	.921	.949	.976	1.010	1.042	1.076	1.114	1.154	1.202	1.263	1.405
59	.618	.644	.670	.696	.722	.748	.775	.801	.828	.856	.884	.912	.939	.973	1.005	1.039	1.077	1.117	1.165	1.226	1.368
60	.584	.610	.636	.662	.688	.714	.741	.767	.794	.822	.849	.878	.905	.939	.971	1.005	1.043	1.083	1.131	1.192	1.334
61	.549	.575	.601	.627	.653	.679	.706	.732	.759	.787	.815	.843	.870	.904	.936	.970	1.008	1.048	1.096	1.157	1.299
62	.515	.541	.567	.593	.619	.645	.672	.698	.725	.753	.781	.809	.836	.870	.902	.936	.974	1.014	1.062	1.123	1.265
63	.483	.509	.535	.561	.587	.613	.640	.666	.693	.721	.749	.777	.804	.838	.870	.904	.942	.982	1.030	1.091	1.233
64	.450	.476	.502	.528	.554	.580	.607	.633	.660	.688	.716	.744	.771	.805	.837	.871	.909	.949	.997	1.058	1.200
65	.419	.445	.471	.497	.523	.549	.576	.602	.629	.657	.685	.713	.740	.774	.806	.840	.878	.918	.966	1.027	1.169
66	.388	.414	.440	.466	.492	.518	.545	.571	.598	.626	.654	.682	.709	.743	.775	.809	.847	.887	.935	.996	1.138
67	.358	.384	.410	.436	.462	.488	.515	.541	.568	.596	.624	.652	.679	.713	.745	.779	.817	.857	.905	.966	1.108
68	.329	.355	.381	.407	.433	.459	.486	.512	.539	.567	.595	.623	.650	.684	.716	.750	.788	.828	.876	.937	1.079
69	.299	.325	.351	.377	.403	.429	.456	.482	.509	.537	.565	.593	.620	.654	.686	.720	.758	.798	.840	.907	1.049
70	.270	.296	.322	.348	.374	.400	.427	.453	.480	.508	.536	.564	.591	.625	.657	.691	.729	.769	.811	.878	1.020
71	.242	.268	.294	.320	.346	.372	.399	.425	.452	.480	.508	.536	.563	.597	.629	.663	.701	.741	.783	.850	.992
72	.213	.239	.265	.291	.317	.343	.370	.396	.423	.451	.479	.507	.534	.568	.600	.634	.672	.712	.754	.821	.963
73	.186	.212	.238	.264	.290	.316	.343	.369	.396	.424	.452	.480	.507	.541	.573	.607	.645	.685	.727	.794	.936
74	.159	.185	.211	.237	.263	.289	.316	.342	.369	.397	.425	.453	.480	.514	.546	.580	.618	.658	.700	.767	.909
75	.132	.158	.184	.210	.236	.262	.289	.315	.342	.370	.398	.426	.453	.487	.519	.553	.591	.631	.673	.740	.882
76	.105	.131	.157	.183	.209	.235	.262	.288	.315	.343	.371	.399	.426	.460	.492	.526	.564	.604	.652	.713	.855
77	.079	.105	.131	.157	.183	.209	.236	.262	.289	.317	.345	.373	.400	.434	.466	.500	.538	.578	.620	.687	.829
78	.053	.079	.105	.131	.157	.183	.210	.236	.263	.291	.319	.347	.374	.408	.440	.474	.512	.552	.594	.661	.803
79	.026	.052	.078	.104	.130	.156	.183	.209	.236	.264	.292	.320	.347	.381	.413	.447	.485	.525	.567	.634	.776
80	.000	.026	.052	.078	.104	.130	.157	.183	.210	.238	.266	.294	.321	.355	.387	.421	.458	.499	.541	.608	.750
81	—	.000	.026	.052	.078	.104	.131	.157	.184	.212	.240	.268	.295	.329	.361	.395	.433	.473	.515	.582	.724
82	—	—	.000	.026	.052	.078	.105	.131	.158	.186	.214	.242	.269	.303	.335	.369	.407	.447	.489	.556	.698
83	—	—	—	.000	.026	.053	.079	.105	.132	.160	.188	.216	.243	.277	.309	.343	.381	.421	.463	.530	.672
84	—	—	—	—	.000	.026	.053	.079	.106	.134	.162	.190	.217	.251	.283	.317	.355	.395	.437	.504	.645
85	—	—	—	—	—	.000	.027	.053	.080	.108	.136	.164	.191	.225	.257	.291	.329	.369	.417	.478	.620

Example: Total kw input of load from wattmeter reading 100 kw at a power factor of 60%. The leading reactive kvar necessary to raise the power factor to 90% is found by multiplying the 100 kw by the factor found in the table, which is .849. Then 100 kw × 0.849 = 84.9 kvar. Use 85 kvar.

Reprinted by permission of Federal Pacific Electric Company.

VOLTAGE DROP

Voltage drop on branch circuits and feeders should not exceed 3% according to the National Electrical Code (NEC). In addition, the voltage drop from a feeder circuit current limiting device such as a circuit breaker to the farthest outlet on a branch circuit served by the feeder should not exceed 5%.

To determine the voltage drop, take voltage readings at the branch circuit breaker and at the farthest part to be measured.

In the case where the permissible voltage drop is exceeded, a larger diameter cable and or redistributing the load should be considered.

REDUCING PEAK DEMAND

One of the biggest energy cost-saving potentials is to reduce peak demands. The simplest method to do this relies upon manually scheduling activities so that big power users do not operate at the same time. This is sometimes possible during initial plant start-up where one system can be operated when another is down. The second method relies upon automatic controls which shut off nonessential users during peak periods. Nonessential users such as heating, ventilation and air-conditioning equipment can be automatically controlled through packaged equipment such as load-demand controllers.

LOAD DEMAND CONTROLLERS

The load demand controller is basically a comparator. A comparison is made between the actual rate of energy usage to a predetermined ideal rate of energy usage during the demand interval. As the actual usage rate approaches the ideal usage rate, the controller determines if the present demand will be exceeded. If the determination is positive, the controller will begin to shed loads based upon a predetermined priority. The control action usually occurs during the last few minutes of the demand interval. The loads are automatically restored when the new demand interval is started. Figure 7-5 illustrates a typical

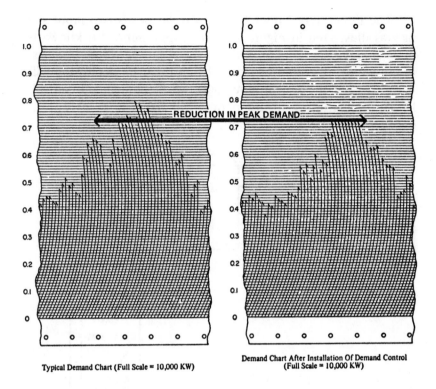

Typical Demand Chart (Full Scale = 10,000 KW)

Demand Chart After Installation Of Demand Control
(Full Scale = 10,000 KW)

**Figure 7-5. Typical Demand Chart Compared
After Installation of a Demand Control**

demand chart before and after the installation of a demand controller.

There are several types of demand controller on the market. Careful consideration should be given to the type of controller specified. Cost and proper application are the primary criteria for choosing the demand controller for the plant. Several commonly used types are:

- Packaged solid-state controllers
- Time-interval reset type
- Sliding-window type
- Computer

The time-interval reset type controller needs two input signals as illustrated in Figure 7-6. The inputs represent kilowatthour energy usage and an interval signal pulse. Before purchasing this unit, it should be verified that the utility company will permit use of the synchronous pulse with the demand controller. Several utilities do not permit this signal to be used; thus another type of controller may be required.

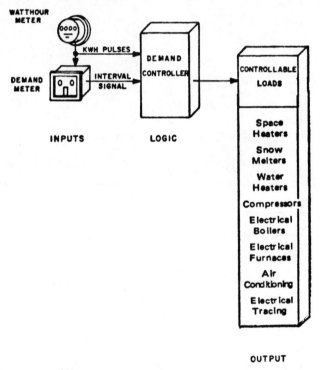

Figure 7-6. Time-Interval Reset Type Controller

The sliding-window type does not require a synchronous pulse. In the sliding-window type power consumption is monitored continuously. The width of the sliding window can be set from five to sixty minutes in five-minute increments. The energy consumed during this interval is proportional to demand. Loads are shed and restored based on predetermined upper and lower thresholds. Predicted usage is calculated based on the consumption during the most recent quarter window width. A scheduling clock can be built into these units allowing for turning loads on and off during specific times of the day.

Computers used for load shedding can also serve several other functions. Computer systems presently offered can be used in conjunction with security and fire-alarm protection. These units also allow for better reporting of energy consumption through audit reports. One feature of computer load shedding is the floating target adjustment. This allows the system to automatically respond to changing conditions in the facility such as weekends, holidays, and unexpected work stoppages.

8

The Utility And Process System Energy Audit

Optimizing utility system performance for steam, air, and water is a very important part of the overall program. This chapter presents utility, combustion and insulation energy audit procedures.

THE COMBUSTION AUDIT

A boiler tuneup should be a high priority on the energy audit program. The reason being that with a minimal cost, high operating savings are achieved.

Techniques used to analyze air/fuel ratios, waste heat recovery, and combustion conservation opportunities are presented in this chapter. For information concerning instrumentation and maintenance, Chapters 3 and 9 should be referred to respectively. Figure 15-24, Chapter 15 illustrates a typical audit data form.

COMBUSTION PRINCIPLES

The boiler plant should be designed and operated to produce the maximum amount of usable heat from a given amount of fuel.

Combustion is a chemical reaction of fuel and oxygen which produces heat. Oxygen is obtained from the input air which also contains nitrogen. Nitrogen is useless to the combustion process. The carbon in the fuel can combine with air to form either CO or CO_2. Incomplete combustion can be recognized by a low CO_2 and high CO content in the stack. Excess air causes more fuel to be burned than required. Stack losses are increased and more fuel is needed to raise ambient air to stack temperatures. On the other hand, if insufficient air is supplied, incomplete combustion occurs and the flame temperature is lowered. The rate of combustion of preheating air is illustrated in Figure 8-1.

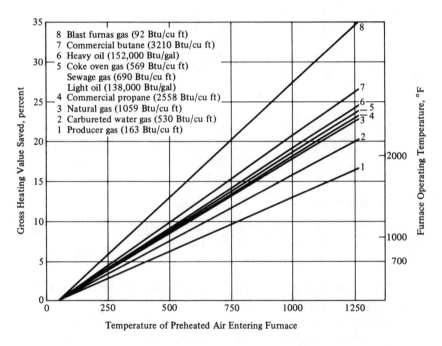

Figure 8-1. Fuel Savings Resulting From Use of Preheated Combustion Air
(Figure adapted with permission from *Plant Engineering.*)

Preheating combustion air has the following advantages.
- Flame temperature is raised, thus permitting air increase in boiler output.
- Higher flame temperature reduces excess air requirements.
- Dual firing is made simpler.

Preheating combustion air is usually accomplished by recovering the waste heat from the stack by utilizing an air-to-air heat exchanger.

Combustion air preheat temperature should be checked against manufacturer's recommendations to insure that the upper limit is not exceeded. Usually combustion air can be preheated up to 600°F for pulverized fuels and 400-450° for other.

BOILER EFFICIENCY

Boiler efficiency (E) is defined as:

$$\% \; E = \frac{\text{Heat out of Boiler}}{\text{Heat supplied to Boiler}} \times 100 \qquad \textit{Formula (8-1)}$$

For steam-generating boiler:

$$\% \; E = \frac{\text{Evaporation Ratio} \times \text{Heat Content of Steam}}{\text{Calorific Value of Fuel}} \times 100$$
$$\textit{Formula (8-2)}$$

For hot water boilers:

$$\% \; E = \frac{\text{Rate of Flow from Boiler} \times \text{Heat Output of Water}}{\text{Calorific Value of Fuel} \times \text{Fuel Rate}} \times 100$$
$$\textit{Formula (8-3)}$$

The relationship between steam produced and fuel used is called the evaporation ratio.

Boilers are usually designed to operate at the maximum efficiency when running at rated output. Figure 8-2 illustrates boiler efficiency as a function of time on line.

Full boiler capacity for heating occurs only a small amount of the time. On the other hand, part loading of 60% or less occurs approximately 90% of the time.

Where the present boiler plant has deteriorated, consideration should be given to replacing with modular boilers sized to meet the heating load.

The overall thermal efficiency of the boiler and the various losses of efficiency of the system are summarized in Figure 8-3.

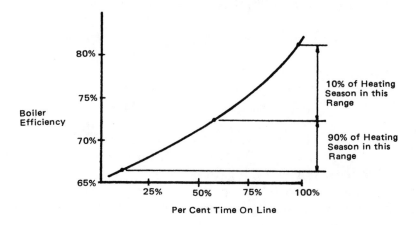

Figure 8-2. Effect of Cycling to Meet Part Loads

---

1.   Overall thermal efficiency . . . .   ———

2.   Losses due to flue gases

    (a)   Dry Flue Gas . . . .   ———

The loss due to heat carried up the stack in dry flue gases can be determined, if the carbon dioxide (CO_2) content of the flue gases and the temperatures of the flue gas and air to the furnace are known.

    (b)   Moisture % Hydrogen . . . .   ———

    (c)   Incomplete combustion . . . .

                                             ———

3.   Balance of account, including radiation and other unmeasured

    losses . . . .   ———

            TOTAL 100%

Figure 8-3. Thermal Efficiency of Boiler

To calculate dry flue gas loss, Formula (8-4) is used.

$$\text{Flue gas loss} = \frac{K\,(T\text{-}t)}{CO_2} \qquad \textit{Formula (8-4)}$$

where

K = constant for type of fuel = 0.39 Coke
0.37 Anthracite
0.34 Bituminous Coal
0.33 Coal Tar Fuel
0.31 Fuel Oil

T = temperature of flue gases in °F

t = temperature of air supply to furnace in °F

CO_2 = percentage CO_2 content of flue gas measured volumetrically.

It should be noted that this formula does not apply to the combustion of any gaseous fuels, such as natural gas, propane, butane, etc. Basic combustion formulas or nomograms should be used in the gaseous fuel case.

To estimate losses due to moisture, Figure 8-4 is used.

The savings in fuel as related to the change in efficiency is given by Formula 8-5.

$$\text{Savings in Fuel} = \frac{\text{New Efficiency-Old Efficiency}}{\text{New Efficiency}} \times \text{Fuel Consumption}$$

$$\textit{Formula (8-5)}$$

Figure 8-5 can be used to estimate the effect of flue gas composition, excess air, and stack temperature on Boiler Efficiency.

BURNERS

The choice of a burner is critical to the whole boiler efficiency operation. The basic requirement of an oil burner is that it change the oil into tiny particles thus exposing the greatest surface area of combustible materials in the shortest possible time. Some burners atomize the oil better than others.

Another important aspect is that the burner have the same operating range or turndown ratio as the boiler. Losses of up to

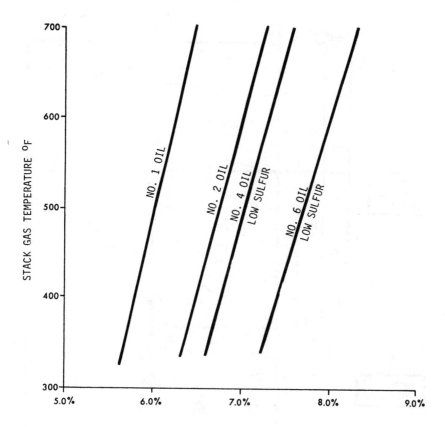

NOTE:
1. The figure gives a simple reference to heat loss in stack gases due to the formation of water in burning the hydrogen in various fuel oils.
2. The graph assumes a boiler room temperature of 80°F.

Figure 8-4. Heat Loss Due to Burning Hydrogen in Fuel
(Source: Instructions For Energy Auditors, Volume 1)

20%* in fuel consumption may be occurring when a poor turn-down ratio burner is matched against a fluctuating steam load. Burners and associated control systems should be able to modu-late through the whole range of output called for by the facility.

---

*Instructions for Energy Auditors, Volume 1 –DOE/CS-0041/12

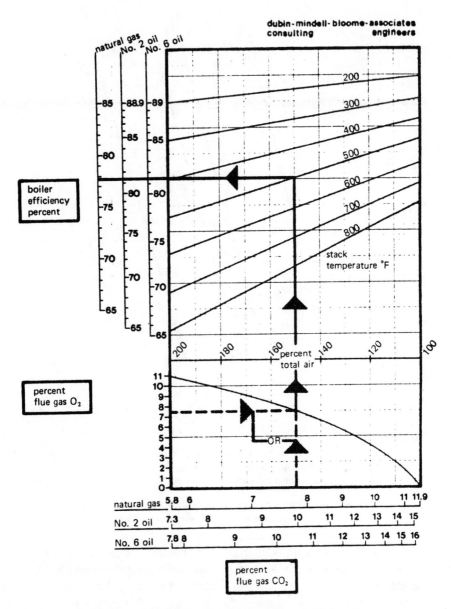

**Figure 8-5. Effect of Flue Gas Composition and Temperature
on Boiler Efficiency**
*(Source: Guidelines For Saving Energy in Existing Buildings—
Engineers, Architects and Operators Manual, ECM-2)*

Burner tips should also be checked, especially if heavier fuels are used. Damaged burner tips should be discarded. Adequate filtering of oil should be provided so that dirt does not get through to burner tips. In addition, burner tips should be periodically cleaned.

In the case of natural gas burners, a check should be made if there is any indication of pulsating or shaking of the boiler. If this phenomenon does occur, this can be corrected by changing burner type, or altering burner gas parts, or changing fuel/air ratios.

WATER TREATMENT AUDIT

Poor quality boiler feed water can inhibit heat transfer and cause corrosion. The chemical water treatment and blowdown requirements can be critical to both efficiency and maintenance.

Blowdown of solids should be kept to a minimum from an energy conservation viewpoint. To determine the optimum operation, the chemical composition of the incoming water and the boiler manufacturer recommendations should be known. Chemical treatment manufacturers are often a good source of information.

RETROFIT DEVICES

There are many new devices on the market that can save energy. Care should be taken to properly install the devices. Improper installation or application could present problems at no fault to the device itself.

AUTOMATIC DAMPERS

A flue gas damper can be used to close the exhaust at the end of the combustion cycle as illustrated in Figure 8-6.

In normal operation, the temperature of the gas will drop rapidly at the end of the combustion cycle. As a result, the temperature-sensing switch contacts will close approximately 90 seconds after the gas valve has been de-energized. Closing of the

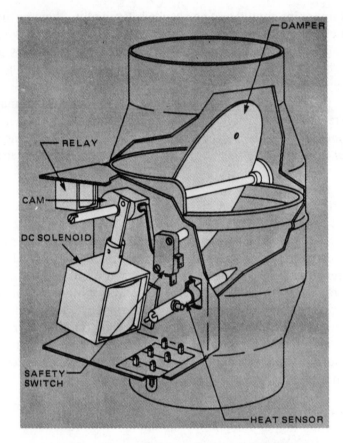

Large clearance around damper gives 2½-sq inch orifice area
for venting gas in event of pilot light outage.

Figure 8-6. Automatic Combustion Damper
(Figure courtesy of Energy Vent, Inc., Dayton, Ohio)

switch contacts will permit supplying of current to the damper's
solenoid actuator for closing of the damper disc. However, if
operation is abnormal and the temperature does not drop after
the gas valve is de-energized, the switch contacts will remain in
an open position to continue venting of the exhaust gases. Also,
this will eliminate the possibility of carbon monoxide build-up
from continued combustion that might result from the gas
valve remaining open, after it has been de-energized. Unless

these devices are properly installed a hazardous condition could occur.

A listing of manufacturers of Retrofit Automatic Dampers for the residential user is listed below:

Abcor Inc., Lowell, Massachusetts
Ad-Vant Industries, Norristown, Pennsylvania
Bryant Division of BDP Corp., Indianapolis, Indiana
Calspan Corp., Buffalo, New York
Werner Diermayer
Energy Vent Inc., Dayton, Ohio
Flair Manufacturing Co., Hauppauge, New York
Penn Division of Johnson Controls, Oak Brook, Illinois
Perfection Corp., Madison, Ohio
Save Fuel Corp., Clarksdale, Mississippi
Thermal Development Corp., Quakertown, Pennsylvania
Trionic Industries, Inc., Harrisburg, Pennsylvania

To determine the potential savings and the risks involved, the Office of Consumer Products of the Department of Energy requested Arthur D. Little, Inc. to conduct a study into these devices.* Some of the conclusions reached are as follows:

Vent dampers will be applicable to approximately 25.5 million out of 46 million homes that have central furnaces. A program for retrofiting vent dampers on existing furnaces will result in a small decrease in the number of furnace-related accidents. This reduction will come about as a result of interest generated in the public concerning energy savings that will result from retrofit of dampers. Homeowners who are interested in reducing their heating bills through the use of vent dampers and/or other energy saving devices will first have their furnace inspected to determine if it is feasible to install such devices. During this inspection, the utility or other service personnel or the oil burner service personnel will have the opportunity to discover hitherto undetected furnace and venting problems such as corroded vent pipes and blocked chimneys that should be immediately corrected. Many furnaces and boilers that are in

---

* Contract No. CR 04-60663-00, Task Order No. 93

need of total replacement either because they are inefficient or unsafe will be identified in this process.

The total accidents and fatalities due to vent dampers might be

Total Accidents   = one every 1.4 years
Total Fatalities   = 0.26 per year (one every 3.8 years)

It is important to recognize the level of uncertainty of the above estimates. For example, when it is stated that the expected accident rate is 0.69 per year, this means that the actual accident rate is *probably* not higher than 10 times this value (6.9 per year) and almost certainly not higher than 100 times this value (69 per year).

The report concludes that all risk can not be eliminated. A comparison of various risks indicates that risk due to dampers is the smallest of the most common causes of accidents such as travel, weather, etc.

A major conclusion is that the cooldown of the heat exchanger is much more significant than the loss of room air in its potential for automatic dampers. Cooldown losses represent about 40 percent of the total loss. *Approximately 40 percent of the energy conservation potential of vent dampers is attributable to recovering heat that is rejected from the furnace or boiler as air flows through and cools off the heat exchanger.* An additional 40 percent represents the loss of conditioned air associated with this heat exchanger draft (draft hood air) over and above the normal vent flows which would occur without a furnace. The balance (20 percent) is attributable to normal vent losses of room temperature air at flow rates not induced by the heat exchanger cooldown. The validity of this 40/40/20 breakdown is supported with field test data. The additional savings in the summertime due to reduced infiltration load on the air-conditioner as a result of the damper is negligible.

The relatively significant heat exchanger cooldown losses explains why the percentage savings are much higher in the South/West regions than in the Northeast/North Central regions, where loss of room air is more critical.

INSULATION REFIT KIT FOR
DOMESTIC WATER HEATERS

Domestic water heaters traditionally do not have an installed insulation jacket. Electric and gas water heater insulation kits to reduce losses from these heaters are presently on the market.

Figures 8-7 and 8-8 illustrate the payback periods and estimated savings as a result of using the kits. As with any new product, safety considerations are of most importance. The most serious concern is that the wire temperature leads to electric water heaters are not raised by the insulation to cause an electrical problem. In a 1979 bulletin, *Safety News* warned against careless use of electrical water heater insulation kits.

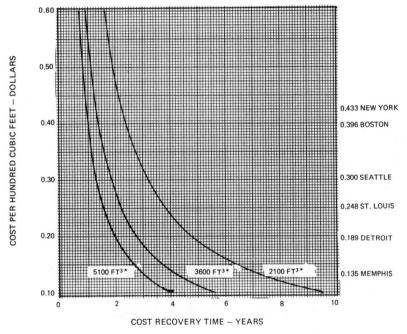

* PROJECTED ANNUAL SAVINGS

**Figure 8-7. Cost-Effective Analysis of Insulation Refit Kit
for Domestic Gas Water Heaters**
(Source: ERDA Report PO NOSWA76-3813 and WA-76-3814)

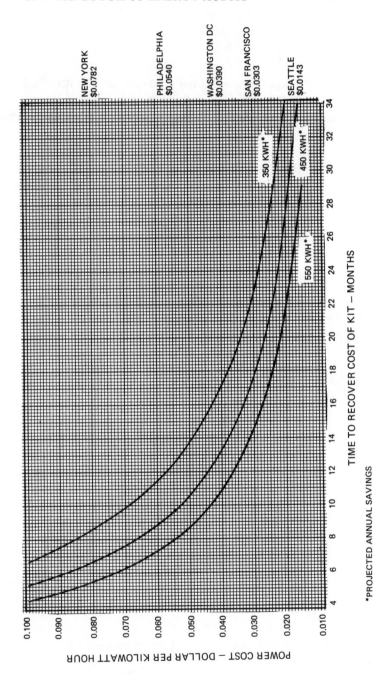

*PROJECTED ANNUAL SAVINGS

Figure 8-8. Cost Effective Analysis of Insulation Refit Kit for Domestic Electric Water Heaters
(Source: ERDA Report PO NOS WA76-3813 and WA-76-3814)

Complete acceptance of the products hinges in part on UL listing, which has not yet occurred as of this writing. It is the author's feelings that the two devices previously mentioned, when properly installed are safe and do save significantly on energy.

FLAKY PRODUCTS AND SERVICES

As with any new technology, care should be given to "fly-by-night con artists." The market place will clean itself, but in the meantime many people will be hurt. The example of the "unturned automobile" should not be overlooked. If the automobile was "unturned" and fitted with an energy saving carburetor, the end result may be a savings in gasoline. The question asked is whether the savings is the result of the carburetor or a tune-up which had to be done after the unit was installed.

COMPRESSED AIR AUDIT

Air leaks are a major energy loss as indicated in Table 9-3, Chapter 9. Doubling the size of air leak increases the loss four times, as illustrated in Figure 8-9.

The energy audit should determine pressure requirements of each user. If the pressure of the distribution system can be lowered savings will be realized, as illustrated by Figure 8-10. If only one or two users require a higher pressure, it may be desirable to purchase a smaller compressor for these users.

A third area to check is the temperature of the incoming air. The lower the inlet air temperature, the greater the volume of air that can be delivered at room temperature. Thus the installation of a manual inlet damper may be justified. This would permit use of outside air during winter and inside air during summer.

INSULATION

Savings as a result of using the optional economic insulation thickness has been estimated as 1,400 trillion BTUs.* To cal-

---

* "Economic Thickness For Industrial Insulation," Conservation Paper 46, U.S. Government Printing Office.

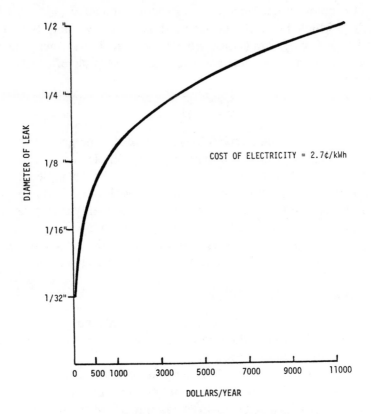

Figure 8-9. Cost of Air Leaks at 100 PSI
(Source: Instructions For Energy Auditors, Volume II)

culate economic thicknesses for piping applications, a good reference is "Economic Thickness of Industrial Insulation," which is available from the U.S. Government Printing Office. Access to computer programs using the method outlined in this reference are available from:

Thermal Insulating Manufacturers Association (TIMA)
7 Kirby Plaza
Mount Kisco, NY 10549

Figure 8-11 illustrates minimum recommended pipe size insulation for each pipe diameter size. Insulation applications for ducts, equipment and pipe are illustrated in Figure 8-12.

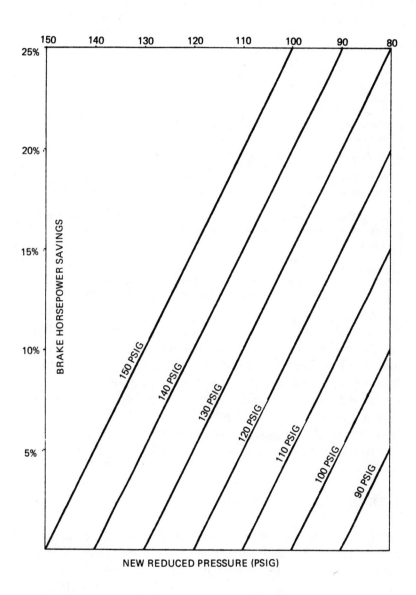

Figure 8-10. Savings with Reduction in Pressure
(Source: Instructions for Energy Auditors, Volume II)

Piping System	Temperature Range °F	Insulation Thickness Inches
Heating		
High pressure steam	306 to 400	1.5 – 2.0
Medium pressure steam	251 to 305	1.0 – 1.5
Low pressure steam	up to 250	1.0
Condensate	190 to 220	1.0
Hot water	up to 200	1.0
Hot water	over 200	1.0
Cooling		
Chilled water	40 to 60	.75 – 1.0
Refrigerant and Brine	below 32	1.0 – 1.5

A WORD OF WARNING: Make absolutely sure that the pipe or vessel to be insulated is properly primed with zinc or silicone coating before installing the insulation.

Figure 8-11. Minimum Piping Insulation
(Source: Instructions for Energy Auditors, Volume II)

Several manufacturers offer access to computer program simulations by use of a touch dial telephone and an assigned user number. These programs can calculate economic thickness for tanks as well as equipment and piping. To use these programs the user dials the computer telephone number and then talks to a computer by touching numbers on the telephone. In a simulated voice the computer transmits the economic thickness. The detailed analysis is given to the user by a local sales representative.

ECONOMIC ANALYSIS

The primary function of insulation is to reduce the loss of energy from a surface operating at a temperature other than ambient. The economic use of insulation reduces plant operating expenditures for fuel, power, etc.; improves process efficiency; increases system output capacity, or may reduce the required capital cost.

Insulation types	Temperature range, °F	Conductivity Btu per hr per deg F per sq ft per in.	Density lb per cu ft	Application
DUCT SYSTEMS				
Boards and blankets with vapor barrier on one side	Up to 250°F	0.23 to 0.36	9.75 to 6.0	Ducts—hot or cold
Thermal and acoustical duct liner blankets and boards	Up to 250°F 4000 to 6000 fpm	0.20 to 0.48	1.5 to 3.0	Ducts—hot or cold and acoustical treatment
Glass fiber boards, 1 in. thick	Up to 250°F 2400 fpm 2 in. WG	0.21 to 0.29	1.5 to 6.0	Rectangular ducts hot or cold
Rigid and flexible preinsulated ducts	Up to 250°F 2400 to 5400 fpm 1.5 to 4 in. WG	0.23 to 0.26	5.0	Round ducts
EQUIPMENT				
Urethane foam	−270 to 225	0.11 to 0.14	2.0	Tanks and vessels
Glass fiber blankets	−270 to 450	0.17 to 0.60	0.60 to 3.0	Chillers, tanks (hot and cold) process equipmt.
Elastomeric sheets	−40 to 220	0.25 to 0.27	4.5 to 6.0	Tanks and chillers
Glass fiber boards	Ambient to 850	0.23 to 0.36	1.6 to 6.0	Boilers, tanks, and heat exchangers
Calcium-silicate boards, blocks	450 to 1200	0.22 to 0.59	6.0 to 10	Boilers, breechings, and chimney liners
Mineral fiber blocks	to 1900	0.36 to 0.90	13.0	Boilers and tanks

Figure 8-12. Representative Insulation Applications
*(Source: Thermal Insulation Guide for Ducts, Equipment and Piping,
Robert W. Roose—HPAC)*

Insulation types	Temperature range, °F	Conductivity Btu per hr per deg F per sq ft per in.	Density lb per cu ft	Application
PIPE				
Urethane foam	−400 to 300	0.11 to 0.14	1.6 to 3.0	Hot and cold pipes
Cellular glass blocks	−350 to 500	0.20 to 0.75	7.0 to 9.5	Tanks and piping
Glass fiber blanket for wrapping	−120 to 550	0.15 to 0.54	0.60 to 3.0	Piping and pipe fittings
Glass fiber preformed shapes	−60 to 450	0.22 to 0.38	0.60 to 3.0	Hot and cold pipes
Glass fiber mats	−150 to 700	0.21 to 0.38	0.60 to 3.0	Piping and pipe fittings
Elastomeric pre-formed shapes and tape	−40 to 220	0.25 to 0.27	4.5 to 6.0	Piping and pipe fittings
Glass fiber with vapor barrier jacket	−20 to 150	0.20 to 0.31	0.65 to 2.0	Refrigerant lines, dual temperature lines, chilled water lines, fuel oil piping
Glass fiber without vapor barrier jacket	to 500	0.20 to 0.31	1.5 to 3.0	Hot piping
Cellular glass blocks and boards	70 to 900	0.20 to 0.75	7.0 to 9.5	Hot piping
Urethane foam blocks and boards	200 to 300	0.11 to 0.14	1.5 to 4.0	Hot piping
Mineral fiber pre-formed shapes	to 1200	0.24 to 0.63	8.0 to 10	Hot piping
Mineral fiber blankets	to 1400	0.26 to 0.56	8.0	Hot piping
Glass fiber field applied jacket for exposed lines	500 to 800	0.21 to 0.55	2.4 to 6.0	Hot piping
Mineral wool blocks	850 to 1800	0.36 to 0.90	11.0 to 18.0	Hot piping
Calcium-silicate blocks	1200 to 1800	0.33 to 0.72	10.0 to 14.0	Hot piping

Figure 8-12. Representative Insulation Applications (concluded)

There are two costs associated with the insulation type chosen: a cost for the insulation itself, and a cost for the energy lost through this thickness. The total cost for a given period is the sum of both costs.

The optimum economic thickness is that which provides the most cost-effective solution for insulating and is determined when total costs are a minimum. Since the solution calls for the sum of the lost energy and insulation investment costs, both costs must be compared in similar terms. Either the cost of insulation must be estimated for each year and compared to the average annual cost of lost energy over the expected life of the insulation, or the cost of the expected energy loss each year must be expressed in present dollars and compared with the total cost of the insulation investment. The former method, making an annual estimate of the insulation cost and comparing it to the average expected annual cost of lost energy, is the method used in this analysis.

9

Maintenance And Energy Audits

An audit for a good preventive maintenance program as well as good housekeeping methods is essential. Probably no single one area offers the best rate of return and is the most overlooked and underemphasized area. This chapter will illustrate both the administrative and technical areas that make up a good preventive maintenance program.

This section includes material contributed by Richard Fessler, Director of Energy, Marriott Corporation.

WORK ASSIGNMENTS

Each major item of equipment must show a history of maintenance and repair. A procedural system of indexing scheduled work and quality control should be established by the supervisor in conjunction with the company's standards of performance.

Personnel assigned to the maintenance control system must be made familiar with all work items. Thus assignments are to be regularly rotated so as to familiarize each man with the equipment.

TRAINING

Periodically, personnel will be requested to attend manufacturers' seminars on maintenance methods for physical plant, building, kitchen equipment, etc.

Typical Manufacturer	*Equipment Type*
A – Sellers Manufacturing Company –	Boilers
B – Hobart Manufacturing Company –	Kitchen Equipment, Dishwashers, etc.
C – Gaylord Manufacturing Company –	Kitchen Exhaust Hoods
D – Vogt Manufacturing Company –	Ice Machines
E – Traulsen –	Reach-In, Pass-Through Refrigeration
F – Groen –	Steam Kettles, Tilting Fry Pans
G – Etc. –	

To assure skilled maintenance personnel and maintenance supervisors, an apprentice mechanics training program should be initiated. The maintenance supervisor will be responsible for the work progression and technical training of the apprentice.

PREVENTIVE MAINTENANCE PROCEDURES

The preventive maintenance (PM) program is a method of budgeting and controlling maintenance expense. It pinpoints problem areas, it helps avoid repetitive maintenance, excessive parts replacement, and purchasing errors. Thus, money spent on a well-planned system of preventive maintenance reduces profit loss due to breakdown, emergency work, and related parts failures.

In order to introduce controls, the PM program must be effective but very simple to avoid assigning administrative chores to maintenance for recordkeeping, etc. When maintenance fills out a simplified work ticket, illustrated in Figure 9-1, the data acquired helps pinpoint costs to accomplish the following:

- Show areas of high cost.
- Change criteria of new construction to reduce high-cost areas.
- Set incentive goals for satisfaction of work.
- Eliminate high-priced skilled labor performing mediocre, unskilled chores.
- Point out high-cost areas to obtain help from qualified technicians, controllers, etc.

NAME: _____

BILLET #: _____   Code Description

SHIFT: _____

	OPERATION #	HOURS	CODE
1			
2			
3			
4			
5			
6			
7			
8			
OVER-TIME			

REMARKS: _____

_____

_____

CODES: A   APPRENTICE
        MJ MECHANIC (JUNIOR)
        M   MECHANIC
        S   SUPERVISOR
        CL CLERK

Code Description

AM	Administration
AC	Air Conditioning
B	Boilers
C	Carts
D	Malicious Damage
EP	Electrical Power
EL	Lighting
EV	Elevators
G	Building Maintenance General
H	Heating
K	Kitchen Equipment
LS	Landscaping & Site Work
M	Miscellaneous
P	Plumbing
PM	Preventative Maintenance
R	Refrigeration
T	Supervisor's Technical Time
V	Ventilation

1	Boiler Room
2	Dry Storage
3	Cafeteria
4	Restrooms & Locker Rooms
5	Assembly Area
6	Dishroom
7	Gift Shop
8	Loading Dock
9	General Storage Area
10	General Offices
11	Miscellaneous

Figure 9-1. Simplified Work Ticket

The coding on the ticket will enable study of the shift for more effective coverage of the operation after evaluation of the time cards. Information on time tickets, such as the nature of breakdown and what action was taken to correct it, is only valuable to supervisory personnel for evaluation of satisfactory performance of maintenance duties.

The information needed to reduce costs in PM is compiled from data collected from high-cost areas. This appears in the labor required to effectively maintain the operation and the labor needed for an effective PM program.

A typical coding system is as follows:

AM — **Administration** —is directed to the maintenance supervisor so as to pinpoint his administrative duties vs. his technical supervision.

AC — **Air-Conditioning** —is to point out costs in this area to take corrective steps in future program criteria.

B — **Boiler** —would pertain to breakdown, lack of PM, etc. It can be directly attributed to that area of time required to maintain service.

C — **Carts (Rolling Stock)** —would be maintenance of casters, modules, baker's racks, dunnage racks, portable mop sinks, etc. It would enable us to pinpoint areas such as specifying heavier duty casters, welding in key point areas, etc.

D — **Malicious Damage** —would include mistreating equipment (carts, kitchen equipment, etc.)

EP — **Electrical Power** --would entail the following: from the service entrance, main disconnect, electricity to source of lighting, power to all equipment, etc.

EL — **Lighting** —will encompass the area of lamp replacement and maintenance of the lighting system throughout the operation.

EV — **Elevators** —where applicable, will deal strictly in the area that is directly pertaining to the satisfactory function of the elevator.

G — **Building Maintenance (General)** —will cover the areas of painting, tile replacement, roof repair, windows, etc.

H — **Heating** —will deal in the areas of what means the building is being heated, such as steam, HVAC units, space heaters, etc.

K — **Kitchen Equipment** —would entail all equipment which includes ranges, conveyors, dishwashers, etc.

LS — **Landscaping & Site Work** —would encompass the exterior of the building such as lawn, trees, sprinkler system, paving and striping of roads and lots.

M — **Miscellaneous** —will be used in areas that have not been covered by defined codes.

P — **Plumbing** —will deal with the areas of water, sewer, industrial wastes, grease traps, septic tanks, etc.

PM — **Preventive Maintenance** —will cover time and location spent on preventive maintenance program so as to pinpoint high PM areas.

R — **Refrigeration** —will cover the areas of maintaining compressors, condensers, evaporative coils on all walk-ins, reach-throughs, and pass-throughs.

T — **Supervisor's Technical Time** —will cover the amount of time actually spent in supervising maintenance in the field.

V — **Ventilation** —will cover the areas of the supply air system and exhaust.

To further pinpoint costs numbers should be assigned to descriptive areas. For example:

1. Boiler Room
2. Dry Storage
3. Cafeteria
4. Restroom and Locker room
5. Assembly Areas
6. Dishroom
7. Gift Shop
8. Loading Dock
9. General Storage Areas
10. General Offices
11. Miscellaneous

The purpose for setting up these codes is to shorten the time for filling out the time tickets, which could be a time-consuming and meaningless task when the ultimate goal is to reduce costs and pinpoint high-cost areas. Naturally, as the system is introduced, other codes will be initiated to cover areas that have not been covered in the start-up of the preventive maintenance program.

To keep personality out of the PM program and to reduce administrative chores of the mechanics, helpers, etc., each maintenance supervisor or mechanic assigned (whichever the case may be) will assign a billet number to each maintenance mechenic, helper, etc. The explanation of these codes is as follows:

A	Apprentice	A	A-1 _____	Series
MJ	Mechanic (Junior)	MJ	MJ-2 _____	Series
M	Mechanic	M	M-3 _____	Series
S	Supervisor	S	S-4 _____	Series
CL	Clerk	CL	CL-5 _____	Series

Example: John Smith: M-3 _____ (will be mechanic's billet #). In case John Smith leaves the company, the new employee will be assigned the same billet number for payroll purposes, etc.

The time ticket attached covers an eight-hour shift, but an area has been designated for overtime which will require an explanation from _____ .

The steps required for a fully encompassing preventive maintenance program are described in this section. Each step must be performed initially and then added to and revised as new equipment is purchased or existing equipment requires more frequent maintenance.

The initial organization and subsequent administration of the program is the responsibility of the supervisor of maintenance.

PREVENTIVE MAINTENANCE SURVEY

This survey is made to establish a list of all equipment on the property that requires periodic maintenance and the maintenance that is required. The survey should list all items of equipment according to physical location. The survey sheet should list the following columns:
1. Item
2. Location of Item
3. Frequency of Maintenance
4. Estimated Time Required for Maintenance
5. Time of Day Maintenance Should Be Done
6. Brief Description of Maintenance To Be Done

PREVENTIVE MAINTENANCE SCHEDULE

The preventive maintenance schedule is prepared from the information gathered during the survey. Items are to be arranged on schedule sheets according to physical location. The schedule sheet should list the following columns:

1. Item
2. Location of Item
3. Time of Day Maintenance Should Be Done
4. Weekly Schedule with Double Columns for Each Day of the Week (one column for "scheduled" and one for "completed")
5. Brief Description of Maintenance To Be Done
6. Maintenance Mechanic Assigned To Do the Work

USE OF PREVENTIVE MAINTENANCE SCHEDULE

At some time before the beginning of the week, the supervisor of maintenance will take a copy of the schedule. The copy that the supervisor prepares should be available in a three-ring notebook. He will go over the assignments in person with each mechanic.

After the mechanic has completed the work, he will note this on the schedule by placing a check under the "completed" column for that day and the index card system for cross-checking the PM program.

The supervisor of maintenance or the mechanic will check the schedule daily to determine that all work is being completed according to the plan. At the end of the week, the schedule will be removed from the book and checked to be sure that all work was completed. It will then be filed.

USE OF THE SCHEDULE TO RECORD REPAIRS

Any repairs or replacement of parts on a particular piece of equipment should be noted on the preventive maintenance schedule. The work done should be written in the weekly schedule section or reference should be made to an attached sheet if more space is necessary. This will provide a history of repairs or replacements on each piece of equipment.

The supervisor of maintenance or mechanic should analyze these schedules twice a year to determine if certain pieces of equipment are requiring more than acceptable maintenance and if replacement of the piece of equipment is necessary.

Figure 9-2 illustrates a form used by the supervisor of maintenance, lead mechanic, etc., for accumulating cost and labor information on a weekly, monthly, and yearly basis. The accumulated information pinpoints high-cost areas, preventive maintenance labor, etc., plus the necessary information for yearly budgeting and other purposes.

The index card system illustrated in Figure 9-3 will become a source of data collecting plus a cross check on preventive maintenance schedules and the analyzing time needed to perform PM work for future maintenance schedules. When the initial program goes into effect, it will require estimating the time required to perform PM on equipment. The data collected will also compile a record of which type motor belts, filters, etc., will be needed to reduce inventory, etc.

The card will be placed in a waterproof enclosure and attached to or located near the equipment which will require preventive maintenance. This will eliminate PM being performed in the office, since the mechanic will fill out the required information listed on the index card and will be responsible if the PM work was not performed. It would further help the supervisor of maintenance or lead mechanic to evaluate the mechanic's performance. See Figure 9-4.

PREVENTIVE MAINTENANCE TRAINING

The supervisor of maintenance or mechanic is responsible for assisting department heads in the training of employees in handling, daily care, and the use of equipment. When equipment is mishandled, he must take an active part in correcting this through training.

SPARE PARTS

All too often equipment is replaced with the exact model as presently installed. Excellent energy conservation opportunities exist in upgrading a plant by installing more efficient replace-

ACTUAL MAINTENANCE COST EXPENDITURES	Weekly			TOTAL COST OF ESTIMATED MAINTENANCE EXPENDITURE......
		REMOVED/EXIST. INVENTORY		
		AIR CONDITIONING		
		BOILERS		
		CARTS		
		ELECTRICAL		
		LIGHTING		
		BLDG. MAINTENANCE (GEN.)		
		HEATING		
		KITCHEN EQUIPMENT		
		LAND & SITE WORK		
		MISCELLANEOUS		
		PLUMBING		
		PREVENTATIVE MAINTENANCE		
		REFRIGERATION		
		VENTILATION		
		LABOR		
		OVERTIME		

Figure 9-2. Maintenance Cost Expenditure Form

DAILY   WEEKLY   MONTHLY   6 MONTHS   YEARLY

MECHANIC ASSIGNED FOR COMPLETION
BILLET #   AMOUNT OF TIME   DATE

Figure 9-3. Maintenance Index Card System

	DAILY	WEEKLY	MONTHLY	6 MONTHS	YEARLY
	BILLET #	AMOUNT OF TIME		REMARKS	
JAN					
FEB					
MAR					
APR					
MAY					
JUN					
JUL					
AUG					
SEP					
OCT					
NOV					
DEC					

Figure 9-4. Recording Performance Comments Form

ment parts. Consideration should be given to the following:
- Efficient line motor to replace standard motors
- Efficient model burners to replace obsolete burners
- Upgrading lighting systems.

How many times are steam traps replaced with a size corresponding to the pipe thread size? Instead of this energy inefficient procedure, before a steam trap is replaced the correct orifice size should be determined. In this way the steam trap will be checked periodically for correct sizing. When a discharge pipe needs to be replaced because it has corroded, a check should be made to determine if a larger size diameter pipe should be used as its replacement. The larger diameter pipe reduces pipe friction losses, thus saving energy.

EQUIPMENT MAINTENANCE

When equipment is properly maintained energy will be saved. This section contains representative equipment and types of maintenance checks to be performed. In addition to equipment checks, leaks in steam, water, air and other utilities should be made and uninsulated or damaged insulation, furnace refractory damages, etc. should be recorded and corrected.

Figures 9-5 and 9-6 illustrate maintenance survey and log book forms respectively.

EQUIPMENT PM AND OPERATIONS

BOILERS

Operating and maintenance procedures depend on the type of boiler, the fuel used, and the manufacturer's instructions. Permanent records should be kept covering all inspections, testing, and servicing.

A general maintenance checklist is illustrated in Figure 9-7. A specific form similar to this figure should be incorporated into the overall PM program based on the details of the unit in operation.

DATE	OPERATIONS REQUEST		MAINTENANCE			
		DATE	CODE	BILLET #	ACTION TAKEN	

Figure 9-5. Operations Maintenance Log Book

Item	Location of Item	Code	Frequency of Maintenance	Est. Time Required	Time of Day	Description of Maintenance

Maintenance Department

Operation No.

Figure 9-6. Preventive Maintenance Survey Form

System	Daily Requirements	Weekly	Monthly	Annual
Blowdown and Water Treatment	• Check that blowdown valve does not leak. • Make sure blowdown is not excessive.		• Make sure that solids are not built-up.	
Exhaust Gases	• Check temperature at two different firings	• Measure exhaust gas temperature and composition at selected firings and adjust to recommended values.	• Same as weekly. • Compare with readings of previous months	• Same as weekly. • Record reference data
Burner	• Check controls are operating properly. • Burner may need cleaning several times daily if #6 fuel is used.	• Clean burner pilot pilot assemblies. • Check condition of spark gap, electrode, burner.	• Same as weekly.	• Same as weekly. • Clean and recondition
Feedwater Systems	• Check & correct unstable water level. • Causes of unstable conditions: contaminants, overload, malfunction.	• Check control by stopping feedwater pump and allow control to stop fuel flow.		• Clean condensate receivers, de-aeration system. • Check pumps.
Steam Pressure	• Check for excessive loading on boiler which will cause excessive variations in pressure.			
Air Temperature in Boiler Rooms	• Check that temperature in boiler room is within acceptable range			

Figure 9-7. Boiler Operations and Maintenance Requirements.

System	Daily Requirements	Weekly	Monthly	Annual
Relief Valve		• Check if relief valve leaks.		• Remove and recondition.
Boiler Operating Characteristics		• Observe flame failure system & characteristics of flame.		
Combustion Air Supply			• Check that adequate openings exist for combustion air inlet. • Clean inlet if fouled.	
Fuel System			• Check pumps, filters, pressure gauges and transfer lines. • Clean filters as required.	• Clean and recondition system.
Belts and Packing Glands			• Check belts for proper tension and damage. • Check packing glands for leakage and proper compressions.	
Air Leaks			• Check for leaks around access openings and flame scanner.	

Air Leaks Waterside & Fireside Surfaces	• Clean surfaces according to manufacturer's recommendations.
Refractor on Fireside	• Repair refractor.
Electrical Systems	• Clean electrical terminals and replace defective parts.
Hydraulic & Pneumatic Valves	• Check all operations and repair all leakages.
Start-Up and Operation	• Check during start-up and operation.
Records	• Record type and amount of fuel used, exhaust gas temperature, and firing position and boiler room temperature.

Figure 9-7. Boiler Operations and Maintenance Requirements (concluded)

OVENS (Monthly)

1. Inspect compartment for proper primary and secondary air conditions.
2. Regulate automatic pilot and safety valve for proper operation.
3. Check motor, belts, fans, on convection ovens.
4. Adjust thermostat for accurate calibration.
5. Check oven doors for (heat loss) tight fit.
6. Clean and adjust orifice and burner to rated BTU input.
7. Lubricate gas valves.
8. Adjust burner flame for proper gas/air mix.

PUMPS

Based on the pump manufacturer's recommendations, a PM Form of checks to be made should be incorporated. Checks should include:
1. Clean inside pump casing periodically and check impellor for wear or damage.
2. Check gland stuffing boxes and repack where necessary.
3. Check and adjust drives (as for fans).
4. Check nonreturn valves, pressure by-pass valves, etc., for correct and effective operation.

COMPRESSORS AND EVAPORATORS

1. *Weekly Checklist*
   a. Box temperature
   b. Thermostat setting
   c. Oil level of compressor (where appropriate)
   d. Flood back to compressor—no frost on compressor
   e. Operation of condenser and evaporator fans. Clean.
   f. Clean evaporator coils, pan and fans
   g. Leaks and oil spots
   h. Synchronization of timers (where applicable)
   i. Receiver temperature should be warm
   j. Short cycling
   k. Over heater strips, hardware

2. *Semi-Annual Checklist*
   a. Bank water level and immersion heater
   b. Leak test entire system
   c. Grease bearings on belt-driven fans
   d. Tighten all electrical terminals
   e. Check discharge pressure, receiver pressure, evaporator pressure, interstage pressure, and suction pressure as per manufacturer's recommendations
   f. Check expansion valve
   g. Check volts and amps of compressor and evaporator
   h. Noncondensibles in system
   i. Lowside pressure control setting. Cut in and cut out according to installation or condensed instruction.

Note: Do not make pressure adjustments without gauges installed, or without first checking recommended pressure setting in the manufacturer's instructions.

The ratio of brake horsepower consumed per ton of refrigerant output can vary considerably with the cleanliness of the condenser and evaporation. Table 9-1 indicates the measured variations of a nominal 15-ton capacity machine having a reciprocating compressor.

Table 9-1. The Effects of Poor Maintenance on the Efficiency of a Reciprocating Compressor, Nominal 15-Ton Capacity

Conditions	(1) °F	(2) °F	(3) Tons	(4) %	(5) HP	(6) HP/T	(7) %
Normal	45	105	17	—	15.9	0.93	—
Dirty Condenser	45	115	15.6	8.2	17.5	1.12	20
Dirty Evaporator	35	105	13.8	18.9	15.3	1.10	18
Dirty Condenser and Evaporator	35	115	12.7	25.4	16.4	1.29	39

(1) Suction Temp, °F
(2) Condensing Temp, °F
(3) Tons of refrigerant
(4) Reduction in capacity %
(5) Brake horsepower
(6) Brake horsepower per Ton
(7) Percent increase in compressor bh per/ton

It can be seen that in the worst case, a reduction in capacity of some 25% occured with an increase of 39% in power requirement per ton of refrigerant.

REFRIGERATION MAINTENANCE

1. Manufacturer's specifications should be followed for selection of *all* lubricants and refrigerants.
2. Inspect and repair any damage to insulation on duct work and piping to avoid temperature loss and damage from condensation.
3. Check for plugged spray nozzles on condenser.
4. Check for dirt on fan blades or rotors causing an unbalanced condition and vibration. Do not paint fan blades.
5. Do not over-lubricate blower bearings. This will avoid oil or grease being thrown on blades and acting as catch agents for dust and dirt.
6. Check for wasted condenser and cooling water in terms of gallons per minute per ton of refrigeration.
7. Check controls on outdoor air sources, so that outside air supply is increased when sufficiently cool to replace refrigerated air.
8. Check for air leakage around doors and transoms through worn weather stripping.
9. Check for worn gaskets on refrigerator doors.
10. Check pump impellers and packings on circulating pumps.
11. Check for clean condensers to avoid poor heat transfer.
12. Check for excessive head pressure and proper suction pressure for longer life of compressor.
13. Check for possibilities of reclaiming condensing water where applicable.
14. Check defrosting cycles to avoid power loss from frost buildup.
15. Check for condition of compressor valves and pistons.
16. Check air cool condenser for fin damage and clean.
17. Seasonal Maintenance. Towards the end of the cooling season, a complete check should be made of air-condi-

tioning equipment while it is still performing. The following should be included:

a. Possible replacement of controls, belts, air filters, refrigerant filter driers, and insulation.

b. Check to see whether units are increasing in power consumption or cooling water requirements. Taking one unit at a time out of service, service it for idleness, drain water, back-off packing glands, drain oil, flush bearings, add new oil, and clean catch pans and tanks.

c. Check for worn parts and compression clearance. The above work should be done regardless of how well the machinery has operated during the previous season.

Table 9-2 shows the measured effect of dirty evaporators and condensers on a nominal 520-ton absorption chiller.

Table 9-2. The Effects of Poor Maintenance on the Efficiency of an Absorption Chiller, 520-Ton Capacity

Condition	Chilled Water °F	Tower Water °F	Tons	Reduction in Capacity %	Steam lb/ton/H	Per Cent
Normal	44	85	520	—	18.7	—
Dirty Condenser	44	90	457	12	19.3	3
Dirty Evaporator	40	85	468	10	19.2	2.5
Dirty Condenser and Evaporator	40	90	396	23.8	20.1	7.5

A reduction in output of 23.8% occurs at the worst case with an increase in steam consumption of 7-5% per ton of refrigerant.

FANS

1. Wheel shaft bearings on belt-driven units of all types with prelubricated pillow blocks and grease fittings should be relubricated every three (3) years. For normal operating conditions, use a grease conforming to NLGI No. 2 consistency.

Motor bearings are prelubricated and should be relubricated every three (3) to five (5) years. Consult instructions on motor. Motors not having pipe plugs or grease fittings in bearing housing can be relubricated by removing end shields from motor.

2. Check belt tension every six (6) months. Belt should depress its width when pressed firmly inward at mid-way point between the pulleys. Too much tension will damage bearings; belt should be tight enough to prevent slippage. When replacing belt, replace motor sheave if "shoulder" is worn in groove. Do not replace with a larger diameter pulley as this will overload the motor.

3. Clean fan (or blower) blades and check for blade damage, which may cause out-of-balance running.

4. Check fan casing and duct connections for air leakage.

FILTERS, COILS, STRAINERS, DUCTS, AND REGISTERS

1. *Filters*—Manufacturer's recommendations regarding the method and interval of cleaning/replacement should be followed. The manually-serviced type air filter requires periodic cleaning or replacement. The usual indication that cleaning/replacement is required is either (a) a decrease in air flow through the filter (up to 10%), or (b) an increase in resistance across the filter (more than 100%).

   Large installations having a number of filters, can arrange a maintenance program of cleaning/replacement on a rotated basis at a regular interval. In certain large duct installations and central air-handling units, it is possible to install simple manometers to indicate the pressure differential across the filter.

   Self-cleaning filters and precipitators should also be examined periodically to observe expiration of the disposable media or accumulation of sludge into the collecting pan. Many manufacturers provide indicators for their equipment to show when servicing is required.

2. *Coils*—The efficient operation of both cooling and heating coils depends largely upon the cleanliness of the heat-

transfer surface. Finned tube surfaces require particular attention and can be cleaned with detergents and high-pressure water using portable units.

Spray coil units may require chemical treatment for the build-up of algae and slime deposited by cooling water. Chemical cleaning can be most effective, but caution must be exercised with the choice of chemicals on certain metal surfaces.

3. *Strainers*—Regular cleaning of strainer screens keeps pressure losses in liquid systems to a minimum, thus saving pumping energy. It may be possible to replace fine-mesh strainer baskets with large mesh, without endangering the operation of the system. This again will reduce the pressure loss in the system and save pumping energy.

4. *Ducts*—Periodic opening and cleaning of the inside of ducts, plenum chambers, air-handling units, etc., to remove residually deposited dust and particulate matter. This will assist in keeping down the duty of the air filter, and maximizing the period between air filter servicing.

5. *Registers*—Periodically check for accumulation of material or other foreign matter behind registers. Check also the register seal to the duct, to ensure that all the conditioned air louvres are in the direction required.

Adjustable registers should be checked for setting, as these are sometimes moved by accident or by unauthorized personnel.

ELECTRIC MOTORS

Inspection of electric motors will cover the following:
1. Check electric starter contactors, and loose wire connections.
2. Using a meter, check the starting load and running load against rated loads.
3. Adjust the belt tension to a slight slackness on the top side.
4. Align the belt to avoid damage to belts, bearings, and excessive electrical consumption.

5. Check bearings for wear, dust and dirt.
6. Check internal insulation to see that it is free of oil.
7. Check commutator slots and motor housing for dust and good air circulation.
8. Examine fusing and current limiting devices for protection while starting and then while running.
9. Check brushes for wear.

LEAKS – STEAM, WATER, AND AIR

The importance of leakage cannot be understated. If a plant has many leaks, this may be indicative of a low standard of operation involving the loss not only of steam, but also water, condensate, compressed air, etc.

If, for example, a valve spindle is worn, or badly packed, giving a clearance of 0.010 inch between the spindle, for a spindle of ¾-inch diameter, the area of leakage will be equal to a 3/32-inch diameter hole. Table 9-3 illustrates fluid loss through small holes:

Table 9-3. Fluid Loss Through Small Holes

| Diameter of Hole | Steam – lb/hour | | Water – gals/hour | | Air SCFM |
	100 psig	300 psig	20 psig	100 psig	80 psig
1/16"	14	33	20	45	4
1/8"	56	132	80	180	16
3/16"	126	297	180	405	36
1/4"	224	528	320	720	64

Although the plant may not be in full production for every hour of the entire year (i.e., 8760 hours), the boiler plant water systems and compressed air could be operable. Losses through leakage are usually, therefore, of a continuous nature.

THERMAL INSULATION

Whatever the pipework system, there is one fundamental—it should be adequately insulated. Table 9-4 gives a guide to the degree of insulation required. Obviously there are a number of

Table 9-4. Pipe Heat Losses

Pipe Dia Inches	Surface Temp°F	Insulation Thickness Inches	Heat Loss (BTU/Ft/Hr)		Insulation Efficiency
			Uninsulated	Insulated	
4	200	1½	300	70	76.7
	300	2	800	120	85.0
	400	2½	1500	150	90.0
6	200	1½	425	95	78.7
	300	2	1300	180	85.8
	400	2½	2000	195	90.25
8	200	1½	550	115	79.1
	300	2	1500	200	86.7
	400	2½	2750	250	91.0

types of insulating materials with different properties and at different costs, each one of which will give a variancy return on capital. Table 9-4 is based on a good asbestos or magnesia insulation, but most manufacturers have cataloged data indicating various benefits and savings that can be achieved with their particular product.

STEAM TRAPS

The method of removing condensate is through steam trapping equipment. Most plants will have effective trapping systems. Others may have problems with both the type of traps and the effectiveness of the system.

The problems can vary from the wrong type of trap being installed, to air locking, or steam locking. A well-maintained trap system can be a great steam saver. A bad system can be a notorious steam waster, particularly where traps have to be bypassed or are leaking.

Therefore, the key to efficient trapping of most systems is good installation and maintenance. To facilitate the condensate removal, the pipes should slope in the direction of steam flow. This has two obvious advantages in relationship to the removal of condensate; one is the action of gravity, and the other the pushing action of the steam flow. Under these circumstances the strategic siting of the traps and drainage points is greatly simplified.

One common fault that often occurs at the outset is installing the wrong size traps. Traps are very often ordered by the size of the pipe connection. Unfortunately the pipe connection size has nothing whatsoever to do with the capacity of the trap. The discharge capacity of the trap depends upon the area of the valve, the pressure drop across it, and the temperature of the condensate.

It is therefore worth recapping exactly what a steam trap is. It is a device that distinguishes between steam and water and automatically opens a valve to allow the water to pass through but not the steam. There are numerous types of traps with various characteristics. Even within the same category of traps, e.g., ball floats or thermoexpansion traps, there are numerous designs, and the following guide is given for selection purposes:

1. Where a small amount of condensate is to be removed an expansion or thermostatic trap is preferred.

2. Where intermittent discharge is acceptable and air is not a large problem, inverted bucket traps will adequately suffice.

3. Where condensate must be continuously removed at steam temperatures, float traps must be used.

4. When large amounts of condensate have to be removed, relay traps must be used. However, this type of steam trap is unlikely to be required for use in the food industry.

To insure that a steam trap is not stuck open, a weekly inspection should be made and corrective action taken. Steam trap testing can utilize several methods to insure proper operation:

- Install heat sensing tape on trap discharge The color indicates proper operation.

- Place a screw driver or more sophisticated acoustical instrument to the ear lobe with the other end on the trap. If the trap is a bucket-type, listen for the click of the trap operating.

CONTROL DEVICES

The functional operation of control equipment is of no use unless the equipment operates correctly at the required set point. Periodic checking and recalibration of all control equipment is an essential aspect of energy conservation.

1. *Thermostats*—In many cases, thermostats can be checked with a mercury-in-glass thermometer, and calibration adjustments can be made. Temperature differential for a signal is not usually adjustable. If it is found that the differential is too great, then usually it is necessary to replace the unit. Checks should be made at both maximum and minimum set positions.

2. *Humidistats*—These can be checked with a wet and dry bulb thermometer. Most units can be easily recalibrated, but operating differentials across a set point cannot usually be adjusted.

3. *Control Valves*—These should be checked and adjusted for operation by monitoring the actuating signal with a known standard,* or by using an auxiliary signal for an alternative corrected source.

ADJUSTMENTS

1. *Actuators*—These should be checked for operation (and repetition of operation) from a signal. Length of stroke, or angle of arc should be checked to ensure full operational movement.

2. *Linkages*—Check for ease of motion; lubricate fulcrum and check for heat. Check locking devices on adjustable linkages and make sure that they are in the original position determined during the testing and balancing of the system.

3. *Motor Drives*—These are used for the control of some

---

* Direct acting valves—mercury/glass thermometer
  Pneumatic valves—pressure gauge
  Electrically operated valves—ammeter/voltmeter.

types of valves, dampers, etc. Check for length of stroke/ angle of arc, security of fixing, and adjust where required,

4. *Manual Dampers*—Check that these are set at positions determined during the testing and balancing of the system. Check for leakages around the spindle, and check that the quadrant permits full open/close operation of the blade. Check that the blades give a tight shut-off.

5. *Registers*—Check that these are set to discharge the air in the direction required. Make sure that short-circuiting of delivered conditioned air into the return air system *does not* occur.

10

Case Study: Energy Audit For Educational Facilities

by JOHN BAUMGARTEL
Energy Conservation and Management Division
New Mexico State Office of Energy

INTRODUCTION

Over 60 million Americans, about one in four, are directly involved in the education process.[1] Saving energy in schools is a highly visible project, many people will see the work being done.

Many schools were designed and built before the 1973 oil embargo, and, as a result, the first-cost considerations greatly outweighed the effects of operating costs. A great many of our schools are simple buildings with very unsophisticated heating and ventilation systems allowing little or no opportunity to change the control settings to save utility costs.

In addition to building design limitations, the educational funding process does not lend itself to capital modifications for energy efficiency. Capital projects tend to get funding which increase the space for educational program areas and those which might reduce utility bills do not get funded. This, combined with poorly trained maintenance personnel, leaves the schools' administrators in a difficult position to save energy.

The Federal government has realized that schools are in this dilemma, rising utility bills and no funding available to upgrade inefficient buildings. The National Energy Act signed by President Carter November 9, 1978, allocates not less than 900 million dollars to identify those schools needing assistance and to design, purchase, and install the equipment to make them efficient. These dollars must be matched by state or local funds and the regulations[2] are quite stringent concerning the information upon which grants are based.

As a whole, energy audits in schools identify energy wasteful buildings, instruct their operators in the efficient operation and maintenance of the building, and identify attractive energy retrofit projects the costs of which may be partially borne by the Federal government. The benefits of these audits are retaining school dollars in educational programs rather than in utility budgets and reducing the 5% of the nation's heating bill attributable to educational facilities.[3]

HOW DOES ONE STUDY THE ENERGY USE IN SCHOOLS?

The total square footage of educational facilities in the United States was estimated in 1977 to be over seven billion square feet.[4] To accomplish energy audits on this huge building sector would require a tremendous number of manhours of effort. How does the structure of schools lend itself to energy audits?

Elementary and secondary schools have the same elements appearing in every one, and, furthermore, each of these elements has similarities in energy use levels. Each high school in the country has, for example, one or more classrooms, a gymnasium, a library, and administration area, etc. One way to examine schools is to examine each of these elements and combine the results. Two methods using this approach are the "workbook" and the "computer audit." The workbook approach leads the auditor through a step-by-step calculation procedure in which hidden factors govern the results for each school element. The computer audit approach requires the auditor to collect certain information about each building element from which the energy use features can be calculated.

The ultimate and most productive energy analysis requires the full participation of an engineer. This effort will be required before any dollars will be spent on capital modifications. The workbook or computer audit in no way replaces the engineer's analysis, but allows the use of paraprofessionals and a systematized audit to identify the facilities for which the engineer's analysis is most likely to uncover cost-effective retrofits.

This chapter will describe one computer audit that is available for use in elementary and secondary schools. The computer program was developed by Educational Facilities Laboratory, Inc. under contracts with the Federal Energy Administration and later with the Department of Energy. A method for collecting the data, running the program, and using the output reports will be presented along with an illustrative example from New Mexico's Public School Energy Audit Program.

The energy audit procedure described in this chapter includes the following:
1. Data Collection
   - Scheduling and Introduction
   - Data Prepared in Advance by School Personnel
   - Auditor Visit
   - Other Data Collection
2. Data Analysis
   - Selection of Method
   - Data Editing and Correction
   - GAP 4 Program
3. Reporting Results
   - To School Administration
   - For Federal Grants Eligibility

PROGRAM BACKGROUND

The Educational Facilities Laboratory (EEL) after studying the available algorythms used in analyzing energy consumption in buildings, realized that a complete ASHRAE-type analysis for a school would be beyond their cost parameters. A large sample of school buildings was selected and their characteristics summarized. Statistically they fell into three generic categories, pre-World War II schools, post-World War II finger plans schools, and artificial environment schools. Using the Meriwether program, each generic type was studied carefully using sample schools from different climate-design zones. It was discovered that the consumption for a school could be accurately predicted from a few key data elements. For example, the date of construction and a code indicating that unit ventilators are used for classroom heating is sufficient information for the computer to make an accurate guess of the electrical and gas consumption. The date of construction is used to identify the generic type from which a baseline energy use can be determined, and the use of unit ventilators adds a watts-per-square-foot correction. The result is a statistical energy use for the school if it were operated in a normally efficient manner.

The GAP 4 version incorporates a survey of capital modifications which may prove to be cost-effective for the school. The cost for each modification varies from state to state and must be established and introduced into the program. The savings in electrical consumption and cost are calculated for each modification in each building space. The payback in years is calculated for three rates of fuel escalation and for two methods of financing, pay-as-you-go and sold bonds.

CAPITAL MODIFICATIONS CONSIDERED BY GAP 4

1. Replace existing lighting with (1) improved flourescent, or (2) high-intensity discharge type.
2. Damper the gravity relief vents.
3. Weatherstrip and/or caulk windows.
4. Replace glass with insulated panels.
5. Double glaze windows.
6. Increase roof insulation by adding (1) blow wool to attic, (2) batts above existing ceiling, (3) rigid insulation at next reroofing, (4) suspended ceiling with batts.
7. Add radiation setback by thermostat.

8. Add air system setback.
9. Eliminate multizone overlap.
10. Replace absorption chillers with centrifugal units.
11. Install separate domestic hot water system.
12. Install modular boiler(s).
13. Modify pumps and controls for sequenced or variable speed operation.
14. Cover swimming pool.

CODE OPERATION COSTS

Education Facilities Laboratory, Inc. will process Elementary Schools (PS-41 Forms) for $50.00 each and Secondary Schools (PS-42 Forms) for $75.00 each. Running schools, including key entry, costs less than $2.00 each when undertaken on a large number of schools, more than 200.

DATA COLLECTION

This section includes the major steps that must be taken to gather the data to calibrate and run the Public Schools Energy Conservation Service (PSECS) energy analysis program, PSECS GAP 4, which was developed under Federal grant by Educational Facilities Laboratory, Inc., 3000 Sand Hill Road, Menlo Park, CA 94025.

INTRODUCTION AND SCHEDULING

Introduce the energy audit program to the school personnel. It is always best to contact the district office before talking to the school representative. Describe the federal program and other goals of the audit and indicate that the audit will uncover ways in which the school can be operated to save energy and dollars. Get confirmation for the date and time your auditor will visit the school, and inform the school staff that the auditor will need to visit mechanical-electrical rooms and that it would be most convenient to have a (the) custodian assigned to unlock doors and explain the systems. Finally specify the information that school personnel must prepare in advance of the auditor's visit.

INFORMATION PREPARED IN ADVANCE
BY SCHOOL PERSONNEL

Ask the principal or school energy manager to prepare the following and have them ready when the auditor arrives:

1. *Plot Plan*—An 8½" by 11" sketch showing the parcel of land and the outlines of each building.
2. *Floor Plan*—An 8½" by 11" sketch of the floor plan of each building. The dates of construction of buildings or parts of buildings must be indicated, and the area in square feet of each room must be indicated. The total area in square feet should be indicated for each building. The school staff may have building plans from which the areas may be taken, or may request the shop or industrial arts class to take on the project of preparing the floor plans.
3. *Energy Consumption Data*—The total 12-month consumption data for each fuel type and the units by which it is measured. The school representative can request this from his business office, district office or from the utility itself. If more than one school is to be audited, the 12-month data for each school must be for the same period as all other schools. Along with each energy type, the rate schedule should be submitted.

Beside providing data that would take the auditor much extra time to collect, asking school staff to provide the above items has the effect of including them in the program and encouraging them to look at their buildings and utility bills.

AUDITOR VISIT TO SCHOOL

The auditor should arrive at the school very nearly at the specified time, and, if he will be late, the school should be notified. The auditor should have a clipboard, a camera, a hand-held calculator, a tape measure (6-foot), blank data collection forms (PS-42 form for secondary school and PS-41 form for elementary school), and instructions for completing forms. Forms and instructions can be obtained from Educational Facilities Laboratory, Inc.

1. *Principal's Meeting*—The auditor should first meet with the principal and energy officer to collect the prepared data and ask for a place to use as a base—often the teachers' lounge or a conference room is best. Interview the principal to get these data:
   - ADA (average daily attendances)
   - Schedules of use for various building subspaces
   - Boiler operation.
2. *Quick Walk Through*—Walk quickly through the building and stop at base.
3. *Determine Plan*—Plan the order in which you will examine the facilities and mark your floor plan to indicate dates of construction of each general area. Ask custodian to show you the mechanical rooms and which space each heats.
4. *Building Examination*—Proceed carefully through the school, filling in the line of information on the data form as you go through each space. Ask the custodian to open locked doors if required. Check for accuracy the first few room areas indicated on the floor plan. If they are accurate, only spot check the remainder; however, if they are not accurate, you must either measure as you go or work with architectural plans to complete this information. Do not accept the custodian's explanations unless he proves to be very knowledgeable. Quite often custodians have only been assigned the building a short while or have not really been given the authority to change or adjust the HVAC systems controls, so they really do not understand these systems.

   Record boiler and chiller sizes. Establish "watts-per-square-foot" for each space by counting bulbs and dividing by space square footage. The custodian can usually tell you the wattage of inaccessible bulbs. Determine ratings of special equipment, such as forges and kilns. Establish the wattage of outdoor lighting used for sports, security, parking, etc.

   Double check the form to make sure that all information is recorded. Go back and record anything missed on the first time through.

5. *Closing Meeting with Principal*—Stop back to speak with the principal to ask any last questions and to thank him for his assistance. If possible, let him know when he will see the report.

6. *Take Photograph*—Take one photograph of the main entrance face of the building. This photograph serves two purposes, first it improves the appearance of the report and second it will serve as a memory refresher to an auditor who has visited 20 or more schools.

7. *Special Notes*—Before leaving the school, record any special comments that you will need to decipher the computer results or comments reflecting situations encountered for which there was no way to record the information. For example, record: wall and roof constructions for which there are no codes; notes to describe metering arrangements which will not allow actual and calculated energy uses to be compared.

OTHER DATA COLLECTION

1. *Identify school numbering system*—Find out if there exists a state numbering system for schools. It will save tremendous amounts of confusion if you are able to use an existing, and widely supported, numbering system instead of establishing a new one.

2. *Calibrate cost factors and boiler sizing equation*—Both the cost factors and the boiler sizing parameter in the GAP-4 program have been established based on nationwide statistics. The cost factors should be checked and corrected by a professional cost estimator. The boiler sizing equation is used to size boilers when the boiler rating cannot be determined in the field. (Author's Note: about one out of ten boilers has no rating.) Find out the actual sizes of boilers and compare those with the GAP-4 calculations and correct the equation.

Determine:
- Elevation
- Weather

  Heating and Cooling Degree Days, National Oceanic and Atmospheric Administration, "Climatological Data," Environmental Data and Information Service, Asheville Climatic Center, Asheville, NC, Design Conditions.

  "Engineering Weather Data," Air Force Manual, AFM 88-8, Chapter 6.
- Rate Schedules

  For each district a set of representative rates for each fuel type must be established. Use the schedules submitted by the schools.

DATA ANALYSIS

There are two ways to produce the analysis with the now completed data bank. The first option is to mail the completed forms along with a fee, to Educational Facilities Laboratory, Inc. The second option is to run the program yourself or through a local consulting firm. The method described in this section applies to the second option, you run the program yourself.

OVERVIEW OF THE COMPUTER PROCESSING PHASE

The GAP-4 computer code has two main parts. The first part, called EDIT 4, screens all the school data files and indicates to the operator the existence of data elements missing, out of appropriate range, or out of match with other data elements. The second part, called GAP-4, produces the school and district summary reports. In the following descriptions, card procedures will be used; however, GAP-4 will accommodate tape input as well.

DATA HANDLING

Obtain services to have cards punched from data forms. Establish early the procedures you will use for changing and deleting cards. Prepare a district file deck with district cards first, followed by all the school decks.

Retain a file folder for each school. Keep in the school folder the notes concerning the metering and wall types, as these notes will help you account for anomalous analysis reports. Also, the folder should contain the floor and plot plan, energy consumption figures and rate schedules.

Run the EDIT 4 program against the district file deck. Study the output carefully and identify any data elements that are incorrect. Some data errors can be corrected by studying the information in the school folder; however, others will require a telephone call to the school.

Run the EDIT 4 program against the corrected district data file to establish the correctness. This output will then become the listing of the data to be run on GAP-4.

GAP-4 PROGRAM

Run the GAP-4 program against the corrected district file deck. Study the output done with school file notes and make any final corrections that surface. If necessary, rerun GAP-4 to produce final reports.

CASE STUDY—MEMORIAL MIDDLE SCHOOL

In the fall of 1978 the National Energy Act was finally passed by the Congress. New Mexico began a large-scale public school energy audit program to take advantage of the grants for energy audits included in the Act. This program has been described previously and will not be detailed here.

Twelve energy auditors were hired in November 1978, and trained to collect the GAP-4 data. The training included three days of lecture and two days of field work. Auditors were selected from applicants who had an engineering or architectural degree and experience in the design or modifications of HVAC systems or in energy auditing.

DATA COLLECTION

School personnel were requested to prepare school plot plans and floor plans and to send them to the Energy and Minerals Department before the auditors began. The floor plan for Memorial Middle School is shown in Figure 10-1. Notice that the square footages of all rooms are indicated on the floor plan. This maximized the use of school personnel and minimized the auditor time at the school. The school personnel were also asked to gather and compile their energy consumption figures for June 1977 through July 1978.

Energy and Minerals Department staff scheduled the energy auditor to visit Memorial Middle School on January 9, 1979. This school required the auditor to spend one-half day at the school to complete the PS-42 data form. The auditor followed the procedure described previously and completed the data forms. Figure 10-2 shows the completed PS-42 data form for Memorial Middle School.

Energy and Minerals Department staff collected the other data required to run GAP-4; cost variables for construction were developed by a professional estimator and are not shown here. Heating and cooling degree-days were from the source listed in the section on Other Data Collection. The elevation was also found with the weather data. The public schools in New Mexico have in existence a numbering system, so the district number used was 69 and the school number 31. Figure 10-3 shows the completed district record form for district 69. "TDB," "TWB," "TSB," and "TDW," came from Air Force Manual 88-8. "TDB" is the 10% dry-bulb temperature; "TWB" is the 10% wet-bulb temperature; "TSB" is the 1% wet-bulb temperature; and "TDW" is the 99% winter dry-bulb temperature. These values

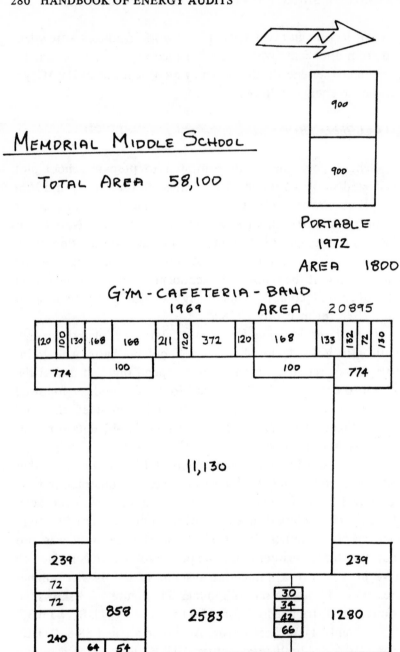

MEMORIAL MIDDLE SCHOOL

TOTAL AREA　58,100

PORTABLE
1972
AREA　1800

900

900

GYM - CAFETERIA - BAND
1969　　　AREA　20895

| 120 | 100 | 130 | 168 | 168 | 211 | 120 | 372 | 120 | 168 | 133 | 182 | 72 | 130 |

| 774 | 100 | | | 100 | 774 |

11,130

| 239 | | 239 |

72					
72	858	2583	30 34 42 66	1280
240	64 54			

Figure 10-1. Floor Plan for

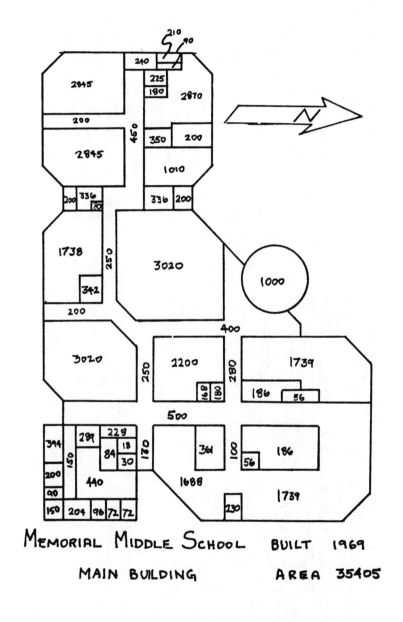

MEMORIAL MIDDLE SCHOOL   BUILT 1969

MAIN BUILDING   AREA 35405

Memorial Middle School

PS 42
SECONDARY FORM

The base year for this form is: 7 7 7 9
If another base year is used, enter here: [ ]

DISTRICT

A GENERAL

	SCHOOL NAME	GRADES HOUSED	TOTAL FLOOR AREA SQ. FT.	PSECS USE ONLY		REGULAR SESSION		SUMMER SESSION	
						AVERAGE DAILY ATTEND.	CLASS DAYS	AVERAGE DAILY ATTEND.	CLASS DAYS
0 0 6 7 0 3 1	MEMORIAL MIDDLE SCH	6-8	58100			475	180		

B

HOT WATER FOOD SERVICE ENERGY USE

FOOD SERVICE

SERV. HW	FUEL	# DAILY FULL PREP MEALS	# DAILY WARM UP MEALS
0 3		22	679

POOL

HEAT	OPER.	WATER TEMP.	COVER	SURFACE AREA SQ. FT.	# DAYS HEATED

ELECTRICITY

BASE YEAR USAGE KWH	DEMAND	PRESENT COST / KWH
323820		

PRIMARY FUEL

TYPE	BASE YEAR USAGE	PRESENT UNIT PRICE
23	7192	

SECONDARY FUEL

TYPE	BASE YEAR USAGE	PRESENT UNIT PRICE

SITE LIGHTING

INSTL. KW	H/W FALL	H/W WINTER	H/W SPRING	H/W SUMMER

C

CENTRAL BOILERS & CHILLERS

BOILERS

TYPE	NUMBER	FUEL 1	FUEL 2	COMB. EFFECT	INPUT RATING LEAD (MBH)	# DAYS LEAD FIRED
GROUP 1	0 6					
GROUP 2	0 7					
GROUP 3	0 8					
GROUP 4	0 9					

CHILLERS

TYPE	NUMBER	TOWER FUEL	RATED TONS

SPECIAL EQUIPMENT

FUEL	INPUT RATING KBTU or KW	TOTAL HOURS REG. SESSION	TOTAL HOURS SUMMER SESSION
KILNS / FORGES	1	11	10
KILNS / FORGES			
KILNS / FORGES			
OTHER			

PARKING

SECURITY

ATHLETICS

OTHER

PSECS PUBLIC SCHOOLS ENERGY CONSERVATION SERVICE

PLEASE REFER TO THE INSTRUCTION MANUAL BEFORE STARTING WORK ON THIS FORM.

BOX B

COL. 11   SERVICE HOT WATER
Boiler and/or electric heater(s) 1
Boiler and/or gas heater(s) 2
Boiler and/or oil heater(s) 3
Boiler only source 8

COL. 12   FUELS
Electricity 1
Natural gas or LPG 2
Oil 3
Coal 4
Wood, steam 5

COL. 21   POOL HEATING
Electric pool heater 1
Natural gas pool heater 2
Oil pool heater 3
By Boiler Group 1 5
By Boiler Group 2 6
By Boiler Group 3 7
By Boiler Group 4 8

COL. 32   POOL COVER
No cover .... blank
Cover 1

BOX C

COL. 11
Steam 1
Hot water 2
Steam boiler converting to hot water 3
Modular steam 4
Modular hot water 5

COL. 18, 19, 29, 33   FUELS
(See Box B12 for fuel codes)

COL. 20   BOILER OPERATION
Boilers used only as needed 1
Lead on, lag as needed 2
All on line during load period 3

COL. 51, 65   FUEL TYPE
All electric 10
Natural gas, therms 21
Natural gas, CCF 22
Natural gas, MCF 23
LPG, gallons 25
No. 2 Fuel Oil gallons 31
No. 4 Fuel Oil gallons 32
No. 5 Fuel Oil gallons 33
No. 6 Fuel Oil gallons 34
Hard Coal, tons 41
Soft Coal, tons 42
Street Steam, MLBS 51

COL. 26   CHILLER TYPE
Electric reciprocating 1
Electric centrifugal 2
Absorption 3
Steam turbine 4
Gas engine 5

COL. 28   COOLING TOWER
Cooling tower 1
Air-cooled 2

● Indicates starting point for that item only. All other items are right justified.

D BUILDING CONSTRUCTION MECHANICAL SYSTEMS SCHEDULE

Space	Line	Descr.: Year Opened	Plan	# Ext. Classrms	# Bldgs	Floor Area Sq. Ft.	Roof: Roof Area Sq. Ft.	Skylight Area Sq. Ft.	Roof Code	Wall: Code	Ext. Doors	Lights: Watts/Sq. Ft.	Type	Window Area: GL-BLK DBL-GL Sq. Ft.	Single Glass Sq. Ft.	Cond.	Temp.: Day	Night	Mechanical Systems: Non Air Type	Non Air Heat	Air Supply	Air Exhaust	Air Heat	Cool % Cooled	Cool Source	Cool Reheat	# Air Units	Mon.–Fri. Reg.: Days/Wk.	Hrs/Day	Summer: Days/Year	Days/Wk.	Hr./Day	% Used	Sat.–Sun.: Days/Year	Hrs/Day	% Used	Evening: Nights/Year	Hrs/Day	% Used
AUDITORIUM	1 1																																						
GYMNASIUM	2 1	69	4			11130	11130		41	56		1.1	3		100	1	68	55	2	4								5	06										
SHOWER/LOCKER	3 1	69	4			4210	4210		41	56		1.3	2				68	60	2	4								5	06										
KITCHEN	6 0	69	6			1460	1460		53	56		1.6	2				70	60	3	4								5	04										
CAFETERIA	6 1	69	6			2583	2583		53	58		2.2	2		198	1	68	55	3	4								5	03										
BAND RM	6 6	69	3			1512	1512		53	56		2.0	2				68	55	3	4								5	05										
CONNECTING CORRIDOR	8 0																																						
GEN'L AREA 1	8 1	69	3	22	2	35405	35405		53	56		1.4			60	1	68	60	3	4								5	07										
GEN'L AREA 2	8 2																																						
GEN'L AREA 3	8 3																																						
GEN'L AREA 4	8 4																																						
PORTABLES	8 9	72	1	02	1	1800	1800		52	57	2	1.6	2		40	1	68	60	3	4								5	06										

ANSWER FOR TYPICAL CLASSROOM

TOTAL FLOOR AREA (MUST = A 38): 58100

PSECS PUBLIC SCHOOLS ENERGY CONSERVATION SERVICE

PLEASE REFER TO THE INSTRUCTION MANUAL BEFORE STARTING WORK ON THIS FORM.

BOX D

COL. 13 — PLAN TYPE
(Special Spaces Lines 11 & 21)
- Freestanding ... 1
- Attached by short side ... 2
- Attached by long side ... 3
- Attached by two sides ... 4
- Partially enclosed (3 or more sides) ... 5
- Attached by 3 sides or fully enclosed ... 6
- Basement ... 7

(Gen'l Areas Lines 81 to 89)
- Single-loaded corridor ... 1
- Double-loaded corridor ... 2
- Compact, big room, pods ... 3
- As 3 but with interior courts ... 4

COL. 33, 35 — ROOF, WALL INSULATION
See Appendices 1 and 2 for codes.

COL. 41 — LIGHTING TYPE
- Incandescent ... 1
- Fluorescent ... 2
- Mercury-vapor, other HID ... 3

COL. 49 — WINDOW CONDITION
- Tight fit, little air leakage ... 1
- Medium fit, some air leakage ... 2
- Loose fit, great air leakage ... 3

NON-OUTSIDE AIR SYSTEMS
COL. 54 — TYPE
- Radiators, radiant panels ... 1
- Unit heater(s), fan coil unit(s) ... 2
- Furnace(s) ... 3
- Heat pump(s) ... 6

COL. 55 & 58 — HEAT SOURCE
- Hot water or steam, Boiler Group 1 ... 1
- Hot water or steam, Boiler Group 2 ... 2
- Electric coils ... 3
- Direct-fired gas ... 4
- Direct-fired oil ... 5
- Small packaged boilers ... 7
- Hot water or steam, Boiler Group 3 ... 8
- Hot water or steam, Boiler Group 4 ... 9
- Not heated (58 only) ... blank

AIR SYSTEMS
COL. 56 — SUPPLY
- Windows only ... blank
- Transfer air ... 1
- House fans ... 2
- Unit ventilators ... 4
- Single duct, single zone ... 5
- Heat pump(s) ... 6
- Multizone, dual duct ... 7
- Variable volume ... 8

COL. 57 — EXHAUST
- Windows only ... blank
- Gravity relief ... 1
- Powered fans ... 3
- Transfer air ... 4
- Return to system + ducted ... 5
- Return to system – plenum ... 6

COL. 58 — HEAT SOURCE
(See COL. 55)

COOLING
COL. 59 — PER CENT COOLED
- 0 to 10 per cent ... blank
- 11 to 25 per cent ... 1
- 26 to 50 per cent ... 2
- 51 to 75 per cent ... 3
- 76 to 100 per cent ... 4

COL. 60 — COOLING SOURCE
- Direct expansion (DX) ... 1
- Chilled water from chiller #1 ... 2
- Chilled water from chiller #2 ... 3
- Evaporative (swamp) cooler(s) ... 5
- Heat pump ... 6
- Chilled water from chiller #3 ... 8
- Chilled water from chiller #4 ... 9

COL. 61 — REHEAT
- Steam ... 1
- Hot water ... 2
- Electricity ... 3
- Hot refrigerant gas ... 4

COL. 71, 75 80 — PER CENT USED
- 1 to 25 per cent ... 1
- 26 to 50 per cent ... 2
- 51 to 75 per cent ... 3
- 76 to 100 per cent ... 4

Figure 10-2. Completed PS-42 Form for Memorial Middle School

PSECS   PUBLIC SCHOOLS ENERGY CONSERVATION SERVICE   PS 40

General Instructions

It is essential that all data forms be filled out accurately and completely. Before filling out forms PS41 and PS42, please read the instruction manual carefully.

Instructions for Completing Form PS40

1. *Complete lines A, B, & C of the DISTRICT DATA RECORD* on this page. Item A53, Cooling Degree Days, and item A57, Heating Degree Days, should be completed if at all possible. Cooling Degree Days may be omitted if no air condition is reported.

4. On the back of this form are the Rate Schedule form and instructions. *Please read the instructions carefully and fill out the form accordingly.*

5. *Send all forms (PS40/41/42), floor plans as requested in the instruction manual, and check,* to:

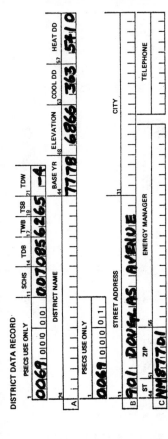

PSECS

PS 40

PSECS USE ONLY	EFFECTIVE DATE MO. DAY YR.	RATE BLOCK #1 COST	LIMIT	RATE BLOCK #2 COST	LIMIT	RATE BLOCK #3 COST	LIMIT	RATE BLOCK #4 COST	LIMIT	RATE BLOCK #5 COST	LIMIT	RATE BLOCK #6 COST
	11 13 15	18	22	29	33	40	44	51	55	62	66	73
0 0 5 1 0 0 0 1 1 1 ELECTRIC RATES	0 9 01 78	.045	2,000.031	31.75		101.61						
0 0 6 1 0 0 0 1 2 GAS RATES	1 30 78	2.59										
0 0 6 1 0 0 0 1 3 OIL RATE	01 1 57 78	0.41										
1 0 0 0 1 4 COAL RATE												
0 0 6 1 0 0 0 1 5 OTHER FUEL RATES	01 1 57 78	0.36										

INSTRUCTIONS FOR FILLING OUT RATE SCHEDULE

Enter on this form the rate schedule or flat rate for fuel and/or electricity in your district. If individual schools are billed differently, please follow these instructions:

1) If one or more schools have a unique flat rate, or are billed according to a flat rate while the rest of the district is billed according to a rate schedule, enter the "Present Unit Cost" in the appropriate columns in Box B on the PS41/42 form for each of those schools. Enter on this form the flat rate or rate schedule which applies to the rest of the district.

2) If one or more schools are billed according to a rate schedule different from that of the majority of district schools, enclose a copy of that schedule indicating the school(s) to which it applies. Enter on this form the rate schedule which applies to the majority of your district schools.

The rate schedule form is divided into rate blocks which are defined as follows: A given number of fuel or electricity units billed at the same rate or cost constitutes a RATE BLOCK. Each rate schedule is composed of two or more rate blocks.

Columns 11 — 16   Effective Date
Enter the month, day, and year in which the rate schedule became effective.

Columns 18 — 21   Rate Block 1, Cost
Enter the fuel or electricity rate for the first rate block. Be sure to enter the figure above the appropriate arrow head. *Decimal points occupy a full space.*

Columns 22 — 28   Rate Block 1, Limit
Enter the figure which marks the upper limit of the first rate block. Example: If the cost is $.04 for the first 200,000 units, enter 200,000 as the limit.

Columns 29 — 32   Rate Block 2, Cost
Enter the fuel or electric rate for the second rate block.

Columns 33 — 39   Rate Block 2, Limit
Enter the figure which marks the upper limit of the second rate block. This should be a cumulative limit. For example: If the cost in Block 1 applies to the first 200,000 units, and the cost in block 2 applies to the next 400,000 units, the limit for block 2 is 600,000 units.

Enter data for as many rate blocks as are appropriate, following the instructions given for Rate Block 2.

Figure 10-3. District Record Form for Memorial Middle School

can be found in the Air Force Manual AFM 88-8. The abbreviations are from the data form, PS-40.

The energy auditor who visited Memorial Middle School recorded two notes describing unusual conditions. The first indicated that the main building was originally designed for "open classroom concept" teaching and was later partitioned into classrooms. He indicated that he had made the best approximation possible to record the "number of exterior classrooms" required in columns 14 and 15 for General Area 1. He also indicated that 267 of the "fully prepared meals," Box B columns 13 to 16, were served to students from an adjacent elementary school.

DATA ANALYSIS

The data record on the PS-42 form for Memorial Middle School was key entered along with that for the other schools in the district and the district record form. This data was then processed by the EDIT-4 program and found to be complete and ready for GAP-4 processing.

The GAP-4 computer program was installed on the University of New Mexico IBM 360 computers. The GAP-4 program was run against the data for district 69. The output is described in the following paragraphs.

1. *PS8C—Summary of Capital Modifications*—The PS8C report is shown in Figure 10-4. This report summarizes the capital modifications appropriate for each space of Memorial Middle School. From the left, the report lists the modification, the estimated capital cost, the total dollars saved per year, the cost and units saved for electricity and fuel, respectively, and the payback for each of two methods of payment for three fuel escalation rates. The list of all the modifications considered in GAP 4 along with the cost of each is shown in Figure 10-5.

2. *PS-8—Self-Help Audit Program*—Figure 10-6 shows the PS-8 report for Memorial Middle School. The report is self-explanatory. This report compares the actual consumption to the "Guideline," the energy consumption that would be required if Memorial Middle were operated at normal efficiency.

3. *PS8B—Self-Audit Criteria*—The PS8B report is shown in

Figure 10-7. This report shows the operating schedule that would allow Memorial Middle to operate at the "Guideline" consumption indicated in the PS-8 report. The notes following the operating schedule indicate operating conditions and maintenance procedures which can be employed at Memorial Middle to insure that the "Guideline" consumption levels can be reached.

4. *PS-5—PSECS Summary Report on Energy Conservation* —This report, shown in Figure 10-8, is a summary for district 69. From the left, this report lists the school, grade levels and square footage. For electricity and fuel, the report lists the actual and "Guideline" use, the savings, the percent savings and the dollar savings. The savings are totaled for each fuel type and school.

ENERGY AUDIT RESULTS

The GAP-4 report presents the level of consumption that Memorial Middle School will require to maintain an efficient level of operation. The operating schedule and notes in the PS8B report are the methods to reduce current consumption to the "Guideline" level. In addition, the capital modifications presented in the PS8C represent a preliminary list of options to be considered by the school for installation to reduce consumption below the guideline level.

The GAP-4 district summary, the PS-5 report, can be used by district staff to evaluate the performance of the schools in their district. In New Mexico, the schools' operating budgets are paid by the state through the Public School Finance Division. The Public School Finance Division intends to use the GAP-4 district summary reports to help establish the budget requirements for utilities in each district. Districts will then be funded only to the level of the "Guideline" values. This, needless to say, will be a powerful force to get school personnel to employ the GAP-4 recommendations and reduce the energy use in their schools.

AUDIT COSTS

The energy audits of public schools using the GAP-4 pro-

PS-8C   PSECS SURVEY OF MODIFICATIONS FOR
31   MEMORIAL MIDDLE SCH

AREA 58100. SQUARE FEET   4/1/79   59

MODIFICATIONS AND PAYOFF PERIODS

MODIFICATION	ESTIMATED CAPITAL COST DOLLARS	ESTIMATE ANNUAL TOTAL COST DOLLARS	ELECTRICITY COST	ELECTRICITY KWH	HEATING COST	HEATING FUEL UNITS SAVINGS	PAYOFF PERIOD AT FUEL ESCALATION OF 0 PERCENT PAYG	0 PERCENT BOND	10 PERCENT PAYG	10 PERCENT BOND	20 PERCENT PAYG	20 PERCENT BOND
GYMNASIUM (1969)												
REDUCE GLASS BY 50. PCT	$ 335.	$ 12.	$ 0.	0.	$ 12.	7.	28.0	44.5	14.0	17.8	10.3	12.6
SET DAY STATS AT 65.		$ 11.	$ 0.	0.	$ 11.	6.						
MARGINAL HR/DAY-REG SES		$ 72.	$ 72.	2326.	$ 0.	0.						
SHOWER/LOCKER (1953)												
REMOVE 53. 40W TUBES	$ 95.	$ 104.		3350.	$ -19.	-11.						
OR												
RADIATION SETBACK *	$ 320.	$ 114.	$ 0.	0.	$ 114.	67.	2.8	4.5	2.6	3.9	2.4	3.5
MARGINAL HR/DAY-REG SES		$ 23.	$ 23.	642.	$ 0.	0.						
KITCHEN (1969)												
SET DAY STATS AT 68.		$ 0.	$ 0.	0.	$ 0.	0.						
MARGINAL HR/DAY-REG SES		$ 14.	$ 14.	444.	$ 0.	0.						
CAFETERIA (1969)												
REDUCE GLASS BY 50. PCT	$ 663.	$ 24.	$ 0.	0.	$ 24.	14.	28.0	44.5	14.0	17.8	10.3	12.6
MARGINAL HR/DAY-REG SES		$ 33.	$ 33.	1080.	$ 0.	0.						
MUSIC ROOM (1969)												
MARGINAL HR/DAY-REG SES		$ 18.	$ 18.	575.	$ 0.	0.						
GENERAL AREA (1969)												
REDUCE GLASS BY 50. PCT	$ 4422.	$ 158.	$ 0.	0.	$ 158.	93.	26.0	44.5	14.0	17.8	10.3	12.6
MARGINAL HR/DAY-REG SES		$ 225.	$ 225.	7252.	$ 0.	0.						

BOND = MONIES BORROWED AT 4.9 PER CENT FOR 20 YEARS

PAYG = PAY AS YOU GO FINANCING FROM OPERATING BUDGET

* = CONTROL MODIFICATIONS WILL REQUIRE AN ADDITIONAL ONE TIME EXPENDITURE OF APPROXIMATELY $1000 FOR BUILDING WIRING, ETC.

**** = INDICATES PAYOFF PERIOD IN EXCESS OF 99.9 YEARS

FUEL TYPE AND UNITS ARE NATURAL GAS MCF   AT $1.690
                       ELECTRICITY KWH   AT $0.031

Figure 10-4. PS8C Survey of Modifications for Memorial Middle School

```
                    PUBLIC SCHOOLS ENERGY CONSERVATION SERVICE
                    ENERGY MANAGEMENT REPORTS PS-5 AND PS-3
    THESE REPORTS WERE PREPARED ON  4/ 1/79 AT THE REQUEST OF
                              BY              ENERGY & MINERALS
                                                  DEPARTMENT
        901 DOUGLAS AVENUE                   SANTA FE, NEW MEXICO, 87503
                      NM   87701            PHONE 505-827-2471
    THE FOLLOWING RENOVATION COSTS WERE USED TO ESTIMATE CAPITAL COSTS
    FOR THE PS-RC SURVEY OF MODIFICATIONS

            CAPITAL MODIFICATION            COSTING UNIT         COST PER UNIT
```

CAPITAL MODIFICATION	COSTING UNIT	COST PER UNIT
REPLACE EXISTING LIGHTING		
WITH IMPROVED FLUORESCENT	SQUARE FOOT	$ 1.40
WITH HID TYPE SYSTEM	SQUARE FOOT	$ 0.50
DAMPER GRAVITY RELIEFS	SQUARE FOOT	$ 0.10
SEAL WINDOWS	SQUARE FOOT OF WINDOW	$ 1.50
REDUCE GLASS AREA (REPLACE WITH INSULATED PANEL		
PRE-1945 SCHOOL	SQUARE FOOT OF WINDOW	$ 8.37
POST-WAR SCHOOL	SQUARE FOOT OF WINDOW	$ 6.70
DOUBLE-GLAZE WINDOWS		
PRE-1945 SCHOOL	SQUARE FOOT OF WINDOW	$ 15.75
POST-WAR SCHOOL	SQUARE FOOT OF WINDOW	$ 14.00
INCREASE ROOF INSULATION (4 METHODS)		
1. BLOW WOOL INTO ATTIC	SQUARE FOOT OF ROOF	$0.00 + $0.02/R
2. BATTS ABOVE EXIST CEILG	SQUARE FOOT OF ROOF	$0.00 + $0.02/R
3. RIGID INSULATION, REROOF	SQUARE FOOT OF ROOF	$0.67 + $0.09/R
4. SUSPEND CEILING & BATTS	SQUARE FOOT OF ROOF	$0.17 + $0.09/R
RADIATION SETBACK BY THERMOSTAT	BOILER SET	$ 320.00
ADD AIRSYSTEM SETBACK	AIR HANDLING UNIT	$ 32.00
ELIMINATE MULTIZONE OVERLAP	AIR HANDLING UNIT	$ 422.00
REPLACE ABSORPTION CHILLERS		
WITH CENTRIFUGAL UNITS	TON OF COOLING	$ 235.00
INSTALL SEPARATE DOMESTIC		
HOT WATER HEATERS	STUDENT	$ 1.54
INSTALL MODULAR BOILERS	BOILER INPUT MBH	$ 11.50
MODIFY PUMPS FOR SEQUENCED		
OR VARIABLE SPEED OPERATION	BOILER SET	$4800.00
COVER SWIMMING POOL	SQUARE FOOT OF POOL SURFACE	$ 0.70

Figure 10-5. Capital Modifications List

gram are cost-effective. Besides being a basis for current recommendations, the data collected can be updated annually and a new set of "Guidelines" calculated each year. The cost to collect data, key enter it, run EDIT-4, make data corrections, run GAP 4 and administer the project was about $112,000, or $160 per school. This is about 0.4 cents per square foot.

REFERENCES

1. *Energy and Educational Facilities: Costs and Conservation*, Educational Facilities Laboratory, Menlo Park, CA.
2. Department of Energy, "Energy Measure and Energy Audits Grants Programs for Schools and Hospitals and Buildings Owned by Units of Local Government and Public Care Institutions," *Federal Register*, Vol. 44, No. 84, April 2, 1979.
3. John Baumgartel, "Energy Audit for New Mexico's Public Schools," Proceedings of The National Conference on Energy Auditing and Conservation, held March 14 and 15, 1979, unpublished at this date.

```
                    ** PS-8   SELF-HELP AUDIT PROGRAM **
      4/ 1/79
      PS8A  ENERGY CONSERVATION REPORT ON-
                    PLANT NAME        MEMORIAL MIDDLE SCH 6-8
                    STATE ID#            69      31
                    DISTRICT
      AREA   58100. SQUARE FEET              1977/1978 ENROLLMENT    475.
      DURING 1977/1978 PORTIONS OF THIS SCHOOL WERE USED FOR THE
      SCHOOL DAY PLUS
      DURING 1977/1978 THIS SCHOOL WAS USED FOR THE SCHOOL DAY ONLY.
      ***********************************ENERGY SAVINGS**************************
      FOR THIS SCHOOL *PSECS* ESTIMATES THAT ENERGY USE REDUCTIONS OF
                          63.9 PER CENT IN ELECTRICITY
                          68.7 PER CENT IN OTHER FUELS
      ARE POSSIBLE WITHOUT CHANGING EDUCATIONAL OR COMMUNITY USE AND
      WITH LITTLE OR NO ADDITIONAL EXPENDITURE
                                      ACTUAL USE     GUIDELINE      ESTIMATED
                                      1977/1978      1977/1978      SAVINGS

      NATURAL GAS    MCF               7992.          2503.            5489.
                                                                   $ 9276.

      ELECTRICITY    KWH              323820.        116986.         206834.
                                                                   $  6412.

      TOTAL ESTIMATED SAVINGS                                       $ 15688.
      THESE ESTIMATES ARE BASED UPON A COMPARISON OF THIS PLANT WITH
      THE PSECS COMPUTER MODEL ADJUSTED FOR LOCATION AND GENERAL USE.
      UNUSUAL DESIGN FEATURES MAY INVALIDATE THESE FINDINGS.
      *********************************************************************
```

Figure 10-6. PS-8 Self-Audit Report for Memorial Middle School

4. References for PSECS GAP 4:
    a. Phase I Report, Public Schools Energy Conservation Service–FEA Contract C-04-50047-00, October 1975.
    b. Phase II Report, Public Schools Energy Conservation Service–FEA, Contract C-04-50047-01, February 1977.
    c. A Manual for the Operation and Maintenance of the Public Schools Energy Conservation Service, FEA, Contract C-04-50047-01, February 1977.
    Supporting documents for GAP 4 are:
    d. Manager's Manual, Phase III, Public Schools Energy Conservation Service, U.S. Department of Energy Grant EM-78-6-01-5169, November 1978.
    e. Supporting Materials Document, Phase III, Public Schools Energy Conservation Service, U.S. Department of Energy Grant EM-78-6-01-5169, November 1978.
    f. Computer Operator's Manual, Phase III, Public Schools Energy Conservation Service, U.S. Department of Energy Grant EM-78-6-01-5169, November 1978.

```
*****PS8B   SELF-AUDIT CRITERIA FOR MEMORIAL MIDDLE 6-8 *****
```

SPACE TYPE	LIGHTING WATTS/SQ FT ACTUAL / PSECS	SEE HEAT NOTE	HEATING ON SPACE TEMPERATURE ON REGULAR ACTUAL / PSECS	ON SETBACK ACTUAL / PSECS	SYSTEM HOURS PER WEEK ON REGULAR ACTUAL / PSECS	ON SETBACK ACTUAL / PSECS	COOLING SPACE TEMPERATURE ACTUAL / PSECS	SYSTEM HOURS PER WEEK ACTUAL / PSECS
GYMNASIUM	1.1 1.1	2	64.F 65.F	55.F 55.F	38.	130.		
SHOWER/LOCKER	1.3 0.8	2	68.F 68.F	62.F 62.F	39.	130.		
KITCHEN	1.6 1.6	2	70.F 68.F	60.F 60.F	29.	140.		
CAFETERIA	2.2 2.2	2	64.F 64.F	55.F 55.F	33.	145.		
MUSIC ROOM	2.0 2.0	2	68.F 68.F	55.F 55.F	33.	135.		
GENERAL AREA 1969	1.4 1.4	2	68.F 68.F	50.F 50.F	43.	125.		
CORRIDORS	1.4 1.0	2	58.F 60.F	60.F 60.F	43.	125.		
PORTABLES 1972	1.6 1.6	2	63.F 68.F	60.F 60.F	38.	130.		

```
**** NOTES TO TABLE ****
```

NOTE 2. SYSTEM PUT ON NIGHT SETTING FROM END OF DAILY USE TO
START OR WARM UP PERIOD. USE OF DAILY DAMPERS
IF NGT THUS PERMITS SETBACK. HR BEGINS AS EARLY
AS 2 294 IF EXPERIMENTATION INDICATES ADEQUATE BUILD-
ING HEAT REENTION.

AIR SYSTEM OPERATING CONDITIONS

HEATING: SUPPLY OR MIXED AIR TEMPERATURE 60F
SUPPLY AIR: SPECIAL USE SPACES 1.5 CFM/SQ FT
UNIT GENERAL AREAS 1.2 CFM/SQ FT
FRESH AIR: SPECIAL USE SPACES 45 REPORTED
UNIT GENERAL AREAS 7.5 CFM/PUPIL

DEFINITIONS OF TERMS USED

REG = OCCUPIED CONDITIONS, SO-CALLED DAY SETTING.
SETBACK = UNOCCUPIED CONDITIONS, NIGHT SETTING.

```
**** MECHANICAL SYSTEMS ****
```

THIS SECTION CONTAINS SUGGESTIONS FOR REDUCING ENERGY WASTAGE
IN THE MAINTENANCE AND OPERATIONS OF THE MECHANICAL PLANTS.
CAN BE FOUND IN PS-3C TABLE OF MODIFICATIONS. THESE SUGGESTIONS

NON-BOILER HEATING PLANTS-

THESE ARE FAST PICK-UP SYSTEMS WHICH CAN BE OPERATED TO
CLOSELY MATCH THE BUILDING OCCUPANCY. OPERATE EACH
SETTING MORE THAN 35. HOURS PER WEEK. NO UNIT ON DAY

INSPECT, CLEAN, ADJUST AND REPAIR ALL ELEMENTS AT LEAST
ONCE A YEAR.

Figure 10-7. PS8B Self-Audit Criteria for Memorial Middle School

PS-5 PSECS SUMMARY REPORT ON ENERGY CONSERVATION FOR

4/1/79

DISTRICT NAME
DISTRICT ADDRESS   901 DOUGLAS AVENUE N   37701
ENERGY MANAGER
STATE ID#   59

DISTRICT DATA 1977/1978   363. CLG D-D   5410. HTG D-D

PLANT	GRADES	AREA	ELECTRIC ENERGY 1977/1978					FUEL ENERGY 1977/1978					TOTAL SAVINGS
			KBTU/SQ FT/YEAR ACTUAL	GUIDEL	SAVING	PCT	SAVINGS DOLLARS	KBTU/SQ FT/YEAR ACTUAL	GUIDEL	SAVING	PCT	SAVINGS DOLLARS	
MEMORIAL MIDDLE	6-8	58100.	19.02	6.87	12.15	54.	$ 5412.	110.26	34.53	75.73	69.	$ 9276.	$ 15688.
LEGION PARK ELEM	1-5	16451.	18.71	10.41	8.29	44.	$ 1239.	60.12	42.61	11.51	19.	$ 399.	$ 1639.
DOUGLAS ELEMENTA	K-3	10075.	5.97	3.68	2.29	38.	$ 341.	109.95	65.09	44.86	41.	$ 953.	$ 1284.
GALLINAS ELEMENT	4-5	8910.	10.34	5.96	4.38	42.	$ 354.	29.06	29.81	0.00	0.	$ 0.	$ 354.
MORA AVENUE ELEM	K-5	7636.	13.62	10.12	3.50	26.	$ 243.	76.84	43.06	33.77	44.	$ 544.	$ 786.
ROBERTSON HIGH S	7-12	155318.	7.88	6.42	1.46	19.	$ 2074.	91.13	54.74	26.39	29.	$ 8697.	$ 10771.
SAPELLO ELEMENTA	1-5	8614.	3.29	3.29	0.00	0.	$ 0.	109.97	48.61	61.36	56.	$ 1993.	$ 1993.
TOTALS PLANTS (7)							$ 10655.					$ 21862.	$ 32516.

Figure 10-8. PS-5 District Summary Report—District 69

11

Case Study:
Energy Audit
For Hospitals

by NICK CHOKSI
Certified Test & Balance Company, Inc.

The Energy Management program applied by Certified Test & Balance Company (CTB)* is divided into three major categories:

1. Audit
2. Modifications
3. Monitoring

To modify, redesign, or retrofit a building system, a thorough energy audit is necessary. The audit cannot be a "walk-thru" done with a clipboard and pencil, or just sitting at the drawing board with the design drawings. It must be a detailed study through the application of proven engineering, coupled with the actual field measurements of the equipment performance and its operation. Understanding the intended design and operation of each system with the building and how the energy actually is used is critical.

CTB takes full responsibility of any modifications and keeps constant monitoring of consumption and savings. Any

---

* CTB is a technical service firm with management, engineering and installation capabilities.

modifications performed must have a major impact on the quality of the system's performance, and must have a minor effect on the environmental conditions.

AUDIT

Energy audits, simple in concept, actually require complex and thorough research by knowledgeable and competent persons to provide practical and realistic results. Constant consideration of codes and patient comfort is necessary when developing an energy audit for any type of health-care facility.

After extensive audit work, CTB has established the following five major steps for preparing an integrated energy audit:
1. Energy inventory
2. Engineering overview
3. Data collection
4. Analysis
5. Final report

ENERGY INVENTORY

The inventory defines the energy-using functions and the amount of energy used by each. It is very important to acquire an energy consumption history for a facility by plotting at least the past three years of energy consumption. The records of energy used by major equipment such as chillers, boilers, etc., should be available to help make preliminary comparisons for major functions and relate them to the total consumption.

Data more than three years old is usually not available or either it is inaccurate or poorly recorded. Whenever energy records for individual units are not available, they are obtained in the data-collection step.

To compare the energy consumption from one year to the next and to compare individual facilities, it is essential to derive a comparative consumption unit. Although it is possible to compare the energy usage and cost-effectiveness based on the number of beds, patients, staff days, etc., experience has shown that proper comparisons can be achieved when the ratio of total energy in BTU per square foot per year is obtained.

Because of the rapid expansion in the health-care field, 60 to 70 percent of the facilities audited have undergone construction within the previous three-year interval. Usually the cost of energy used during construction phases is included as part of the total cost for the fiscal year, and no separate metering is obtained to evaluate consumption properly. Justifiable corrections are made in the consumption for proper comparisons.

The comparison can also be made based upon the BTU per square foot per degree-day, per day basis. The ratio of BTU per square foot per year is called the Energy Usage Index. The EUI is obtained for all types of energy used.

Due to the variety of space uses in the health-care facilities, such as kitchen, laundry, outpatient care, surgery, etc., various types of ventilation and heating/cooling systems are used. It therefore becomes impossible to use one common BTU/sq ft/ year factor and come up with a standard of comparison.

Each energy source, as well as total consumption, are calculated in the different comparative units, and plotted on the graph as required. Figure 11-1 shows a typical computer printout showing the electrical, fuel, and total consumption for Leila Hospital in Battle Creek, Michigan for the year of 1976.

ENGINEERING OVERVIEW

The engineering overview includes the collection of architectural, mechanical, electrical, and control drawings. Preliminary on-site operations start with a meeting with the chief engineer and his staff to familiarize them with the procedures for data collection and data reporting. It is not practical to conduct a full energy audit without the full cooperation and commitment of the operating engineer and his staff.

Again, because of the expansion phases of most health-care facilities, it is usually not possible to obtain proper historical data. The majority of facilities have several sets of drawings for the same area at each stage of remodeling or change, and yet none of them are up-dated or accurate enough to reflect actual existing conditions.

Understanding and organizing the documents becomes a

ELECTRICAL CONSUMPTION RECORD

LEILA POST HOSP 76

YEAR 1976

MONTH		HEATING DEGREE DAYS	COOLING DEGREE DAYS	ELECTRICAL	
				KWH	MBTU
JAN	29	1420	0	521600	1780221
FEB	30	980	0	524800	1791142
MAR	28	835	0	518400	1769299
APR	29	526	27	611200	2086026
MAY	30	342	4	603200	2058722
JUN	29	18	158	668800	2282614
JUL	31	0	239	777600	2653949
AUG	30	32	161	670400	2288075
SEP	30	185	49	653200	2229372
OCT	32	591	0	601600	2053261
NOV	32	999	0	588800	2009574
DEC	32	1415	0	606400	2069643

GROSS CONDITIONED AREA 262944

GROSS AREA 295595

	COST		
BTU/°/DAY/SQFT	TOT.ELEC.	CENT/KWH	CENTS /SQFT
.146	17106.66	3.2797	5.7872
.206	15064.43	2.8705	5.0963
.256	15596.35	3.0086	5.2763
.440	18526.07	3.0311	6.2674
.671	19112.88	3.1686	6.4659
1.513	20089.31	3.0038	6.7962
1.212	22190.07	2.8537	7.5069
1.337	18196.82	2.7143	6.1560
1.074	19170.60	2.9349	6.4854
.367	16077.59	2.6725	5.4391
.213	15643.94	2.6569	5.2924
.155	16020.65	2.6419	5.4198

Figure 11-1 (a). Electrical Consumption Record—Leila Hospital—1976

```
FUEL CONSUMPTION RECORD
YEAR 1976                    LEILA POST HOSP 76

MONTH        HEATING COOLING       FUEL
             DEGREE  DEGREE
             DAYS    DAYS     MCF       MBTU

  JAN  31   1420        0   10140.38  10545995
  FEB  29    980        0    8427.39   8764486
  MAR  31    835        0    8478.39   8817526
  APR  30    526       27    6347.36   6601254
  MAY  31    342        4    5056.35   5258604
  JUN  30     18      158    4641.39   4827046
  JUL  31      0      239    3931.37   4088625
  AUG  31     32      161    4165.34   4331954
  SEP  30    185       49    4666.38   4853035
  OCT  31    591        0    6166.36   6413014
  NOV  30    999        0    9095.35   9459164
  DEC  31   1415        0    9931.36  10328614


   GROSS CONDITIONED AREA 262944

   GROSS AREA 295595

                              COST
                                      CENTS
BTU/°/DAY/SQFT  FUEL          $/MCF   /SQFT

       .810    12862.08       1.27   4.3513
      1.043    10172.69       1.21   3.4414
      1.152    11961.44       1.41   4.0466
      1.346     9063.40       1.43   3.0662
      1.659     8251.31       1.63   2.7914
      3.093     7419.55       1.60   2.5100
      1.867     6043.08       1.54   2.0444
      2.449     7022.39       1.69   2.3757
      2.339     7375.05       1.58   2.4950
      1.184    10523.20       1.71   3.5600
      1.068    13770.10       1.51   4.6584
       .797    15762.17       1.59   5.3324
```

Figure 11-1 (b). Fuel Consumption Record—Leila Hospital—1976

LEILA POST HOSP 76ENERGY CONSUMPTION RECORD

GROSS CONDITIONED AREA 262944

YEAR 1976   GROSS AREA 295595

COST

MONTH	MBTU	BTU/o/DAY/SQ.FT	TOTAL	CENTS /SQ.FT
JAN	12326216	.957	29968.74	10.1384
FEB	10555628	1.249	25237.12	8.5377
MAR	10586825	1.408	27557.79	9.3228
APR	8687280	1.786	27589.47	9.3335
MAY	7317326	2.330	27364.19	9.2573
JUN	7109660	4.606	27508.86	9.3063
JUL	6742574	3.079	28233.15	9.5513
AUG	6620029	3.786	25219.21	8.5317
SEP	7082407	3.413	26545.65	8.9804
OCT	8466275	1.551	26600.79	8.9991
NOV	11468738	1.280	29414.04	9.9508
DEC	12398258	.951	31782.82	10.7522

BTU/SQ.FT/YEAR =   369969.77
TOTAL ENERGY COST =   333021.83
AVERAGE COST IN CENTS/SQFT/MONTH = 9.3885

Figure 11-1 (c). Energy Consumption Record—Leila Hospital—1976

major function. The intent of this phase is to gather as much information as possible and verify it with on-site inspections of every system and area.

The engineering overview is divided into six major categories:

1. Air handling systems
2. Heating systems and controls
3. Cooling systems and controls
4. Electrical systems
5. Building envelope
6. Miscellaneous, such as kitchen, laundries, occupancy schedules, etc.

DATA COLLECTION

The data collection is a major and most important phase of an energy audit. A qualified team of engineers and technicians develop the format of required data collection by utilizing various special data sheets. These data-collection forms are used to gather the maximum possible information with the utmost accuracy. The forms were developed to identify and evaluate every possible energy transfer point and its relationship in the overall system.

Data collection, under actual operating conditions, records quantities, pressures, temperatures, flows, and conditions of components and total system for each category. (Refer to the sample sheet, Figure 15-8 in Chapter 15.)

The building envelope data includes exterior exposures, type of structure and its condition, types and areas of windows and doors and their leakage factors, interior loads, occupancy schedules, etc.

ANALYSIS

The intent of the analysis is to evaluate the energy economics and the dollar economics simultaneously and to help the building engineer and facility administrator understand, evaluate and implement the audit.

The tremendous variety of Energy Conservation Opportunities (ECOs) are reviewed based on the engineering overview and the actual field data obtained. How much energy and money will possible actions save? Will they conform to health codes? What will they cost to implement? Will they reduce or increase maintenance problems? All these questions are reduced to dollar economics.

The interrelations of ECOs in the entire analysis process is complex and is shown as a flow diagram in Figure 11-2.

Once an energy conservation opportunity is identified, it must be verified that enough actual field data is available to confirm the savings. If proper information is not available from the field data or developed during the engineering overview, further research is necessary. If enough information is available, the savings can be accurately calculated. CTB's in-house computer and special programming are used to verify and justify the ECOs whenever possible.

A majority of the ECOs can be performed at nominal cost by the facility's maintenance department, although others require moderate or extensive costs to implement. And one ECO will affect another. For example, a reduction in lighting will reduce the cooling load for the internal zones year-round. It will also reduce the cooling load in summer for the exterior zones, but it will increase the required heating load during the winter.

The computer programs CTB has developed allow analysis of these complex ECO interrelations. Substitute values can be entered to evaluate any variables within proposed design changes.

Hospital codes are very restrictive. Even though the Hill-Burton code is widely used and it allows recirculation of the air in operating rooms as well as delivery rooms, fire codes restrict the use of recirculated air. Any modifications recommended for energy savings must be evaluated in terms of applicable codes, and facility accreditation requirements must be reviewed prior to any change.

Alternate methods to implement an ECO are reviewed with cost justification. Value engineering analyses are performed, and the return on investment for each ECO and related alternatives is evaluated.

FINAL REPORT

Results and recommendations are collated into the final re-

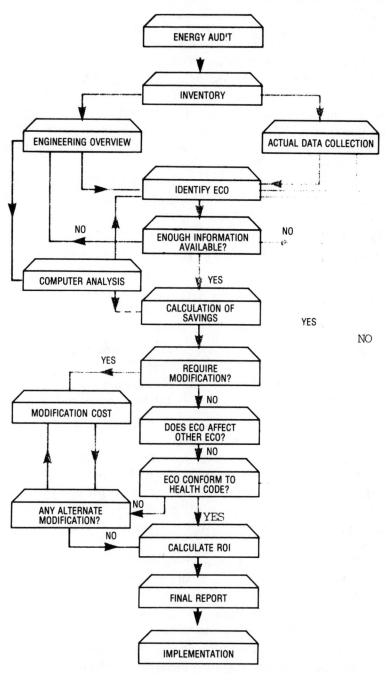

Figure 11-2. Logic Diagram for Hospital Energy Audits

port, which is divided into two sections. First the economic analysis, and second the technical report with collected data.

The economical analysis division contains both narrative and graphic elements and a concise summary with a brief engineering follow-up to justify listed savings. The engineering follow-up indicates the recommendations and cost-saving opportunities that are also applicable but not economically feasible. Whenever applicable a life-cycle cost analysis is made with fixed return on investment in mind.

Time frame and initial cost of the audit limit in-depth cost studies for every ECO. Also, if the implementation will not follow immediately, a detailed cost analysis is not justified. To justify expenditures for alternative ECOs, the following rating combinations have been found to be practical and understandable:

Rating	First Cost
A	Little or none
B	Moderate
C	High

Rating	Energy Saving Potential
1	High
2	Moderate
3	Little

For example, an ECO rated A-1 involves little or no first cost, but promises high energy savings.

The technical section of the report is primarily designed for use by the facility's engineering and maintenance staffs. This section includes the complete data collection for every system, showing performance, physical conditions, and efficiencies. Each system is identified with a schematic showing the flows, temperatures, pressure drops, etc.

The technical report also identifies the maintenance problems observed for each system and the causes of energy waste together with the precautions necessary.

This same format, without the added complexities of health codes and sensitive patient conditions, can be applied to almost any building with major central energy consuming systems.

The following case history illustrates the results of a typical audit application.

MODIFICATIONS

Leila Hospital, comprising 295,595 square feet of total area in 1976, used 369,969 BTU/sq ft/year. The hospital expanded with an additional 12,000 square feet of trauma and emergency area in 1977. Two air-handling systems, fourteen exhaust fans, and individual system pumps added 47 HP to the existing building load. In addition to this horsepower, a 100-ton chiller, associated cooling tower, and pumps were installed.

Due to the added square feet of the trauma area and the consumption during the construction period it was very difficult to determine the actual additional consumption for the added equipment, since it was not submetered.

Figure 11-3 shows the breakdown of building identification, including its square-foot area and the general use of this area.

Building Name	Sq Ft Area	Conditioned Area	Use of the Space
"A" Wing	19,200	15,360	Offices
"B" Wing	76,990	65,450	ICU, PCU, Offices, Patient Rooms
"C" Wing	151,110	151,110	Patient, Surgery, Kitchen, etc.
62 Addition	12,900	12,900	Outpatient, Pharmacy, etc.
Lodge	19,780	9,890	
Trauma	11,934	11,934	Emergency & Minor Surgery
Laundry	3,170	3,170	Laundry
Professional	5,065	5,065	Doctors Offices
Boiler Room	7,380	0	Boilers & Chillers
Total Area =	307,529	274,879	

Figure 11-3. Building Identification

LIGHTING MODIFICATIONS

During the field data-collection period it was observed that basic operational and maintenance changes would have to be made to improve occupant comfort conditions. Minor control calibrations and modifications were necessary for every system.

A lighting survey was made on a room-by-room basis identifying the footcandle level and the light density in watts per square feet. Recommendations for lighting reductions were submitted to plant operations based upon safety and productivity of the occupants. Recommended footcandle levels as well as the output improvement of clean fixtures were also submitted.

Total recommended reduction in lighting was 6160 watts since most of the lighting in the patient area is comprised of spot-lighting only. All the corrections were completed by the hospital employees at a very minimal cost. Several rooms were left untouched as requested by the department heads. Actual reduction in lighting was 5500 watts and the equivalent savings due to reduced lighting was $1,050.00 per year.

MODIFICATIONS TO SYSTEM ACS #6
SERVING THE PATIENT AREA

It was observed during the audit stage that the system E-1 serving surgery exhaust, E-7 toilet exhaust, and return fan E-8 share a common exhaust louver. Figure 11-4 indicates the flow schematic of the system. The outside air damper was handling 8134 CFM and the return air damper was wide open and handling 11,062 CFM. Design requirements of the supply fan were 15,955 CFM while the supply fan was handling 19,196 CFM and the return fan was handling 6483 CFM.

Temperature and CFM readings obtained during the audit indicated that the common exhaust louver was working as a partial fresh-air intake louver to compensate for the deficiency. The exhaust from surgery and toilet was recirculated throughout the patient rooms. This problem was due to improper controls and improper setting during the initial start-up. With improper setting of the dampers and higher temperature air from the toilet and surgery exhaust being recirculated, this system was not taking full advantage of the free cooling available.

Several major balancing dampers were installed for proper zone balancing, as none were installed during the original construction stage. Design CFM for the patient rooms is based upon the minimum outside air change required by the Department of Public Health, and cannot be revised even though the actual CFM requirement was lower. CFM levels in the interior rooms were reduced to meet the new load requirements.

After proper control changes, recalibration of hot-deck temperature to work on an automatic sliding scale, and proper set-

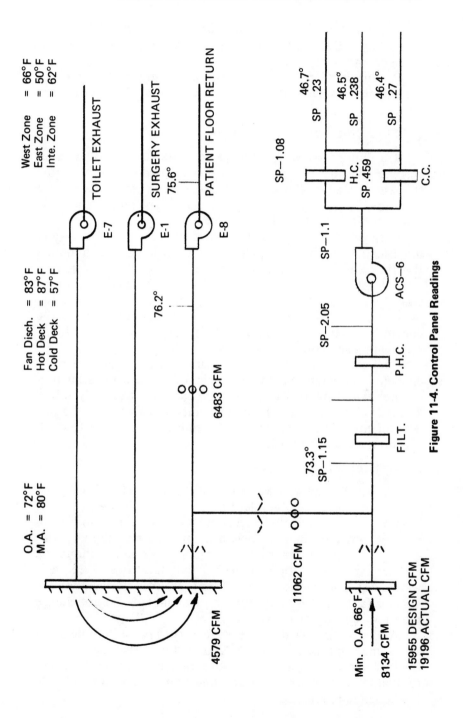

Figure 11-4. Control Panel Readings

ting of the fresh-air and return-air dampers to work on the proper economizer cycle, the system was rebalanced to obtain proper comfort conditions.

Patient comfort and implementation of the health code was the major consideration, with energy savings of secondary importance for this individual system.

CENTRAL CHILLED WATER SYSTEM

The chilled water system was used on a year-round basis wasting considerable amounts of energy predominantly during the winter season. Before CTB's involvement the chillers were shut down during the winter and a significant temperature rise was noticed throughout the building.

Lack of a full chilled water layout and several earlier system modifications within the buildings, made it impossible to define the full scope of the problem. Chilled water flow schematics were developed and made positive that no cross connection of chilled water and hot water existed as suspected by the hospital maintenance staff. Various control changes, calibration of the controls, and minor operational changes reduced the simultaneous heating and cooling situations.

CTB worked closely with the plant operation department to educate the operators in the principles of the new operating procedures with the end result of a reduction of roughly 4,000 hours of chiller operation and its connected accessories. Cost of implementing this work was $8,000 and the savings due to modifications were $18,000.

SYSTEM ACS #1

The ACS #1 system was serving the surgery area. During the past a booster fan on the inlet of ACS #1 was installed with the intention of keeping the surgery under positive pressure. CFM readings obtained in the ductwork for ACS #1 supplying surgery, and exhaust fan serving surgery, with and without the booster fan in operation, indicated that the surgery area as a whole was under positive condition. It was noticed that the booster fan installed in series with the main unit did not change the CFM capacity of the system ACS #1.

Added balancing dampers were necessary to complete the air balance and maintain the design air flow. The ductwork for the fresh-air intake was revised and proper air balancing was performed to maintain the comfort condition and still comply with the design requirements.

FOUR-PIPE RADIATION SYSTEM

The patient rooms in building "C" were supplied with the code-required tempered air through system ACS #6. The same patient rooms were served by the four-pipe radiant panels, supplying either heating or cooling as required by the room thermostat.

Figure 11-5 shows the general layout of the area. During the spring and fall when temperature variation is high, cooling and heating requirements are changing depending upon the solar and transmission losses. The room calls for heat during the night which is provided by the radiant panels, and calls for cooling during the day which is also provided by the panels. When this change-over takes place, the water which was inside the panel transfers from one system to the other. This intermixing of the system water created more problems and confusion.

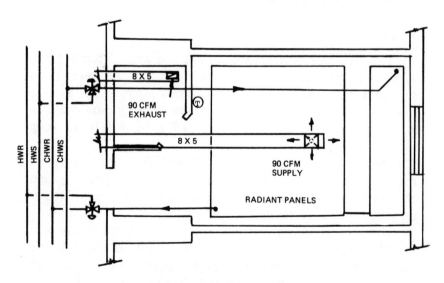

Figure 11-5. General Layout

Operational changes for the heating and cooling pumps and the proper sliding-scale temperature controller for the air-handling unit zones, avoided the continuous intermixing of the chilled water and hot water, and provided better comfort conditions to the occupant as well.

TEMPERATURE CONTROL

Various temperature control modifications were made throughout the complex in all air-handling units, convertors, reheat systems and perimeter radiation systems. The control modifications were designed to reduce the simultaneous heating and cooling conditions noted during the audit. Manual summer/winter operations were converted to automatic giving better comfort and reduced manhours for proper operation of the systems.

Revised temperature control drawings were made for the hospital showing the "as installed" conditions.

Overall savings due to temperature control modifications and recalibration were difficult to calculate due to various conditions for every system. However, substantial reductions in consumption resulted since the simultaneous heating and cooling was virtually eliminated.

SYSTEM ACS #2

The ACS #2 system was serving the administrative area, which was occupied for ten hours a day, and the sterile linen storage area, which was occupied for 24 hours a day. System shutdown was not practical without making major modifications in the system. These modifications will be looked into during the second stage of the program.

The system was designed to handle 100% outside air year-round. It is a low-pressure reheat system. The reheat system was used for heating the perimeter offices during the winter, as no other means of heating was provided.

The general exhaust system serving the administrative area was discharging the exhaust air in the equipment room. It was possible to install ductwork from the general exhaust fans to the supply air plenum of system ACS #2 and gain full advantage of the economizer cycle by utilizing the return air.

Cost of the above modifications, including the engineering, ductwork change, and control modifications, was only $7,400, while estimated savings for the modifications came to $4,500 per year.

POWER FACTOR CORRECTION

The measured power factor in the building for the past several years was 0.75. The hospital was paying a penalty of approximately $500 per month because of this lower power factor.

Two separate lines were supplying the power in the buildings. Several options were considered for power factor correction. After careful analysis it was determined from an economical standpoint that it was cheaper to install the capacitor banks on the secondary side of the transformers with a disconnect switch.

One negative result of the capacitor bank on the secondary side of the transformer was that it created a false signal to the master Simplex clock system. The master clock, which generates the signals and resets all the subordinate clocks on a twelve-hour basis, would not function properly with the power factor capacitors connected. Modified signal generators were provided by Simplex to correct the problems.

Total cost of the power factor correction work was $8,000 including the modifications to the Simplex system. Savings due to the power factor correction were equal to $6,000/year, the same as the penalty charge. New power factor varies from 0.87 to 0.92, giving a credit when power factor is above 0.9.

REVISED AIR QUANTITIES

The constant change of the rooms' usage, the reduced lighting load and the design based upon the peak requirements, are the biggest waste factors for any system and especially reheat systems. CFM quantities were recalculated based upon the new room usage, internal loads and the operating conditions. Main considerations were given to meet the health-code requirements for proper outside and total air changes. Proper pressure relation was maintained as required by the Department of Public Health.

All calculations in system reductions were based on actual field data information collected by our technicians and not on nameplate or existing drawing information. Total reduction in outside air quantities from the actual operating conditions was 10,778 CFM or equal to 11%.

Simultaneous reduction in exhaust CFM was obtained to maintain the positive/negative pressure relationships within the building as conditions required. Secondary beneficial results were obtained in the reduction of fan motor horsepower.

With the overall system reductions, the hospital now operates without utilizing the new 100-ton chiller system installed during the trauma center addition. Also, temperature and GPM readings show that a substantial reserve capacity is now available from the two original chillers.

SYSTEM OPERATIONS DURING UNOCCUPIED PERIODS

System ACS #4 and exhaust fan E-5 were serving the kitchen and dining area and were running on a 24-hour-a-day basis. It was not necessary to operate this system on a continuous basis, and a fixed shutdown schedule was not possible due to variable occupancy times. Manual shutdown periods were established with the help of the department head.

System ACS #7, serving the X-ray area, was operated on a continuous basis. System operation was reduced to occupied hours only giving a greater energy savings.

Cost of the work—none.

INSULATION

The steam pipes and condensate return pipe in the crawl space along with all the steam risers and the condensate return risers were not insulated in the corridors of building "A." Heating in the building was provided by the radiators and cooling with the window units. Steam risers located inside the rooms were insulated, but the steam pipes, connecting risers, and the radiators were not insulated.

Several of the manual valve handles were broken and valves were wide open. All the manual valve handles were repaired and valves were made operable before new insulation was installed.

A survey was made on a room-by-room basis to come up

with the proper sizes of the pipe and their length to calculate the heat loss and estimate the insulation cost. Figure 11-6 represents the accumulated sizes and length of the steam and condensate return pipes to be insulated.

Due to the uninsulated steam pipes in the crawl space, uninsulated risers, uninsulated pipes up to the radiators and broken valve handles, lower floors were always overheated while the upper floors were always cold. Windows were kept open on the lower floors to compensate the overheating problems during the winter.

All the steam and condensate return pipes in the crawl space, risers in the corridors, and steam pipes up to the radiators were insulated. The repair work for valves and handles was done by the plant operation personnel. Cost of the insulation work was $7,210, and estimated savings per year was $4,500.

Pipe Sizes	Steam Pipe	Condensate Pipe	Remarks
¾"∅	80'	—	Copper tubes
1"∅	80'	185'	
1¼"∅	250'	—	
1½"∅	40'	500'	
2"∅	—	300'	
3"∅	50'	200'	
3"∅	500'	—	Replaced old insulation with new.

Figure 11-6. Steam and Condensate Distribution

FAN COIL UNITS

Fan coil units serving intensive and pediatric care were having problems maintaining the proper comfort levels in the rooms. One, two, or three fan coils were serving the rooms depending upon the size of the room, and one controller was providing the desired temperature. Three-speed blowers serving the fan coils in several cases were discharging less air at high-speed settings than recommended by the manufacturer for the lower speed output.

The combination of dirty coils and blower squirrel cages diminished the air flow through the unit. Faulty control valves would cause one unit to supply cooling while the others would supply heating to the same space.

CTB, along with plant operations personnel, checked every fan coil, identified the problems and developed a schedule for plant operations people to perform the required work, to assure the proper operation of the units. The operation of the system was shown to the nurses, recommending its use as necessary, and with their cooperation significant reduction in energy and complaints was achieved.

A practical training seminar on a question-and-answer basis was conducted with the maintenance staff, and was found to be very helpful. The understanding of the system, enthusiasm, and confidence of the maintenance staff were found to be the major factors in any management program. Any energy conservation measure performed cannot be successful without the help of the operational people and understanding of the occupant.

MONITORING

The integration between one energy conservation step to the other, the human factors involved, and the operational problems restricted CTB from coming up with the exact cost savings for every ECO. When work is completed as recommended, the energy savings are the difference between monthly consumption from one year to the next. Cost savings are equal to the energy savings times the cost for that month.

Figure 11-7 shows the continuous monitoring of the savings and their equivalent dollar value due to modifications. Assumption is made here that no additional equipment is added and the weather conditions remain the same as an average for each month. The billing days difference will average out on a yearly basis.

Since the hospital has gone through a major renovation and an addition of 12,000 square feet of trauma center during the last six months of 1977, the consumption shown in Figure 11-7 does not represent real savings.

The energy consumption for the system installed, and the additional energy required for heating and cooling the trauma center were calculated. Using the calculated KWH and MCF consumption for the trauma center and adding them to the past year's consumption, the actual savings were calculated. Figure 11-8 shows the actual savings based upon the added load.

Total cost of the project, including the audit, was $73,000. The annual savings, using the actual consumption rather than estimated savings, indicates that the actual savings are $52,217 for the first year and increases as the cost of energy increases. The annual savings with the added trauma center load considered equals $70,000.

In summary, it can be said that the energy conservation work performed saved energy, provided a better environment, reduced the complaint level and gave a better understanding of the system to the operators. As built, ductwork drawings showing new CFM levels, the operating data points such as static pressure, temperature, amperage and RPM for every air-handling unit were provided to the maintenance staff.

All the work completed so far is for the air-handling systems only. No major modifications for the chilled-water systems, boilers or heating system were made during the first phase. No modifications to the work in the new trauma center were performed since these systems were still under one-year installing contractor's warranty. CTB is in the process of providing the chilled-water system modifications and alterations of the heating system based upon the life-cycle costing.

The program was successful due to the help of the plant operating staff. Without their cooperation, constant innovation, and eagerness to improve the system, it would have been impossible to achieve these results. The people operating the buildings are involved in the systems' operation, and are the key to the success of an energy program.

A knowledgeable building operator versed in the systems' actual operating characteristics is more valuable to efficient energy savings than many sophisticated computer systems.

LEILA HOSPITAL

MONTH	KWH FOR 77-78	KWH FOR 78-79	SAVINGS IN KWH	SAVINGS IN DOLLARS
MAR	5584000.00	4704000.00	880000.00	3573.72
APR	5840000.00	5008000.00	832000.00	3977.55
MAY	6560000.00	6368000.00	192000.00	944.00
JUN	7428000.00	6736000.00	692000.00	2336.34
JUL	7552000.00	6928000.00	624000.00	1742.16
AUG	7296000.00	6768000.00	528000.00	1473.11
SEPT	7712000.00	6704000.00	1008000.00	3010.92
OCT	5824000.00	6367000.00	- 543000.00	1529.72
NOV	6528000.00	5360000.00	1168000.00	4293.05
DEC	6048000.00	4272000.00	1776000.00	6192.62
JAN	5840000.00	4352000.00	1488000.00	4427.02
FEB	6016000.00	4080000.00	1936000.00	6570.80
		TOTAL DOLLARS SAVED		37011.56

MONTH	MCF FOR 77-78	MCF FOR 78-79	SAVINGS IN MCF	SAVINGS IN DOLLARS
MAY	4450.31	5309.80	—	1762.86
JUN	4392.38	4031.90	859.49	740.88
JUL	3767.20	3978.50	360.48	439.32
AUG	4824.50	4157.60	211.30	1391.06
SEPT	4565.60	4280.00	666.90	522.58
OCT	6305.60	6925.90	285.60	1193.16
NOV	8201.10	7466.60	—	1413.17
DEC	10155.80	8439.60	620.30	3301.26
JAN	12526.90	11332.60	734.50	2303.46
FEB	11025.40	9176.10	1716.20	3561.45
MAR	10076.60	7409.60	1194.30	5143.03
APR	5938.60	5822.20	1849.30	224.59
			2667.00	
			116.40	
		TOTAL DOLLARS SAVED		15206.14

Figure 11-7. Continuous Monitoring of Savings

KWH

(1)	(2)	(3)	(4)	(5)	(6)	(7)	(8)	(9)	(10)	(11)
Time Period	Prior Years' Consumption	Average Cost ¢/KWH	Added KWH	Total Est. KWH *2+4	Actual KWH	Present Avg. Cost ¢/KWH	Estimated Cost *5X7 100	Actual Cost	Actual Savings *8−9	Remarks
1-77/6-77	3,448,000	3.0603	0	3,448,000	3,597,200	2.9677	102,326.29	$106,017.88	−3,691.16	Added KWH is
7-77/12-77	3,898,000	2.7457	0	3,898,000	4,096,000	2.9105	113,451.29	120,316.45	−6,865.16	for Trauma Center
1-78/6-78	3,597,200	2.9677	215,832	3,813,032	3,467,200	3.7146	141,638.88	127,662.21	13,976.67	HVAC equipment
7-78/12-78	4,096,000	2.9105	215,832	4,311,832	3,639,900	3.0914	132,002.42	110,783.68	21,218.74	and lighting only.
1-79/3-79	1,656,000	2.9999	0	1,656,000	1,276,800	3.278	54,285.50	41,854.99	12,430.51	

CTB's work started 3/1/78. Savings based upon nine months of '78 and three months of '79 equal to $43,000.00.

MCF

(1)	(2)	(3)	(4)	(5)	(6)	(7)	(8)	(9)	(10)	(11)
1-77/6-77	43,091.26	1.425	0	43,091.26	44,050.84	1.76	75,840.61	77,749.67	−1,909.06	Added MCF is
7-77/12-77	37,956.16	1.6033	0	37,956.16	37,819.80	1.97	74,773.63	73,398.15	1,375.48	for 20,000 sq ft
1-78/6-78	44,050.84	1.76	2,850	46,900.84	48,910.1	2.03	95,208.70	99,233.69	−4,024.99	of added Trauma
7-78/12-78	37,819.80	1.97	2,850	40,669.80	35,247.3	1.96	79,712.80	68,697.40	11,014.78	Center and HVAC
1-79/3-79	33,628.9	2.02	0	33,628.9	27,918.3	1.92	64,567.49	53,817.60	10,749.80	equipment only.

*Pertains to column numbers.
**Projected savings from 4/79 to 6/79 for fuel is $5,200.00.

Figure 11-8. Actual Savings Based Upon Added Load

12

Energy Audits Of Government Buildings

The material presented in this chapter is based upon "Federal Management in the Federal Government," DOE/S–0005, and "Energy Conservation Self-Evaluation Manual for Federal Managers." The latter work was sponsored by the Chicago Federal Executive Board. Appreciation is given to the authors and agencies who participated in these projects.

The Federal Government is the single largest user of energy in the nation, accounting for 2.2 percent of the energy used in the United States in 1977. This energy is used within the Federal Government by almost six million people, in more than 400,000 buildings and in operating more than 650,000 vehicles of all types. This amount of energy would be sufficient to:

- Heat 11 million homes for one year
- Operate 18 million automobiles—as many automobiles as are currently registered in the States of New York and California combined—for one year.

Federal energy use by fuel type is shown in Table 12-1. The major portion (62 percent) of the energy used is in the form of petroleum fuels. More than 175 million barrels of petroleum products were used in 1977. If petroleum fuels consumed in the generation of electricity are included, the total increases to 194 million barrels of oil, or 69 percent.

Federal energy use for fiscal years 1975 through 1977 is summarized in Table 12-2. Individual agency results are presented for the 20 largest energy users, while results for the 46 agencies that use relatively little energy are combined.

Table 12-1. Fuel Use By Type in the Federal Government in FY 1977

Fuel Type	Amount		Percent of Total
	Trillion Btu	Million Barrels of Oil Equiv. (MBOE)	
Jet Fuel	619.35	106.54	37.73
Diesel and Petroleum Distillates	195.67	33.65	11.92
Fuel Oil	121.47	20.89	7.40
Gasoline	63.85	10.98	3.89
Navy Special	9.39	1.62	0.57
Aviation Gasoline	8.81	1.52	0.53
Petroleum Fuels Subtotal	1018.54	175.20	62.04
Electricity	425.16	73.13	25.90
Natural Gas	138.87	23.89	8.46
Coal	49.25	8.47	3.00
Other*	9.72	1.65	0.60
Total All Fuels	1641.54	282.34	100.00

* Other fuels include propane and purchased steam.
Source: Department of Energy.

The buildings category includes all energy used to operate a building, such as for heating, cooling and ventilating, water heating and lighting, but excludes roadways, parking lot lighting, etc., which are now included in this category. Energy used for other purposes, such as for vehicles, the operation of communications and navigation systems, large computers, and for research, test and production equipment, will be reported under general operations in the future.

The ten largest energy-using agencies account for over 98 percent of the energy consumed by the executive branch of the Federal Government. These agencies in order of energy use, are:

- Department of Defense
- Department of Energy
- U.S. Postal Service

Table 12-2. Federal Government Energy Consumption FY 1975 to FY 1977*

(Figures are in Trillions of Btu and Million Barrels of Oil Equivalent (MBOE))

Agency	FY 1975 (BASE YEAR)			FY 1976			FY 1977		
	Buildings & Facilities	Vehicles & Equipment	Total	Buildings & Facilities	Vehicles & Equipment	Total	Buildings & Facilities	Vehicles & Equipment	Total
DOD	470.99	899.78	1,370.77	457.40	816.32	1,273.72	454.92	849.55	1,304.47
DOE	82.00	1.63	83.63	85.42	1.78	87.20	84.00	1.85	85.85
USPS	44.27	11.24	55.51	43.70	11.32	55.02	47.20	11.74	58.94
GSA	44.68	.18	44.86	43.66	.17	43.83	43.61	.18	43.79
VA	38.59	.62	39.21	35.83	.63	36.46	37.31	.61	37.92
DOT	15.97	10.98	26.95	14.80	12.21	27.01	15.88	12.43	28.31
NASA	25.20	1.72	26.92	24.24	1.62	25.86	22.35	1.73	24.08
Interior	11.23	3.55	14.78	11.05	3.85	14.90	11.56	3.66	15.22
Agriculture	6.76	5.17	11.93	6.06	5.55	11.61	5.48	5.29	10.77
HEW	8.52	.74	9.26	8.82	.77	9.59	9.24	.69	9.93
Justice	4.83	1.86	6.69	4.98	2.20	7.18	5.36	2.09	7.45
Treasury	1.98	2.22	4.20	1.96	2.22	4.18	2.03	2.23	4.26
Commerce	2.39	1.13	3.52	2.45	1.42	3.87	2.43	1.39	3.82
Panama Canal	1.38	1.30	2.68	1.35	1.17	2.52	1.36	1.26	2.62
Labor	1.40	.25	1.65	1.34	.29	1.63	1.46	.30	1.76
TVA	.25	.51	.76	.35	.55	.90	.60	.55	1.15
EPA	.43	.13	.56	.44	.12	.56	.44	.12	.56
HUD	—	.37	.37	—	.31	.31	—	.31	.31
CSC	—	.10	.10	—	.10	.10	—	.10	.10
SBA	—	.08	.08	—	.08	.08	—	.09	.09
Others	.03	.11	.14	.03	.12	.15	.03	.11	.14
Totals									
Btu	760.89	943.68	1,704.57	743.88	862.80	1,606.68	745.26	896.28	1,641.54
MBOE	130.87	162.31	293.19	127.95	148.40	276.35	128.18	154.16	282.34
Annual Savings From FY 75									
Btu	—	—	—	17.01	80.88	97.89	15.63	47.40	63.03
MBOE	—	—	—	2.93	13.91	16.84	2.69	8.15	10.84
Cumulative Savings From FY 75									
Btu	—	—	—	—	—	—	32.64	128.28	160.92
MBOE	—	—	—	—	—	—	5.62	22.06	27.68

* Savings totals may not equal sums due to rounding.
Source: Department of Energy.

- General Services Administration
- Veterans Administration
- Department of Transportation
- National Aeronautics and Space Administration
- Department of the Interior
- Department of Agriculture
- Department of Health, Education and Welfare.

The remaining 56 agencies account for less than 1.6 percent of the total energy used.

FEDERAL BUILDINGS PROFILE

Twenty-three agencies of the Federal Government own or lease about 2.7 billion square feet of space in more than 403,000 buildings. The following six agencies account for over 90 percent of the energy used in buildings owned and operated by the executive branch of the Federal Government.

- Department of Defense
- Department of Energy
- General Services Administration
- National Aeronautics and Space Administration
- U.S. Postal Service
- Veterans Administration

The Department of Defense is the largest building owner with 317,000 buildings, totaling more than 1.8 billion square feet of floor space.

Agencies that do not own buildings lease space directly, or are tenants in buildings leased by other agencies. The Federal Government currently leases 220 million square feet of floor space, or 8.1 percent of the total floor area it occupies.

The Federal Government owns and operates a wide range of buildings of various types. As shown in Figure 12-1, these buildings use differing amounts of energy. Research and development and industrial buildings are the most energy intensive, with housing and storage being the least. These preliminary results are based upon historical data of undetermined accuracy. Agencies are developing more accurate information to determine these energy use baselines on a gross square-foot basis.

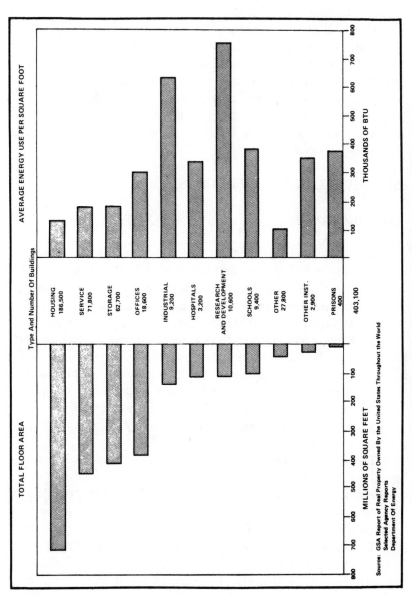

Figure 12-1. Federal Building Categories—Total Floor Area and Energy Use

The goals for the Federal buildings programs are to reduce energy use by 20 percent in existing buildings and by 45 percent in new buildings by FY 1985.

The high energy usage of Btu/square foot shown in Figure 12-1, and the increasing emphasis on reducing this consumption is bound to make energy audits in this area a high priority. The material presented in the next section is based on a program developed by the Chicago Federal Executive Board. The aim of the program is to increase the awareness of the energy manager to how energy is used in the building and to identify energy conservation opportunities.

SELF-EVALUATION CHECKLISTS

INTRODUCTION

The self-evaluation checklists are to be used to:
1. Determine the major factors of energy consumption in the federal facility and determine factors contributing to the overall energy usage in the specific area.
2. Discover transferable techniques for saving energy.
3. Provide guidance to federal facility managers to pinpoint modifications in building systems and operational practices that would result in reducing energy consumption.
4. Identify areas where additional information would be helpful and constructive suggestions welcome.
5. Reinforce the importance of energy conservation and its place in our National Energy Policy.

The initiative and the responsibility of corrective actions remain with the individual manager. To aid in this analysis, these self-evaluating checklists have been developed. They provide the manager with an indication of the factors of thermal performance which require correction.

The checklists consist of separate sections or areas of evaluation. A relative numerical value has been assigned to those specific conditions that effect the energy loss in these areas. Additional instructions are also provided in the self-evaluating checklists to assist in completion of the form and provide consistency of results between federal facilities. When completing the forms using these instructions and computing a resultant overall score for each section, both strong and weak areas become apparent. This scoring method is valid for each of the sections as well as for each item within a section.

The purpose of these checklists is to assist in dealing with the "How" of starting an energy management program. In this handbook space does not permit listing the recommendations of possible remedies for the twenty evaluation sections. Each manager must determine the best use of budgeted expenditures for reducing energy consumption.

INSTRUCTIONS FOR SELF-EVALUATION CHECKLISTS

To demonstrate the use of self-evaluating checklists, an example is presented as follows:

Seven windows are used to demonstrate the typical checklist shown in the following example. Note that each window condition is assigned a value if the condition applies. The overall rating for the windows listed is 51 percent. This rating scale of 51 percent indicates that corrective action is required in this area since its rating is only half of the maximum score of 100 allowable.

Although the example covers only seven windows, a typical building evaluation will include hundreds of windows. Each form provides for the listing of 25 windows. A sufficient number of forms should be used to list each window as an individual item.

For record-keeping purposes, it is suggested that each window be assigned an "address" which will serve to positively identify that opening for all references regarding that window. Architectural building exterior elevation drawings will be useful as a means of tabulating and recording work on windows.

There are twenty categories or evaluation sections, as follows:
1. Window
2. Door
3. Ceiling
4. Wall
5. Roof

EVALUATOR A. AUD

DATE 5/10/74

UNIT NAME Anywhere

SHEET NO. 1

NO.	LOCATION	RATING VALUE MAX. = 10	Storms	Solar Protection	Tight Fit	Minor Infiltration	Major Infiltration	Cannot Be Opened	Can Be Opened	Weather Stripped								TOTAL POINTS
			2	2	2	1	0	3	0	1							
1	Bldg. 4, Room 401		2			1			0	1							4
2	Bldg. 4, Room 402			2	2			3		1							8
3	Bldg. 4, Room 609					1			0	1							2
4	Bldg. 4, Room 102		2	2	2			3		1							10
5	Bldg. 4, Room 104, W1		2			1			0	1							4
6	Bldg. 4, Room 104, W2		2				0		0	1							3
7	Bldg. 4, Room 104, W3		2		2				0	1							5
25	GRAND TOTAL																36

WINDOW CONDITIONS

$$\text{RATING SCORE} = 100 \times \frac{36}{(7)(10)} = 51\%$$

6. Storage Area
7. Shipping and Receiving
8. Illumination
9. Food Area
10. Heat Generation
11. Heat Distribution
12. Cooling Generation
13. Cooling Distribution
14. Electrical Power Distribution
15. Hot Water Service
16. Laundry
17. Compressed Air
18. Water
19. Process Heating
20. Transportation

Completion of these 20 forms by the manager and/or his staff will provide the current status of energy consumption in those areas identified as needing the most attention. Recommendations to improve any faulty conditions should be evaluated using an energy savings cost analysis for these 20 parameters to ensure that the greatest energy savings per dollar are attained.

Each of the 20 sections will be evaluated on a separate rating schedule. There are three parts to each section:

1. Recommendations for improvements (not included in this text)
2. Instructions for evaluating ratings
3. Checklist

Specific conditions in each category are determined by completing the corresponding checklist. Each item being evaluated is identified and located in the appropriate space on the form. An example would be Building 4, Room 406, Window 1.

Each of the specific conditions listed on the checklist is evaluated for each item. The instruction sheet provides guidance in properly identifying correct conditions. The assigned value for each existing condition should be listed in the proper column to credit the item being evaluated. Total points for each item are determined and this total listed in the item total points column.

Each form will accommodate 25 items of similar nature, such as 25 windows or 25 doors. As many forms as are necessary to list all similar items on an individual line should be used. The total points for each section are determined by adding all item total points for that section.

Using the following scoring formula, the rating score of each of the 20 sections should be individually calculated.

$$\text{Rating Score} = \frac{(100) \times (\text{Point Total for Section})}{(\text{No. of Items}) \times (\text{Maximum Rating Value in Section})}$$

This rating score is then applied to the following table which indicates the urgency of corrective action.

Range of
Rating Score   *Action Required*

Range of Rating Score	Action Required
0 – 20	Immediate Corrective Action Required
20 – 40	Urgent Corrective Action Required
40 – 60	Corrective Action Required
60 – 80	Evaluation for Potential Improvement Required
80 – 100	No Corrective Action Required

Recommendation sheets are included in the government guide that list several methods to improve the score in each section. These recommendations are general in nature. The recommendation that is prevalent in all sections is: Education and training of personnel to reduce energy consumption. It is critical that managers realize the importance of the individual's role in a personal commitment to energy conservation. Employee awareness of energy consumption and its reduction should be given high priority when establishing energy conservation policies and practices.

In the following pages are checklists and instruction for their use for each of the 20 sections.

WINDOW RATING INSTRUCTIONS

2 points if the window has storm windows adequate for cold weather protection. The storm windows must fit tightly and block the wind from entering around the window.

2 points if the window has protection from the direct sun during warm weather. Solar protection can be part of the building design such as overhang, awnings or physical shields. Protection can also be tinted or reflective film applied to the windows, double-glazed windows, solar screening or trees blocking out direct sunlight.

2 points for a tight fitting window. A window is tight fitting if the infiltration will not be detected around the window during a windy day. The window must fit well and all caulking must be in place. Weatherstripping will contribute to a tight fit.

1 point if the wind has some infiltration around the window. The window should fit fairly well and not be loose and rattle.

0 points if infiltration can be felt to a large degree. The window is loose in the frame and caulking is missing or in poor condition.

3 points if the window is designed so physically it cannot be opened.

0 points if it can be opened. If it can be opened, it will be opened to "regulate" room temperature.

1 point if window is weatherstripped all around and the weatherstripping is in good condition.

SELF-EVALUATING CHECKLIST FOR WINDOWS

			WINDOW CONDITIONS																TOTAL POINTS
EVALUATOR																			
DATE																			
UNIT NAME			Storms	Solar Protection	Tight Fit	Minor Infiltration	Major Infiltration	Cannot Be Opened	Can Be Opened	Weather Stripped									
SHEET NO.																			
NO.	LOCATION	RATING VALUE MAX. = 10	2	2	2	1	0	3	0	1									
1																			

DOOR RATING INSTRUCTIONS

This section applies to all doors that open to the outside and all doors that open to an unconditioned space such as warehouses and storerooms.

2 points   if door is part of an air-lock system.
1 point   if door has a closer which may be either spring, air or hydraulic.
1 point   if door closer does not have a hold-open feature.
0 points   if door closer has a hold-open feature.
2 points   if door fits snugly into the door frame with no loose condition and where no infiltration exists around the edges.
1 point   if door is an average fit and can be slightly rattled in the frame and has a slight infiltration around the edges.
0 points   if door is loose in the frame and infiltration exists.
2 points   if weatherstripping exists on all four edges and is in good condition. (Thresholds with elastic or fiber to close the space, and astragals on double doors are considered weatherstripping.)
1 point   if weatherstripping exists on jambs and head only.
0 points   if no weatherstripping exists or if it exists and is in poor condition.
1 point   if door is protected from outside wind. This can be building design, wind screen or shrubbery.

SELF-EVALUATING CHECKLIST FOR EXTERIOR DOORS

NO.	LOCATION	RATING VALUE MAX. = 10	Air Lock	Door Has Closer	Closer Has No Hold-Open	Closer Has a Hold-Open	Snug Fit	Average Fit	Loose Fit	Weather Strip 4 Edges	Weatherstrip Jamb Head	No Weatherstrip	Wind Screens or Other									TOTAL POINTS
			2	1	1	0	2	1	0	2	1	0	1									
1																						

EVALUATOR _____   DATE _____   UNIT NAME _____   SHEET NO. _____

DOOR CONDITIONS

CEILING RATING INSTRUCTIONS

1 point   if a drop ceiling exists.
1 point   if insulation exists above ceiling on top floor below roof or mechanical space.
1 point   if space above drop ceiling is mechanically vented. Natural draft is not considered mechanical venting.
2 points   if all panels are in place and in good condition, no broken or missing panels are present.
1 point   if panels are broken or in poor condition.
0 points   if panels are missing or removed and out of place.

			CEILING CONDITIONS																	
EVALUATOR																					
DATE																					
UNIT NAME																					
SHEET NO.			Drop Ceiling	Insulated Drop Ceiling	Insulated Reg. Ceiling	Space Not Mech. Vented	All Panels in Place	Panels Broken	Panels Missing											TOTAL POINTS
NO.	LOCATION	RATING VALUE MAX. = 6	1	1	1	1	2	1	0											
1																					

WALL RATING INSTRUCTIONS

3 points   if wall is designed to resist outside temperature differential. Insulation is present to substantially change heat transfer time.

0 points   if wall is merely a physical separation without adequate insulating qualities.

2 points   if outside wall surface has solar protection such as light finish, is heavily shaded or has physical sun screens.

2 points   if surfaces of walls are in good repair and not damaged.

1 point   if inside is in average condition with a few small cracks in the surface and smaller plaster sections missing.

0 points   if wall has openings to unconditioned space; i.e., plumbing or duct openings not closed.

SELF-EVALUATING CHECKLIST FOR EXTERIOR WALLS

			WALL CONDITIONS																	
EVALUATOR																				
DATE																				
UNIT NAME																				
SHEET NO.			Insulated	Not Insulated	Solar Protection	Watertight	Cracked or Broken	Open to Noncondition Sp.											TOTAL POINTS
NO.	LOCATION	RATING VALUE MAX. = 7	3	0	2	2	1	0											
1																				

ROOF RATING INSTRUCTIONS

2 points   if roof insulation is in dry condition.
0 points   if roof insulation is in poor condition, wet, aged, brittle, cracked, etc., or if no insulation exists.
1 point   if roof has a reflective surface; this may be the type of material used or the color and condition of surface (gravel, etc.).
1 point   if mechanical ventilation exists between roof and ceiling below. This should be properly sized so adequate air flow exists.
2 points   if no leaks exist in the roof.
1 point   if minor leaks exist.
0 points   if there are many leaks.

SELF-EVALUATING CHECKLIST FOR ROOFS

			ROOF CONDITIONS														
EVALUATOR																	
DATE																	
UNIT NAME																	
SHEET NO.			Dry Insulation	Wet Insulation	Reflective Surface	Ventilation Under Roof	No Leaks	Small Leaks	Many Leaks								TOTAL POINTS
NO.	LOCATION	RATING VALUE MAX. = 6	2	0	1	1	2	1	0								
1																	

STORAGE AREA RATING INSTRUCTIONS

1 point   if area is not temperature controlled.
1 point   if the doors are kept closed.
2 points   if there are no windows in the area.
1 point   if one window is in the area.
0 points   if two or more windows are in the area.
2 points   if area is used as it was designed.
0 points   if area is used for storage but designed for other usage.

SELF-EVALUATING CHECKLIST FOR STORAGE AREAS

			STORAGE AREA CONDITIONS														
EVALUATOR																	
DATE																	
UNIT NAME																	
SHEET NO.			Not Conditioned	Door Closed	No Windows	One Window	Two or More Windows	Used as Designed	Not Used as Designed								TOTAL POINTS
NO.	LOCATION	RATING VALUE MAX. = 6	1	1	2	1	0	2	0								
1																	

SHIPPING AND RECEIVING AREA RATING INSTRUCTIONS

3 points   if the shipping and receiving area is well protected from outside temperature.

1 point   if the shipping and receiving area is reasonably protected from outside air entry.

0 points   if the shipping and receiving area has no protection from the ambient. This would be an open area directly exposed to the outside conditions.

1 point   if individual truck stalls exist so the unused areas can be closed.

0 points   if one large area exists and the entire dock must be exposed if a single truck is loaded or unloaded.

1 point   if the doors are closed when not in use.

0 points   if the doors are left open as a matter of convenience.

1 point   if the area does not receive conditioned air.

0 points   if the area receives conditioned air.

SELF-EVALUATING CHECKLIST FOR SHIPPING AND RECEIVING AREAS

EVALUATOR_____				SHIPPING AND RECEIVING CONDITIONS																
DATE_____ UNIT_____ NAME SHEET NO. _____			Weather Prot. Good	Weather Prot. Average	Weather Prot. Poor	Individual Stalls	One Large Area	Doors Closed	Doors Opened	Not Temp. Cond.	Temp. Cond.									TOTAL POINTS
NO.	LOCATION	RATING VALUE MAX. = 6	3	1	0	1	0	1	0	1	0									
1																				

ILLUMINATION RATING INSTRUCTIONS

1 point   if extensive decorative lighting has been eliminated where used for reasons of appearances (not security, walkway lighting and other necessities).

1 point   if lighting has been arranged to illuminate only the work area.

0 points   if lighting has been designed to illuminate the entire room to a working level.

2 points   if light fixture diffuser is clean and clear.

1 point   if diffuser is slightly yellowed or dirty.

0 points   if diffuser is noticeably yellowed or dust is visible. This restriction can amount to 10% or more of the light flux being transmitted.

2 points   if fixture internal reflective surface is in good condition (the paint is reflective and clean).

1 point   if the fixture internal reflective surface gives dirt indication on clean white cloth.

0 points   if the reflective surface is yellowed and dull.

1 point   if fluorescent lights are used for all illumination.

0 points   if incandescent lights are used.
1 point   if lights are properly vented so the heat can escape to ceiling space, providing that ceiling space is ventilated to prevent heat build-up.
1 point   if lights are turned off when area is not occupied.
1 point   if illumination level is adequate for designed usage.
0 points   if area is "over illuminated" for designed usage.*
0 points   if two or more lamps have blackened ends or are glowing without lighting.

SELF-EVALUATING CHECKLIST FOR ILLUMINATION

EVALUATOR _____

DATE _____

UNIT NAME _____

SHEET NO. _____

NO.	LOCATION	RATING VALUE MAX. = 10	No Decorative Ltg.	Light Work Area	Light Entire Room	Diffusers Good	Diffusers Average	Diffusers Poor	Reflection Good	Reflection Average	Reflection Poor	Flourescent Lights	Incandescent Lights	Lights Vented	Lights Turned Off	Illumination Adeq.	Excessive Illumination			TOTAL POINTS
			1	1	0	2	1	0	2	1	0	1	0	1	1	1	0			
1																				

*Note: Momentarily disconnect lamps until level is reached which is adequate for the intended function. The following light meter readings will assist in determination of average adequate light levels. These are below Illumination Engineering Society recommendations in some instances. Absence of reflected glare is mandatory for reading tasks requiring careful fixture placement.

Corridors, lobbies	—10-15 footcandles average
Typing areas	—50 footcandles in area of work, 20 elsewhere
Storerooms	—5 footcandles
Prolonged reading task areas	—50 footcandles
Kitchens	—50 footcandles in areas of work, 20 elsewhere
Laboratories	—50 footcandles in areas of work
Toilet rooms	—20 footcandles at mirrors

Federal Energy Administration
Recommended Maximum Lighting Levels

Task or area	Footcandle levels	How measured
Hallways or corridors	10±5	Measured average, minimum 1 footcandle.
Work and circulation areas surrounding work stations	30±5	Measured average.
Normal office work, such as reading and writing (on task only), store shelves, and general display areas	50±10	Measured at work station.

Task or area	Footcandle levels	How measured

Prolonged office work
which is somewhat difficult
visually (on task only) . . . . 75±15 . . . . . .Measured at work station.
Prolonged office work
which is visually difficult
and critical in nature
(on task only) . . . . .100±20 . . . . . .Measured at work station.

FOOD AREA RATING INSTRUCTIONS

2 points   if the food preparation equipment is only energized when actually needed. This includes, but is not limited to, ovens, warmers, steam tables, delivery equipment and coffee urns.

0 points   if equipment is turned on and left on all day.

1 point   if refrigerator and freezer doors are kept tightly closed.

0 points   if refrigerator and freezer doors can be left ajar.

1 point   if faucets and valves are in good condition and not leaking.

0 points   if faucets and valves are leaking. Leaks may be external or internal in the system.

3 points   if doors between kitchen area and other areas are kept closed.

2 points   if adequate vent hoods are used over heat-producing equipment.

1 point   if some vent hoods are used over heat-producing equipment.

0 points   if no or inadequate vent hoods are used.

1 point   if ventilation air supply is adequate to remove most of the heat produced by the kitchen equipment.

2 points   if refrigerator equipment is in good repair, seals are good, condenser is clean, air passage over condenser is clear.

1 point   if refrigeration equipment is in average condition, dust and dirt exist on condensers but the air flow is not restricted, door gaskets seal all around although they may have lost some resiliency.

0 points   if refrigeration equipment is in poor condition, a large collection of dust and dirt on the condenser or the fins may be bent to restrict air flow, door gaskets do not seal all around, are brittle, broken or missing.

3 points   if heat-recovery systems are utilized. These can be applied to the exhaust air, the hot waste water or on the refrigeration equipment.

SELF-EVALUATING CHECKLIST FOR FOOD AREA

				FOOD AREA CONDITIONS															
EVALUATOR___ DATE___ UNIT NAME___ SHEET NO.___			Equipment Turned Off	Equipment Left On	Refrig. Doors Closed	Refrig. Doors Ajar	Faucets Not Leaking	Faucets Leaking	Access Doors Closed	Good Vent Hoods	Average Vent Hood	Poor Vent Hood	Adequate Ventilation	Refrig. Equip. Good	Refrig. Equip. Average	Refrig. Equip. Poor	Heat Recovery System			TOTAL POINTS
NO.	LOCATION	RATING VALUE MAX. = 15	2	0	1	0	1	0	3	2	1	0	1	2	1	0	3			
1																				

HEATING SYSTEM (GENERATION) RATING INSTRUCTIONS

2 points   if the insulation is in good condition with no broken or missing sections. The insulation must not be wet, crumbly or cracked.

1 point   if insulation is in average condition with small sections broken or missing. The insulation must not be wet or crumbly.

0 points   if insulation is in poor condition with sections missing, broken, wet, crumbly or cracked.

2 points   if flanges, valves and regulators are insulated with removable lagging.

2 points   if the steam system has no leaks.

1 point   if the steam system has minor leaks around valve packing, shaft seals, etc.

0 point   if the steam system has many leaks, valves, regulators and traps have dripping leaks, steam plumes, etc.

1 point   if boiler combustion controls are automatic.

1 point   if definite standard operating procedures are used. These should be written and posted near the boiler control panel.

1 point   if each boiler has an individual steam flow meter.

1 point   if each boiler has an individual make-up water meter.

1 point   if each boiler has an individual fuel flow meter.

1 point   if a definite preventive maintenance schedule is followed.

0 points   if equipment is maintained or repaired only when it breaks down.

3 points   if an energy recovery system is used. This may be a heat exchanger of water to water, an air wheel or any of several types in common use.

2 points   if heat generation is controlled by a system using an economizer system by comparing inside and outside temperature.

SELF-EVALUATING CHECKLIST FOR HEAT GENERATION

EVALUATOR_____

DATE_____

UNIT NAME _____

SHEET NO. _____

NO.	LOCATION	RATING VALUE MAX. = 17	Insulation Good	Insulation Average	Insulation Poor	Flanges Insulated	No Leaks	Some Leaks	Many Leaks	Auto Controls	Standard Op. Procedure	Steam Meter	Fuel Meter	Make-Up Water Meter	Preventive Maintenance	Fix as Required Schedule	Energy Recovery	Economizer Controls			TOTAL POINTS
			2	1	0	2	2	1	0	1	1	1	1	1	1	0	3	2			
1																					

HEATING SYSTEM (DISTRIBUTION) RATING INSTRUCTIONS

2 points   if insulation is in good condition with no broken or missing sections. The insulation must not be wet, crumbly or cracked.

1 point   if insulation is in average condition with small sections broken or missing. The insulation must not be wet, crumbly or cracked.

0 points if insulation is in poor condition with sections missing, broken, wet, crumbly or cracked.

2 points if flanges, valves and regulators are insulated with removable lagging.

2 points if the steam system has no leaks.

1 point if the steam system has minor leaks around valve packing, shaft seals, etc.

0 points if the steam system has many leaks, valves, regulators and traps have dripping leaks, steam plumes, etc.

2 points if the control system to each area is adequate. The control system shall maintain the temperature in each room close to the thermostat setting.

1 point if the control system to each area is only a general control without the ability to control each room.

0 points if the control system has little or no control over the area temperature. Also included here is a control system that allows the heating and cooling systems to oppose each other in the same general area.

1 point if definite standard operating procedures are used. These should be written and posted.

1 point if a definite preventive maintenance schedule is followed.

0 points if equipment is maintained or repaired only when it breaks down.

1 point if the area is conditioned only when occupied. This will apply especially to auditoriums, work rooms, hobby shops, TV rooms, etc.

0 points if the area is conditioned all the time regardless of occupancy.

2 points if the zone control is good and certain areas can be secured when not in use or require less temperature conditioning.

1 point if the zone control only allows general areas to be secured when conditions dictate.

0 points if zone control cannot be secured without securing a large general area.

SELF-EVALUATING CHECKLIST FOR HEAT DISTRIBUTION

EVALUATOR_____

DATE_____

UNIT_____
NAME

SHEET NO. _____

NO.	LOCATION	RATING VALUE MAX. = 13	Insulation Good	Insulation Average	Insulation Poor	Flanges Insulated	No Leaks	Some Leaks	Many Leaks	Control Good	Control Average	Control Poor	Standard Op. Procedure	Preventive Maintenance	Fix as Required	Condition as Required	Constant Conditioning	Zone Control Good	Zone Control Average	Zone Control Poor	TOTAL POINTS
			2	1	0	2	2	1	0	2	1	0	1	1	0	1	0	2	1	0	
1																					

COOLING SYSTEM (GENERATION) RATING INSTRUCTIONS

2 points if the insulation is in good condition with no broken or missing sections. The insulation must not be wet, crumbly or cracked. Closed cell insulation will be considered average condition because of deterioration that occurs in this type of material.

1 point	if insulation is in average condition with small sections broken or missing. The insulation must not be wet or crumbly. The outside shell of open cell insulation must be intact with only minor breaks.
0 points	if insulation is in poor condition with sections missing, broken, wet, crumbly or cracked.
1 point	if flanges and valves are insulated.
1 point	if definite standard operating procedures are used. These should be written and posted near the control panel.
1 point	if unit has an individual watt-hour meter so the real-time power consumption can be determined.
1 point	if a definite preventive maintenance schedule is followed.
0 points	if equipment is maintained or repaired only when it breaks down.
3 points	if an energy recovery system is used. This may be a heat exchanger of water to water, an air wheel or any of several types in common use.
2 points	if outside air is utilized to help condition areas that require cooling even on cold days.
1 point	if the fresh air ratio is regulated by comparing inside requirements with outside temperatures.

SELF-EVALUATING CHECKLIST FOR COOLING SYSTEM GENERATION

EVALUATOR_____

DATE_____

UNIT NAME _____

SHEET NO. _____

NO.	LOCATION	RATING VALUE MAX. = 12	Insulation Good	Insulation Average	Insulation Poor	Flanges Insulated	Standard Op. Procedure	Ind. Power Meter	Preventive Maintenance	Fix as Required	Energy Recovery	Outside Air Used	Req. Fresh Air								TOTAL POINTS
			2	1	0	1	1	1	1	0	3	2	1								
1																					

COOLING SYSTEM (DISTRIBUTION) RATING INSTRUCTIONS

2 points	if the insulation is in good condition with no broken or missing sections. The insulation must not be wet, crumbly or cracked. "Closed cell" insulation will be considered average condition because of deterioration that occurs in this type of material.
1 point	if insulation is in average condition with small sections broken or missing. The insulation must not be wet, crumbly. The outside shell of "open cell" insulation must be intact with only minor breaks.
0 points	if insulation is in poor condition with sections missing, broken, wet, crumbly or cracked.
1 point	if flanges and valves are insulated.
1 point	if definite standard operating procedures are used. These should be written and posted near the control panel.

2 points   if the control system to each area is adequate. The control system shall maintain the temperature in each room close to the thermostat setting.

1 point   if the control system to each area is only a general control without the ability to control each room.

0 points   if the control system has little or no control over the area temperature. Also included here is a control system that allows the heating and cooling systems to oppose each other in the same general areas.

1 point   if a definite preventive maintenance schedule is followed.

0 points   if equipment is maintained or repaired only when it breaks down.

1 point   if the area is conditioned only when occupied. This will apply especially to auditoriums, work rooms, hobby shops, TV rooms, etc.

0 points   if the area is conditioned all the time regardless of occupancy.

2 points   if the zone control is good and certain areas can be secured when not in use or require less temperature conditioning.

1 point   if the zone control only allows general areas to be secured when conditions dictate.

0 points   if zone control cannot be secured without securing a large general area.

SELF-EVALUATING CHECKLIST FOR COOLING DISTRIBUTION

EVALUATOR _____
DATE _____
UNIT _____
NAME
SHEET NO. _____

NO.	LOCATION	RATING VALUE MAX. = 11	Insulation Good	Insulation Average	Insulation Poor	Flange Insulated	Standard Op. Procedure	Controls Good	Controls Average	Controls Poor	Preventive Maintenance	Fix as Required	Condition as Required	Constant Conditioning	Zone Control Good	Zone Control Average	Zone Control Poor					TOTAL POINTS
			2	1	0	2	1	2	1	0	1	0	1	0	2	1	0					
1																						

ELECTRICAL POWER DISTRIBUTION RATING INSTRUCTIONS

2 points   for operation of a recording ammeter.

1 point   for hourly electrical usage pattern of building being determined.

1 point   for study of electrical requirements with the Power Company staff.

1 point   for installation of a power peak warning system.

1 point   for analysis to eliminate power peak demands.

1 point   if a definite standard operating procedure is used. This shall be written and posted near the control panel.

1 point   if definite preventive maintenance schedule is followed.

0 points   if equipment is maintained or repaired only when it breaks down.

2 points   for overall system Power Factor of 90 percent or above at main service.

SELF-EVALUATING CHECKLIST FOR ELECTRICAL POWER DISTRIBUTION

EVALUATOR			POWER DISTRIBUTION CONDITIONS																		
DATE																					
UNIT NAME																					
SHEET NO.			Recording Meter	Usage Pattern	Power Co. Coord.	Power Peak Warning	Power Demand Limited	Standard Op. Procedure	Preventive Maintenance	Fix as Required	90% Power Factor									TOTAL POINTS
NO.	LOCATION	RATING VALUE MAX. = 10	2	1	1	1	1	1	1	0	2									
1																					

HOT WATER SERVICE RATING INSTRUCTIONS

2 points if the insulation is in good condition with no broken or missing sections. The insulation must not be wet, crumbly or cracked.

1 point if insulation is in average condition with small sections broken or missing. The insulation must not be wet or crumbly.

0 points if insulation is in poor condition with sections missing, broken, wet, crumbly or cracked.

1 point if faucets and valves are in good repair.

0 points if faucets and valves leak externally or internally.

1 point if definite standard operating procedures are used. These should be written and posted.

1 point if a definite preventive maintenance schedule is followed.

0 points if equipment is maintained or repaired only when it breaks down.

SELF-EVALUATING CHECKLIST FOR HOT WATER SERVICE

EVALUATOR			HOT WATER SERVICE CONDITIONS																		
DATE																					
UNIT NAME																					
SHEET NO.			Insulation Good	Insulation Average	Insulation Poor	No Faucet Leaks	Faucet Leaks	Standard Op. Procedure	Preventive Maintenance	Fix as Required											TOTAL POINTS
NO.	LOCATION	RATING VALUE MAX. = 5	2	1	0	1	0	1	1	0											
1																					

LAUNDRY RATING INSTRUCTIONS

2 points   if overall equipment is in good condition. This means all equipment is operating per manufacturers' specifications. There are no leaks; gaskets and seals are all functioning properly, nothing is "jury rigged" to enable it to work, and equipment is used for its designed function, etc.

1 point   if overall equipment is in average shape. Equipment condition will deteriorate over time due to normal usage. If equipment has been in use for a few years it should be placed in this category.

0 points   if equipment is in poor condition. This includes leaks, malfunctioning equipment, improperly adjusted components, bypassing manufacturers' operational procedures, etc.

1 point   if faucets, valves and traps are in good condition. Faucets should not leak, valves should seal tight and traps cannot have any blow by.

3 points   if energy recovery systems are used. These can be any of several systems on the market today.

1 point   if the laundry hot water generator is secured during laundry off periods such as evenings and weekends. An analysis should be made of each hot water system to determine the recovery time to ensure hot water is available when required.

2 points   if the insulation is in good condition with no broken or missing sections. The insulation must not be wet, crumbly or cracked.

1 point   if insulation is in average condition with small sections broken or missing. The insulation must not be wet, or crumbly.

0 points   if insulation is in poor condition with sections missing, broken, wet, crumbly or cracked.

2 points   if flanges, valves and regulators are insulated with removable lagging.

1 point   if definite standard operating procedures are used. These should be written and posted.

1 point   if a definite preventive maintenance schedule is followed.

0 points   if equipment is maintained or repaired only when it breaks down.

SELF-EVALUATING CHECKLIST FOR LAUNDRY

			LAUNDRY CONDITIONS																
EVALUATOR			Equip. Condition Good	Equip. Condition Average	Equip. Condition Poor	No Leaks	Energy Recovery System	Hot Water Gen. Secured	Insulation Good	Insulation Average	Insulation Poor	Flanges Insulated	Standard Op. Procedure	Preventive Maintenance	Fix as Required					TOTAL POINTS
NO.	LOCATION	RATING VALUE MAX. = 13	2	1	0	1	3	1	2	1	0	2	1	1	0					
1																				

COMPRESSED AIR SERVICE RATING INSTRUCTIONS

1 point	if outlets and valves are in good repair.
0 points	if outlets and valves leak externally or internally.
1 point	if compressors are properly sized to shave peak demands.
1 point	if additional compressors are brought on line as demand requires and not run continuously.
1 point	if definite standard operating procedures are used. These should be written and posted.
1 point	if a definite preventive maintenance schedule is followed.
0 points	if equipment is maintained or repaired only when it breaks down.

SELF-EVALUATING CHECKLIST FOR COMPRESSED AIR

EVALUATOR _____

DATE _____

UNIT NAME _____

SHEET NO. _____

COMPRESSED AIR CONDITIONS

NO.	LOCATION	RATING VALUE MAX. = 5	No Outlet Leaks	Outlet Leaks	Compressors Sized	Compressors on Demand	Standard Op. Procedure	Preventive Maintenance	Fix as Required												TOTAL POINTS
			1	0	1	1	1	1	0											
1																				

WATER SERVICE RATING INSTRUCTIONS

1 point	if faucets and valves are in good repair.
0 points	if faucets and valves leak externally or internally.
1 point	if definite standard operating procedures are used. These should be written and posted.
1 point	if a definite preventive maintenance schedule is followed.
0 points	if equipment is maintained or repaired only when it breaks down.
1 point	if there is no equipment that uses once-through cooling water and discharges to sewer.
1 point	if water-consuming equipment is turned off when not in use.

SELF-EVALUATING CHECKLIST FOR WATER

EVALUATOR _____

DATE _____

UNIT NAME _____

SHEET NO. _____

WATER CONDITIONS

NO.	LOCATION	RATING VALUE MAX. = 5	No Faucet Leaks	Faucet Leaks	Standard Op. Procedure	Preventive Maintenance	Fix as Required	No Equip. Use Water Once	Equipment Off											TOTAL POINTS
			1	0	1	1	0	1	1											
1																				

PROCESS HEATING RATING INSTRUCTIONS

1 point   if the flue gas waste heat from processing equipment is extracted to heat relatively low temperature makeup, process and space heating water.

2 points   if all high-temperature piping, ovens, dryers, tanks and processing equipment are covered with suitable insulating material. The insulation must not be wet, crumbly or cracked.

0 points   if insulation is in poor condition with sections missing, broken, wet, crumbly or cracked.

1 point   if definite standard operating procedures are used. These should be written and posted near the control panel.

1 point   if gas-heated equipment is checked for combustion efficiency on a regular basis.

1 point   if a definite preventive maintenance schedule is followed.

0 points   if equipment is maintained or repaired only when it breaks down.

SELF-EVALUATING CHECKLIST FOR PROCESS HEATING

			PROCESS HEATING CONDITIONS																			
EVALUATOR			Flue Gas Waste Heat	High Temp. Areas Insulated	Insulation Poor	Exhaust Process Air	Standard Op. Procedure	Combustion Efficiency	Preventive Maintenance	Fix as Required													TOTAL POINTS
NO.	LOCATION	RATING VALUE MAX. = 6	1	2	0	1	1	1	1	0													
1																							

VEHICLE OPERATIONS/MAINTENANCE RATING INSTRUCTIONS

2 points   if a driver training course in economical operation is utilized.

2 points   if the fueling of vehicles is supervised and controlled.

2 points   for the maintenance of vehicles on a scheduled basis.

3 points   if there is an operating program on van pool and/or car pool.

0 points   if vehicles are observed operating with tires underinflated.

1 point   if a vehicle operating schedule procedure is in effect.

0 points   if vehicles are dispatched without regard for optimum use.

1 point   if mileage and fuel consumption data is available to all drivers.

SELF-EVALUATING CHECKLIST FOR VEHICLE OPERATIONS/MAINTENANCE

			VEHICLE OPERATIONS/MAINTENANCE CONDITIONS																							
			Economical Training	Supervised Fueling	Scheduled Maintenance	Van/Car Pool	Underinflated Tires	Dispatch Schedules	No Display Schedules	Mileage/Fuel Data															TOTAL POINTS
NO.	LOCATION	RATING VALUE MAX. = 10	2	2	2	3	0	1	0	1															
1																									

EVALUATOR_____

DATE_____

UNIT NAME_____

SHEET NO. _____

13

Case Study: Energy Audit Of Food Service Facilities

by RICHARD FESSLER
Marriott Corporation

Optimizing energy utilization for food service kitchens is extremely important when it is realized that these facilities are found in schools, hospitals, commercial and institutional buildings, as well as food-processing centers and restaurants.

Over the last several years there has been a continued increase in the use of energy-consuming equipment in the foodservice kitchens. This is especially true in new and modernized facilities. The food service industry has come to realize the benefits to be gained in cooking more efficiently.

Because of the national energy situation, food service personnel must become more aware, not only of the importance of using energy, but also how it is used in the kitchen—and to use it more efficiently. It is the manager's and Engineering Department's responsibility to help in every way possible to manage energy resources. Using energy efficiently, to some people, means simply to turn the equipment off. But it is really more than that. It also means turning equipment on at the right time.

In the case of cooking equipment, it also means setting controls to the correct temperatures for each operation and reducing the temperature for idle or slack periods of time. It really means *managing* energy. Paying attention to the types of utensils

342

used and the ways they are used is important. The condition and manner in which equipment is used has an effect on the amount of energy it will consume. To save energy may require the changing of work schedules, food preparation methods, and, yes, the retraining of kitchen personnel.

There is a great variety of food service equipment. There is even a greater variety of food preparation procedures and combinations of equipment in the various types of kitchens.

The food service manager is the expert in food preparation, but he may not have looked closely at his operation from an energy management point of view.

COOKING EQUIPMENT

Energy management principles or techniques which apply to cooking equipment are:
- Preheat only the equipment or portion of the equipment that will be used.
- Preheat equipment just before using, as specified.
- Reduce temperature or turn equipment off during slack periods of the day.
- Use full production capacity of equipment when possible or practical.
- Select the correct size of equipment for the cooking job.
- Use cooking equipment as recommended by the manufacturer.
- Maintain equipment in good repair.
- Keep equipment clean and schedule cleaning to prevent energy waste.

There is nothing complicated about these ideas. Any cook can easily learn to follow them. All the cook has to do is think about what his food production requirements are going to be for a particular meal preparation period.

Now let's apply these principles or management techniques to each of the major types of cooking equipment.

PREHEAT ONLY THE EQUIPMENT THAT WILL BE USED

To apply the first energy management principle, the food

service manager must schedule his food production requirement, cooking on as few pieces of equipment as possible. He must give some thought to the variety and quantities of food to be cooked and the time required to cook each. It may also be possible to finish some foods requiring short cooking cycles, such as gravies, on the same equipment after cooking some foods requiring longer cooking cycles, but which can be and are normally held for a longer period of time before serving.

PREHEAT EQUIPMENT JUST BEFORE USING

To apply the principle of preheating equipment just before using requires knowing how much time is required to preheat each piece of equipment to operating temperatures. The preheat time may vary not only for each type of equipment, but also for some of the different models of the same types of equipment. For example, some fryers will preheat to operating temperature in 4½ minutes, some require 5 minutes and others require as much as 6 minutes to preheat.

Often, the difference in time is so short that it is not necessary to burden ourselves to learn them for each model of equipment. The approximate time required to preheat the various types and sizes of cooking equipment is in the energy operating information tables for ranges, ovens, fryers, griddles and broilers which can be obtained through the Energy Department.

REDUCE TEMPERATURE OR TURN EQUIPMENT OFF DURING SLACK PERIODS OF THE DAY

Slack periods of the day means after the principal meal periods are over. During slack periods, a good energy management practice is to turn the cooking equipment off or set the controls back to a lower temperature.

The table on Electric Fryer Energy Operating Information shows that less than one-half of the energy is required to maintain a fryer at 200°F than at an operating temperature of 350° F. It also shows that the time to recover from 200°F to 350°F is only 2 minutes for the smaller fryers. If a food service operator has several fryers, one may be left on, idling at operating temperature, set one back to 200°F and turn the rest of them off. The same thing could be done with griddles, ranges and convection ovens.

At first glance it would seem that it would require less energy to allow a griddle to idle at operating temperature than to allow it to cool and have to preheat it again in an hour. This is not the case. It will take the average griddle 2½ to 3 hours to cool down to room temperature from an operating temperature of 400°F. Using the 36-inch, 12-kw griddle as determined by the equipment identification plate, the energy saved if the griddle were cooled down to room temperature could be calculated as follows:

Savings = 1,808 watthour x 3 hours − 2,400 watthours
= 5,424 watthours − 2,400 watthours
= 3,024 watthours

Making this calculation for the other types of cooking equipment would produce similar results. The conclusion is that energy can be saved, and it would be a good management practice to turn equipment off anytime that doing so does not interfere with production requirements.

USE FULL PRODUCTION CAPACITY WHEN POSSIBLE OR PRACTICAL

Cooking at full production capacity of the equipment means cooking full loads on every cooking cycle. It also means cooking one load right after another. This prevents wasting energy during the cooking cycle for maintaining part of the equipment, such as one-half of an oven cavity, idle at operating temperature.

It is good management to load and unload equipment as fast as possible. This reduces the total time that equipment must be heated for each meal cooking period.

If foods requiring different temperatures are to be baked in the same equipment, one following the other, the foods requiring the lowest temperatures should be cooked first, if practical.

The question arises as to when is it and when is it not practical to cook at full production capacity of equipment one load right after another. Foods cooked to order and foods having a short life in the finished state must be cooked to fit the demand. This may include such foods as fried and scrambled eggs, fried potatoes, pancakes, steaks, Texas toast, etc. It may not be practical to cook these foods at the full production capacity of the equipment. The equipment used to cook foods to order and foods with short finished life most often are fryers, griddles and broilers.

Equipment may be used to full production capacity when cooking foods that may be cooked ahead of time, or partially cooked and held to be finished later. This may include breads and to some extent, chicken and hamburger patties. Foods only partially cooked may include hamburger patties and steaks.

Ovens, both deck ovens and convection ovens, are usually used to cook foods ahead of time. Partial cooking of foods may be done in ovens and later finished on griddles. Chef uses his own discretion.

SELECT THE CORRECT SIZE OF EQUIPMENT FOR THE COOKING OPERATION

Selecting the correct size of equipment for each particular operation simply means using the small item if only small loads are to be cooked, rather than preheating a large one. In the case of griddles, ranges or ovens, only the number of sections needed should be used.

USE EQUIPMENT PROPERLY

Probably the greatest waste of energy in cooking, except for leaving equipment idling at operating temperature, is improper use of equipment. This is also a cause of improperly finished food products which also waste energy because some of the foods must be thrown out and more foods cooked.

To assure efficient heat transfer from hot plates and french plates of ranges, and hearths of deck ovens, only heavy, flat-bottomed pots and pans should be used. Pans that are bent or warped not only waste energy, but also result in uneven finishing of the product.

On french plates, the pot should cover the entire surface of the plate and not extend over the edge of the french plate more than one inch.

Ovens are designed to accommodate standard size bake pans properly. When smaller pans are used, the oven is not being used to its full production capacity.

Proper loading and unloading of foods into or on equipment is important. Overloading the fryer basket so that part of the food is not submerged, results in part of the load to be thrown away or an inferior grease-soaked product being served.

Placing pans too close to the sides, back, or front of ovens causes poor circulation of hot air in the cavity, resulting in improperly cooked foods, wasted food, and wasted energy.

Excessive opening of oven doors or frequent peeking into the oven wastes heat and may result in a poor quality product. Slow loading and unloading of ovens, especially convection ovens, causes not only a waste of heat but may cool the oven down enough to cause a poor product.

Loading ovens and fryers before they have become completely saturated with heat can also result in a poor quality finished food product.

Oven doors can be easily checked to be sure they are closing properly. A tight door seal is not as important on convection ovens as it is on deck ovens, but excessive leakage will waste energy.

Burned-out indicator lamps should be replaced so that the cook can tell if the equipment is on and when it has reached the desired operating temperature.

Because of expansion and contraction due to heating and cooling, heating elements sometimes become loose on the griddles and ranges. It is not very easy to check these but the loose element problem can be easily recognized. On griddles, and ranges in particular, the preheating will be slow and inefficient. Griddles may have hot and cold spots because of the inefficient transfer of heat. Hot and cold spots on griddles can result in wasting food, time, and energy.

KEEP EQUIPMENT CLEAN AND SCHEDULE
CLEANING TO PREVENT WASTING ENERGY

Cooking equipment will use less energy if it is kept clean. Spills and splatters should be cleaned as they happen throughout the day. (CLEAN AS YOU GO.) This will make the equipment easier to clean later. Burned-on spillage and food particles will result in poor performance of the equipment and produce an inferior or unacceptable product. For example, large spillage on the hearth of a deck oven will act as insulation and cause uneven transfer of heat to the bottom of a baking pan. Particles of food that are burned onto the griddle may stick to the next load of food causing it to be wasted. Excessive buildup of burned-on food particles on a griddle will cause uneven heat transfer and can result in unacceptable products. Unnecessary or excessive cleaning by burning off of the heating elements on fryers will also waste energy.

The grease in fryers should be kept clean. This prevents a poor finished food product which in turn may require cooking more food. Fans on convection ovens should be kept clean to provide maximum air delivery and assure even heating throughout the oven cavity. It is also important to keep the breather space below the door on deck ovens clean. This allows for expansion of air when it is heated and prevents the door from being forced open which in turn results in uneven baking and energy loss.

Cleaning of equipment should be scheduled so as not to require using additional energy in the cleaning process. For instance, clean equipment before it cools down, if it is the type that is easier to clean when it is warm. The cooking surface of a griddle is easier to clean if it is cleaned before it cools much below 200°F. The grease chute and drip tray are easier to clean if done before the grease congeals.

When commercial oven cleaners are used, requiring a hot oven for cleaning of the exterior surfaces and around the door, they should be applied while the oven is still above 200°F. If only a damp cloth or mild detergent is required for cleaning the oven, it can be done easier if the oven is allowed to cool. Convection ovens are best cleaned when they are cool enough to handle comfortably.

If the heating elements on fryers are to be burned off, do so at the close of the day before they cool. However, it is important to allow the grease to drip off the elements before burning them off to prevent fires. The fat may be strained anytime after it cools enough to handle. However, it should be done before it congeals to prevent reheating it. Splatters and spills may be cleaned from the exterior surfaces of the fryer anytime.

A range may be cleaned anytime after it is cool enough to handle. Since the range top operates at a temperature high enough to burn the hot plates clean, only the exterior surfaces need to be wiped with a damp cloth. To clean the range oven, follow suggestions for cleaning a deck oven.

To perform an energy audit in a food service facility requires a knowledge of the energy consumption for various types of equipment. Tables 13-1 through 13-5 illustrate energy operating data for typical equipment.

REFRIGERATION EQUIPMENT

Refrigerators and freezers work more hours than any other equipment in the kitchen. Good energy management requires applying the following:

- Make sure that door gaskets are cleaned and fit properly.
- Place refrigerated and frozen foods into refrigerator or freezer immediately upon receiving from the delivery.
- Do not place hot foods in refrigerator or freezer.
- Do not open doors frequently or hold them open for long periods of time.
- Keep evaporator coils or walls free of excessive frost.
- Keep condenser coils free of dust, lint or obstructions that tend to reduce air circulation (proper circulation is of utmost importance for proper operation).
- Make sure equipment is not located in a hot environment.
- Maintain equipment in good repair (maintenance).

Table 13-1. Energy Operating Information for Electric Fryer

Capacity	Nameplate KW	Minutes to Preheat to 350°F	Watthours to Preheat	watthours to Maintain at 350°F	Watthours to Maintain at 200°F	Minutes to Recover from 200°F to 350°F
12 lbs	4.5	4½	338	400	190	2
15 lbs	4.5-6	4½	450	485	230	2
28 lbs	12	5	1,000	770	360	2
45 lbs	18	6	1,800	1,050	495	2-3
50 lbs*	22	6	2,200	836	390	2-3
60 lbs	18	8	2,400	1,300	520	3-4

*High speed deep well fryer.

Table 13-2. Energy Operating Information for Electric Griddle

Griddle Size in Width	Nameplate KW	Minutes to Preheat to 350°F	Minutes to Preheat to 400°F	Watthours to Preheat to 350°F / 400°F	Watthours to Maintain 400°F	Watthours to Maintain 200°F	Minutes to Recover from 200°F to 350°F
18 inch	3	7	12	350 / 600	500	200	9
24 inch	6	7	12	700 / 1,200	980	390	9
24 inch	8	7	12½	935 / 1,670	1,200	480	9
30 inch	6.5	7	12	760 / 1,300	925	370	9
36 inch	12	7	12	1,400 / 2,400	1,808	725	9
36 inch	16.5	7	12	1,926 / 3,300	2,100	840	9
48 inch	22	7	12	2,570 / 4,400	2,800	1,100	9
72 inch	32	7	12	3,735 / 6,400	4,200	1,800	9

Table 13-3. Energy Operating Information for Electric Deck Oven

Type Oven	Size	KW Input	Minutes to Preheat	Watthours to Preheat	Watthours to Maintain				
					300°F	350°F	400°F	450°F	550°F
All purpose	1 pan	6	20	2,000	487	594	702	810	
All purpose	2 pan	6.2	36	3,720	531	649	767	88	
Bake	2 pan	6.2	30	3,100	510	623	737	850	
Bake	4 pan	7.5	90	11,250	660	807	953	1,100	
Bake	6 pan	11	120	22,000	1,020	1,247	1,473	1,700	
Pizza	6 pizza (2 pan)	7.2	45	5,400	4.0	507	599	691	875
*Polythermic Bake	2 pan	6.2	30	3,100	510	625	740	860	
*Polythermic	2 pan	6.2	36	3,720	535	650	770	890	
All purpose *Polythermic Pizza	6 pizzas	7.2	45	5,400	410	510	600	695	885

*Plus 1/8 HP motor for circulating air.

Table 13-4 (a). Energy Operating Information for Electric Convection Oven

Nameplate KW	Minutes to Preheat	Watthours to Preheat	*Watthour to Maintenance at 350°F
11	9	1,605	1,917
11	10	1,835	1,800
11	10	1,835	2,100
15.5	9	1,650	2,300

*Various sizes of bake cavities.

Table 13-4 (b). Energy Operating Information for Microwave Oven

Nameplate Wattage (Operating Wattage)	Watts Output Into Cavity	Watthours to Maintain Idle	Standby Wattage
1,500	650	200	0
2,200	1,000	275	0
2,400	1,000	290	0
3,500	1,300	375	0
5,400	2,700	450	0

Table 13-5. Energy Operating Information for Electric Range

Types of Cooking Tops	Manufacturer's Nameplate KW	Minutes to Preheat to 400°F	Watthours to Preheat to 400°F	Minutes to Preheat to 900°F	Watthours to Preheat to 900°F	Watthours to** Maintain at 350°F
Divided Top	15.3	12	3,060	30	7,650	2,200
French Plates	10-12	3	500-600	8	1,333-1,600	200-300*
Griddle Top	16.5	12.5	3,438			2,160

*Each french plate on low setting.

**Also, low setting with three heat and infinite heat switches.

MAKE SURE DOOR GASKETS
ARE CLEAN AND FIT SNUGLY

The dollar bill test is used to determine the condition of a refrigerator or freezer door gasket. In this test, the bill is placed on the refrigerator mullion and the door is closed on it. If the bill is held securely in place by the door gasket, it is considered to fit snugly enough. The test should be made for the entire length of the gasket. If it is not held securely, the door should be adjusted and/or the gasket replaced. In the absence of a bill, a 3x5 card or other piece of paper may be used. Visual inspection will also sometimes reveal a worn or deteriorated door gasket. Gaskets should be maintained properly and kept clean and free of food particles.

PLACE REFRIGERATED AND FROZEN FOODS INTO
REFRIGERATOR OR FREEZER IMMEDIATELY UPON ARRIVAL

If frozen and refrigerated foods are allowed to remain on the loading dock or in the receiving area, they will absorb heat and then require more energy to cool to the desired or safe holding temperature. Check for over-thawed foods.

DO NOT PLACE HOT FOOD IN REFRIGERATOR OR
FREEZER UNLESS ABSOLUTELY NECESSARY

Food should be cooled as near to room temperature as practical before placing it into the refrigerator.

DO NOT OPEN DOORS FREQUENTLY OR HOLD
THEM OPEN FOR LONG PERIODS OF TIME

When doors are opened, cold air escapes from the refrigeration unit and is replaced with warm moist air. The warm air adds heat and the moisture increases frosting of the evaporator.

To eliminate frequent opening of doors, all of the foods that will be needed for a meal preparation should be removed at the same time. The same applies to placing foods into the units.

The foods should be assembled on a cart or a table near the door of the refrigeration equipment so that they can all be quickly loaded at the same time. Food should be so placed that it is easily accessible for quick removal. Some foods can be identified more quickly if they are placed in see-through containers, or properly marked for visual identification. Adequate lighting and clean lenses on lighting fixtures will help in finding desired foods more quickly. Turn lights off when feasible.

KEEP EVAPORATOR COILS FREE OF EXCESSIVE FROST

Walk-in and some reach-in or roll-in refrigeration equipment use a bank of evaporator coils to pick up heat from inside of the refrigerator or freezer. Many of the reach-in or roll-in units have evaporator coils wrapped around the outside of the interior wall and pick up heat through the walls of the unit.

Ice or frost collected on the evaporator coils or the walls acts as an insulator for the coils and makes it more difficult for the refrigerant to pick up the heat from inside of the refrigerator or freezer. Some units automatically defrost every 24 hours. Others must be defrosted by turning the compressor off periodically. Defrosting should be performed when approximately one-quarter inch of frost or ice has accumulated on the coils and before circulation of air through the coils is hampered. Keeping foods in covered or sealed containers helps to prevent moisture from escaping from the foods and reduces the amount of moisture that collects on the evaporator coils. Note: during inventory, doors should be closed and/or temperature adjusted to eliminate frost build-up on coils.

KEEP CONDENSER COILS FREE OF DUST, LINT OR OBSTRUCTIONS THAT TEND TO REDUCE AIR CIRCULATION

It is natural for condenser coils to attract dust and lint and also it seems natural for people to stack boxes, cartons, etc. around the condenser coils of refrigerators and freezers.

Anything that reduces air circulation through and around the condenser reduces the efficiency of the unit and thus wastes energy. Fan blades that are dusty are also less efficient in delivering air through the coils.

Dust may be removed with a brush, but the best tool is a vacuum cleaner. A vacuum cleaner picks up dust for easy disposal, rather than scattering it around the kitchen and depositing part of it back on the coils.

MAKE SURE EQUIPMENT IS NOT LOCATED IN A HOT ENVIRONMENT

Refrigeration equipment should not be placed near heat-generating equipment. If it must be so placed, it should be shielded to prevent or reduce the effect of the heat-generating equipment. Some kitchen make-up air may be brought in around the refrigeration equipment. When refrigerators and freezers are located in a separate room or when the compressors and condensors are remotely located in a separate room from the kitchen, the room should have adequate ventilation and the air should circulate freely. If the condensers are located out-of-doors they should be shielded from the hot sun and kept free of obstructions such as weeds or grass.

MAINTAIN EQUIPMENT IN GOOD REPAIR

Equipment always works better and more efficiently if it is kept in good repair. This includes keeping drive belts properly adjusted and replacing them when they are worn. Suspension springs should be replaced when they become weak or break. The equipment should be kept fully charged with refrigerant. When a unit is low on refrigerant it will run excessively and fail to cool the inside of the refrigerator or freezer to the desired temperature.

KITCHEN VENTILATING SYSTEM

Food service kitchens have a special ventilating system. A hood is placed over the cooking equipment to remove smoke, vapors, food odors and heat generated by the cooking processes.

The *design* rates for air flow through the kitchen ventilating system are prescribed by law. These same rates are recommended by the National Fire Protection Association. They are: Wall hood—100 CFM/square foot hood face; Island hood—150 CFM/square foot hood face; Shelf hood—300 CFM/foot (length of shelf).

Air must be brought into the kitchen to replace the large amounts of air that are exhausted. Some of this make-up air is brought in from the dining areas, but most of it is brought into the kitchen directly from the outside. The outside air may have to be heated in the winter and cooled in the summer. In some cases the air is cooled with evaporative equipment and in other cases with refrigeration equipment.

This heating and cooling of large amounts of make-up air wastes energy. This is especially true if the make-up air is cooled with refrigeration equipment.

The codes do not say that the ventilating equipment must be operated at full capacity or at the prescribed ventilating rates. They just state that *"it must be so designed."* Also, these design criteria make no distinction between gas and electric equipment.

When there is little or no cooking, it is not necessary to ventilate the kitchen at the full design rate. Larger ventilating systems may have more than one exhaust fan. Only the fans needed to remove the smoke, vapors, food odors and heat generated at any one time need be turned on. In case of a single fan system, two-speed or three-speed fan can reduce the exhaust air flow.

The few energy management principles applicable to kitchen ventilating systems are simple to apply. They are:
- Operate only the number of exhaust fans required to capture cooking vapors and smoke.
- Operate two-speed fans or three-speed fans at the lowest speed required to capture cooking vapors and smoke.
- Turn fans off when not needed.
- Keep filters clean to assure proper flow of air through ventilating system. This will also keep motors from overloading with proper air flow.

OPERATE ONLY THE NUMBER OF EXHAUST FANS REQUIRED TO CAPTURE COOKING VAPORS AND SMOKE

The ventilating system should be operated with the smallest number of fans which will capture all of the food cooking vapors and smoke. It can be assumed that the latent heat will also be captured and removed. The manner and location of the make-up air supply, and the types and location of cooking equipment will provide the best ventilation. This is best determined by experimenting with the operation of the system.

When forced make-up air is used for the kitchen, certain make-up air fans should be interlocked electrically with certain exhaust fans. Thus when a fan is turned off to reduce the amount of air exhausted, the make-up air will be reduced by the same amount.

OPERATE TWO-SPEED OR THREE-SPEED FANS AT THE LOWEST SPEED REQUIRED TO CAPTURE COOKING VAPORS AND SMOKE

Many single-fan ventilating systems do not have a two-speed or three-speed fan. The cost of changing the fan should be weighed against the energy savings by operating the system at a lower ventilation rate. Most of the savings would be in the heating and cooling of make-up air.

TURN FANS OFF WHEN NOT NEEDED

It makes sense to turn exhaust fans off when they are not needed to remove smoke and vapors, or to keep the kitchen cool. The natural updraft through the ventilating hood will provide some ventilation for the kitchen. It may be enough to capture the smoke and vapors with limited cooking.

KEEP FILTERS CLEAN TO ASSURE PROPER FLOW OF AIR THROUGH THE VENTILATING SYSTEM

Filters should be kept clean to assure a free flow of air through the system.

When grease extractors are used in a ventilating system there is no cleaning problem, except for emptying the grease receptacle and wiping down the hood at the end of the day. Manufacturers of these grease extractors claim that the extractors will not accumulate enough lint, dust, and grease to require washing more than once or twice each year.

When filters are used (older installations), they must be cleaned as often as necessary. Although cleaning of the filters is a messy job, it is a simple operation. The filters may be removed and put through the dishwasher anytime the system is shut down. The frequency of washing filters depends on the cooking operation. It varies from approximately once per week to once per month. Check with a warewashing chemical vendor for proper cleaning product.

To make it easier to apply energy management principles, the Energy Audit Form, Figure 13-1 has been developed. The use of this form is left up to the food service manager and will vary according to each situation and need. Completing the form and analyzing the situation are the first steps in establishing an energy conservation program for the operation.

Operating hints for cooking equipment are summarized in Figure 13-2.

Organize your workload.
Vents are important.
Eliminate problems with good cleaning procedures.
No peeking.
Fat level should be maintained.
Remember not to overload baskets.
Your produce depends on the frying fat.
Elements need to be cleaned also.
Reset thermostats when not in use.
Remember to keep door closed.
Every so often clean condenser coils and fan.
Food should be cooled before placing into refrigerator.
Refrigerant levels should be checked.
Ice should not be allowed to build up.
Gaskets and seals should be in good condition.
Remember to preheat and stagger.
Arrange pots close together.

Need to use lids and as little water as possible.
Good cleaning procedures.
Evaluate types of controls used.
Stagger and preheat.
Traces of sediment and particles should be removed.
Each day check water levels on kettles and pressure relief valves on cookers.
Allow pressure to reach 0 before opening door.
Maintain door gaskets.
Manufacturer's instructions should be followed.
Instruct personnel to shut off ventilation hoods when cooking is complete.
Shut off booster heaters after using dishwasher.
Check with maintenance if you suspect a malfunction.

Figure 13-1. Energy Conservation Operating Hints

Major Type of Cooking Equipment	Number	Major Type of Cooking Equipment	Number
Ranges	_____	Fryers	_____
Deck Ovens	_____	Griddles	_____
Convection Ovens	_____	Broilers	_____
Microwave Ovens	_____	Other	_____

Operating Procedures

	Yes	No
Is only the equipment preheated that will be used?	____	____
Suggestions: _____		
Is the equipment being preheated just before it is going to be used?	____	____
Suggestions: _____		
Is temperature reduced or equipment turned off during slack periods of the day?	____	____
Suggestions: _____		
Is the full production capacity of equipment used?	____	____
When practical, are ovens fully loaded for each baking cycle?	____	____
Is another load put on right after one has been removed?	____	____
Suggestions: _____		
Is the correct size of equipment used for the cooking operation?	____	____
Suggestions: _____		
Is equipment used properly:		
Are pots and pans with flat bottoms used on range hot plate and hearths of deck ovens?	____	____
Do pots used on french plates cover the entire surface of the plate?	____	____
Are fryer baskets sometimes overfilled?	____	____
Are standard sized pans used in ovens to prevent waste of space?	____	____
Is care taken to space pans an equal distance from walls (sides, front and back) of convection ovens?	____	____
Is a timer used in baking operations to prevent opening of oven doors unnecessarily?	____	____
Is the deck oven damper closed, except when baking very moist products?	____	____
Are microwave ovens being used for large quantity primary cooking functions?	____	____
Suggestions: _____		

Figure 13-2. Energy Audit- Cooking Equipment Form

Maintenance of Equipment

	Yes	No
Are indicator lights working on all of the equipment?	___	___
Are indexes and numbers on control knobs clearly visible?	___	___
Are thermostat bulbs and capillary tubes properly fastened in place on fryers and deck ovens?	___	___
Do oven doors close properly?	___	___
Are there light and dark spots on griddle surfaces indicating a burned-out or loose element?	___	___
Are thermostats periodically checked?	___	___

Suggestions: _____

Cleaning of Equipment

Is equipment kept clean?	___	___
Is spillage cleaned up as it happens throughout the day?	___	___
Is there build-up of food on hearths of deck ovens, griddling surfaces and grates of broilers?	___	___
Are heating elements kept clean on fryers?	___	___
Is the breather space on deck ovens clear of crumbs or other food particles?	___	___
Are contact surfaces on ovens and oven doors clean so that doors will close properly?	___	___

Suggestions: _____

Do you have any questions?	___	___

Question: _____

Figure 13-2. Energy Audit—Cooking Equipment Form (concluded)

14

Certification, Qualifications, And Training Of Energy Auditors

Many states have initiated certification processes to ensure that energy auditors are qualified. The trend will continue due in part to the requirements of the Federal Government. The burden to ensure that the auditor is qualified rests with the states. The form of certification will vary from state to state.

The first certification program was initiated by the State of Iowa. The Iowa program requires that an auditor be a registered professional engineer, that he complete a two-day training program, and pass a one-day test. The test is based on an actual audit of a previously instrumented building. The two-day training program contains the subjects outlined in Figure 14-1.

The survey procedure outlined in the Iowa program includes the comparison of a calculated Building Index with a specified norm. If the Index does not fall within acceptable bounds, the building is classified as energy excessive, warranting the implementation of further energy-audit procedures.

Other criteria specified are in accordance with the following standards:

Comfort Envelope—ASHRAE Standard 55-74, "Thermal Environmental Conditions for Human Occupancy"

Introduction
- Types and classes of Audits
- Cost of Audits (*Federal Register* 42 (125): 33164
- Conflict of Interest
- Definition of an Energy
- Requirements of a Good Audit

Instructions & Forms for a Class "A" Energy Audit
- Building Energy Management Index (BEMI)
- Indoor Environments
- Building/Structures
- HVAC and Service Water Heating Systems
- Lighting & Electrical Distribution

Evaluation Criteria
- BEMI Criteria
- Indoor Thermal & Ventilation Criteria
- Envelope Criteria
- HVAC & Service Water Heating Criteria
- Lighting & Electrical Distribution Criteria

Economic Analysis
- Life Cycle Cost Procedure
- Economic Analysis Comparison
- Commercial Building Ownership Energy Conservation Cost Analysis Model
- Decision Procedure
- Computer Systems
- Service Life Statistics
- Interest Table

Recommended Action
- Implementation of Energy Conservation Opportunities
- Monitoring & Reevaluation

Figure 14-1. Iowa's Energy Auditor Certification Program

Ventilation Criteria- ASHRAE STandard 62-73, "Standards
for Natural and Mechanical Ventilation"
Available from American Society of Heating, Refrigeration and
Air-Conditioning Engineers, Inc. (ASHRAE), 345 East 47th St.,
New York, New York.

Air Movement Criteria—Air Diffusion Performance Index
"Air Diffusion Dynamics, Theory, Design and Application," R. G. Nevins, Business News Publishing Company,
Birmingham, Michigan, 1976.

In addition criteria are established based on ASHRAE 90-75 in the Iowa State Energy Code for the following items:
- Envelope Criteria
- Cooling & Air Leakage
- Combustion Heating Systems
- COP
- Air Distribution
- Piping Insulation
- Service Water
- Oil- and Gas-Fired System
- Electric Water Heating
- Lighting
- Motors
- Power Factor

The auditor proceeds to compare the building with the established criteria. Energy excessive buildings are then investigated in detail to determine energy conservation opportunities to be applied.

The life-cycle costing (LCC) approach is emphasized. The methods employed in the LCC analysis also include formulas to account for fuel escalation.

In addition to the Iowa program, the State of Kentucky initiated an eligibility program in 1979 for energy auditors. The program consists of a training program with no examination. "Guidelines for Saving Energy in Existing Buildings," ECM-1 and ECM-2, are used as the reference texts.

Another type of program was initiated in Massachusetts. The qualifications of the auditor are based on the evaluation of a questionnaire.

Late in 1979, California and Florida initiated programs to develop certification and training.

In addition, in 1979 the U.S. Department of Energy awarded a contract to Booze, Hamilton and Allen to arrive at guidelines, audit and qualifications for program managers.

The problems in defining auditor qualifications are to first determine what is to be done, the qualifications required to do that specific portion, and the funds available.

In lieu of state and Federal regulations, the following guidelines are offered.

GUIDELINES FOR THE SELECTION OF ENERGY AUDITOR TECHNICIANS AND ENERGY AUDITOR ANALYZERS

WHO DOES WHAT?

The energy audit process of any building involves the following steps:

Step 1 Gathering of data to determine how the energy is used and how it is lost.

Step 2 Analysis of the data gathered to determine the alternatives for reducing energy consumption based on a predetermined payback period.

Step 3 Recommendation of the energy conservation measures to be performed.

Step 4 Engineering the energy conservation details.

Step 5 Installation of the energy conservation system.

Step 6 Determining whether the energy conservation installation has saved the predicted quantity.

The traditional roles of the engineer and contractor are illustrated in Steps 4 and 5.

Steps 1, 2, 3, and 6 can be performed by several types of firms and/or individuals. The gathering of data (Step 1) can be performed by an engineering technician working under the guidance of an experienced energy engineer. Steps 2, 3 and 6 need to be implemented by qualified energy engineering/consulting firms.

WHAT TYPES OF FIRMS DO ENERGY ENGINEERING WORK?

Traditional mechanical and electrical engineering firms are developing expertise in energy engineering. In addition many firms who previously specialized in environmental engineering are working in this field.

Many contracting firms have added to their staff experienced engineers to help them implement the noncontracting aspects.

Management consulting firms have added engineers to their staff to work on energy engineering projects.

Since energy engineering is multidisciplined, various engineering disciplines can implement an energy engineering project.

DETERMINING WHO IS QUALIFIED

Consulting in energy conservation is no different than any other specialty. Several criteria apply:

- Has the firm performed similar services for another client? If so, the names and addresses should be obtained and individuals contacted. At least three references should be obtained.
- Who will be in charge of the project and what are the individual's qualifications. (The supervisor should have a degree from an accredited engineering college or university, or be a registered professional engineer, or be a registered architect. In addition, the individual in charge should have at least four years of relevant experience.)
- Who will do the actual survey. Be careful if students or underqualified individuals are used. The Energy Auditor Technician should have had at least two years of college, training in energy audit work, and have a good understanding of the type of business.
- Be cautious of manufacturers who offer energy audit engineering services. You should determine if they have a vested interest in the product they are recommending.
- Be cautious of unrealistic claims as to savings from using audit services.
- Be cautious of contracts which use a percent of savings to determine energy audit fees.

LOCATING AN ENERGY AUDIT ENGINEERING FIRM

Many consultants with whom you are presently doing business may have developed an energy audit capability. If you are satisfied with their work they should be contacted first. It is important to have confidence in the firm chosen.

Engineering and contracting firms should be contacted through organizations such as the National Society of Professional Engineers, American Consulting Engineers Council, Mechanical Contractors Association of America, etc.

In addition, engineering societies have a list of members in their area of expertise, and directories from associations such as the American Society of Heating, Refrigeration, and Air-Conditioning Engineers, the Association of Energy Engineers, and the American Institute of Architects should be reviewed.

OBTAINING QUOTATIONS

First determine what steps should be bid on. Is a turnkey job required (Steps 1-6) or are bids for certain steps to be obtained separately? Once the scope of the project is determined, quotations should be obtained from three potential firms.

TYPES OF CONTRACTS

There are several types of contracts to consider. Traditional contracts apply, such as lump-sum and cost-plus. In addition, bidders may be requested to guarantee that the projected savings will actually be met. If a guarantee is stipulated, the energy consumption before needs to be known and the savings should be measurable.

Many times individuals use a combination of contracts. Such as Steps 1, 2, 3, 4, and 6 on a cost-plus basis while the installation phase is a lump-sum price.

In conclusion, it is the opinion of the author that with any new field a very small percentage of practitioners will be unqualified and may even be unscrupulous. The free market place has a tendency to weed out these individuals. In the long term qualified energy auditors will dominate whether or not a certification process is established.

The certification process is the result of the state's desire to meet implied Federal regulations. Since this is the case, the professional community will aid in the process to ensure that the certification requirements are as meaningful as possible.

15

A Compendium Of Handy Working Aids

This chapter contains tables, figures, and forms which supplement the information presented in the foregoing chapters. Several examples of energy audit forms are presented in this chapter. Feel free to modify these forms to meet your requirements.

INTEREST TABLES

WEATHER DATA

ENERGY AUDIT FORMS

CONVERSION FACTORS

Table 15-1. 10% Interest Factor

Period n	Single-payment compound-amount (SPCA) Future value of $1 $(1 + i)^n$	Single-payment present-worth (SPPW) Present value of $1 $\dfrac{1}{(1 + i)^n}$	Uniform-series compound-amount (USCA) Future value of uniform series of $1 $\dfrac{(1 + i)^n - 1}{i}$	Sinking-fund payment (SFP) Uniform series whose future value is $1 $\dfrac{i}{(1 + i)^n - 1}$	Capital recovery (CR) Uniform series with present value of $1 $\dfrac{i(1 + i)^n}{(1 + i)^n - 1}$	Uniform-series present-worth (USPW) Present value of uniform series of $1 $\dfrac{(1 + i)^n - 1}{i(1 + i)^n}$
1	1.100	0.9091	1.000	1.00000	1.10000	0.909
2	1.210	0.8264	2.100	0.47619	0.57619	1.736
3	1.331	0.7513	3.310	0.30211	0.40211	2.487
4	1.464	0.6830	4.641	0.21547	0.31547	3.170
5	1.611	0.6209	6.105	0.16380	0.26380	3.791
6	1.772	0.5645	7.716	0.12961	0.22961	4.355
7	1.949	0.5132	9.487	0.10541	0.20541	4.868
8	2.144	0.4665	11.436	0.08744	0.18744	5.335
9	2.358	0.4241	13.579	0.07364	0.17364	5.759
10	2.594	0.3855	15.937	0.06275	0.16275	6.144
11	2.853	0.3505	18.531	0.05396	0.15396	6.495
12	3.138	0.3186	21.384	0.04676	0.14676	6.814
13	3.452	0.2897	24.523	0.04078	0.14078	7.103
14	3.797	0.2633	27.975	0.03575	0.13575	7.367
15	4.177	0.2394	31.772	0.03147	0.13147	7.606
16	4.595	0.2176	35.950	0.02782	0.12782	7.824
17	5.054	0.1978	40.545	0.02466	0.12466	8.022
18	5.560	0.1799	45.599	0.02193	0.12193	8.201
19	6.116	0.1635	51.159	0.01955	0.11955	8.365
20	6.727	0.1486	57.275	0.01746	0.11746	8.514
21	7.400	0.1351	64.002	0.01562	0.11562	8.649
22	8.140	0.1228	71.403	0.01401	0.11401	8.772
23	8.954	0.1117	79.543	0.01257	0.11257	8.883
24	9.850	0.1015	88.497	0.01130	0.11130	8.985
25	10.835	0.0923	98.347	0.01017	0.11017	9.077
26	11.918	0.0839	109.182	0.00916	0.10916	9.161
27	13.110	0.0763	121.100	0.00826	0.10826	9.237
28	14.421	0.0693	134.210	0.00745	0.10745	9.307
29	15.863	0.0630	148.631	0.00673	0.10673	9.370
30	17.449	0.0573	164.494	0.00608	0.10608	9.427
35	28.102	0.0356	271.024	0.00369	0.10369	9.644
40	45.259	0.0221	442.593	0.00226	0.10226	9.779
45	72.890	0.0137	718.905	0.00139	0.10139	9.863
50	117.391	0.0085	1163.909	0.00086	0.10086	9.915
55	189.059	0.0053	1880.591	0.00053	0.10053	9.947
60	304.482	0.0033	3034.816	0.00033	0.10033	9.967
65	490.371	0.0020	4893.707	0.00020	0.10020	9.980
70	789.747	0.0013	7887.470	0.00013	0.10013	9.987
75	1271.895	0.0008	12708.954	0.00008	0.10008	9.992
80	2048.400	0.0005	20474.002	0.00005	0.10005	9.995
85	3298.969	0.0003	32979.690	0.00003	0.10003	9.997
90	5313.023	0.0002	53120.226	0.00002	0.10002	9.998
95	8556.676	0.0001	85556.760	0.00001	0.10001	9.999

Table 15-2. 12% Interest Factor

Period n	Single-payment compound-amount (SPCA) Future value of $1 $(1 + i)^n$	Single-payment present-worth (SPPW) Present value of $1 $\dfrac{1}{(1 + i)^n}$	Uniform-series compound-amount (USCA) Future value of uniform series of $1 $\dfrac{(1 + i)^n - 1}{i}$	Sinking-fund payment (SFP) Uniform series whose future value is $1 $\dfrac{i}{(1 + i)^n - 1}$	Capital recovery (CR) Uniform series with present value of $1 $\dfrac{i(1 + i)^n}{(1 + i)^n - 1}$	Uniform-series present-worth (USPW) Present value of uniform series of $1 $\dfrac{(1 + i)^n - 1}{i(1 + i)^n}$
1	1.120	0.8929	1.000	1.00000	1.12000	0.893
2	1.254	0.7972	2.120	0.47170	0.59170	1.690
3	1.405	0.7118	3.374	0.29635	0.41635	2.402
4	1.574	0.6355	4.779	0.20923	0.32923	3.037
5	1.762	0.5674	6.353	0.15741	0.27741	3.605
6	1.974	0.5066	8.115	0.12323	0.24323	4.111
7	2.211	0.4523	10.089	0.09912	0.21912	4.564
8	2.476	0.4039	12.300	0.08130	0.20130	4.968
9	2.773	0.3606	14.776	0.06768	0.18768	5.328
10	3.106	0.3220	17.549	0.05698	0.17698	5.650
11	3.479	0.2875	20.655	0.04842	0.16842	5.938
12	3.896	0.2567	24.133	0.04144	0.16144	6.194
13	4.363	0.2292	28.029	0.03568	0.15568	6.424
14	4.887	0.2046	32.393	0.03087	0.15087	6.628
15	5.474	0.1827	37.280	0.02682	0.14682	6.811
16	6.130	0.1631	42.753	0.02339	0.14339	6.974
17	6.866	0.1456	48.884	0.02046	0.14046	7.120
18	7.690	0.1300	55.750	0.01794	0.13794	7.250
19	8.613	0.1161	63.440	0.01576	0.13576	7.366
20	9.646	0.1037	72.052	0.01388	0.13388	7.469
21	10.804	0.0926	81.699	0.01224	0.13224	7.562
22	12.100	0.0826	92.503	0.01081	0.13081	7.645
23	13.552	0.0738	104.603	0.00956	0.12956	7.718
24	15.179	0.0659	118.155	0.00846	0.12846	7.784
25	17.000	0.0588	133.334	0.00750	0.12750	7.843
26	19.040	0.0525	150.334	0.00665	0.12665	7.896
27	21.325	0.0469	169.374	0.00590	0.12590	7.943
28	23.884	0.0419	190.699	0.00524	0.12524	7.984
29	26.750	0.0374	214.583	0.00466	0.12466	8.022
30	29.960	0.0334	241.333	0.00414	0.12414	8.055
35	52.800	0.0189	431.663	0.00232	0.12232	8.176
40	93.051	0.0107	767.091	0.00130	0.12130	8.244
45	163.988	0.0061	1358.230	0.00074	0.12074	8.283
50	289.002	0.0035	2400.018	0.00042	0.12042	8.304
55	509.321	0.0020	4236.005	0.00024	0.12024	8.317
60	897.597	0.0011	7471.641	0.00013	0.12013	8.324
65	1581.872	0.0006	13173.937	0.00008	0.12008	8.328
70	2787.800	0.0004	23223.332	0.00004	0.12004	8.330
75	4913.056	0.0002	40933.799	0.00002	0.12002	8.332
80	8658.483	0.0001	72145.692	0.00001	0.12001	8.332

Table 15-3. 15% Interest Factor

Period n	Single-payment compound-amount (SPCA)	Single-payment present-worth (SPPW)	Uniform-series compound-amount (USCA)	Sinking-fund payment (SFP)	Capital recovery (CR)	Uniform-series present-worth (USPW)
	Future value of $1 $(1 + i)^n$	Present value of $1 $\dfrac{1}{(1 + i)^n}$	Future value of uniform series of $1 $\dfrac{(1 + i)^n - 1}{i}$	Uniform series whose future value is $1 $\dfrac{i}{(1 + i)^n - 1}$	Uniform series with present value of $1 $\dfrac{i(1 + i)^n}{(1 + i)^n - 1}$	Present value of uniform series of $1 $\dfrac{(1 + i)^n - 1}{i(1 + i)^n}$
1	1.150	0.8696	1.000	1.00000	1.15000	0.870
2	1.322	0.7561	2.150	0.46512	0.61512	1.626
3	1.521	0.6575	3.472	0.28798	0.43798	2.283
4	1.749	0.5718	4.993	0.20027	0.35027	2.855
5	2.011	0.4972	6.742	0.14832	0.29832	3.352
6	2.313	0.4323	8.754	0.11424	0.26424	3.784
7	2.660	0.3759	11.067	0.09036	0.24036	4.160
8	3.059	0.3269	13.727	0.07285	0.22285	4.487
9	3.518	0.2843	16.786	0.05957	0.20957	4.772
10	4.046	0.2472	20.304	0.04925	0.19925	5.019
11	4.652	0.2149	24.349	0.04107	0.19107	5.234
12	5.350	0.1869	29.002	0.03448	0.18448	5.421
13	6.153	0.1625	34.352	0.02911	0.17911	5.583
14	7.076	0.1413	40.505	0.02469	0.17469	5.724
15	8.137	0.1229	47.580	0.02102	0.17102	5.847
16	9.358	0.1069	55.717	0.01795	0.16795	5.954
17	10.761	0.0929	65.075	0.01537	0.16537	6.047
18	12.375	0.0808	75.836	0.01319	0.16319	6.128
19	14.232	0.0703	88.212	0.01134	0.16134	6.198
20	16.367	0.0611	102.444	0.00976	0.15976	6.259
21	18.822	0.0531	118.810	0.00842	0.15842	6.312
22	21.645	0.0462	137.632	0.00727	0.15727	6.359
23	24.891	0.0402	159.276	0.00628	0.15628	6.399
24	28.625	0.0349	184.168	0.00543	0.15543	6.434
25	32.919	0.0304	212.793	0.00470	0.15470	6.464
26	37.857	0.0264	245.712	0.00407	0.15407	6.491
27	43.535	0.0230	283.569	0.00353	0.15353	6.514
28	50.066	0.0200	327.104	0.00306	0.15306	6.534
29	57.575	0.0174	377.170	0.00265	0.15265	6.551
30	66.212	0.0151	434.745	0.00230	0.15230	6.566
35	133.176	0.0075	881.170	0.00113	0.15113	6.617
40	267.864	0.0037	1779.090	0.00056	0.15056	6.642
45	538.769	0.0019	3585.128	0.00028	0.15028	6.654
50	1083.657	0.0009	7217.716	0.00014	0.15014	6.661
55	2179.622	0.0005	14524.148	0.00007	0.15007	6.664
60	4383.999	0.0002	29219.992	0.00003	0.15003	6.665
65	8817.787	0.0001	58778.583	0.00002	0.15002	6.666

Table 15-4. 20% Interest Factor

Period n	Single-payment compound-amount (SPCA) Future value of $1 $(1 + i)^n$	Single-payment present-worth (SPPW) Present value of $1 $\dfrac{1}{(1 + i)^n}$	Uniform-series compound-amount (USCA) Future value of uniform series of $1 $\dfrac{(1 + i)^n - 1}{i}$	Sinking-fund payment (SFP) Uniform series whose future value is $1 $\dfrac{i}{(1 + i)^n - 1}$	Capital recovery (CR) Uniform series with present value of $1 $\dfrac{i(1 + i)^n}{(1 + i)^n - 1}$	Uniform-series present-worth (USPW) Present value of uniform series of $1 $\dfrac{(1 + i)^n - 1}{i(1 + i)^n}$
1	1.200	0.8333	1.000	1.00000	1.20000	0.833
2	1.440	0.6944	2.200	0.45455	0.65455	1.528
3	1.728	0.5787	3.640	0.27473	0.47473	2.106
4	2.074	0.4823	5.368	0.18629	0.38629	2.589
5	2.488	0.4019	7.442	0.13438	0.33438	2.991
6	2.986	0.3349	9.930	0.10071	0.30071	3.326
7	3.583	0.2791	12.916	0.07742	0.27742	3.605
8	4.300	0.2326	16.499	0.06061	0.26061	3.837
9	5.160	0.1938	20.799	0.04808	0.24808	4.031
10	6.192	0.1615	25.959	0.03852	0.23852	4.192
11	7.430	0.1346	32.150	0.03110	0.23110	4.327
12	8.916	0.1122	39.581	0.02526	0.22526	4.439
13	10.699	0.0935	48.497	0.02062	0.22062	4.533
14	12.839	0.0779	59.196	0.01689	0.21689	4.611
15	15.407	0.0649	72.035	0.01388	0.21388	4.675
16	18.488	0.0541	87.442	0.01144	0.21144	4.730
17	22.186	0.0451	105.931	0.00944	0.20944	4.775
18	26.623	0.0376	128.117	0.00781	0.20781	4.812
19	31.948	0.0313	154.740	0.00646	0.20646	4.843
20	38.338	0.0261	186.688	0.00536	0.20536	4.870
21	46.005	0.0217	225.026	0.00444	0.20444	4.891
22	55.206	0.0181	271.031	0.00369	0.20369	4.909
23	66.247	0.0151	326.237	0.00307	0.20307	4.925
24	79.497	0.0126	392.484	0.00255	0.20255	4.937
25	95.396	0.0105	471.981	0.00212	0.20212	4.948
26	114.475	0.0087	567.377	0.00176	0.20176	4.956
27	137.371	0.0073	681.853	0.00147	0.20147	4.964
28	164.845	0.0061	819.223	0.00122	0.20122	4.970
29	197.814	0.0051	984.068	0.00102	0.20102	4.975
30	237.376	0.0042	1181.882	0.00085	0.20085	4.979
35	590.668	0.0017	2948.341	0.00034	0.20034	4.992
40	1469.772	0.0007	7343.858	0.00014	0.20014	4.997
45	3657.262	0.0003	18281.310	0.00005	0.20005	4.999
50	9100.438	0.0001	45497.191	0.00002	0.20002	4.999

Table 15-5. 25% Interest Factor

Period n	Single-payment compound-amount (SPCA)	Single-payment present-worth (SPPW)	Uniform-series compound amount (USCA)	Sinking-fund payment (SFP)	Capital recovery (CR)	Uniform-series present-worth (USPW)
	Future value of \$1 $(1 + i)^n$	Present value of \$1 $\dfrac{1}{(1 + i)^n}$	Future value of uniform series of \$1 $\dfrac{(1 + i)^n - 1}{i}$	Uniform series whose future value is \$1 $\dfrac{i}{(1 + i)^n - 1}$	Uniform series with present value of \$1 $\dfrac{i(1 + i)^n}{(1 + i)^n - 1}$	Present value of uniform series of \$1 $\dfrac{(1 + i)^n - 1}{i(1 + i)^n}$
1	1.250	0.8000	1.000	1.00000	1.25000	0.800
2	1.562	0.6400	2.250	0.44444	0.69444	1.440
3	1.953	0.5120	3.812	0.26230	0.51230	1.952
4	2.441	0.4096	5.766	0.17344	0.42344	2.362
5	3.052	0.3277	8.207	0.12185	0.37185	2.689
6	3.815	0.2621	11.259	0.08882	0.33882	2.951
7	4.768	0.2097	15.073	0.06634	0.31634	3.161
8	5.960	0.1678	19.842	0.05040	0.30040	3.329
9	7.451	0.1342	25.802	0.03876	0.28876	3.463
10	9.313	0.1074	33.253	0.03007	0.28007	3.571
11	11.642	0.0859	42.566	0.02349	0.27349	3.656
12	14.552	0.0687	54.208	0.01845	0.26845	3.725
13	18.190	0.0550	68.760	0.01454	0.26454	3.780
14	22.737	0.0440	86.949	0.01150	0.26150	3.824
15	28.422	0.0352	109.687	0.00912	0.25912	3.859
16	35.527	0.0281	138.109	0.00724	0.25724	3.887
17	44.409	0.0225	173.636	0.00576	0.25576	3.910
18	55.511	0.0180	218.045	0.00459	0.25459	3.928
19	69.389	0.0144	273.556	0.00366	0.25366	3.942
20	86.736	0.0115	342.945	0.00292	0.25292	3.954
21	108.420	0.0092	429.681	0.00233	0.25233	3.963
22	135.525	0.0074	538.101	0.00186	0.25186	3.970
23	169.407	0.0059	673.626	0.00148	0.25148	3.976
24	211.758	0.0047	843.033	0.00119	0.25119	3.981
25	264.698	0.0038	1054.791	0.00095	0.25095	3.985
26	330.872	0.0030	1319.489	0.00076	0.25076	3.988
27	413.590	0.0024	1650.361	0.00061	0.25061	3.990
28	516.988	0.0019	2063.952	0.00048	0.25048	3.992
29	646.235	0.0015	2580.939	0.00039	0.25039	3.994
30	807.794	0.0012	3227.174	0.00031	0.25031	3.995
35	2465.190	0.0004	9856.761	0.00010	0.25010	3.998
40	7523.164	0.0001	30088.655	0.00003	0.25003	3.999

Table 15-6. 30% Interest Factor

Period n	Single-payment compound-amount (SPCA) Future value of $1 $(1 + i)^n$	Single-payment present-worth (SPPW) Present value of $1 $\dfrac{1}{(1 + i)^n}$	Uniform-series compound-amount (USCA) Future value of uniform series of $1 $\dfrac{(1 + i)^n - 1}{i}$	Sinking-fund payment (SFP) Uniform series whose future value is $1 $\dfrac{i}{(1 + i)^n - 1}$	Capital recovery (CR) Uniform series with present value of $1 $\dfrac{i(1 + i)^n}{(1 + i)^n - 1}$	Uniform-series present-worth (USPW) Present value of uniform series of $1 $\dfrac{(1 + i)^n - 1}{i(1 + i)^n}$
1	1.300	0.7692	1.000	1.00000	1.30000	0.769
2	1.690	0.5917	2.300	0.43478	0.73478	1.361
3	2.197	0.4552	3.990	0.25063	0.55063	1.816
4	2.856	0.3501	6.187	0.16163	0.46163	2.166
ᵥ5	3.713	0.2693	9.043	0.11058	0.41058	2.436
6	4.827	0.2072	12.756	0.07839	0.37839	2.643
7	6.275	0.1594	17.583	0.05687	0.35687	2.802
8	8.157	0.1226	23.858	0.04192	0.34192	2.925
9	10.604	0.0943	32.015	0.03124	0.33124	3.019
10	13.786	0.0725	42.619	0.02346	0.32346	3.092
11	17.922	0.0558	56.405	0.01773	0.31773	3.147
12	23.298	0.0429	74.327	0.01345	0.31345	3.190
13	30.288	0.0330	97.625	0.01024	0.31024	3.223
14	39.374	0.0254	127.913	0.00782	0.30782	3.249
15	51.186	0.0195	167.286	0.00598	0.30598	3.268
16	66.542	0.0150	218.472	0.00458	0.30458	3.283
17	86.504	0.0116	285.014	0.00351	0.30351	3.295
18	112.455	0.0089	371.518	0.00269	0.30269	3.304
19	146.192	0.0068	483.973	0.00207	0.30207	3.311
20	190.050	0.0053	630.165	0.00159	0.30159	3.316
21	247.065	0.0040	820.215	0.00122	0.30122	3.320
22	321.184	0.0031	1067.280	0.00094	0.30094	3.323
23	417.539	0.0024	1388.464	0.00072	0.30072	3.325
24	542.801	0.0018	1806.003	0.00055	0.30055	3.327
25	705.641	0.0014	2348.803	0.00043	0.30043	3.329
26	917.333	0.0011	3054.444	0.00033	0.30033	3.330
27	1192.533	0.0008	3971.778	0.00025	0.30025	3.331
28	1550.293	0.0006	5164.311	0.00019	0.30019	3.331
29	2015.381	0.0005	6714.604	0.00015	0.30015	3.332
30	2619.996	0.0004	8729.985	0.00011	0.30011	3.332
35	9727.860	0.0001	32422.868	0.00003	0.30003	3.333

Table 15-7. 40% Interest Factor

Period n	Single-payment compound-amount (SPCA) Future value of $1 $(1 + i)^n$	Single-payment present-worth (SPPW) Present value of $1 $\dfrac{1}{(1 + i)^n}$	Uniform-series compound-amount (USCA) Future value of uniform series of $1 $\dfrac{(1 + i)^n - 1}{i}$	Sinking-fund payment (SFP) Uniform series whose future value is $1 $\dfrac{i}{(1 + i)^n - 1}$	Capital recovery (CR) Uniform series with present value of $1 $\dfrac{i(1 + i)^n}{(1 + i)^n - 1}$	Uniform-series present-worth (USPW) Present value of uniform series of $1 $\dfrac{(1 + i)^n - 1}{i(1 + i)^n}$
1	1.400	0.7143	1.000	1.00000	1.40000	0.714
2	1.960	0.5102	2.400	0.41667	0.81667	1.224
3	2.744	0.3644	4.360	0.22936	0.62936	1.589
4	3.842	0.2603	7.104	0.14077	0.54077	1.849
5	5.378	0.1859	10.946	0.09136	0.49136	2.035
6	7.530	0.1328	16.324	0.06126	0.46126	2.168
7	10.541	0.0949	23.853	0.04192	0.44192	2.263
8	14.758	0.0678	34.395	0.02907	0.42907	2.331
9	20.661	0.0484	49.153	0.02034	0.42034	2.379
10	28.925	0.0346	69.814	0.01432	0.41432	2.414
11	40.496	0.0247	98.739	0.01013	0.41013	2.438
12	56.694	0.0176	139.235	0.00718	0.40718	2.456
13	79.371	0.0126	195.929	0.00510	0.40510	2.469
14	111.120	0.0090	275.300	0.00363	0.40363	2.478
15	155.568	0.0064	386.420	0.00259	0.40259	2.484
16	217.795	0.0046	541.988	0.00185	0.40185	2.489
17	304.913	0.0033	759.784	0.00132	0.40132	2.492
18	426.879	0.0023	1064.697	0.00094	0.40094	2.494
19	597.630	0.0017	1491.576	0.00067	0.40067	2.496
20	836.683	0.0012	2089.206	0.00048	0.40048	2.497
21	1171.356	0.0009	2925.889	0.00034	0.40034	2.498
22	1639.898	0.0006	4097.245	0.00024	0.40024	2.498
23	2295.857	0.0004	5737.142	0.00017	0.40017	2.499
24	3214.200	0.0003	8032.999	0.00012	0.40012	2.499
25	4499.880	0.0002	11247.199	0.00009	0.40009	2.499
26	6299.831	0.0002	15747.079	0.00006	0.40006	2.500
27	8819.764	0.0001	22046.910	0.00005	0.40005	2.500

Table 15-8. 50% Interest Factor

Period n	Single-payment compound-amount (SPCA) Future value of $1 $(1 + i)^n$	Single-payment present-worth (SPPW) Present value of $1 $\dfrac{1}{(1 + i)^n}$	Uniform-series compound-amount (USCA) Future value of uniform series of $1 $\dfrac{(1 + i)^n - 1}{i}$	Sinking-fund payment (SFP) Uniform series whose future value is $1 $\dfrac{i}{(1 + i)^n - 1}$	Capital recovery (CR) Uniform series with present value of $1 $\dfrac{i(1 + i)^n}{(1 + i)^n - 1}$	Uniform-series present-worth (USPW) Present value of uniform series of $1 $\dfrac{(1 + i)^n - 1}{i(1 + i)^n}$
1	1.500	0.6667	1.000	1.00000	1.50000	0.667
2	2.250	0.4444	2.500	0.40000	0.90000	1.111
3	3.375	0.2963	4.750	0.21053	0.71053	1.407
4	5.062	0.1975	8.125	0.12308	0.62308	1.605
5	7.594	0.1317	13.188	0.07583	0.57583	1.737
6	11.391	0.0878	20.781	0.04812	0.54812	1.824
7	17.086	0.0585	32.172	0.03108	0.53108	1.883
8	25.629	0.0390	49.258	0.02030	0.52030	1.922
9	38.443	0.0260	74.887	0.01335	0.51335	1.948
10	57.665	0.0173	113.330	0.00882	0.50882	1.965
11	86.498	0.0116	170.995	0.00585	0.50585	1.977
12	129.746	0.0077	257.493	0.00388	0.50388	1.985
13	194.620	0.0051	387.239	0.00258	0.50258	1.990
14	291.929	0.0034	581.859	0.00172	0.50172	1.993
15	437.894	0.0023	873.788	0.00114	0.50114	1.995
16	656.841	0.0015	1311.682	0.00076	0.50076	1.997
17	985.261	0.0010	1968.523	0.00051	0.50051	1.998
18	1477.892	0.0007	2953.784	0.00034	0.50034	1.999
19	2216.838	0.0005	4431.676	0.00023	0.50023	1.999
20	3325.257	0.0003	6648.513	0.00015	0.50015	1.999
21	4987.885	0.0002	9973.770	0.00010	0.50010	2.000
22	7481.828	0.0001	14961.655	0.00007	0.50007	2.000

Table 15-9. 5 Year Escalation Table

Source: Brown & Yanuck

Present Worth of a Series of Escalating Payments Compounded Annually
Discount-Escalation Factors for N = 5 Years

Discount Rate	Annual Escalation Rate					
	.10	.12	.14	.16	.18	.20
0.10	5.000000	5.279234	5.572605	5.880105	6.202627	6.540569
0.11	4.866862	5.136200	5.420152	5.717603	6.029313	6.355882
0.12	4.738562	5.000000	5.274242	5.561868	5.863289	6.179066
0.13	4.615647	4.869164	5.133876	5.412404	5.704137	6.009541
0.14	4.497670	4.742953	5.000000	5.269208	5.551563	5.847029
0.15	4.384494	4.622149	4.871228	5.131703	5.404955	5.691165
0.16	4.275647	4.505953	4.747390	5.000000	5.264441	5.541511
0.17	4.171042	4.394428	4.628438	4.873699	5.129353	5.397964
0.18	4.070432	4.287089	4.513947	4.751566	5.000000	5.259749
0.19	3.973684	4.183921	4.403996	4.634350	4.875619	5.126925
0.20	3.880510	4.084577	4.298207	4.521778	4.755725	5.000000

Table 15-9. 5 Year Escalation Table (concluded)

Discount Rate	.10	.12	.14	.16	.18	.20
0.21	3.790801	3.989001	4.196400	4.413341	4.640260	4.877689
0.22	3.704368	3.896891	4.098287	4.303947	4.529298	4.759649
0.23	3.621094	3.808179	4.003835	4.208479	4.422339	4.645864
0.24	3.540773	3.722628	3.912807	4.111612	4.319417	4.536517
0.25	3.463301	3.640161	3.825008	4.018249	4.220158	4.431144
0.26	3.388553	3.560586	3.740376	3.928286	4.124553	4.329514
0.27	3.316408	3.483803	3.658706	3.841442	4.032275	4.231583
0.28	3.246718	3.409649	3.579870	3.757639	3.943295	4.137057
0.29	3.179393	3.338051	3.503722	3.676771	3.857370	4.045902
0.30	3.114338	3.268861	3.430201	3.598653	3.774459	3.957921
0.31	3.051452	3.201978	3.359143	3.523171	3.694328	3.872901
0.32	2.990618	3.137327	3.290436	3.450224	3.616936	3.790808
0.33	2.931764	3.074780	3.224015	3.379722	3.542100	3.711472
0.34	2.874812	3.014281	3.159770	3.311524	3.469775	3.634758

Annual Escalation Rate

Table 15-10. 10 Year Escalation Table

Present Worth of a Series of Escalating Payments Compounded Annually   Source: Brown & Yanuck

Discount-Escalation Factors for N = 10 Years

Discount Rate	Annual Escalation Rate					
	.10	.12	.14	.16	.18	.20
0.10	10.000000	11.056250	12.234870	13.548650	15.013550	16.646080
0.11	9.518405	10.508020	11.613440	12.844310	14.215140	15.741560
0.12	9.068870	10.000000	11.036530	12.190470	13.474590	14.903510
0.13	8.650280	9.526666	10.498990	11.582430	12.786980	14.125780
0.14	8.259741	9.084209	10.000000	11.017130	12.147890	13.403480
0.15	7.895187	8.672058	9.534301	10.490510	11.552670	12.731900
0.16	7.554141	8.286779	9.099380	10.000000	10.998720	12.106600
0.17	7.234974	7.926784	8.693151	9.542653	10.481740	11.524400
0.18	6.935890	7.585595	8.312960	9.113885	10.000000	10.980620
0.19	6.655455	7.273785	7.957330	8.713262	9.549790	10.472990
0.20	6.392080	6.977461	7.624072	8.338518	9.128122	10.000000
0.21	6.144593	6.699373	7.311519	7.987156	8.733109	9.557141

Table 15-10. 10 Year Escalation Table (concluded)

Discount Rate	Annual Escalation Rate					
	.10	.12	.14	.16	.18	.20
0.22	5.911755	6.437922	7.017915	7.657542	8.363208	9.141752
0.23	5.692557	6.192047	6.742093	7.348193	8.015993	8.752133
0.24	5.485921	5.960481	6.482632	7.057347	7.690163	8.387045
0.25	5.290990	5.742294	6.238276	6.783767	7.383800	8.044173
0.26	5.106956	5.536463	6.008083	6.526298	7.095769	7.721807
0.27	4.933045	5.342146	5.790929	6.283557	6.824442	7.418647
0.28	4.768518	5.158489	5.585917	6.054608	6.568835	7.133100
0.29	4.612762	4.984826	5.392166	5.838531	6.327682	6.864109
0.30	4.465205	4.820429	5.209000	5.634354	6.100129	6.610435
0.31	4.325286	4.664669	5.035615	5.441257	5.885058	6.370867
0.32	4.192478	4.517015	4.871346	5.258512	5.681746	6.144601
0.33	4.066339	4.376384	4.715648	5.085461	5.489304	5.930659
0.34	3.946452	4.243845	4.567942	4.921409	5.307107	5.728189

Table 15-11. 15 Year Escalation Table

Source: Brown & Yanuck

Present Worth of a Series of Escalating Payments Compounded Annually
Discount-Escalation Factors for N = 15 Years

Discount Rate	Annual Escalation Rate					
	.10	.12	.14	.16	.18	.20
0.10	15.000000	17.377880	20.199780	23.549540	27.529640	32.259620
0.11	13.964150	16.126230	18.690120	21.727370	25.328790	29.601330
0.12	13.026090	15.000000	17.332040	20.090360	23.355070	27.221890
0.13	12.177030	13.981710	16.105770	18.616160	21.581750	25.087260
0.14	11.406510	13.057790	15.000000	17.287320	19.985530	23.169060
0.15	10.706220	12.220570	13.998120	16.086500	18.545150	21.442230
0.16	10.068030	11.459170	13.088900	15.000000	17.244580	19.884420
0.17	9.485654	10.766180	12.262790	14.015480	16.066830	18.477610
0.18	8.953083	10.133630	11.510270	13.118840	15.000000	17.203010
0.19	8.465335	9.555676	10.824310	12.303300	14.030830	16.047480
0.20	8.017635	9.026333	10.197550	11.560150	13.148090	15.000000

Table 15-11. 15 Year Escalation Table (concluded)

Discount Rate	Annual Escalation Rate					
	.10	.12	.14	.16	.18	.20
0.21	7.606115	8.540965	9.623969	10.881130	12.343120	14.046400
0.22	7.227109	8.094845	9.097863	10.259820	11.608480	13.176250
0.23	6.877543	7.684317	8.614813	9.690559	10.936240	12.381480
0.24	6.554501	7.305762	8.170423	9.167798	10.320590	11.655310
0.25	6.255518	6.956243	7.760848	8.687104	9.755424	10.990130
0.26	5.978393	6.632936	7.382943	8.244519	9.236152	10.379760
0.27	5.721101	6.333429	7.033547	7.836080	8.757889	9.819020
0.28	5.481814	6.055485	6.710042	7.458700	8.316982	9.302823
0.29	5.258970	5.797236	6.410005	7.109541	7.909701	8.827153
0.30	5.051153	5.556882	6.131433	6.785917	7.533113	8.388091
0.31	4.857052	5.332839	5.872303	6.485500	7.184156	7.982019
0.32	4.675478	5.123753	5.630905	6.206250	6.860492	7.606122
0.33	4.505413	4.928297	5.405771	5.946343	6.559743	7.257569
0.34	4.345926	4.745399	5.195502	5.704048	6.280019	6.933897

Table 15-12. 20 Year Escalation Table

Present Worth of a Series of Escalating Payments Compounded Annually   Source: Brown & Yanuck

Discount-Escalation Factors for N = 20 Years

Discount Rate	Annual Escalation Rate					
	.10	.12	.14	.16	.18	.20
0.10	20.000000	24.295450	29.722090	36.592170	45.308970	56.383330
0.11	18.213210	22.002090	26.776150	32.799710	40.417480	50.067940
0.12	16.642370	20.000000	24.210030	29.505430	35.181240	44.614710
0.13	15.259850	18.243100	21.964990	26.634490	32.502270	39.891400
0.14	14.038630	16.694830	20.000000	24.127100	29.298170	35.789680
0.15	12.957040	15.329770	18.271200	21.929940	26.498510	32.218060
0.16	11.995640	14.121040	16.746150	20.000000	24.047720	29.098950
0.17	11.138940	13.048560	15.397670	18.300390	21.894660	26.369210
0.18	10.373120	12.053400	14.201180	16.795710	20.000000	23.970940
0.19	9.686791	11.240870	13.137510	15.463070	18.326720	21.860120
0.20	9.069737	10.477430	12.186860	14.279470	16.844020	20.000000

Table 15-12. 20 Year Escalation Table (concluded)

Discount Rate	Annual Escalation Rate					
	.10	.12	.14	.16	.18	.20
0.21	8.513605	9.792256	11.340570	13.224610	15.527270	18.353210
0.22	8.010912	9.175267	10.579620	12.282120	14.355520	16.890730
0.23	7.555427	8.618459	9.895583	11.438060	13.309280	15.589300
0.24	7.141531	8.114476	9.278916	10.679810	12.373300	14.429370
0.25	6.764528	7.657278	8.721467	9.997057	11.533310	13.392180
0.26	6.420316	7.241402	8.216490	9.380883	10.778020	12.462340
0.27	6.105252	6.862203	7.757722	8.823063	10.096710	11.626890
0.28	5.816151	6.515563	7.339966	8.316995	9.480940	10.874120
0.29	5.550301	6.198027	6.958601	7.856833	8.922847	10.194520
0.30	5.305312	5.906440	6.609778	7.437339	8.416060	9.579437
0.31	5.079039	5.638064	6.289875	7.054007	7.954518	9.021190
0.32	4.869585	5.390575	5.995840	6.702967	7.533406	8.513612
0.33	4.675331	5.161809	5.725066	6.380829	7.148198	8.050965
0.34	4.494838	4.949990	5.475180	6.084525	6.795200	7.628322

Table 15-13. 25 Year Escalation Table

Present Worth of a Series of Escalating Payments Compounded Annually   Source: Brown & Yanuck

Discount-Escalation Factors for N = 25 Years

Discount Rate	Annual Escalation Rate					
	.10	.12	.14	.16	.18	.20
0.10	25.000000	31.865200	41.106320	53.601680	70.564800	93.655670
0.11	22.274290	28.147300	36.015560	46.600790	60.902930	80.290840
0.12	19.947090	25.000000	31.724440	40.726100	52.831280	69.172270
0.13	17.954600	22.319250	28.088180	35.775160	46.062280	59.885280
0.14	16.240260	20.023840	25.000000	31.588360	40.363340	52.100020
0.15	14.759290	18.054030	22.361690	28.031930	35.544750	45.549220
0.16	13.473700	16.354530	20.098800	25.000000	31.457960	40.015540
0.17	12.353390	14.883200	18.150720	22.405330	27.975900	35.325790
0.18	11.372780	13.603090	16.465880	20.171380	25.000000	31.332130
0.19	10.511130	12.485400	15.003900	18.244120	22.445120	27.921080
0.20	9.750687	11.505170	13.729700	16.574780	20.242060	25.000000

Table 15-13. 25 Year Escalation Table (concluded)

Discount Rate	Annual Escalation Rate					
	.10	.12	.14	.16	.18	.20
0.21	9.077086	10.642450	12.614860	15.122300	18.335780	22.484980
0.22	8.477970	9.879775	11.635230	13.853700	16.680780	20.310570
0.23	7.943212	9.203218	10.771510	12.741780	15.237640	18.424540
0.24	7.464020	8.600633	10.006940	11.763090	13.975170	16.783950
0.25	7.033149	8.062115	9.327539	10.898610	12.866100	15.350750
0.26	6.644423	7.579059	8.721850	10.132420	11.888750	14.094100
0.27	6.292513	7.144263	8.179757	9.450517	11.023780	12.988500
0.28	5.972860	6.751540	7.692956	8.841652	10.255930	12.012060
0.29	5.681642	6.395750	7.254285	8.296204	9.571679	11.146980
0.30	5.415556	6.072358	6.857835	7.805839	8.960096	10.377850
0.31	5.171707	5.777494	6.498275	7.363513	8.411343	9.691441
0.32	4.947592	5.507914	6.171175	6.963300	7.917555	9.077091
0.33	4.741089	5.260696	5.872792	6.600113	7.471690	8.525357
0.34	4.550347	5.033445	5.599819	6.269493	7.068001	8.028274

Table 15-14. Degree Day Data

(Source: Cooling and Heating Load Calculation Manual ASHRAE GRP 158)

Average Winter Temperature and Yearly Degree Days for Cities in the United States and Canada[a,b,c] (Base 65°F)

State	Station	Avg. Winter Temp.[d] F	Degree-Days Yearly Total	State	Station	Avg. Winter Temp. F	Degree-Days Yearly Total
Ala.	Birmingham	A	54.2	2551	Calif.	Bakersfield	A	55.4	2122
	Huntsville	A	51.3	3070		Bishop	A	46.0	4275
	Mobile	A	59.9	1560		Blue Canyon	A	42.2	5596
	Montgomery	A	55.4	2291		Burbank	A	58.6	1646
						Eureka	C	49.9	4643
Alaska	Anchorage	A	23.0	10864					
	Fairbanks	A	6.7	14279		Fresno	A	53.3	2611
	Juneau	A	32.1	9075		Long Beach	A	57.8	1803
	Nome	A	13.1	14171		Los Angeles	A	57.4	2061
						Los Angeles	C	60.3	1349
Ariz.	Flagstaff	A	35.6	7152		Mt. Shasta	C	41.2	5722
	Phoenix	A	58.5	1765					
	Tucson	A	58.1	1800		Oakland	A	53.5	2870
	Winslow	A	43.0	4782		Red Bluff	A	53.8	2515
	Yuma	A	64.2	974		Sacramento	A	53.9	2502
						Sacramento	C	54.4	2419
Ark.	Fort Smith	A	50.3	3292		Sandberg	C	46.8	4209
	Little Rock	A	50.5	3219					
	Texarkana	A	54.2	2533					

[a] Data for United States cities from a publication of the United States Weather Bureau. *Monthly Normals of Temperature, Precipitation and Heating Degree Days*, 1962, are for the period 1931 to 1960 inclusive. These data also include information from the 1963 revisions to this publication, where available.

[b] Data for airport station, A, and city stations, C, are both given where available.

[c] Data for Canadian cities were computed by the Climatology Division, Department of Transport from normal monthly mean temperatures, and the monthly values of heating days data were obtained using the National Research Council computer and a method devised by H. C. S. Thom of the United States Weather Bureau. The heating days are based on the period from 1931 to 1960.

[d] For period October to April, inclusive.

Table 15-14. Degree Day Data (con't)

State	Station		Avg. Winter Temp. F	Degree-Days Yearly Total
Calif. (Con'td)	San Diego	A	59.5	1458
	San Francisco	A	53.4	3015
	San Francisco	C	55.1	3001
	Santa Maria	A	54.3	2967
Colo.	Alamosa	A	29.7	8529
	Colorado Springs	A	37.3	6423
	Denver	A	37.6	6283
	Denver	C	40.8	5524
	Grand Junction	A	39.?	5641
	Pueblo	A	40.4	5462
Conn.	Bridgeport	A	39.9	5617
	Hartford	A	37.3	6235
	New Haven	A	39.0	5897
Del.	Wilmington	A	42.5	4930
D.C.	Washington	A	45.7	4224
Fla.	Apalachicola	C	61.2	1308
	Daytona Beach	A	64.5	879
	Fort Myers	A	68.6	442
	Jacksonville	A	61.9	1239
	Key West	A	73.1	108
	Lakeland	C	66.7	661
	Miami	A	71.1	214
	Miami Beach	C	72.5	141
	Orlando	A	65.7	766
	Pensacola	A	60.4	1463

State	Station		Avg. Winter Temp. F	Degree-Days Yearly Total
Iowa	Burlington	A	37.6	6114
	Des Moines	A	35.5	6588
	Dubuque	A	32.7	7376
	Sioux City	A	34.0	6951
	Waterloo	A	32.6	7320
Kans.	Concordia	A	40.4	5479
	Dodge City	A	42.5	4986
	Goodland	A	37.8	6141
	Topeka	A	41.7	5182
	Wichita	A	44.2	4620
Ky.	Covington	A	41.4	5265
	Lexington	A	43.8	4683
	Louisville	A	44.0	4660
La.	Alexandria	A	57.5	1921
	Baton Rouge	A	59.8	1560
	Lake Charles	A	60.5	1459
	New Orleans	A	61.0	1385
	New Orleans	C	61.8	1254
	Shreveport	A	56.2	2184
Me.	Caribou	A	24.4	9767
	Portland	A	33.0	7511
Md.	Baltimore	A	43.7	4654
	Baltimore	C	46.2	4111
	Frederich	A	42.0	5087

State	City		Temp	Deg.
	Tallahassee	A	60.1	1485
	Tampa	A	66.4	683
	West Palm Beach	A	68.4	253
Ga.	Athens	A	51.8	2929
	Atlanta	A	51.7	2961
	Augusta	A	54.5	2397
	Columbus	A	54.8	2383
	Macon	A	56.2	2136
	Rome	A	49.9	3326
	Savannah	A	57.8	1819
	Thomasville	C	60.0	1529
Hawaii	Lihue	A	72.7	0
	Honolulu	A	74.2	0
	Hilo	A	71.9	0
Idaho	Boise	A	39.7	5809
	Lewiston	A	41.0	5542
	Pocatello	A	34.8	7033
Ill.	Cairo	C	47.9	3821
	Chicago(O'Hare)	A	35.8	6639
	Chicago(Midway)	A	37.5	6155
	Chicago	C	38.9	5882
	Moline	A	36.4	6408
	Peoria	A	38.1	6025
	Rockford	A	34.8	6830
	Springfield	A	40.6	5429
Ind.	Evansville	A	45.0	4435
	Fort Wayne	A	37.3	6205
	Indianapolis	A	39.6	5699
	South Bend	A	36.6	6439

State	City		Temp	Deg.
Mass.	Boston	A	40.0	5634
	Nantucket	A	40.2	5891
	Pittsfield	A	32.6	7578
	Worcester	A	34.7	6969
Mich	Alpena	A	29.7	8506
	Detroit(City)	A	37.2	6232
	Detroit(Wayne)	A	37.1	6293
	Detroit(Willow Run)	A	37.2	6258
	Escanaba	C	29.6	8481
	Flint	A	33.1	7377
	Grand Rapids	A	34.9	6894
	Lansing	C	34.8	6909
	Marquette	C	30.2	8393
	Muskegon	A	36.0	6696
	Sault Ste. Marie	A	27.7	9048
Minn.	Duluth	A	23.4	10000
	Minneapolis	A	28.3	8382
	Rochester	A	28.8	8295
Miss.	Jackson	A	55.7	2239
	Meridian	A	55.4	2289
	Vicksburg	C	56.9	2041
Mo.	Columbia	A	42.3	5046
	Kansas City	A	43.9	4711
	St. Joseph	A	40.3	5484
	St. Louis	A	43.1	4900
	St. Louis	C	44.8	4484
	Springfield	A	44.5	4900
Mont.	Billings	A	34.5	7049
	Glasgow	A	26.4	8996
	Great Falls	A	32.8	7750

Table 15-14. Degree Day Data (con't)

State	Station		Avg. Winter Temp, F	Degree-Days Yearly Total
Mont. (Con'td)	Havre	A	28.1	8700
	Havre	C	29.8	8182
	Helena	A	31.1	8129
	Kalispell	A	31.4	8191
	Miles City	A	31.2	7723
	Missoula	A	31.5	8125
Neb.	Grand Island	A	36.0	6530
	Lincoln	C	38.8	5864
	Norfolk	A	34.0	6979
	North Platte	A	35.5	6684
	Omaha	A	35.6	6612
	Scottsbluff	A	35.9	6673
	Valentine	A	32.6	7425
Nev.	Elko	A	34.0	7433
	Ely	A	33.1	7733
	Las Vegas	A	53.3	2709
	Reno	A	39.3	6332
	Winnemucca	A	36.7	6761
N.H.	Concord	A	33.0	7383
	Mt. Washington Obsv.		15.2	13817
N.J.	Atlantic City	A	43.2	4812
	Newark	A	42.8	4589
	Trenton	C	42.4	4980

State	Station		Avg. Winter Temp, F	Degree-Days Yearly Total
	Columbus	A	39.7	5660
	Columbus	C	41.5	5211
	Dayton	A	39.8	5622
	Mansfield	A	36.9	6403
	Sandusky	C	39.1	5796
	Toledo	A	36.4	6494
	Youngstown	A	36.8	6417
Okla.	Oklahoma City	A	48.3	3725
	Tulsa	A	47.7	3860
Ore.	Astoria	A	45.6	5186
	Burns	C	35.9	6957
	Eugene	A	45.6	4726
	Meacham	A	34.2	7874
	Medford	A	43.2	5008
	Pendleton	A	42.6	5127
	Portland	A	45.6	4635
	Portland	C	47.4	4109
	Roseburg	A	46.3	4491
	Salem	A	45.4	4754
Pa.	Allentown	A	38.9	5810
	Erie	A	36.8	6451
	Harrisburg	A	41.2	5251
	Philadelphia	A	41.8	5144
	Philadelphia	C	44.5	4486

State	City			
N.M.	Albuquerque	A	45.0	4348
	Clayton	A	42.0	5158
	Raton	A	38.1	6228
	Roswell	A	47.5	3793
	Silver City	A	48.0	3705
N.Y.	Albany	A	34.6	6875
	Albany	C	37.2	6201
	Binghamton	A	33.9	7286
	Binghamton	C	36.6	6451
	Buffalo	A	34.5	7062
	New York (Cent. Park)	C	42.8	4871
	New York (LaGuardia)	A	43.1	4811
	New York (Kennedy)	A	41.4	5219
	Rochester	A	35.4	6748
	Schenectady	C	35.4	6650
	Syracuse	A	35.2	6756
N. C.	Asheville	C	46.7	4042
	Cape Hatteras	A	53.3	2612
	Charlotte	A	50.4	3191
	Greensboro	A	47.5	3805
	Raleigh	A	49.4	3393
	Wilmington	A	54.6	2347
	Winston-Salem	A	48.4	3595
N. D.	Bismarck	A	26.6	8851
	Devils Lake	C	22.4	9901
	Fargo	A	24.8	9226
	Williston	A	25.2	9243
Ohio	Akron-Canton	A	38.1	6037
	Cincinnati	C	45.1	4410
	Cleveland	A	37.2	6351
	Pittsburgh	A	38.4	5987
	Pittsburgh	C	42.2	5053
	Reading	C	42.4	4945
	Scranton	A	37.2	6254
	Williamsport	A	38.5	5934
R. I.	Block Island	A	40.1	5804
	Providence	A	38.8	5954
S. C.	Charleston	A	56.4	2033
	Charleston	C	57.9	1794
	Columbia	A	54.0	2484
	Florence	A	54.5	2387
	Greenville-Spartenburg	A	51.6	2980
S. D.	Huron	A	28.8	8223
	Rapid City	A	33.4	7345
	Sioux Falls	A	30.6	7839
Tenn.	Bristol	A	46.2	4143
	Chattanooga	A	50.3	3254
	Knoxville	A	49.2	3494
	Memphis	A	50.5	3232
	Memphis	C	51.6	3015
	Nashville	A	48.9	3578
	Oak Ridge	C	47.7	3817
Tex.	Abilene	A	53.9	2624
	Amarillo	A	47.0	3985
	Austin	A	59.1	1711
	Brownsville	A	67.7	600
	Corpus Christi	A	64.6	914
	Dallas	A	55.3	2363
	El Paso	A	52.9	2700

Table 15-14. Degree Day Data (concluded)

State	Station	Avg. Winter Temp, F	Degree-Days Yearly Total
Texas (Con'td)	Fort Worth	A	55.1	2405
	Galveston	A	62.2	1274
	Galveston	C	62.0	1235
	Houston	A	61.0	1396
	Houston	C	62.0	1278
	Laredo	A	66.0	797
	Lubbock	A	48.8	3578
	Midland	A	53.8	2591
	Port Arthur	A	60.5	1447
	San Angelo	A	56.0	2255
	San Antonio	A	60.1	1546
	Victoria	A	62.7	1173
	Waco	A	57.2	2030
	Wichita Falls	A	53.0	2832
Utah	Milford	A	36.5	6497
	Salt Lake City	A	38.4	6052
	Wendover	A	39.1	5778
Vt.	Burlington	A	29.4	8269
Va.	Cape Henry	C	50.0	3279
	Lynchburg	A	46.0	4166
	Norfolk	A	49.2	3421
	Richmond	A	47.3	3865
	Roanoke	A	46.1	4150
Wash.	Olympia	A	44.2	5236
	Seattle-Tacoma	A	44.2	5145

Prov.	Station	Avg. Winter Temp, F	Degree-Days Yearly Total
Alta.	Banff	C	—	10551
	Calgary	A	—	9703
	Edmonton	A	—	10268
	Lethbridge	A	—	8644
B. C.	Kamloops	A	—	6799
	Prince George*	A	—	9755
	Prince Rupert	C	—	7029
	Vancouver*	A	—	5515
	Victoria*	A	—	5699
	Victoria	C	—	5579
Man.	Brandon*	A	—	11036
	Churchill	A	—	16728
	The Pas	C	—	12281
	Winnipeg	A	—	10679
N. B.	Fredericton*	A	—	8671
	Moncton	C	—	8727
	St. John	C	—	8219
Nfld.	Argentia	A	—	8440
	Corner Brook	C	—	8978
	Gander	A	—	9254
	Goose*	A	—	11887
	St. John's*	A	—	8991
N. W. T.	Aklavik	C	—	18017
	Fort Norman	C	—	16109
	Resolution Island	C	—	16021

	Seattle	C	46.9	4424
	Spokane	A	36.5	6655
	Walla Walla	C	43.8	4805
	Yakima	A	39.1	5941
W. Va.	Charleston	A	44.8	4476
	Elkins	A	40.1	5675
	Huntington	A	45.0	4446
	Parkersburg	C	43.5	4754
Wisc.	Green Bay	A	30.3	8029
	La Crosse	A	31.5	7589
	Madison	A	30.9	7863
	Milwaukee	A	32.6	7635
Wyo.	Casper	A	33.4	7410
	Cheyenne	A	34.2	7381
	Lander	A	31.4	7870
	Sheridan	A	32.5	7680

N. S.	Halifax	C	—	7361
	Sydney	A	—	8049
	Yarmouth	A	—	7340
Ont.	Cochrane	C	—	11412
	Fort William	A	—	10405
	Kapuskasing	C	—	11572
	Kitchner	C	—	7566
	London	A	—	7349
	North Bay	C	—	9219
	Ottawa	C	—	8735
	Toronto	C	—	6827
P.E.I.	Charlottetown	C	—	8164
	Summerside	C	—	8488
Que.	Arvida	C	—	10528
	Montreal*	A	—	8203
	Montreal	C	—	7899
	Quebec*	A	—	9372
	Quebec	C	—	8937
Sasks	Prince Albert	A	—	11630
	Regina	A	—	10806
	Saskatoon	C	—	10870
Y. T.	Dawson	C	—	15067
	Mayo Landing	C	—	14454

*The data for these normals were from the full ten-year period 1951-1960, adjusted to the standard normal period 1931-1960.

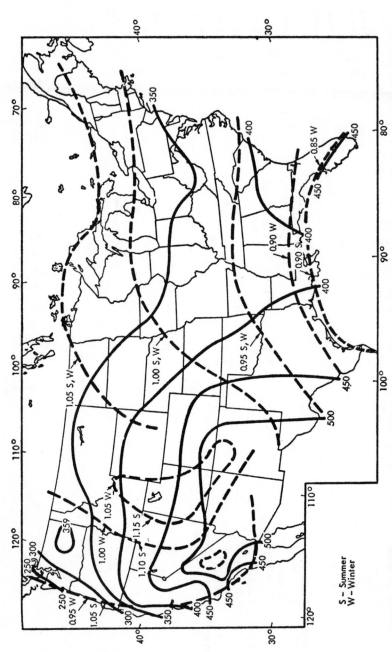

ANNUAL MEAN DAILY INSOLATION (solid lines), in Langleys, and summer and winter clearness numbers (broken lines) are plotted on United States map. Note: To convert Langleys per day to Btu/ft2 day multiply number in figure by 3.69.

Figure 15-1. Annual Mean Daily Insolation
(Courtesy of Heating/Piping/Air Conditioning, Sept. 1966)

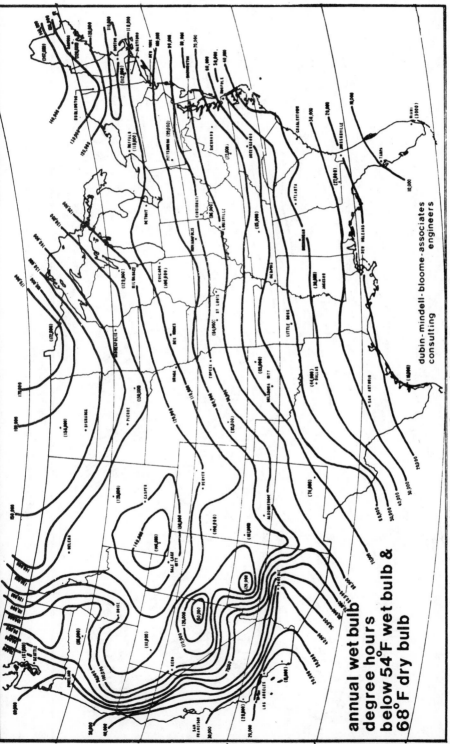

Figure 15-2

(Source: Guidelines for Saving Energy in Existing Buildings—Building Owners and Operators Manual, ECM-1)

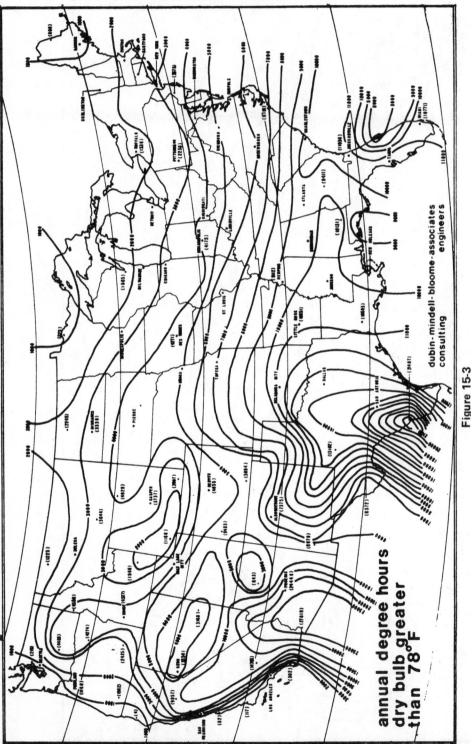

**annual degree hours
dry bulb greater
than 78°F**

dubin·mindell·bloome·associates
consulting   engineers

Figure 15-3

(Source: Guidelines for Saving Energy in Existing Buildings—Building Owners and Operators Manual, ECM-1)

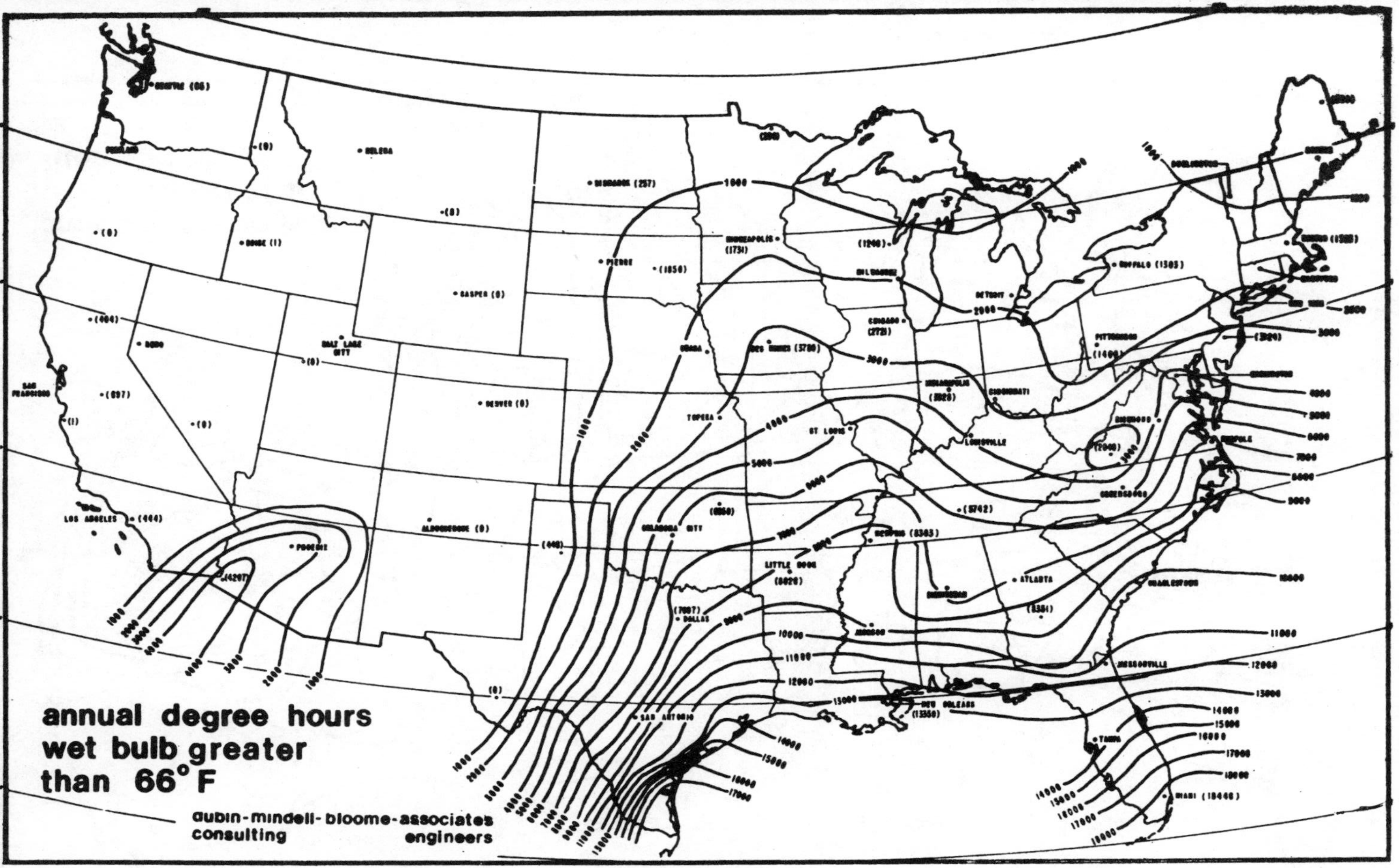

annual degree hours wet bulb greater than 66°F

aubin-mindell-bloome-associates consulting engineers

Figure 15-4

(Source: Guidelines for Saving Energy in Existing Buildings—Building Owners and Operators Manual, ECM-1)

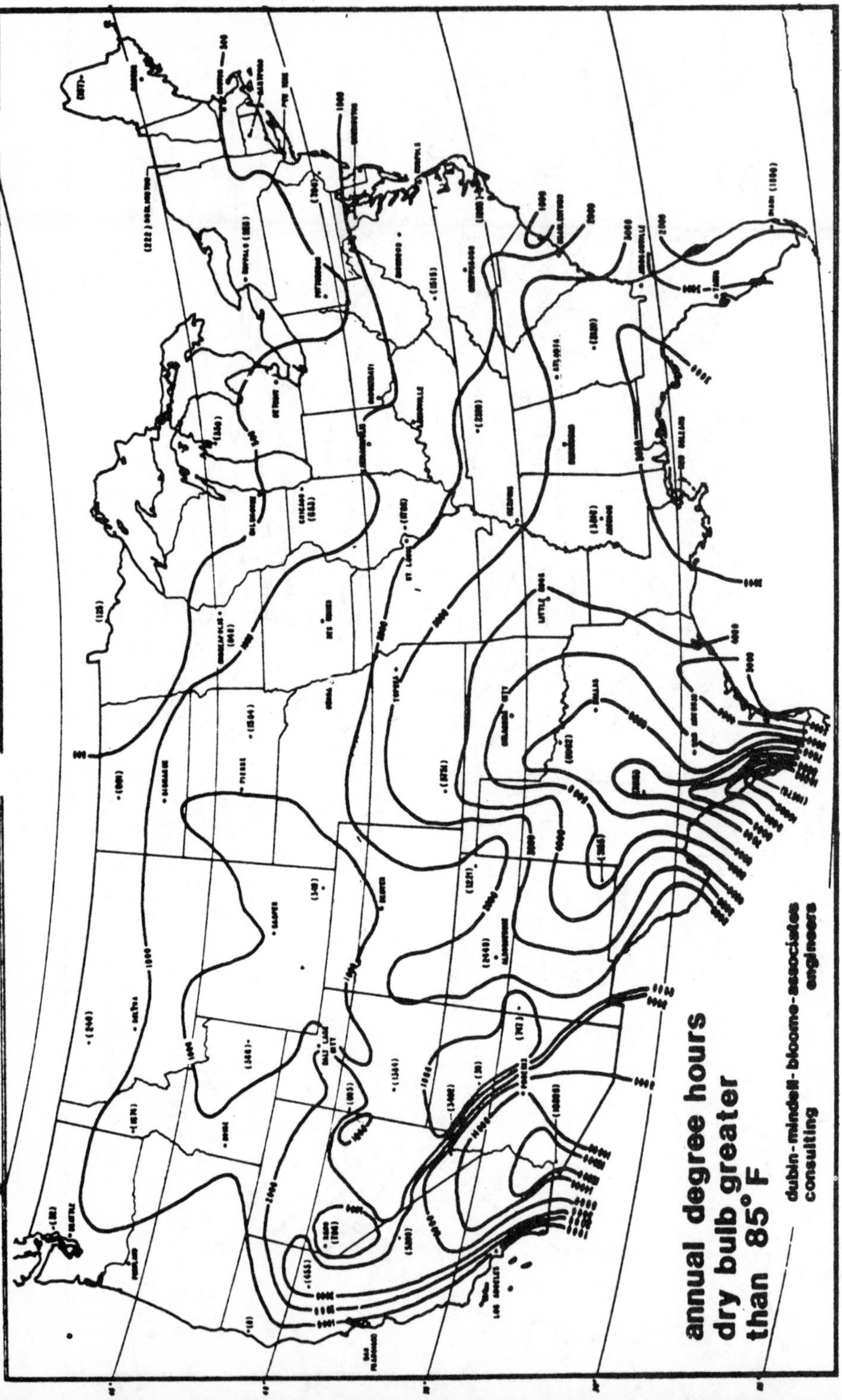

annual degree hours dry bulb greater than 85° F

dubin - mindell - bloome - associates
consulting   engineers

Figure 15-5

(Source: Guidelines for Saving Energy in Existing Buildings—Building Owners and Operators Manual, ECM-1)

BUILDING _____   YEAR _____

MONTH*	HEATING DEGREE DAYS	COOLING DEGREE DAYS	ELECTRICITY				OIL				NATURAL GAS				COAL □ WOOD □	PURCHASED STEAM □ OTHER			TOTAL ENERGY COST
			QUANTITY KWH	COST (DOLLARS)			QUANTITY GALLONS		COST (DOLLARS)		QUANTITY MCF	COST (DOLLARS)			QUANTITY UNIT		COST (DOLLARS)		
				TOTAL $	$/KWH	$/MMBTU		$/GAL.	TOTAL $	$/MMBTU		TOTAL $	$/MCF	$/MMBTU		TOTAL $	$/UNIT	$/MMBTU	
1	2	3	4	5	6	7	8	9	10	11	12	13	14	15	16	17	18	19	20
JANUARY																			
FEBRUARY																			
MARCH																			
APRIL																			
MAY																			
JUNE																			
JULY																			
AUGUST																			
SEPTEMBER																			
OCTOBER																			
NOVEMBER																			
DECEMBER																			
ANNUAL TOTALS																			
ANNUAL AVERAGES																			

* Or comparable time period

ELECTRICITY = 3412 Btu/Kwh
GAS = 1030 Btu/CF

OIL: #2 = .139 MMBTU/gal
      #4 = .150 MMBTU/gal
      #5 = .152 MMBTU/gal
      #6 = .153 MMBTU/gal

MCF = 1000 cubic feet of gas
MMBTU = one million Btu

Figure 15-6. Energy Management Form

1. *Gross Annual Fuel and Energy Consumption*

Line No.

	A	B	C
		Conversion Factor	Thousands of BTUs/yr
		x 138 (1) =	
		x 146 (2) =	
1. Oil—gallons			
		x 1.0 (3) =	
2. Gas—Cubic Feet		x 0.8 (4) =	
3. Coal—Short tons		x 26,000 =	
4. Steam-Pounds x 10³		x 900 =	
5. Propane Gas—lbs		x 21.5 =	
6. Electricity—KW.Hrs		x 3.413 =	

7. Total BTUs X 10³/yr . . . . _____

8. BTUs x 10³/Yr/Per Square Foot of Floor Area _____

(Line 7 + Figure 4, Line 7)

Use for (1) No. 2 Oil; (2) No. 6 Oil; (3) Natural Gas; (4) Mfg. Gas

2. *Annual Fuel and Energy Consumption for Heating*

Line No.

	A	B	C
		Conversion Factor	Thousands of BTUs/yr
		x 138 (1) =	
9. Oil—gallons		x 146 (2) =	
		x 1.0 (3) =	
10. Gas—Cubic Feet		x 0.8 (4) =	
11. Coal—Short tons		x 26,000 =	
12. Steam—Pounds x 10³		x 900 =	
13. Propane Gas—lbs		x 21.5 =	
14. Electricity—KW.Hrs		x 3.413 =	

15. Total BTUs x . . . . = _____

16. BTUs x 10³/Yr Per Square Foot of Floor Area _____

(Line 15   Line 7)

3. *Annual Fuel and Energy Consumption for Domestic Hot Water*

Line No.

	A	B	C
		Conversion Factor	Thousands of BTUs/Yr
17. Oil—Gallons		x 138 (1) =	
		x 146 (2) =	

Figure 15-7. Energy Use Audit Form
(Source: Guidelines for Saving Energy in Existing Buildings—Building Owners and
Operators Manual, ECM-1)

	A	B	C
		Conversion Factor	Thousands of BTUs/Yr
18. Gas–Cubic Feet	_____	x 1.0 (3) =	_____
		x 0.8 (4) =	
19. Coal- Short Tons	_____	x 26,000 =	_____
20. Steam-Pounds x 10³	_____	x 900 =	_____
21. Propane Gas- lbs	_____	x 21.5 =	_____
22. Electricity KW.Hrs	_____	x 3.413 =	_____
23. Total BTUs/Yr x 10³	. . . .		_____
24. BTUs x 10³Yr/Per Square Foot of Floor Area			_____

(Line 23 + Figure 4, Line 7)

4.   Annual Fuel and/or Energy Consumption for Cooling (Compressors & Chillers)

Line No.	A	B	C
		Conversion Factor	Thousands of BTUs/Yr
a) if absorption cooling			
		x 138 (1) =	_____
25. Oil Gallons	_____	x 146 (2) =	_____
		x 1.0 (3) =	_____
26. Gas- Cubic Feet	_____	x 0.8 (4) =	_____
27. Coal- Short Tons	_____	x 26,000 =	_____
28. Steam Pounds x 10³	_____	x 900 =	_____
29. Propane Gas lbs	_____	x 21.5 =	_____
30. Total BTUs/yr x 10³	. . . .		_____
31. BTUs x 10³/Yr Per Square Foot of Floor Area			_____

(Line 30 + Figure 4, Line 7)

b) if electric cooling

	A	B	C
32. Electricity- KWH	_____	x 3.413 =	_____
33 BTUs x 10³/Yr Per Square Foot of Floor Area			_____

(Line 32 + Figure 4, Line 7)

5.   Estimated Annual Energy Consumption for Interior Lighting

Line No.	A	B	C
		Conversion Factor	Thousands of BTUs/Yr
34. KWH	_____	x 3.413 =	_____

Fig. 10, Line 3 x Fig. 10, Line 33 (1)

35. BTUs x 10³/Yr/Per Square Foot of Floor Area _____
(Fig. 10, Line 35, Col. C + Fig. 4, Line 7)

6.   Estimated Annual Electrical Energy Consumption for all Motors and Machines if Building and Hot Water are Not Electrically Heated: (1)

36. Total KW Hrs _____ Less KW Hrs Lighting_____ = _____ KW Hrs
(Line 22, Col. A)

37. KW Hrs/Yr/Sq Ft floor area = _____ (1)
(Line 37 Col. C + Fig. 4, Line 7)

38. BTUs x 10³/Yr/Sq Ft floor area = (Line 37) x 3.431 _____ (2)

(1) and (2). If building heat and hot water are electrically heated, deduct the KW Hrs/Yr per sq ft and BTUs/Yr per sq ft for heating and hot water. (Lines 37 and 38)

Figure 15 7. Energy Use Audit Form (concluded)

PROJECT NO. _____

Job Name _____

System No. _____ Type _____ O.A.T. _____ Date _____

Location _____ Tested By _____ Time of Day _____

1. DRIVE INFORMATION

Motor Manufacturer . . . . . _____ , Frame Size _____

Motor HP . . . . _____

Phases . . . . _____

Amperage . . . . . .Rated _____ Actual _____

Voltage . . . . . . .Rated _____ Actual _____

Fan RPM . . . . . . .Regular _____ Actual _____

Fan Manufacturer . . . . . _____

Fan Type . . . . _____

Motor Sheave Position, Type, and Size . . . . _____

Shaft Diameter . . . . . . _____

Key Size . . . . _____

NOTE: ALL TEMPERATURES MUST BE TAKEN AT THE SAME TIME: AND TIME OF DAY, WHEN THE READINGS ARE TAKEN MUST BE INDICATED.

2. FAN DATA

Does system have return fam? . . . . .Yes _____ No _____

If Yes, Fan No. . . . . . . _____

CFM (Design) . . . . . . .Supply _____ Return _____ O.A. _____

CFM (Actual) . . . . . . .Supply _____ Return _____ O.A. _____ at _____ ΔP (inches H_2O)

SP Filters . . . . . . .Inlet _____ Discharge _____

SP PH Coil . . . . . . .Inlet _____ Discharge _____

SP H Coil · · · · · · · · · · · Inlet _____ Discharge _____
SP C Coil · · · · · · · · · · · Inlet _____ Discharge _____
SP Sup. Fan · · · · · · · · · · Inlet _____ Discharge _____
SP Ret. Fan · · · · · · · · · · Inlet _____ Discharge _____
Temp. Readings · · · · · · · · RAT ___ RFDT ___ MAT ___ PHDT ___
HCDT ___ CCDT ___ SFDT ___

3. COIL DATA

Preheat Coil · · · · · · · · · EWT ___ LWT ___ GPM ___ PDPH ___
Heating Coil · · · · · · · · · EWT ___ LWT ___ GPM ___ PDPH ___
Cooling Coil · · · · · · · · · EWT ___ LWT ___ GPM ___ PDPH ___
Reheat Coil · · · · · · · · · · EWT ___ LWT ___ GPM ___ PDPH ___
For dual duct · · · · · · · · · HDT ___ CDT ___
Discharge for multizone (zone temps- °F) · · · · · · · · · ·

Z_1 ___ Z_2 ___
Z_3 ___ Z_4 ___ Z_5 ___ Z_6 ___
Z_7 ___ Z_8 ___ Z_9 ___ Z_{10} ___

4. COMPONENT CONDITION (VISUAL INSPECTION)

Casing or Plenum · · · · · · · · Heavy Leaks ___ Medium Leaks ___ Nominal ___
Outside Air Louver · · · · · · · · Clean ___ Dirty ___ Clogged ___
Filters · · · · · · · · Clean ___ Dirty ___ Clogged ___
Filter Face Area ___ Ft^2 Air Velocity Across Filter Face ___ GPM
Cooling Coil · · · · · · · · Clean ___ Dirty ___ Clogged ___
Heating Coil · · · · · · · · Clean ___ Dirty ___ Clogged ___

Figure 15-8. HVAC System Data
(Source: Certified Test & Balance Company, Inc., Chicago, Illinois)

Control Dampers
(Leakage in closed position) . . . . High _____ Normal _____ Low _____

Belts . . . . Tight _____ Loose _____ Worn _____ Good _____

5. AIR DISTRIBUTION

Is ductwork leaking? . . . . .Heavy _____ Medium _____ Light _____

Is ductwork insulated/lined? . . . . .Interior _____ Exterior _____ No _____

Is ductwork accessible to repair leaks? . . . . . . .Yes _____ No _____

Does system have manual balancing dampers at zones or mains? . . . . . . .Yes _____ No _____

Do supply outlets have dampers? . . . . .Yes _____ No _____

Do return outlets have dampers? . . . . .Yes _____ No _____

6. REMARKS:

_____

_____

_____

_____

_____

_____

_____

_____

_____

_____

Figure 15-8. HVAC System Data (concluded)

PROJECT NO. _____

JOB NAME _____   DATE _____

SYSTEM NO. _____   LOCATION _____   O.A.T. ___ _____

TESTED BY _____

EWT . . . . ACTUAL _____   DESIGN _____

LWT . . . . ACTUAL _____   DESIGN _____

COIL NO.	AREA SERVED	ACTUAL				DESIGN			
		CFM	EAT	LAT	AIR PD	CFM	EAT	LAT	AIR PD

REMARKS:

Figure 15-9. Reheat Coil Data
(Source: Certified Test & Balance Company, Inc., Chicago, Illinois)

DATE _____

PREPARED BY: _____

PROJECT NO. _____

JOB NAME:

AREA SERVED	GROSS SQ. FEET	SYSTEM SERVING	WEEKDAYS		SATURDAY		SUNDAYS/HOLIDAYS	
			NO. OF OCCU-PANTS	OCCUPANCY TIME A.M. P.M.	NO. OF OCCU-PANTS	OCCUPANCY TIME A.M. P.M.	NO. OF OCCU-PANTS	OCCUPANCY TIME A.M. P.M.

Figure 15-10. Building Occupancy Schedule

(Source: Certified Test & Balance Company, Inc., Chicago, Illinois)

JOB NAME _____

PREPARED BY _____

DATE _____

PROJECT NO. _____

SYSTEM NUMBER	DESIGN		ACTUAL		REMARKS:
	TOTAL CFM	OUTSIDE AIR	TOTAL CFM	OUTSIDE AIR	

NOTE: These readings should be obtained by traverse and O.S. setting kept on minimum position ONLY.

Figure 15-11. CFM Audit

(Source: Certified Test & Balance Company, Inc., Chicago, Illinois)

PROJECT NO. _____

JOB NAME _____ DATE _____

UNIT NO. _____ TYPE _____ (Steam-to-water/Water-to-water) _____

LOCATION _____ TESTED BY _____

Steam Pressure (PSIG) · · · · · · · · Actual _____ Design _____

Flow Rate (GPM) · · · · · · · · · Actual _____ Design _____

Pressure Drop · · · · · · · · · Actual _____ Design _____

EWT · · · · · · · · · Actual _____ Design _____

LWT · · · · · · · · Actual _____ Design _____

Reset Control · · · · · · · · Automatic _____ Manual _____

REMARKS:

Figure 15-12. Hot Water Convertor Data
(Source: Certified Test & Balance Company, Inc., Chicago, Illinois)

PROJECT NO. _____

JOB NAME _____ DATE _____

SYSTEM NO. _____ MACHINE NO. _____ REFRIGERANT TYPE _____

LOCATION _____ TESTED BY _____

COOLER:

GPM Capacity · · · · · · · · Actual _____ Design _____

Pressure Drop · · · · · · · · Actual _____ Design _____

EWT · · · · · · · · · Actual _____ Design _____

LWT · · · · · · · · Actual _____ Design _____

CONDENSER:

GPM Capacity · · · · · · · · Actual _____ Design _____

Pressure Drop · · · · · · · · Actual _____ Design _____

EWT · · · · · · · · · Actual _____ Design _____

LWT · · · · · · · · Actual _____ Design _____

REMARKS:

Figure 15-13. Absorption Refrigeration Machine Data
(Source: Certified Test & Balance Company, Inc., Chicago, Illinois)

1. **GENERAL INFORMATION**

   IDENTITY:

   Surveyed by: _____

   Survey Date: _____

   OPERATION _____

   Address _____

   Type(s) of occupancy _____

   Name of person in charge of energy _____

   _____

   _____

   PHYSICAL DATA:

   Building orientation _____

   No. of floors _____

   Floor area, gross, square feet _____

   Net air conditioned square feet _____

   Construction type: _____

   Walls (masonry, curtain, frame, etc.)

   N _____ S _____ E _____ W _____

Figure 15-14. Building Information

Roof:

Type: Flat _____   Color: Light _____

Pitched _____   Dark _____

Glazing:

Exposure   *Type   %Glass/Exterior wall area

N   _____   _____

S   _____   _____

E   _____   _____

W   _____   _____

*Type: Single, double, insulating, reflective, etc.

Glass shading employed outside (check one)

Fins _____   Overhead _____   None _____   Other _____

Glass shading employed inside (check one):

Shades _____ Blinds _____ Drapes, open mesh _____ Drapes opaque _____ None _____ Other _____

SKETCH OF BUILDING SHOWING PRINCIPLE DIMENSIONS:

BUILDING TYPE:

All electric _____

Gas total energy _____

Oil total energy _____

Other _____

BUILDING OCCUPANCY AND USE:

Weekdays: Occupied by:* _____ people from _____ to _____ (hours)

_____ | | | | |
_____ | | | | |

Saturdays:

Sundays, holidays

Hours air conditioned: Weekdays from _____ to _____ ; Saturdays _____ to _____ Sundays, holidays from _____ to _____

*(Account for 24 hours a day. If unoccupied, put in zero)

2. **ENVIRONMENTAL CONDITIONS**

OUTDOOR CONDITIONS

Winter: Day _____ °F. dB _____ mph wind   Night _____ °F. dB _____ mph wind

Summer: Day _____ °F. dB _____ mph wind   Night _____ °F. dB _____ mph wind

MAINTAINED INDOOR CONDITIONS:

Winter: Day _____ °F. dB _____ %rh   Night _____ °F. dB _____ %rh

Summer: Day _____ °F. dB _____ %rh   Night _____ °F. dB _____ %rh

Figure 15-14. Building Information (con't)

3.   **SYSTEMS AND EQUIPMENT DATA**

HVAC SYSTEMS:

Air handling systems (check as appropriate):

Perimeter system designation:

Single zone _____ Multizone _____

Fan coil _____ Induction _____

Variable air volume _____ Dual duct _____

Terminal reheat _____ Self-contained _____

Heat pump _____

Interior system designation:

Fan coil _____ Variable air volume _____

Single zone _____ Other (describe) _____

Principle of operation:

Heating-cooling-off _____

Air volume variation _____

Air mixing control _____

Temperature variation _____

Interior:

Heating-cooling-off _____

Air volume variation _____

Temperature variation _____

4. AIR HANDLING UNIT – SUPPLY, RETURN, EXHAUST

System Description _____

_____

Horsepower _____   OSA Dampers - Yes ☐   No ☐   M.A. Setting _____ °F

Location _____   Area Served _____

Terminal Units: Quantity _____   Type _____

Operations (Start-Stop)   Start Time   Stop Time

Monday thru Friday   _____   _____

Saturday   _____   _____

Sunday   _____   _____

Holiday   _____   _____

Method of Start-Stop   Time Clock ☐   Manual ☐   Other ☐

Figure 15-14. Building Information (con't)

5. **AIR HANDLING UNIT — SUPPLY, RETURN, EXHAUST**

System Description _____

_____

_____

Horsepower _____ OSA Dampers - Yes ☐ No ☐ M.A. Setting _____ °F

Location _____ Area Served _____

Terminal Units: Quantity _____ Type _____

Operations (Start-Stop)   Start Time   Stop Time

Monday thru Friday   _____   _____

Saturday   _____   _____

Sunday   _____   _____

Holiday   _____

Method of Start-Stop   Time Clock ☐   Manual ☐   Other ☐

6. COOLING PLANT

Chillers: Number_____ Total Tonnage/KW_____

Chilled Water Pumps_____ Total HP_____

Condensed Water Pumps_____ Total HP_____

Cooling Tower Fan(s)_____ Total HP_____

Chilled Water Supply Temp., Setpoint_____ °F

Operations (Start-Stop)   Start Time   Stop Time

Monday thru Friday   _____   _____

Saturday   _____   _____

Sunday   _____   _____

Holiday   _____   _____

Method of Start-Stop   Time Clock ☐   Manual ☐   Other ☐

Figure 15-14. Building Information (con't)

Months Operation per Year _____

Remarks _____

7. **BOILER PLANT**

Boiler No. _____ Size _____ Type _____

Fuel Used _____

Hot Water Supply Setpoint _____ F Steam Pressure Setpoint _____ psi

Number of Pumps _____ Total HP _____

Remarks _____

8. **ROOFTOP/UNITARY SYSTEMS**

Manufacture and Model _____

Quantity _____ Location _____

Cooling Capacity _____ Tons Total _____

Heating Capacity _____ Btu Output _____ Btu Input (Gas/Oil) _____

Electric ☐   Gas ☐   Steam/HW ☐

Single Zone Units _____ Multizone Units _____ Number of Zones _____

O.A. Damper Control _____

Fans: CFM   HP

Supply   _____   _____

Return   _____   _____

Exhaust   _____   _____

Operations   Start Time   Stop Time

Monday-Friday   _____   _____

Saturday   _____   _____

Sunday   _____   _____

Holiday   _____   _____

Figure 15-14. Building Information (con't)

Method of Start-Stop   Time Clock ☐   Manual ☐   Other ☐

9. **EXHAUST, AIR, MAKEUP AIR SYSTEMS**

Designation	Location	Area Served	CFM	HP
_____	_____	_____	_____	_____
_____	_____	_____	_____	_____
_____	_____	_____	_____	_____
		TOTAL _____		

Operating Schedule _____

_____

_____

All fans (supply, return and exhaust):

Location	Horsepower	Type	Method of Operation
_____	_____	_____	_____
_____	_____	_____	_____
_____	_____	_____	_____

Source of heating energy:

Hot water _____ Steam _____ Electric resistance _____ Other _____

Heating plant:

Boiler No. _____ Rating _____ MBH

_____

_____

Boiler type:

Firetube _____ Watertube _____ Elec. resist. _____ Electrode _____ Other _____

Fuel used _____ Standby _____

Hot water supply _____ °F, Return _____ °F

Steam pressure _____ psi

Pumps No. _____ Total HP _____

Room heating units:

Type: Baseboard _____ Convectors _____ Fin tube _____

Ceiling or wall panels _____ Unit heaters _____ Other _____

Cooling plant:

Chillers: No. _____ Total capacity (tons) _____

Type: Centrifugal _____ Reciprocating _____ Absorption _____

Figure 15-14. Building Information (con't)

Capacity controlled by: _____

Chiller operation: Starting controls _____

  Stopping controls _____

Chilled water temp. supply _____ °F, return _____ °F

Condenser water temp. _____ in °F _____ out °F

Heat dissipation device:

  Evaporative condenser _____

  Air cooled condenser _____

  Cooling tower _____

  Condenser/cooling tower fan HP _____

  Heat recovery device: Double bundle condenser _____ Other _____

  Chilled water pumps _____ Total HP _____

  Condenser water pumps _____ Total HP _____

Self-contained units:

  Type: Thru-the-wall-air conditioner _____ Other _____

  No. of units _____ Basic module served _____

  Capacity (tons) _____

10. **ENERGY CONSERVATION DEVICES:**

  Type:

Condenser water used for heating _____

Demand limiters _____

Energy storage _____

Heat recovery wheels _____

Enthalpy control of supply-return-exhaust damper _____

Recuperators _____

Others _____

LIGHTING:

Interior lighting type: _____

Watts/ft2:   Hallway/corridor _____

Work stations _____

Circulation areas within work space _____

On-off from breaker panel _____ Wall switches _____

Control switching _____

Exterior Lighting: Type _____ Total KW _____

DOMESTIC HOT WATER HEATING:

Size _____ Rated input _____ Water Temp. _____ °F

Energy Source: Gas _____, Oil _____, Electric _____, Other _____

Figure 15-14. Building Information (con't)

OTHER EQUIPMENT (Kitchen, etc.):

Equip. Description	Quantity	Size/Capacity in BTU, KW, HP, etc.

11. OPERATING SCHEDULE:

OPERATION (Start-stop)

Equipment description	Weekdays	Saturday	Sunday	Holiday
Refrigeration cycle mach.				
Fans — supply				
Fans — return/exhaust				
Fans — exhaust only				
HVAC auxilliary equip.				
Lighting — interior				
— exterior				
Fan kitchen exhaust				
Elevators				
Escalators				

Domestic hot water ht. _____ _____

Other (describe: _____) _____ _____

12. **LIGHTING**

1. Interior Lighting Type _____

   Watts/Ft.^{2} Offices _____ Other _____

   Total Install KW _____ Foot Candles _____

   On-Off from Breaker Panel? _____

   Wall Switch? _____ Control Switching? _____

   Operating Schedule _____

2. Exterior Lighting Type _____

   Total KW _____

   Operating Schedule _____

3. Remarks _____

   _____

Figure 15-14. Building Information (con't)

13. **UTILITIES**

Electric Utility _____

Rate Schedule _____ Effective _____

Name of Rep _____ Phone _____

Gas Utility _____

Rate Schedule _____ Effective _____

Name of Rep _____ Phone _____

Water Utility _____

Rate Schedule _____ Effective _____

Name of Rep _____ Phone _____

EMERGENCY GENERATORS

Number _____ Size _____ KW _____

How Started: Manual ☐   Auto Switchover ☐

Equipment/Systems Operated: _____

_____

_____

CHECK LIST

	Due Date	Date Complete	By
1. HVAC Survey	_____	_____	_____
2. Lighting & Misc. Survey	_____	_____	_____
3. Utility Bill Analysis	_____	_____	_____
4. Recommendation	_____	_____	_____

Date_____

Figure 15-14. Building Information (concluded)

SUMMARY SHEET

GENERAL INFORMATION

Building/Plant/Business Center: _____

Address: _____

City, State: _____

Building Supervisor: _____

Building Use: _____

TOTALS BY BUILDING LOCATION:

Building Location	Total Area Building Location	Allowance Sq Ft	Total Watt Allowance	Total Connected Load
1		3.0		
2		1.0		
3		0.5		
Interior Total				
		Allowance Ft		
4		5.0		
5		0.5		
Exterior Total				

BUILDING LOCATION DESIGNATIONS:

1 = Office Space/Personnel

2 = Rest, Lunch, Shipping/Warehouse

3 = Malls, Lobby

4 = Building Perimeter, Facade, Canopy

5 = Parking

DETAIL SHEET

GENERAL INFORMATION

Building/Plant/Business Center: _____

Address: _____

BUILDING LOCATION USE: _____

Room Name	Area Sq Ft	Lamp or Fixture Type	Quantity	Watts Unit	Total Connected Load (Watts)
TOTAL					

Figure 15-15. Lighting Audit

TYPICAL LIGHTING FIXTURE WATTAGE

I. FLUORESCENT

Lamp Description	Lamps per / Lamp Fixture / Type	Fixture Wattage*
4 Ft 40 Watt Rapid Start	1-F40T12 2-F40T12 3-F40T12 4-F40T12	50 92 142 184
8 Ft Slimline Instant Start	1-F96T12 2-F96T12 3-F96T12 4-F96T12	100 170 270 340
8 Ft High Output	1-F96T12/HO 2-F96T12/HO 3-F96T12/HO 4-F96T12/HO	140 252 392 504
8 Ft 1500 ma Power Grove, SHO or VHO	1-F96PG17 1-F96T12/SHO or VHO 2-F96PG17 2-F96T12/SHO or VHO 3-F96PG17 3-F96T12/SHO or VHO 4-F96PG17 4-596T12/SHO or VHO	230 450 680 900

II. HIGH INTENSITY DISCHARGE

Lamp Type	Lamp Designation	Watts	Fixture Wattage*
Mercury	MV 100 MV 175 MV 250 MV 400 MV 1000	100 175 250 400 1000	118 200 285 450 1075
Metal Halide	MH 175 MH 250 MH 400 MH 1000	175 250 400 1000	210 292 455 1070
High Pressure Sodium	HPS 70 HPS 100 HPS 150 HPS 250 HPS 400 HPS 1000	70 100 150 250 400 1000	88 130 188 300 465

* Includes Lamp and Ballast Wattage.

Figure 15-15. Lighting Audit (con't)

To plan more adequate lighting, refer to the table below which illustrates the energy used by various types of lighting.

LUMEN/WATT TYPICAL LIGHT SOURCES

Source	Initial Lumens Watt
Low pressure sodium (35 to 180 watts)	133 to 183
High pressure sodium (70 watts to 1,000 watts)	83 to 140
Metal halide (175 watts to 1,000 watts)	80 to 125
Fluorescent (30 watts to 215 watts)	74 to 84
Mercury (100 watts to 1,000 watts)	42 to 62
Incandescent (100 watts to 1,500 watts)	17 to 23

RECOMMENDED REFLECTANCE VALUES

Surfaces	Reflectance (Percent)
Ceiling	80-90%
Walls	40-60%
Desks and Bench Tops, Machines and Equipment	25-45%
Floors	Not less than 20%

Figure 15-15. Lighting Audit (concluded)

OPERATION _____   LOCATION _____   DATE _____

MFG'R.	LIGHT # FIXTURE	LOCATION NO.	WATTS PER FIXTURE	LUMENS	Hrs. Operated Per Day	Days Operated Per Week	KWH Per Per Week	COMMENTS

Figure 15-16. Energy Survey – Lights

OPERATION _____

LOCATION _____

DATE _____

MFG'R.	EQUIPMENT ITEM	LOCATION	ELECTRICAL EQUIPMENT RATED INPUT						COMMENTS
			1 AMPS	2 VOLTS	3 KW* 1 x 2 1000	4 HRS. OPERATED PER DAY	5 DAYS OPERATED PER WEEK	6 KWH PER WEEK 3 x 4 x 5	

1. Fuel or power requirement is usually listed on equipment name plate.
2. To find Btu's per hour for:
   Electricity— multiply amps x volts x 3.413 or watts x 3.413
   Natural Gas— multiply cubic feet per hour x 1,000
   #2 Fuel Oil— multiply gallons per hour x 140,000
   Steam— multiply pounds per hour x 1,000
3. To find cost per hour, multiply the cost per Btu for that unit's fuel (from Worksheet ___ x the Btu's per hour by that unit.

*To find Btu equivalents (expressed in millions) for electricity, multiply kilowatt hours x .0003414.
For natural gas, multiply cubic feet x .001.
For #2 fuel oil, multiply gallons x .14.
For purchased steam, multiply pounds x .001.
To find the cost per million Btu's in each category, divide the total cost in that category by the total Btu's, expressed in millions, for that category.

Figure 15-17. Energy Survey — Electrical Equipment

METER NO. _____
LOCATION _____
STATE _____

MONTHLY ENERGY USE

OPERATION

MONTH	CONSUMPTION KWH	DEMAND KW	RATE	FUEL ADJ. RATE/KWH	COST	65° HEATING DAYS	65° COOLING DAYS	KWH INCREASE OVER PAST YEAR	COST INCREASE OVER PAST YEAR	COST INCREASE FUEL ADJ. RATE OVER/UNDER PAST YEAR
JAN.										
FEB.										
MAR.										
APR.										
MAY										
JUNE										
JULY										
AUG.										
SEPT.										
OCT.										
NOV.										
DEC.										
TOTALS										

	JAN.	FEB.	MAR.	APR.	MAY	JUNE	JULY	AUG.	SEPT.	OCT.	NOV.	DEC.	COMMENTS
% INCREASE COST													
% INCREASE KWH													
% INCREASE FUEL ADJ. RATE													
BASIC RATE INCREASE													

Figure 15-18. Electrical Worksheet

OPERATION _____   LOCATION _____   DATE _____

MFG'R.	EQUIPMENT ITEM	LOCATION	GAS EQUIPMENT RATED INPUT					COMMENTS
			7 BTU PER HOUR	8 CU. FT. PER HR. 7/1000	9 HOURS OPERATED PER DAY	10 DAY'S OPERATED PER WEEK	11 CU. FT. PER WEEK 8 × 9 × 10	

1. Fuel or power requirement is usually listed on equipment name plate.
2. To find Btu's per hour for:
   Electricity— multiply amps x volts x 3.413 or watts x 3.413
   Natural Gas— multiply cubic feet per hour x 1,000
   #2 Fuel Oil— multiply gallons per hour x 140,000
   Steam— multiply pounds per hour x 1,000
3. To find cost per hour, multiply the cost per Btu for that unit's fuel (from Worksheet . . . x the Btu's per hour by that unit.

*To find Btu equivalents (expressed in millions) for electricity, multiply kilowatt hours x .003414.
For natural gas, multiply cubic feet x .001.
For #2 fuel oil, multiply gallons x .14.
For purchased steam, multiply pounds x .001.
To find the cost per million Btu's in each category, divide the total cost in that category by the total Btu's, expressed in millions, for that category.

Figure 15-19. Energy Survey — Gas Equipment

METER NO. _____
LOCATION _____
STATE _____

MONTHLY ENERGY USE _____

OPERATION _____

MONTH	CONSUMPTION CCF	RATE	FUEL ADJ. RATE/CCF	COST	65° HEATING DAYS	65° COOLING DAYS	CCF INCREASE OVER PAST YEAR	COST INCREASE OVER PAST YEAR	COST INCREASE FUEL ADJ. RATE OVER/UNDER PAST YEAR
JAN.									
FEB.									
MAR.									
APR.									
MAY									
JUNE									
JULY									
AUG.									
SEPT.									
OCT.									
NOV.									
DEC.									
TOTALS									

	JAN.	FEB.	MAR.	APR.	MAY	JUNE	JULY	AUG.	SEPT.	OCT.	NOV.	DEC.	COMMENTS
% INCREASE COST													
% INCREASE CCF													
% INCREASE FUEL ADJ. RATE													
BASIC RATE INCREASE													

Figure 15-20. Gas Worksheet

METER NO._____
LOCATION_____
_____STATE_____

MONTHLY ENERGY USE

OPERATION

MONTH	CONSUMPTION GALLONS	RATE	FUEL ADJ. RATE/GAL.	COST	65° HEATING DAYS	65° COOLING DAYS	GAL. INCREASE OVER PAST YEAR	COST INCREASE OVER PAST YEAR	COST INCREASE FUEL ADJ. RATE OVER/UNDER PAST YEAR
JAN.									
FEB.									
MAR.									
APR.									
MAY									
JUNE									
JULY									
AUG.									
SEPT.									
OCT.									
NOV.									
DEC.									
TOTALS									

	JAN.	FEB.	MAR.	APR.	MAY	JUNE	JULY	AUG.	SEPT.	OCT.	NOV.	DEC.	COMMENTS
% INCREASE COST													
% INCREASE GALLONS													
% INCREASE FUEL ADJ. RATE													
BASIC RATE INCREASE													

Figure 15-21. Fuel Oil Worksheet

METER NO._____

LOCATION._____

STATE._____

OPERATION _____

MONTHLY ENERGY USE _____

MONTH	CONSUMPTION LBS.	RATE	FUEL ADJ. RATE/LBS.	COST	65° HEATING DAYS	65° COOLING DAYS	LBS. INCREASE OVER PAST YEAR	COST INCREASE OVER PAST YEAR	COST INCREASE FUEL ADJ. RATE OVER/UNDER PAST YEAR
JAN.									
FEB.									
MAR.									
APR.									
MAY									
JUNE									
JULY									
AUG.									
SEPT.									
OCT.									
NOV.									
DEC.									
TOTALS									

	JAN.	FEB.	MAR.	APR.	MAY	JUNE	JULY	AUG.	SEPT.	OCT.	NOV.	DEC.	COMMENTS
% INCREASE COST													
% INCREASE LBS.													
% INCREASE FUEL ADJ. RATE													
BASIC RATE INCREASE													

Figure 15-22. Steam Worksheet

MONTHLY ENERGY USE_____   METER NO._____
                                                       LOCATION_____
                                                                  STATE_____

                              OPERATION

MONTH	CONSUMPTION GALLONS	RATE	ADJ. RATE/GAL.	COST	65° HEATING DAYS	65° COOLING DAYS	GAL. INCREASE OVER PAST YEAR	COST INCREASE OVER PAST YEAR	COST INCREASE ADJ. RATE OVER/UNDER PAST YEAR
JAN.									
FEB.									
MAR.									
APR.									
MAY									
JUNE									
JULY									
AUG.									
SEPT.									
OCT.									
NOV.									
DEC.									
TOTALS									

	JAN.	FEB.	MAR.	APR.	MAY	JUNE	JULY	AUG.	SEPT.	OCT.	NOV.	DEC.
% INCREASE COST												
% INCREASE GALLONS												
% INCREASE ADJ. RATE												
BASIC RATE INCREASE												

COMMENTS

Figure 15-23. Water Worksheet

Building or location _____

Type (check below)

      Steam boiler _____   Hot water generator _____

      Hot air furnace _____   Other _____

Fuel source: Natural gas _____   #1 Oil _____

              Butane _____   #2 Oil _____

              Propane _____   #6 Oil _____

                                     Other _____

Rated pressure of boiler or generator _____

Measured water or steam system, pressure drop _____ psig

Pump motor: Voltage _____   Amperage _____

                Manufacturer _____   Phases _____

Minimum pressure drop, assuming no corrosion or fouling _____ psig

Nameplate or rated output _____ Btu/hr; Hp

Design heat loss of system _____ Btu/hr

Measured draft pressure $\pm$ _____ in. H_2O

Location of measurement:

_____ Over-the-fire _____ Breaching

Type of draft: _____ Forced _____ Induced

Acceptable draft pressure $\pm$ _____ in. H_2O
    (Refer to table at end of form)

Measured smoke density reading
    (For oil burners only)

Measured CO_2 concentration _____ %

Acceptable CO_2 range _____ %
    (Refer to table at end of form)

Measured stack temperature _____ °F

Measured make-up air (or boiler room air) temperature _____ °F

Net stack temperature = _____ °F

Acceptable net stack temperature _____ °F

Measured boiler efficiency _____ %

RECOMMENDED DRAFT PRESSURES (IN. H_2O)
FOR COMBINATION SYSTEMS

	Location	
Gas or Oil Burners	Over the Fire	Boiler Breaching
Natural or induced draft	−0.02 to −0.05	−0.07 to −0.10
Forced draft	0.70 to 0.10	0.02 to 0.05

Figure 15-24. Combustion System Data
(Source: Manual of Procedures for Authorized Class A Energy Auditors in Iowa)

APPROXIMATE STOICHIOMETRIC AND RECOMMENDED CO_2 CONCENTRATIONS FOR VARIOUS FUELS

	% CO_2	
Gases	*Stoichiometric*	*Recommended Value*
Natural	12	7-10
Propane or Butane	14	8.5-11.5
Fuel Oils		
No. 1 or No. 2	15	9-12
No. 6	16.5	10-14

Figure 15-24. Combustion System Data (concluded)

Table 15-15. List of Conversion Factors

1 U.S. barrel	= 42 U.S. gallons
1 atmosphere	= 14.7 pounds per square inch absolute (psia)
1 atmosphere	= 760 mm (29.92 in) mercury with density of 13.6 grams per cubic centimeter
1 pound per square inch	= 2.04 inches head of mercury
	= 2.31 feet head of water
1 inch head of water	= 5.20 pounds per square foot
1 foot head of water	= 0.433 pound per square inch
1 British thermal unit (Btu)	= heat required to raise the temperature of 1 pound of water by 1°F
1 therm	= 100,000 Btu
1 kilowatt (Kw)	= 1.341 horsepower (hp)
1 kilowatt-hour (Kwh)	= 1.34 horsepower-hour
1 horsepower (hp)	= 0.746 kilowatt (Kw)
1 horsepower-hour	= 0.746 kilowatt hour (Kwh)
1 horsepower-hour	= 2545 Btu
1 kilowatt-hour (Kwh)	= 3412 Btu
To generate 1 kilowatt-hour (Kwh) requires 10,000 Btu of fuel burned by average utility	
1 ton of refrigeration	= 12,000 Btu per hr
1 ton of refrigeration requires about 1 Kw (or 1.341 hp) in commercial air conditioning	
1 standard cubic foot is at standard conditions of 60°F and 14.7 psia.	
1 degree day	= 65°F minus mean temperature of the day, °F
1 year	= 8760 hours
1 year	= 365 days
1 MBtu	= 1 million Btu
1 Kw	= 1000 watts
1 trillion barrels	= 1×10^{12} barrels
1 KSCF	= 1000 standard cubic feet

Note: In these conversions, inches and feet of water are measured at 62°F (16.7°C), and inches and millimeters of mercury at 32°F (0°C).

Index

441